Unions, Radicals, and Democratic Presidents

Unions, Radicals, and Democratic Presidents

Seeking Social Change in the Twentieth Century

MARTIN HALPERN

Contributions in American History, Number 201
Jon L. Wakelyn, Series Editor

Westport, Connecticut
London

Library of Congress Cataloging-in-Publication Data

Halpern, Martin, 1945–
    Unions, radicals, and democratic presidents : seeking social
    change in the twentieth century / Martin Halpern.
        p.   cm. (Contributions in American history ; no. 201)
    Includes bibliographical references and index.
    ISBN 0–313–32471–9 (alk. paper)
    1. Labor unions—United States—History—20th century.
2. Presidents—United States—History—20th century. 3. Social
justice—United States. 4. Socialism—United States. 5. Values—
United States. I. Title. II. Series.
HD6508.H243   2003
331.88'0973'0904—dc21   2003046967

British Library Cataloging in Publication Data is available.

Library of Congress Catalog Card Number: 2003046967
ISBN: 0–313–32471–9
ISSN: 0084–9219

First published in 2003

Praeger Publishers, 88 Post Road West, Westport, CT 06881
An imprint of Greenwood Publishing Group, Inc.
www.praeger.com

Printed in the United States of America

The paper used in this book complies with the
Permanent Paper Standard issued by the National
Information Standards Organization (Z39.48–1984).

10 9 8 7 6 5 4 3 2 1

Copyright Acknowledgments

Grateful acknowledgment is made to the following publishers for kind permission to use earlier versions of the author's previously published essays:

"Children of the Left: Sharing Values Across the Generations," published in Paul Schervish, Virginia Hodgkinson, and Margaret Gates, eds., *Care and Community in Modern Society: Passing on the Tradition of Service to Future Generations* (San Francisco: Jossey-Bass Publishers, Inc., 1995). This material is used by permission of John Wiley & Sons, Inc.

"When Henry Met Franklin," published in Mark Rozell and William Pederson, eds., *FDR and the Modern Presidency: Leadership and Legacy* (Westport, Conn.: Greenwood Publishing, 1997). Reprinted by permission.

"'I'm Fighting for Freedom': Coleman Young, HUAC, and the Detroit Black Community," published in *Journal of American Ethnic History* 17 (Fall 1997): 19–38. Reprinted by permission.

"Arkansas and the Defeat of Labor Law Reform in 1978 and 1994," published in *Arkansas Historical Quarterly* LVII (Summer 1998): 99–133. Reprinted by permission.

"Jimmy Carter and the UAW: Failure of an Alliance," published in *Presidential Studies Quarterly* 26 no. 3 (Summer 1996): 755–777. Reprinted by permission.

The author and publisher are also grateful for permission to use excerpts from the following:

Judy Kaplan and Lin Shapiro, eds., *Red Diaper Babies: Children of the Left: Edited Transcripts of Conferences Held at World Fellowship Center, Conway, New Hampshire, July 31–August 1, 1982, July 9–10, 1983* (Somerville, Mass.: Red Diaper Productions, 1985). Kaplan and Shapiro are also editors of *Red Diapers: Growing Up in the Communist Left* (Urbana: University of Illinois Press, 1998).

For Helen

Contents

Preface

Historical writing stems from the experiences of the person writing as much as from her or his forays into archives, libraries, or living rooms of living persons whose memories one wishes to stir. The research for this book began after my family moved from Lansing, Michigan, to the small university town of Arkadelphia, Arkansas, in 1990. How would my wife and I raise our daughters, then seven and five, and pass on our left-wing values in a Bible Belt town largely devoid of left influences and more than nine hundred miles away from the nearest family member on either side? This personal dilemma led me to respond to a call for papers on "Passing on the Tradition of Caring" issued by Independent Sector, a leading organization in the philanthropic community. I took the opportunity to examine how left-wing parents throughout the twentieth century attempted to pass on their traditions and concepts of caring to their children. The resulting study, "Children of the Left: Sharing Values Across the Generations," is the second of two introductory chapters in the present volume. Chapter 1, "The Labor Movement: Leader of Social Change or Just Another Interest Group?" also was first presented at a philanthropy conference and aims to provide a basic theoretical introduction to the nature of the labor movement and answer critics who tend to dismiss it as irrelevant to the social change process or worse. The remaining chapters in the book carry forward the themes of the influence of labor and the left in the social change process and focus as well on left-center coalitions and presidential politics.

Long before I began the research that resulted in this book, I was an activist in peace, civil rights, and other social-change movements. As a movement activist in the 1960s and 1970s, I sought to find ways to bring about broad-based alliances, conduct militant actions, win specific gains, and strengthen the progressive organizations within which I worked. At the same time, I tried to study and learn along with other participants what our experiences meant for understanding the nature of our society and what it would take to transform it so that caring and social justice, equality and peace would be our fundamental principles. As an activist in local and national campaigns, I found that left leadership and left-center coalitions were crucial ingredients in achieving advances.

Like many young people who were left-minded in the 1960s, I was disappointed in the weakness of the left in our country, especially so since my own parents had brought me up to be a working-class-minded leftist. I set out in my first major project as an historian to find out what happened to the left of my parents' generation. I discovered, as I described in *UAW Politics in the Cold War Era*, that the passage of the Taft-Hartley Act in 1947 was the decisive turning point in leading to the defeat of the left-center coalition in the United Automobile Workers. The UAW defeat led to a turn to the right in the Congress of Industrial Organizations (CIO) as a whole. The shattering of the left-center alliance in the CIO made such coalitions vulnerable in all the CIO unions and elsewhere in American political culture as well. With the CIO embracing the cold war consensus against Communists at home and the Soviet Union abroad, blacklisting and the near destruction of the left soon followed, particularly after Henry Wallace's poor showing in the 1948 election. In addition to the personal unhappiness it caused many left families, the practical exclusion of the left from many arenas of U.S. life during the early cold war years meant that criticism of the nuclear arms race and foreign-policy interventionism was weak, civil rights advances were slowed, and the labor movement became more bureaucratic. My scholarly work reinforced the conclusions I had reached in my personal political activity: that left leadership and left-center coalitions are essential to progressive advances. It also led me to two other ideas. The labor movement is crucial to producing any social changes of consequence in our society. National, particularly presidential, politics can shape what labor and its allies may attempt because they often determine the pattern of labor laws under which the unions must operate in our capitalist culture. Given a political and legal environment which nurtures union rights, unions can empower working people and promote progressive change.

Many people helped me by reading and commenting on one or more chapters of the manuscript, by making suggestions for improvements, or by recommending sources or helping me make contacts important to the study. I wish to thank Jon Wakelyn, Robert Asher, Paul Schervish, Sally Lancaster, John Beck, Paul Mishler, John Graves, James Hodges, Nelson Lichtenstein, Thomas Sugrue, Douglas Fraser, John Barnard, Donna ship of the social-change process and the potential for alliances between the trade unions and social-change advocates outside the labor movement. The closing chapters of the book will examine in depth the role of unions in the recent period.

The concept of social change involves an implicit critique of the existing order of society. Change is necessary, the concept implies. It is not merely or primarily that the lives of individuals need improvement; it is the lives of people (oppressed, exploited, impoverished) as social beings that are in need of improvement. Implied also is that there is a social cause to people's problems, namely the institutional arrangements of the larger society, indeed of the larger *unjust* society. Social change thus stands opposed to the status quo.

Advocates for the status quo may recognize the need to address what they see as abuses or shortcomings in the existing system. Thus, significant charitable aid may be regarded as necessary for those who fall by the wayside in the competitive system. An advocate of the status quo may help those who are unlucky or have a disability but favor the maintenance of existing socioeconomic arrangements because they are just, are based on freedom of the individual, and produce innovation and continually growing wealth for society as a whole. Social-change advocates, on the other hand, seek changes that involve real improvement in the lives of the masses of people and a shift in power toward the non-elite and relatively powerless sectors of society. Social-change advocates see societal injustice, which they wish to see corrected. They may advocate a transformation of the existing social system, substantial change in the system, or merely correction of the specific injustices they see. If they are not advocates of socialism or of radical system changes, even the most moderate social-change advocates diagnose the problems they see as consequences of injustice rather than misfortune, accident, or the inadequacies of the suffering and seek to enhance the power of the powerless as well as ameliorate their material problems.

To what degree was the labor movement a force for social change in the twentieth century? It might be argued that the labor movement is by nature a force for social change since ours is a business civilization. The *first sector*—the private business world—is by far the largest sector of our economy. The owners and managers of these private businesses have predominate—and in some cases total—control over decision-making in the first sector. As a representative of the employees of these private businesses, the labor movement has attempted to gain some say for workers over wages, working conditions, and other matters, or, in other words, to gain some power for the powerless and deprived. The rejoinder to this argument by labor's critics, however, is that, having gained some power for its members, the labor movement very quickly was transformed into a movement focusing only on the needs of its own members and neglecting

CHAPTER 1

The Labor Movement: Leader of Social Change or Just Another Interest Group?

Advocates of social change today seek to produce a just society with genuine respect and dignity for all, with power democratically controlled and distributed, and with full and equal inclusion into all areas of society of groups excluded or limited because of race, gender, age, sexual orientation, ethnicity, or class. When social-change advocates discuss the labor movement, they often focus on the distant past—the brutal suppressions of unions in the nineteenth century, for example, or the dramatic triumph of industrial unionism in the 1930s.[1] Many charge, however, that the labor movement has evolved into a narrowly focused and defensive interest group whose concerns are marginal to the process of social change. Are these claims warranted, or should the labor movement more properly be regarded as an active participant and a leader of the process of social change?

To properly address this contentious issue, this chapter will: (1) define the concept of social change; (2) provide some historical examples to show how the labor movement has, indeed, often been a significant force for social change in the twentieth century; (3) evaluate the principal critiques of the labor movement made by progressives, to wit that it (a) serves only the interests of its members and, in doing so, has often been antagonistic to non-members, including individuals suffering from historic patterns of race and sex bias, and that it (b) has become bureaucratic and focuses primarily on organizational preservation and meeting the needs of its officials; (4) explain the contradictory nature of the labor movement and the historical factors that have led to ups and downs in labor's activism on behalf of social change; and (5) briefly assess the prospects for labor leader-

Are the practitioners of left-center coalition politics likely to find a Democratic presidential candidate who wishes to steer a Rooseveltian left-of-center course, or will they once again be torn between a radical alternative like the Greens and a too-conservative Democratic candidate? The new scale of capital accumulation and the infusion of money into electoral politics tend to promote the ambitions of right-of-center Democratic presidential aspirants. The analysis contained herein of the 2000 election, however, demonstrates that Gore's popular vote victory came from the party's liberal base. The victory of a liberal Democratic aspirant would create a new climate for social advance on issues of peace and justice.

NOTES

1. Karl Marx and Frederick Engels, *Manifesto of the Communist Party* (New York: International Publishers, 1948), 31.

2. I examine the shattering of the left-center coalition in the United Automobile Workers and discuss a rare cold war victory for the left, Young's election as director of organization of the Wayne County CIO in 1947, in *UAW Politics in the Cold War Era* (Albany: State University of New York Press, 1988).

3. I discuss Truman's presidency at length in *UAW Politics.* For labor during the presidency of Woodrow Wilson, see Joseph McCartin, *Labor's Great War: The Struggle for Industrial Democracy and the Origins of Modern American Labor Relations, 1912–1921* (Chapel Hill: University of North Carolina Press, 1997).

4. Taylor Dark, "Organized Labor and the Carter Administration: The Origins of Conflict," in Herbert D. Rosenbaum and Alexej Ugrinsky, eds., *The Presidency and Domestic Politics of Jimmy Carter* (Westport, Conn.: Greenwood Press, 1994), 779; Steve Fraser and Gary Gerstle, eds., *The Rise and Fall of the New Deal Political Order, 1930–1980* (Princeton: Princeton University Press, 1989); Thomas Edsall, *The New Politics of Inequality* (New York: W.W. Norton, 1984); Thomas Ferguson and Joel Rogers, *Right Turn: The Decline of the Democrats and the Future of American Politics* (New York: Hill and Wang, 1986).

intellectuals, students, and other progressive social movements. While retaining the AFL-CIO's long-standing ties to the Democratic party, it has put a new stress on labor's independent political and public relations activities. Left-wing activists are playing an increasing role within the AFL-CIO. On the other hand, a bureaucratic approach to organizing by AFL-CIO officials and the strength of business and conservative opposition have led to limited success thus far.

The renewal of both progressive and radical activism that began in the 1960s became a permanent feature of the political landscape. Progressives and leftists became active in scores of feminist, environmental, consumer, civil rights, peace, anti-imperialist, labor, and economic justice organizations. As in the 1930s, radicals during the 1960s and after developed an institutional base in many communities and faced the challenge of protecting the interests of their constituencies and aspiring at the same time to change the direction of the country. They sought to produce both significant policy changes and a shift in the balance of political power. Throughout the twentieth century, leftists who sought both immediate improvements in the well-being of labor and the oppressed and a fundamental transformation of the U.S. polity have struggled with the practicality of developing a radical political movement to the left of the two major parties. Progressive allies of the left in labor and other social movements have been pulled toward this idea during times of radical upheavals and away from it by the hopes that a Democratic president might help promote social advances and the fears that a Republican president would destroy past gains. The century closed with progressives and radicals feeling betwixt and between by the dangers and opportunities posed by independent political action. The controversy and the outcome are examined in Chapter 9, "Gore or Nader? Progressives, Radicals, Labor, and the 2000 Election." In addition to evaluating the strengths and weaknesses of both Gore's and Nader's candidacies, the chapter also assesses the Clinton presidency and evaluates the charge that Nader cost Gore the presidency.

The immediate prospects for social change declined precipitously in the wake of the Republican-dominated Supreme Court's intervention to award George W. Bush the presidency over Al Gore, the popular vote winner. Note, however, that three of the four important elements for progressive advance were in place at the beginning of the Bush presidency. To a significant degree, the labor movement had been energized by progressive activists. The strength of a highly diversified and contentious left was much greater than its critics realized, if still far short of what it was in the 1930s. Left-center coalitions in such disparate arenas as the women's movement, environmental and electoral politics, immigrant and civil rights, and the anti-globalization movement were as active and as strong as at any time in our history.

Johnson's escalation of the Vietnam War, however, contributed decisively to the closing of a period of social advance and the Republicans gaining control of the presidency.[3]

Although Democrats regained the White House in 1976 with Jimmy Carter's narrow victory, progressives were soon disheartened as public policy lurched to the right. A more highly competitive and globalized economy, a new level of political activism by business, and a fragmentation of the Democratic party contributed to a rightward shift even before Ronald Reagan arrived to take up occupancy in the White House. Taylor Dark adds: "The central pillars of the New Deal order—a politically powerful labor movement, increasing economic growth and federal spending, and a working relationship between Democrats in Congress and the presidency—had all come unstuck." Aware of the difficulties of the moment, the United Automobile Workers (UAW), perhaps the leading embodiment of the liberal politics of the New Deal order, allied with the moderate one-term former Georgia Governor Jimmy Carter, a product of the new, fragmented, media-oriented politics of the 1970s. Despite close personal ties to UAW leaders, Carter failed to make the unions' goals of labor law reform and national health insurance truly his own. The result was a crumbling of the alliance and a failed presidency, as described in Chapter 6, "Jimmy Carter and the UAW: Failure of an Alliance." The UAW's attempt to fashion an alternative progressive politics also failed, and right-of-center approaches percolated in the Democratic party during the Reagan and Bush years.[4]

Another moderate southern Democratic president, Bill Clinton, put even less of a priority on the issue of helping the substantially weakened labor movement of the early 1990s. Chapter 7, "Arkansas and the Defeat of Labor Law Reform in 1978 and 1994," documents Clinton's practical indifference to labor's efforts to pass the workplace fairness bill. Though Clinton succeeded in winning reelection and leaned toward the liberal side of the nation's cultural divide on issues of race and gender, his focus on shepherding the country into a new global age reminds one more of the presidency of William McKinley than that of Franklin Roosevelt.

Despite Clinton's conservatism, the grassroots activism exhibited in Arkansas workers' efforts to pass legislation to counter the business tactic of permanently replacing striking workers heralded the beginning of a new labor upsurge. Chapter 8, "The Crisis of the Labor Movement in the United States and the Search for a New Vision in Domestic and Foreign Affairs," evaluates the efforts of recently elected AFL-CIO President John Sweeney to revitalize the labor movement. The long decline in union membership combined with the Republican takeover of Congress in 1994 led to a successful New Voices insurgency. In attempting to rebuild the union membership base after a period of long decline, the Sweeney leadership has emphasized grassroots militancy and reached out to radical public sympathetic to its inquisitorial goals, the story of Coleman Young's aggressive defense shows that the African American community in Detroit remained relatively immune to the frenzy of the day. Young's actions were popular and contributed to his later electoral successes. Left influence survived in the Detroit black community.

The broad support for Young in the Detroit African American community in 1952 came not only because of his charisma and his standing up to white Southern members of Congress whose positions derived in part from black disfranchisement, but also because of his long-standing role as a leader of left-center coalitions. Young had worked alongside progressives in the 1940s in such organizations as the National Negro Congress, the United Public Workers, the Wayne County CIO Council, and the National Negro Labor Council. The post-World War II red scare caused the isolation of the communist-oriented left and shattered most left-center coalitions. The many legal and economic sanctions made it impossible even for black left-wing groups to continue functioning.[2]

Bereft of the long-standing organizational alliances developed during the Franklin Roosevelt era, many individual leftists nevertheless managed to find new ways to participate in social and political activity. Left-center coalitions emerged once again in new forms in the 1960s. The roles assumed by new left groups in the civil rights advances of the 1960s are well-known, but left-center coalitions played vital, if often barely visible, roles in many other social advances of the period. Chapter 5, "From the Top Down or from the Bottom Up?" John F. Kennedy, Executive Order 10988, and the Rise of Public Sector Unionism," argues that grassroots, left-influenced coalitions contributed to one of the most important, if least heralded, progressive achievements of the postwar period.

Democratic presidents have often been the focus of working-class and progressive hopes. Although Roosevelt was the most successful of Democratic presidents, it was not for lack of opposition. The pressures on Roosevelt from the media support for such a popular rival as Henry Ford were great, as Chapter 3, "When Henry Met Franklin," illustrates. Roosevelt knew he wanted to operate a left-of-center, pro-labor course and was able to ignore these distractions. Although less decisively committed to liberal values than Roosevelt, Presidents Kennedy and Johnson both resolved to actively support the left-progressive civil rights movement in the 1960s. Kennedy's initiative in establishing collective bargaining rights for federal workers, which was continued by Johnson, had significant limitations but gave important encouragement to a grassroots unionization movement that helped public workers to become a central component of the trade union movement and an influential force in the political arena. The passage of the Civil Rights Act of 1964 and the Voting Rights Act of 1965 and the inauguration of the Medicare program established the Johnson presidency as a rival to Roosevelt's as a time of progressive legislative gains.

both sexes and of all races and ethnic groups, and seek the transformation of America's capitalist society into a socialist society run by the working class. Although they are anti-capitalist and acknowledge that they seek to advance the interests of the working class at the expense of the capitalist class, leftists believe that socialism and communism would be a more just society in which all would gain the opportunity to develop to their full potential. "In place of the old bourgeois society, with its classes and class antagonisms," Marx and Engels wrote, "we shall have an association, in which the free development of each is the condition for the free development of all."[1]

The presence of a strong left has been vital to social advances, but it is also the element that has been subject to the most sustained attack throughout much of the century. Without entering into the debate over whether the weakness of the left in the United States is part of an "exceptional" path for our country from a model of "normal" capitalist development, few would dissent from the observation that the position of the left in American society has been a precarious one. Although the words *freedom* and *democracy* were on the lips of opinion leaders throughout the twentieth century, a truly open discussion of radical alternatives has been rare in our history. If quiet but effective limitation of freedom of thought by social and economic pressures has been the norm, the country has also witnessed episodes of severe repression at both the local and national levels. In twentieth-century history, the 1917–1921 and 1947–1959 periods stand out for their repressiveness, but in many communities and in the region of the South, sharp sanctions against left-wing activism were present throughout much of the century. In these circumstances, the very survival of the left seems remarkable. That survival largely has been due to the ability of left-wing parents to pass on their values to their children. As Chapter 2, "Children of the Left: Sharing Values Across the Generations," illustrates, however, that transmission has been contested rather than automatic. There are many influences on the thinking of children of left-wing parents and the adoption of their parents' values is variable. Although the influence of peers on their children is one of the continuing challenges faced by left-wing parents (and, for that matter, by all parents), a turn to repression in the general culture creates special difficulties.

Chapter 4, "'I'm Fighting for Freedom': Coleman Young, HUAC, and the Detroit African American Community," addresses the efforts of the African American left-wing leader and future Detroit mayor to resist McCarthyite inquisitors in 1950s Detroit. Through the holding of local hearings, the House Un-American Activities Committee sought to expose and destroy centers of left-wing power and influence in American society. When HUAC went to Detroit in 1952, the anticommunist hysteria was at a particularly high pitch since the United States was fighting communism in a hot war in Korea. Although HUAC found the media and the general reasons: they felt the "have-nots" were not worthy; they saw their interests as threatened by higher taxes, a more unmanageable workforce, or loss of race and sex privileges; or they feared that the world as they knew it might collapse and be replaced by anarchy, socialism, or communism.

The term *progressive* has been much debated by historians, and many political trends have claimed this identification. Although the content of progressivism changes and develops over time, it is used here to mean that set of changes under discussion in the body politic at a given moment that would improve the lives of working people and the oppressed and make society as a whole more just.

Is the labor movement truly a movement for social change and for a more just society? Chapter 1 evaluates organized labor's role in two important social advances, the adoption of woman's suffrage in 1920 and the passage of the Civil Rights Act of 1964. It also presents a theoretical explanation for the contradictory aspects of the labor movement, the presence within it of conservative as well as progressive trends. Although many scholars and critics argue that organized labor is a special interest group, the contention here is that the labor movement is the most important social-change force in American society.

One part of the progressive trend within the labor movement is the political left. Although non-working class individuals have been part of the political left, the left trend in U.S. politics has had a working-class orientation and has focused on advancing social justice for the oppressed at home and abroad. The left-wing movement's goal has been to transform society as a whole so that encouragement to caring becomes the society's organizing principle. A planned socialist economy would provide jobs, health care, and education for all, while support would be provided for those unable to work. Cooperative values would replace competitive ones. Many nineteenth-century radicals in the labor, Populist, and Socialist movements argued that the growth of monopoly meant that the republican ethic on which the United States was founded could be best preserved by embracing the vision of a *cooperative commonwealth*. Despite many disagreements among themselves, twentieth-century left-wingers continued to look beyond immediate struggles for democratic rights and economic improvements toward a socialist future.

America's left-wing subculture has been modest in size, but its activist orientation and the value it placed on education and culture made it a significant and visible influence on twentieth-century American society. Leftists see themselves as members of a working class oppressed and exploited by the capitalist class. Although members of the working class may seek to advance themselves individually, the left-wing view is that real improvement in the lives of workers comes through collective action. Leftists are those members of the working class who actively organize against oppression and exploitation, promote united action of workers of

Introduction

Twentieth-century progressivism had its ups and downs. The most fruitful periods for progressive social change were those where the following four elements were present: (1) a Democratic president strongly influenced by liberalism; (2) a labor movement energized by progressive activists in its ranks; (3) a left-wing movement focused on organizing large numbers of working people on immediate issues of concern to them; and (4) left-center coalitions at the local and national levels endeavoring to accomplish important social change objectives such as the building of strong unions, making advances toward racial and sexual equality, creating a national health care system, or promoting a sustainable environment, peace, and global justice. Although there have been progressive advances when these elements have not been present, the most sustained periods of social progress, the New Deal and the 1960s, were periods when these four elements were all present to a substantial degree. Not a single element in this mixture, however, even in the most progressive periods, has been uncontested.

Throughout the twentieth century, there was a great deal of contention over each of these elements. Both progressives and their opponents focused on these elements as if they were pressure points in the body politic. Why? What is common to all four elements is the focus on *gaining power* to do something new or *progressive*. It is not merely the expression of visionary ideas or programs that was at stake. Liberal Democratic presidents, an activist labor movement, left-wingers, and left-center coalitions sought to change the balance of power in society so that the "have-nots" had more access and a better life. Conservatives resisted for a variety of

NPU	National Postal Union
NRA	National Recovery Administration
SEIU	Service Employees International Union
UAW	United Automobile Workers
UFT	United Federation of Teachers
UPWA	United Public Workers of America
WSU	Wayne State University Archives of Labor History and Urban Affairs

Abbreviations

AEA	Arkansas Education Association
AFL-CIO	American Federation of Labor and Congress of Industrial Organizations
AFSCME	American Federation of State, County, and Municipal Employees
AFT	American Federation of Teachers
CIO	Congress of Industrial Organizations
CNHI	Committee for National Health Insurance
CP	Communist party
CRC	Civil Rights Congress
DLC	Democratic Leadership Council
DSA	Democratic Socialists of America
EMC	Employee-Management Cooperation
FDR	Franklin Delano Roosevelt
HUAC	House Un-American Activities Committee
IUD	Industrial Union Department
JFK	John F. Kennedy
MBPU	Manhattan-Bronx Postal Union
NA	National Archives
NAFTA	North American Free Trade Agreement
NALC	National Association of Letter Carriers
NEA	National Education Association
NLRB	National Labor Relations Board
NNLC	National Negro Labor Council
NOW	National Organization for Women

Gabaccia, Haroon Khan, Roger Lohmann, George Green, Michael Gold-field, Michael Honey, Kenneth Stein, Martin James, Mark Rozell, Steve Schlossberg, Sidney Fine, Jeannie Whayne, Ronald Bayor, Gary Fink, Robert Zieger, Richard Magat, Hideo Totsuka, Kathleen Frankovic, Barry Burden, Taylor Dark, Lee Lockwood, Michael Wreszin, Ron Halpern, and Helen Webb. I am particularly grateful to my editor, Heather Staines, for her warm encouragement and support.

My research has been facilitated by the helpful and attentive assistance of librarians and archivists at many institutions including Henderson State University, the Archives of Labor History and Urban Affairs at Wayne State University, the Henry Ford Archives, the Franklin Delano Roosevelt Library, the Library of Congress, the National Archives, the John F. Kennedy Library, the Jimmy Carter Library, the New York Public Library, the George Meany Memorial Archives, and the Tamiment Institute of New York University. I wish to thank Alan Hughes for facilitating my use of the records of the Arkansas AFL-CIO and Melba Collins for providing me access to her personal papers.

Numerous individuals shared their stories with me. I wish to thank Douglas Fraser, Leonard Woodcock, Stuart Eizenstat, Melba Collins, Alan Hughes, former Senators Dale Bumpers and David Pryor, former Representative George Crockett, David Moore, Arthur McPhaul, Shelton Tappes, James Jackson, Gordon Brehm, Christopher Alston, Lane Kirkland, Bill Becker, Stanley Nowak, and Harold Shapiro.

Henderson State University has provided me with numerous research grants and other support that greatly facilitated my work on this project. During the course of my stay in Japan, I benefited from the kindness and interest in my work of colleagues in the Faculty of Economics and the American Studies Department of Tohoku University, where I served as a Fulbright lecturer. I was pleased to respond to the request of Hideo Totsuka of the Transnational Center for Labor Studies to provide a picture of the new directions in the U.S. labor movement, my initial work on Chapter 8 herein.

I owe my greatest debt to my wife, Helen Webb, who both discussed the project with me as it was evolving and read and critiqued the entire manuscript. I began the project with the challenge of parenting in mind, and our daughters, Sheila and Leah Webb-Halpern, have shown increasing interest in the project. My hope is that the volume will be of value to them and to all others who continue to seek social change and a just and peaceful world.

movement activist in the 1960s and 1970s, I sought to find ways to bring about broad-based alliances, conduct militant actions, win specific gains, and strengthen the progressive organizations within which I worked. At the same time, I tried to study and learn along with other participants what our experiences meant for understanding the nature of our society and what it would take to transform it so that caring and social justice, equality and peace would be our fundamental principles. As an activist in local and national campaigns, I found that left leadership and left-center coalitions were crucial ingredients in achieving advances.

Like many young people who were left-minded in the 1960s, I was disappointed in the weakness of the left in our country, especially so since my own parents had brought me up to be a working-class-minded leftist. I set out in my first major project as an historian to find out what happened to the left of my parents' generation. I discovered, as I described in *UAW Politics in the Cold War Era,* that the passage of the Taft-Hartley Act in 1947 was the decisive turning point in leading to the defeat of the left-center coalition in the United Automobile Workers. The UAW defeat led to a turn to the right in the Congress of Industrial Organizations (CIO) as a whole. The shattering of the left-center alliance in the CIO made such coalitions vulnerable in all the CIO unions and elsewhere in American political culture as well. With the CIO embracing the cold war consensus against Communists at home and the Soviet Union abroad, blacklisting and the near destruction of the left soon followed, particularly after Henry Wallace's poor showing in the 1948 election. In addition to the personal unhappiness it caused many left families, the practical exclusion of the left from many arenas of U.S. life during the early cold war years meant that criticism of the nuclear arms race and foreign-policy interventionism was weak, civil rights advances were slowed, and the labor movement became more bureaucratic. My scholarly work reinforced the conclusions I had reached in my personal political activity: that left leadership and left-center coalitions are essential to progressive advances. It also led me to two other ideas. The labor movement is crucial to producing any social changes of consequence in our society. National, particularly presidential, politics can shape what labor and its allies may attempt because they often determine the pattern of labor laws under which the unions must operate in our capitalist culture. Given a political and legal environment which nurtures union rights, unions can empower working people and promote progressive change.

Many people helped me by reading and commenting on one or more chapters of the manuscript, by making suggestions for improvements, or by recommending sources or helping me make contacts important to the study. I wish to thank Jon Wakelyn, Robert Asher, Paul Schervish, Sally Lancaster, John Beck, Paul Mishler, John Graves, James Hodges, Nelson Lichtenstein, Thomas Sugrue, Douglas Fraser, John Barnard, Donna

Preface

Historical writing stems from the experiences of the person writing as much as from her or his forays into archives, libraries, or living rooms of living persons whose memories one wishes to stir. The research for this book began after my family moved from Lansing, Michigan, to the small university town of Arkadelphia, Arkansas, in 1990. How would my wife and I raise our daughters, then seven and five, and pass on our left-wing values in a Bible Belt town largely devoid of left influences and more than nine hundred miles away from the nearest family member on either side? This personal dilemma led me to respond to a call for papers on "Passing on the Tradition of Caring" issued by Independent Sector, a leading organization in the philanthropic community. I took the opportunity to examine how left-wing parents throughout the twentieth century attempted to pass on their traditions and concepts of caring to their children. The resulting study, "Children of the Left: Sharing Values Across the Generations," is the second of two introductory chapters in the present volume. Chapter 1, "The Labor Movement: Leader of Social Change or Just Another Interest Group?" also was first presented at a philanthropy conference and aims to provide a basic theoretical introduction to the nature of the labor movement and answer critics who tend to dismiss it as irrelevant to the social change process or worse. The remaining chapters in the book carry forward the themes of the influence of labor and the left in the social change process and focus as well on left-center coalitions and presidential politics.

Long before I began the research that resulted in this book, I was an activist in peace, civil rights, and other social-change movements. As a the needs and injustices inflicted on other powerless members of society. Let us look, then, at more general social-change issues to assess the degree to which labor can be counted as a significant participant in this process.

There are many forms of power-holding in our society. Control of economic resources, of property, is of fundamental importance. Power in the political arena tends to flow from power in the economic realm, but our democratic system does provide others with opportunities to seek changes that may alter existing social arrangements. One of the elementary—but nevertheless portentous—changes is gaining access to the political arena. Prior to the twentieth century, women had voting rights in only four western states with small populations.

The women's suffrage movement, born at Seneca Falls, New York, in 1848, finally burgeoned into a tremendous mass movement in the second decade of the twentieth century and achieved victory in 1920. What role did the working-class movement play in the campaign to achieve women's suffrage? In 1904, socialists began a series of working-women's conferences. In 1908, the socialist women adopted March 8 as a day to agitate for the right to vote. Mass gatherings were held on the east side of New York. In 1910, the International Socialist Congress adopted March 8 as International Women's Day.[2] This was one of the streams of a rising militancy among women in both the United States and Great Britain that brought the women's suffrage issue from the back burner to the center of politics in these two countries.

Influenced by the militant tactics of the British suffrage movement, Harriet Stanton Blatch began another important activist stream when she initiated the formation of the Equality League of Self-Supporting Women in New York. The new organization brought thousands of working women into the struggle for suffrage with new tactics such as open-air meetings, outdoor meetings before factory gates, and the now famous suffrage parades. It recruited women unionists to testify before the state legislature on behalf of women's rights, adding a new vitality and realism to the arguments for women's suffrage. Thus Mary Duffy of the Overall Makers Union testified: "We working women are often told that we should stay at home and then everything will be all right. But we can't stay at home. We have to go out and work.... Gentlemen, we need every help to fight the battle of life, and to be left out by the State just sets up a prejudice against us. Bosses think, and women come to think themselves, that they don't count for as much as men."[3]

Women trade unionists played prominent roles in the suffrage movement. Leonora O'Reilly was a pioneer trade unionist in the Knights of Labor and later served as an organizer for the Women's Trade Union League (WTUL) and president of the Wage Earners Suffrage League. She told a joint meeting of the U.S. Senate Women's Suffrage and Judiciary Committees in 1912: "You can not or will not make laws for us; we must make laws for ourselves. We working women need the ballot for self-protection; that is all there is to it. We have got to have it."[4] Outspoken for suffrage also were Clara Lemlich, the leader of the 1909 Uprising of 20,000 Shirt Waist Makers; Rose Schneiderman of the Cap Makers Union and the WTUL; and Socialist organizers Ida Crouch Hazlett of Colorado, Meta Berger of Wisconsin, Theresa Maikel of New York, and Ella Reeve Bloor of Connecticut.[5]

Women trade unionists and Socialists were also active in the two leading national suffrage organizations, the National American Women Suffrage Association (known as the National) and the Woman's Party. The WTUL had played a vital role in supporting strikes of women garment and clothing workers but, after 1910, increasingly turned its attention to working on the suffrage issue. Margaret Hinchey, a laundry worker hired as a WTUL organizer, worked closely with the National. In February 1914, she went to Rochester and organized 600 working women "to call on President Wilson...and ask him for the vote."[6] When women suffrage advocates were arrested for picketing the White House in 1917 after the United States entered World War I, among those jailed was a group of workers from a Bridgeport munitions plant. "When the women protested against the illegality of their arrests, the bad conditions, and the brutality of their treatment by going on hunger strikes, the authorities...resorted to forced feeding, and made martyrs wholesale."[7] A mass meeting of working-women sponsored by the Seattle Central Labor Council resolved to picket the White House if the jailed suffragists were not immediately freed.[8]

What was the position of male trade unionists in general and of the leadership of the AFL on the issue of women's suffrage? One of the most prominent partisans of women's suffrage was Eugene Debs, leader of the Pullman strike of 1894 and, after 1900, the nation's best-known Socialist. Support for women's suffrage came from less radical laborites as well. At its 1907 convention, the National reported that the AFL, the International Brotherhood of Teamsters, the International Brotherhood of Bookbinders, the United Mine Workers, and fifteen state federations all had endorsed votes for women. Endorsements from additional unions and state federations came in later years. Many of the union resolutions were unanimous.[9] AFL President Samuel Gompers observed in 1915: "The right to use the ballot increases the power and resourcefulness of voters whether they be men or women, and thereby puts them in such a position that they are able to better work out their own industrial problems."[10]

It was, of course, independent women's organizations that played the leading role in the campaign to achieve women's suffrage. Women trade unionists, women Socialists, and working-class women's organizations played important parts in this multi-class effort. Male-dominated labor unions, particularly those influenced by Socialists, tended to be more sympathetic to the women's movement than were other male-dominated organizations. Although some labor activists and labor organizations, including the radical Industrial Workers of the World and some AFL central labor bodies, opposed the women's suffrage movement, the working-class movement in general contributed in important ways to the success of this historic achievement.[11]

The consequences of the women's suffrage victory have often been downplayed in the literature. The hoped-for transformation of American society spoken of by advocates of women's suffrage did not come to pass. Although a new morality did not immediately dominate the U.S. polity, as was the hope of many suffragists, and many forms of inequality still plagued women, the gain of suffrage—the *sin qua non* of full citizenship—was a giant step forward. It became much more difficult to define and isolate women as helpless, dependent, or inferior creatures. Women's participation in the political arena accelerated, and the basis was laid for the modern feminist movement's drive for full equality in economic, social, political, and family life. Major legislative changes sometimes change social relationships and social thinking in fundamentally important ways. In winning the vote, women gained the opportunity to speak for themselves and acquired a slice of power in the democratic system that was previously denied them.

Another major democratic advance of the twentieth century was the civil rights transformation of the 1960s. The upsurge of the modern civil rights movement that began with the Montgomery bus boycott of 1955–56 culminated in two historic pieces of legislation, the Civil Rights Act of 1964 and the Voting Rights Act of 1965. These national legislative achievements reinforced the impact of the grassroots protest activities and resulted in irresistible pressure that ended the system of Jim Crow segregation in the South. The federal government enforced equal access to public accommodations, African American voting rights, and equal-employment opportunity. Although complete equality has yet to be achieved, for the first time since Reconstruction, African Americans gained a share of power in southern society. African American political power grew in the North as well. The fair employment practices clause of the Civil Rights Act led to an increase in professional, skilled, manufacturing, and government jobs for African Americans.

As was the case with the women's suffrage movement, the mass base and leadership of the civil rights movement was composed of members of the oppressed group seeking redress—in this case, African Americans. Similarly, unionists from the oppressed group were among the leaders and activists in the movement. For example, E. D. Nixon of the Sleeping Car Porters Union and the NAACP was a key organizer of the Montgomery bus boycott. The initiative for the famous 1963 March on Washington came from the Negro American Labor Council led by A. Philip Randolph. Randolph and two other African American trade unionists,

Bayard Rustin and Cleveland Robinson, were among the march's most important organizers.[12]

The AFL-CIO played a key role in getting the fair employment practices clause, Title VII, into the 1964 Act. President John F. Kennedy thought it would kill the bill and wanted it as a separate measure. AFL-CIO President George Meany told the House Judiciary Committee in 1963 that the labor movement supported equal employment opportunity laws while employer groups bitterly opposed them:

We need the statutory support of the federal government to carry out the unanimously-adopted principles of the AFL-CIO.... the labor movement is not what its enemies say it is—a monolithic, dictatorial, centralized body that imposes its will on the helpless dues payers. We operate in a democratic way, and we cannot dictate even in a good cause. So, in effect, we need a federal law to help us do what we want to do: mop up those areas of discrimination which still persist in our own ranks.[13]

Although Meany's statement underestimated the degree to which many unions were involved in defending white male job privileges, the AFL-CIO did push hard for the inclusion of Title VII in the civil rights bill and its lobbying was instrumental in the passage of the act.[14]

Meany, of course, was one of the more conservative figures in the U.S. labor movement. Although he supported the civil rights bill, he refrained from participation in or even endorsement of the historic August 28, 1963, March on Washington for jobs and freedom. Two weeks before the march, Meany stopped a move in the AFL-CIO executive council to issue a statement supporting the goals of the march and commending unions that planned to participate.

As a leading cold warrior, moreover, Meany supported the Vietnam War, opposed détente with the Soviet Union, and opposed leftists in U.S. domestic politics.[15] Despite this conservatism, it is impossible to imagine that the civil rights revolution and the Great Society of the mid-1960s would have achieved legislative successes if it had not been for the influence of the labor movement on the Democratic members of Congress. Lyndon Johnson observed in 1965: "The AFL-CIO has done more good for more people than any group in America in its legislative efforts. It doesn't [only] try to do something about wages and hours for its own people. No group in the country works harder in the interests of everyone."[16]

Meany's contribution to social change in the mid-1960s was to lobby for liberal legislation and, in addition, to provide electoral support for pro-civil rights and pro-Great Society candidates. Other labor leaders provided support in additional areas. Prior to the 1963 March on Washington, there was a preliminary civil rights march in Detroit of 150,000 to 200,000 led by Dr. Martin Luther King, Jr., and by Walter Reuther, president of the United Automobile Workers. Reuther and the Industrial Union Department of the

AFL-CIO participated in the March on Washington. An estimated 40,000 of the total of 200,000 to 250,000 marchers were trade unionists.[17] Local union leaders and rank-and-file activists were involved in raising funds and other volunteer activities supporting the civil rights movement. To be sure, the labor movement also included extreme opponents of civil rights along with the radical, liberal, and moderate supporters of civil rights. Many AFL-CIO affiliates in Mississippi, for example, were taken over by Ku Klux Klan members. Even there, however, Claude Ramsay, the president of the state affiliate, was a staunch civil rights supporter whose "life was threatened,...family...harassed, and...was denounced by name at Klan rallies."[18] Ramsay persevered despite great opposition from white union members both because of his own convictions and because of solid support from the national AFL-CIO.

The example of the Mississippi trade unionists who actively supported the Ku Klux Klan makes clear that the labor movement includes within it individuals who strongly oppose changes in the status quo. Less extreme forms of conservatism, such as resistance to affirmative action programs, are also a feature of the labor movement. Nevertheless, an assessment of the historical significance of the labor movement's civil rights record must include the crucial support given to the central legislative triumphs of the era along with shortcomings, particularly in the areas of affirmative action and promotion of African Americans into union leadership ranks.

The labor movement was a factor of some weight in the achievement of two of the most important social changes of the twentieth century. Other examples could be adduced. Nevertheless, it is important to come to grips with what has thus far been only hinted at—the critique of the labor movement offered not by exponents of the status quo but by social-change advocates both outside and inside the labor movement. Of course, a number of conservative critics argue that organized labor is a special interest concerned only about the narrow interests of a group of relatively privileged workers. This charge devastated Walter Mondale's 1984 presidential candidacy, which was strongly supported by the labor movement.[19] Some progressive critics, however, make essentially this same criticism. For example, J. Craig Jenkins cites a survey of advocacy organizations in Washington, D.C. that found that "nonprofit advocates generally...find themselves at odds with the more privatistic positions taken by the special interest representatives of trade associations, corporations, professional societies, and unions."[20] It might be difficult to convince these nonprofit activists that the labor movement is a fundamental force for social change when their own experience is that union representatives oppose their progressive public policy goals.

Unionists tend to reject the special-interest label. For example, as early as 1964, George Meany argued: "The modern labor movement long ago outgrew the role of 'special interest group' in the narrow sense. The AFL-

CIO is made up of 13.5 million men and women who live in every state of the Union, who are engaged in virtually every occupation except business proprietorship, and whose interests, not only as union members but as citizens, embrace every facet of American life. This infinite variety is reflected in the ever-widening scope of the AFL-CIO's legislative program, for we try to represent the needs and aspirations of all workers, in all phases of their lives. Thus we are for more clear trout streams, for a humane immigration policy as well as a shorter work week."[21]

Although the AFL-CIO's legislative program is broadly progressive in a wide variety of areas, the critics raise a number of substantive and serious issues. Unions sometimes falter in representing their members' interests fully and well, as the experience of several unions with concession bargaining in the 1980s demonstrated.[22] The unions' internal political life is sometimes less democratic than some members, opponents of union leaders within the organizations, and outside progressive critics would like.[23] Writing in the 1980s, *New York Times* labor journalist A.H. Raskin contended that "mobsters have achieved [influence] in recent years in a number of important unions."[24] In the 1970s, the unions' record in altering patterns of racial and sexual discrimination was judged less than adequate by members of the affected groups both within and outside the movement, but criticism on this subject diminished in the ensuing years.[25] Similarly, some progressive political activists in the 1970s found AFL-CIO leaders opposing both Democratic party reform and the most liberal Democratic candidates. These disputes also subsided in the 1980s.[26]

Many commentators—including some sympathetic to labor—have concluded that the labor movement is no longer a force for social change. In an analysis of the recent crisis of the U.S. labor movement, Peter Seybold argued that "labor's commitment to mainstream politics and to the Democratic party had a number of contradictory aspects which by the 1980s had stripped labor of its character as a social movement and reduced it to just another special interest group."[27] What was the historical process leading to this development? For Seybold, labor's failures in the 1940s and 1950s to "press the case of society-wide social reforms," to organize the unorganized, and "to encourage rank-and-file activism" led the labor movement to be "content just to be recognized as a major player." As a result, it was unprepared for the assaults from business that came in the 1970s and 1980s. In the 1980s, Seybold stressed, the AFL-CIO, while conducting some efforts to defend unions, supported Reagan administration foreign policy "as if the leaders...expected elites to call off or moderate the corporate offensive against labor once they could conclusively prove to business that the labor movement was thoroughly committed to anticommunism." The AFL-CIO's "pledge of allegiance...to an unsophisticated and dogmatic cold war ideology...distanced itself further from its potential allies in the religious community as well as the peace and anti-intervention movements," Seybold maintained. Moreover, "suppression of dissenters" from the AFL-CIO foreign policy approach "created even more distance between the rank and file and the national federation."[28]

The problem with the critiques of the labor movement is that they tend to become one-sided. They ignore the degree to which the unions do many things well in representing their members' interests, in providing them a modicum of protection, and in speaking out and working for the broader social needs of the deprived in our society. The labor movement is the principal factor in our polity that has attempted to preserve and expand governmentally mandated social welfare. It is the labor movement that pushes for a higher minimum wage to lift more people out of poverty. It is the labor movement that has been the principal institutional support for the campaign for national health insurance.[29] Nevertheless, the flaws to which the critics point are real enough and require explanation.

How do we untangle these contradictory realities—a labor movement often at the center of the social-change process but both flawed in its internal processes and too often on the sidelines or on the wrong side of public policy issues of concern to social-change advocates?

The term *labor movement* implies a social change and activist orientation. Wage earners are seeking change, improvement in their immediate material situations, a greater say at their work sites, and a polity in which their ideas and needs receive due consideration. The labor movement is by nature collectivistic rather than individualistic. Groups of workers who face common problems combine to gain a measure of power for the group and thereby diminish the absolute power of the employer over their work lives. The labor movement by definition is a social-change movement.

Although the labor movement is a social-change movement, it inevitably is less than perfect in embodying within it all the social-change needs of our society. The labor movement is a movement of, by, and for workers. Trade unions as democratic and representative institutions reflect the thinking of their members. The thinking of the membership changes historically due to demographic changes in the workforce and union membership and ideological debates among workers. Some of these debates are unique to workers, but many more are reflective of ongoing debates on cultural, social, and economic issues in our society. To the degree that social change is an effort to seek social justice as well as social power for the powerless, ideological conceptions are central to the issues at hand. Trade unionists, like all other members of society, are influenced by the ideological debates ongoing in our polity on social justice issues. Contends Douglas Fraser, "When a union advocates such issues as affirmative action, welfare benefits, and gun control and speaks out against capital punishment and discrimination on the basis of race, gender, or sexual orientation, you get into difficulty with some of the members." Citing the examples of the bigoted racial campaigns of John Silber in Massachusetts and David

Duke in Louisiana, Fraser observes that the support such candidates get among white blue-collar workers "has a tremendous impact on the union's efforts in politics, in organizing, and in other areas of union activity."[30] Moreover, even on issues in the immediate workplace interest of workers, different groups may have contradictory interests. For example, workers at the Ypsilanti, Michigan, and Arlington, Texas, General Motors plants—both represented by the United Automobile Workers—competed against one another to prevent their factory from closure.

Despite internal divisions among workers and the influence of status quo thinking on working-class people, the labor movement represents the most significant institutional base for social change in the country. This is the case because labor unions are mass membership organizations with a base at the work site, the most critical site of the institutional power of the status quo forces in our society. Recall the dominance of the first sector in day-to-day decision-making in our society. Recall the importance of business influence on decision-makers in the second (public) and third (non-profit) sectors. Organized labor is the only significant institutional factor challenging the powers that be at the source of their power, the private business workplace. Despite the differences among workers, the philosophy of trade unionism reasserts the need for unity of working people against employers and their allies in government. It is the only significant institutional setting in which the ideas emanating from the business community are continuously challenged.

What are the current prospects for labor leadership of the social-change process? What potential is there for alliances between the trade unions and social-change advocates outside the labor movement? To address these questions, we need to evaluate the possible outcomes to labor's current crisis and examine the thinking prevalent among nonlabor social-change advocates.

Social change requires action at the local, national, and international levels. The importance of the international arena becomes obvious when its effect is negative: when our country is mobilized to fight an unjust war to preserve traditional power structures, the opposition to social change at home rises. National resources need to be used to fight the foreign foe, the opponents of social change argue, not for social experimentation.

The idea that real change is local was popular with many veterans of 1960s social-change movements. Given the collapse of the Great Society in the wake of the escalation of the Vietnam War, disillusionment with change at the national level was understandable. In turning toward localism, these activists failed to recognize the factors shaping their own political development. It was, in fact, the successes of the civil rights movement as a national movement seeking congressional legislation, the reforms of the Great Society, and the national protests of the antiwar movement that led many products of the sixties generation to become social-change advocates. Their experience was simultaneously local and national. They partic-ipated in local organizations and activities, but ones that were intimately tied into central events of our national political life. There is a symbiosis between national and local social-change efforts. Neither can get very far without the other. A national effort without a foundation in local commu-nities and workplaces will have very little punch or staying power. Simi-larly, local movements that are isolated from national currents will tend to sputter and be overwhelmed by the forces of the status quo.

Sixties types went into many nooks and crannies of our culture. They went into social work, academia, the civil service, into trade unions, femi-nist, environmental, consumer, and health organizations, the law and pol-itics, and philanthropy. They created new networks, movements, and trends. Many of these activists encourage challenges to the existing order and its institutions and "try to empower disadvantaged people to make permanent improvements in their social and economic environments and in the basic institutions of our society that affect their lives." Many groups emphasize "citizen-based grass roots organizing," create "cooperatives and worker-owned-and-managed enterprises in low-income communi-ties" and seek empowerment of the poor, the disadvantaged, minorities, and women.[31]

Rabinowitz describes a sample of ninety-one projects supported by the new social-change philanthropic network, including many grants that involved funding of working-class community organizations, particularly in African American and Hispanic communities. In New Orleans, for example, the Workers' Rights Action Project focuses on improving work-ing conditions and benefits for low-wage service workers. The Midwest Unemployed Organizing Project negotiates with service providers on behalf of its members and campaigns for jobs, health care, and lower util-ity rates. 9to5, the National Association for Working Women, builds grass-roots organizations that help women office and clerical workers improve working conditions. The Comité de Apoyo a Los Trabajadores Agrícola is an organization of Hispanic agricultural workers in New Jersey, Pennsyl-vania, and Puerto Rico that forms worker committees to push for "mini-mum wages, better housing, and protection from dangerous chemicals, as well as favorable unemployment and pesticide regulations."[32]

Rabinowitz's sample makes clear that some nonlabor social-change advocates are cognizant of the special problems of working-class commu-nities and minority and women workers. Social-change philanthropists have targeted funds to assist working-class people to both improve their material situations and to gain greater say in their working lives and in their communities. Even those organizations that specifically address improving workers' lives, however, seem to shy away from unionization as an explicit goal. In a survey of specific labor-oriented grants by founda-tions, Richard Magat found 300 such grants since the 1980s on a wide variety of topics, including some that assist rank-and-file union groups.[33] If unionization as such is rarely the focal point of grantees or foundations, is it because unionization would spin grantees out of legal 5013(c) nonprofit status? Is it because of hostility to the characteristics of the existing labor movement? Is it because of the preference for local organizing and local autonomy—with the implication that unionization necessarily involves subordination to national bodies such as a national (or international) union and the national AFL-CIO?

Whatever the reasons, the apparent tendency of grantees to distance themselves from the organized labor movement weakens both the grantees and the labor movement. An organization interested in empowering low-income workers on the job will languish if it fails to use the weapon of unionization. Working-class community organizations that distance themselves from the labor movement may make it more difficult to establish themselves on a permanent basis if they hesitate to link themselves with the philosophy and institutional support of the national labor movement.

While the labor movement is the most important institutional base for social-change activism, its own prospects have been troubled since the mid-1970s. There has been a dramatic decline in union density, the percentage of all workers who belong to unions, and an erosion of workers' right to strike. The causes of these difficulties and the efforts to overcome them will be examined in later chapters. Aware of its need for allies, the AFL-CIO in the 1990s was considering the establishment of associate membership status for friends and supporters of labor.[34] The AFL-CIO might also consider creating activist community unions composed of those workers who would like to but do not have unions at their work sites. These community unions would support the AFL-CIO legislative and educational efforts and, at the same time, assist in the unionization of those work sites of its members where circumstances were most promising for such efforts.[35]

The survival of the labor movement should be of concern to all social-change advocates. If there is no strong institutional counterweight to private business power in the first sector, all efforts to bring about changes in the status quo are weakened. Social-change advocates should add to their goals support for educating the public on the importance of the survival of an independent, powerful, national labor movement for the vibrancy of our democracy. It may be that there is no more important social-change effort than ensuring the survival of the labor movement itself.

NOTES

1. See, for example, Frances Fox Piven and Richard A. Cloward, *Poor People's Movements: Why They Succeed, How They Fail* (New York: Random House, 1977).

2. Ella Reeve Bloor, *We Are Many* (New York: International Publishers, 1940), 93.

3. Eleanor Flexner, *Century of Struggle: The Woman's Rights Movement in the United States* (Cambridge, Mass.: Belknap Press, 1959), 249–54.

4. Sarah Eisenstein, *Give Us Bread But Give Us Roses: Working Women's Consciousness in the United States, 1890 to the First World War* (London: Routledge & Kegan Paul, 1983), 155–56. On O'Reilly, see Flexner, *Century of Struggle*, 202.

5. Eisenstein, *Give Us Bread*, 157–60; Mari Jo Buhle, *Women and American Socialism, 1870–1920* (Urbana: University of Illinois Press, 1981), 214–41; Bloor, *We Are Many*, 92–94.

6. Philip Foner, *History of the Labor Movement in the United States*, vol. 6 (New York: International Publishers, 1982), 138. There were tensions over class and ideology within the women's movement. See Eisenstein, *Give Us Bread*, 149, and the document set, Thomas Dublin and Kathryn Kish Sklar, "How Was the Relationship Between Workers and Allies Shaped by the Perceived Threat of Socialism in The New York City Shirtwaist Strike, 1909–1910," <http://womhist.binghamton. edu/shirt/doclist.htm> (accessed December 5, 2002).

7. Flexner, *Century of Struggle*, 285.

8. Philip Foner, *Women and the American Labor Movement: From World War I to the Present* (New York: The Free Press, 1980), 57–58.

9. Ida Husted Harper, *The History of Woman Suffrage*, vol. 5, *1900–1920* (New York: National American Woman Suffrage Association, 1922), 205–6, 249, 281–82.

10. David Morgan, *Suffragists and Democrats: The Politics of Woman Suffrage in American* ([East Lansing]: Michigan State University Press, 1972), 60.

11. Buhle, *Women and American Socialism*, 214–41; Foner, *History of the Labor Movement*, 6:137.

12. Philip Foner, *Organized Labor and the Black Worker, 1619–1973* (New York: Praeger, 1974), 334–50.

13. Archie Robinson, *George Meany and His Times* (New York: Simon & Schuster, 1981), 236.

14. While agreeing that AFL-CIO support was important to the inclusion of FEPC in the civil rights bill, Denton Watson notes that as the bill wound its way through Congress, "the civil rights forces were steadfastly opposing weakening amendments, some of which were also offered by the AFL-CIO to Title VII [the FEPC clause]." Denton L. Watson, *Clarence L. Mitchell, Jr.'s Struggle for the Passage of Civil Rights Laws* (New York: William Morrow, 1990), 547–49, 610. For a polemical debate on the topic, see Herbert Hill, "Meany, Reuther, and the 1964 Civil Rights Act," *New Politics* 7 (Summer 1998), 82–107; Nelson Lichtenstein, "Walter Reuther in Black and White: A Rejoinder to Herbert Hill"; and Herbert Hill, "Lichtenstein's Fictions Revisited: Race and the New Labor History," both in *New Politics* 7 (Winter 1999), 133–63.

15. *New York Times*, August 14, 1963, 21.

16. Quoted in Robinson, *George Meany*, 244 n.

17. Foner, *Organized Labor and the Black Worker*, 347–50.

18. Alan Draper, "Claude Ramsay, the Mississippi AFL-CIO, and the Civil Rights Movement," *Labor's Heritage* 4 (Winter 1992): 4–19.

19. Steven M.. Gillon, *The Democrats' Dilemma: Walter F. Mondale and the Liberal Legacy* (New York: Columbia University Press, 1992).

20. J. Craig Jenkins, "Nonprofit Organizations and Policy Advocacy," in Walter W. Powell, *The Nonprofit Sector: A Research Handbook* (New Haven, Conn.: Yale University Press, 1987), 298.

21. Robinson, *George Meany*, 240.

22. Kim Moody, *An Injury to All: The Decline of Industrial Unionism* (London: Verso, 1988); Charles Craypo, "The Decline in Union Bargaining Power," in Bruce Nissen, ed., *U.S. Labor Relations, 1945–1989: Accommodation and Conflict* (New York: Garland Publishing, 1990), 17–27.

23. Herman Benson, "The Fight for Union Democracy," in Seymour Martin Lipset, ed., *Unions in Transition, Entering the Second Century* (San Francisco: ICS Press, 1986), 323–70.

24. A.H. Raskin, "Labor: A Movement in Search of a Mission," in Lipset, *Unions in Transition*, 15.

25. Deborah E. Bell, "Women and the Rise of Public-Sector Unionism Since the 1960s, in Eileen Boris and Nelson Lichtenstein, eds., *Major Problems in the History of American Workers* (Lexington, Mass.: Heath, 1991), 621–33; Alice H. Cook, "Women and Minorities," in George Strauss, Daniel G. Gallagher, and Jack Fiorito, *The State of the Unions* (Madison, Wis.: Industrial Relations Research Association Series, 1991), 237–57.

26. William Crotty, *Party Reform* (New York: Longman, 1983), 131–33.

27. Peter Seybold, "American Labor at the Crossroads: Political Resurgence or Continued Decline?" in Nissen, *U.S. Labor Relations, 1945–1989*, 46–51.

28. Ibid.

29. Vincente Navarro, "Swaying the Health Care Task Force," *The Nation* 257 (September 6/13, 1993): 230, 246–49.

30. Douglas Fraser, "Inside the 'Monolith,'" in Strauss et al., *State of the Unions*, 413.

31. Alan Rabinowitz, *Social Change Philanthropy in America* (New York: Quorum Books, 1990), 6–8, 11.

32. Ibid., 157–204.

33. Richard Magat, "Organized Labor and Philanthropic Foundations: Partners or Strangers," (paper presented at the Annual Conference of the Association for Research on Nonprofit Organizations and Voluntary Action, Toronto, Canada, October 28–30, 1993).

34. David Brody, *Workers in Industrial America: Essays on the Twentieth Century Struggle*, 2nd ed. (New York: Oxford University Press, 1993), 265 n. 19.

35. For two somewhat different approaches to community unionism, see Michael J. Piore, "The Future of Unions," in Strauss et al., *State of the Unions*, 404–9, and Jeremy Brecher, "Crisis Economy: Born-Again Labor Movement?" *Monthly Review* 34 (March 1984): 12–15.

CHAPTER 2

Children of the Left: Sharing Values Across the Generations

How can we as a society raise our children so that they become adults who care thoughtfully and actively about the needs of others? We must first take note of the fact that our society is not organized to bring about such a goal. There is no central planning in the fields of child development or education, just as there is no central planning of the economy in the United States. Our society does not have a single "we" but rather many competing, conflicting, and cooperating "we's" and "I's." In the cacophony of conflicting subcultures, ideas, and values, it is not surprising that there is no shared goal of raising children to be thoughtful and actively caring about others in society. In practice, much of the responsibility for the transmission of caring values devolves upon the family and the community. In some families and communities, the concept of caring is valued only for members of one's subculture. In some cases, caring is limited to members of one's own family. In other cases, caring is viewed as a delusion: pursuing one's own self-interest is the only meaningful goal.

Although families and communities may wish to transmit caring values to children, the diversity of power centers within our society means that the influences on our children are many and often conflicting. Our children are influenced by their parents, by their extended families, by their teachers and other adults in the school environment, by their peers, and by general societal institutions such as the media, the business community, trade unions, churches, civic organizations, and government. They also may be influenced by neighbors as well as by members of their family's subculture(s).

How important is membership in a caring subculture to the development of children into caring adults? How is the moral development of children brought up in caring subcultures affected by such other variables as the media, the schools, and peer groups? What happens when a caring subculture is out-of-joint with the larger society? Is it able to survive and pass on its traditions to the younger generation?

This chapter examines the attempts of members of one subculture—the left-wing movement in the twentieth-century United States—to pass on caring values to its children. A study of the left's experience is useful because activist caring is at the core of the left's value system rather than a peripheral or subsidiary concern. Moreover, the left, while critical of the existing social system, has not sought to wall off its members into an unchanging sect. Accepting the reality of a rapidly changing society, left-wing families have sent their children into the public educational system to learn and eventually into the market economy to earn a living while attempting to transmit to them the value of caring for their people and all people, for the working class and all oppressed people. Children of the left have faced the problem of coming to grips with ideas and value systems coming from the government, employers, the media, the schools, and peers that conflict with the ideas and values of their parents.

The left has shown a great deal of resilience but has also faced tremendous adversity. As a secular, modern, and egalitarian subculture, the left has supported scientific and technological progress and favored an end to the traditional subordination of minorities and women. The left's philosophical orientation thus allowed it to adapt to rapid changes in twentieth-century American society while at the same time maintaining its core values. For example, left-wing understanding of women's oppression evolved considerably during the course of the century, especially under the impact of the feminist movement that erupted in the 1960s.[1] Because the left is a subculture that defines itself as oppositional to the existing social system, however, it has endured hostility from powerful groups determined to maintain the status quo. The left's experience, therefore, can highlight the workings of subcultural survival mechanisms. The maintenance of alternative subcultures from which grassroots activist movements can develop is an important factor in the struggle for social progress.

The concept of caring is an important component of the left-wing outlook. The director of the Aliyah Senior Citizens Center in Venice, California, the subject of Barbara Myerhoff's anthropological work *Number Our Days,* noted that his mother was

one of the important people in the Russian revolution. She was the first one in our town to carry the Red Flag. She was what you call a humanitarian, a most dedicated person.... In my life, she had the biggest influence.... I do all what I can for humanity, perpetuating the ideas of my mother, so that I want to carry that on for her. I'm not so big, like Abraham, Moses, Christ, and Buddha. But you should know, they too didn't want war. Those people left their footsteps on history, and in my smaller way, I may do that also.[2]

At the most general level, the left's concept of care, helping humanity, is similar to that of the philanthropic community. As is implicit from the juxtaposition of the image of carrying the "Red Flag" and being a humanitarian, to the left being a caring person means being politically active for the working class. Also evident is the left's emphasis on history. Leftists feel connected to the past and the future of their movement. The dedication during difficult times to carry on for the sake of those who went before and for those who will come after provides important sustenance, similar to the spiritual faith of religious people. Although leftists generally favor scientific thinking and contrast it with religious beliefs, Elizabeth Gurley Flynn acknowledged in her autobiography that "in a certain sense," socialism was her religion. "I found the Socialist movement at a very young and impressionable age. To me it was the creed of the brotherhood of man or 'to do on earth as it is in Heaven,' and I was an intense believer in socialism during my whole life."[3]

In her study of the left-wing writer Tillie Olsen, Elaine Neil Orr focuses on the central role of caring in Olsen's vision of social and spiritual transformation. Olsen wrote: "'What's wrong with the world then, that it doesn't ask—and make it possible—for people to raise and contribute the best that is in them.'"[4] For Olsen, caring involves meeting the daily needs of children and others but also encouraging them to develop themselves and contribute to others. Orr explains Olsen's concept of caring and her critical view of the consequences of its practice being limited: "Olsen's 'truth' emerges as an advocacy that all learn the necessary human art of caring and encouraging.... If part of humanity offers all of the 'essential' care—whether that part be the half who are women or the more than half who are working class—those people are denied their human creativity in other areas. On the other hand, to live without offering to someone else 'essential' care and encouragement may be, in Olsen's view, a greater poverty." Orr summarizes Olsen's view: "Care and encouragement, given and received, liberate people toward their fullest being."[5] When left-wingers write specifically about the concept of care, then, they include caring for others in one's family, caring for others through the medium of political and social activism, and the sociable caring provided to friends, neighbors, and strangers.

Having failed thus far to achieve its dream of a transformation of American society, how well has the left-wing fared in the effort to transmit its values to succeeding generations?

The left's concept of activism is based on a unity of the personal interest of the individual with the collective interest of all working people. The left thus recognizes and includes the concept of self-interest in its world view but the left is also a movement with significant psychological and spiritual dimensions. In practice, leftists laud those who make sacrifices to help the working class, the poor and oppressed, and other members of the left-wing movement. In certain periods, most notably during the period of cold war repression of the late 1940s and the 1950s, the need to make sacrifices became overwhelming. The survival of a left-wing movement in the United States was in doubt.

For leftists as for other Americans, personal interests have generally included love, marriage, and children. Although child-rearing styles and practices are quite varied among leftists and have changed with the times, children do have a special place in left-wing philosophy. As people looking to the development of a future society organized on the basis of humanistic values, leftists view their current activities as a contribution to the welfare of their children and of future generations.

Like most other parents, leftists want their children to adopt their values. Didactic instruction in right and wrong behavior and beliefs occurs in left-wing households as in other households. Those who think deeply about how to raise their children know that instruction in caring values entails many layers of involvement with their children. Two such parents were Ethel and Julius Rosenberg, who were arrested, tried on the charge of conspiracy to commit espionage in wartime, and executed in 1953 in what the left viewed as a cold war frame-up. While separated from their two sons, Julius wrote that he and Ethel "shared everything together and gave our all to help our boys develop as healthy, socially concerned human beings, holding dear the principles of democracy, liberty and brotherhood. In our behavior, in our play with them, in the stories we told them and by understanding and devotion to them we gave them more than just parental love. Through them and in them we mentioned a love for humanity for its basic goodness and its inherent creative genius."[6]

As parents who love their children, leftists generally have wanted their children to acquire an education and to make a good living. Leftists advocate education both as an economic tool and as a necessary component of a full, humanistic life. While working for a socialist future, left-wing parents in most cases realize that their children must equip themselves to live in a capitalist society. As people of generally modest means, they want their children to become skillful and "successful" economically without advancing at the expense of others.

To meet the developmental needs of their children, left-wing parents sometimes find it necessary to employ activist techniques on their children's behalf. When her daughter Kim was in junior high school in the 1950s, for example, Rose Chernin went to the school to protest when the principal suggested secretarial school to Kim. "What do you mean giving such advice to this girl?" she asked the principal. "She has straight A's, doesn't she? She's the brightest girl in her class. This girl is going to college. How can you, a woman, advise her to sacrifice this? Don't you know how hard it is already for a girl to make the right choices? Shame on you."[7]

According to left-wing thinking, children will successfully incorporate socialist ideas only if they make sense in terms of their own experience. Each generation finds itself in new historical circumstances and tests out the ideas it learns in childhood in those new conditions. Given this emphasis on youth as a time of testing out ideas, left-wing theory posits the idea that youth should engage in their own autonomous political activity. As a result, the left-wing movement sponsors the development of youth organizations that share the philosophy of the adult movement but allow for independent decision-making by young people.

Youth of left-wing families are influenced not only by their parents but by other individuals and organizations that tend to pull them in the same direction. Often, extended family members, neighbors, and friends are also left-wing activists or are influenced by left-wing thinking and thus reinforce parental ideas. There are meetings and picnics of left-wing organizations. Appropriate books, pamphlets, newspapers, and records are available for children to read and listen to. Depending on their resources, which vary with time and place, left groups sponsor outings, dances, Sunday schools, and summer camps for children and youth.[8]

Although the left-wing movement has multiple channels for influencing the children of its participants, there are substantial competing and sometimes antagonistic influences at work. From teachers, friends at school and in the neighborhood, the mass media, and non-left community organizations and recreational centers, children and youth of left-wing families hear ideas that are different from and often hostile to those of their parents and the left-wing movement. Value formation among children of left-wing families results from the individual child's interaction with parents, peers, the subculture(s) of which they are a part, and the institutions of the larger society. Outcomes vary according to the personality of the child, the characteristics of the parents, political attitudes of peers, the quality of subcultural support systems, and the degree of opposition to or support for progressive values by institutions of the larger society. An examination of parent-child interaction in different historical periods reveals some of the general problems involved in value formation and the specific importance of historical context.

Elizabeth Gurley Flynn was born in 1890 in Concord, New Hampshire. According to her autobiography, her ancestors were "'immigrants and revolutionists'—from the Emerald Isle."[9] Her mother was a tailor and her father was a laborer in the quarries. The family experienced poverty even after her father became a civil engineer. Flynn's hatred of poverty developed when the family lived in the "drab bleak textile center of Manchester [New Hampshire]." She recalled watching a police officer put a "weeping old man" in jail. "He kept assuring us children he had done no wrong, he had no job and no money and no place to sleep. This episode caused me anxiety about all old people."[10]

Both of Flynn's parents were critical thinkers and socialists who stimulated the intellectual growth of their children. "My mother was always interested in public affairs. She early became an advocate of equal rights for women.... Mama was no model housekeeper. But she was interesting and different and we loved her dearly.... All during our childhood she read aloud to us—from Irish history, poetry, fairy stories."[11] Her mother "was firm in teaching us respect for other people's nationality, language and religion."[12] Flynn recalled her mother's special place in the South Bronx community where the family settled in 1900: "She was a good neighbor in time of need. She helped the sick, advised on domestic problems, and when she baked pies and cakes she shared them with the neighborhood children. It was a calamity to the areas when she moved away to Brooklyn in the late twenties."[13]

Flynn became interested in socialist ideas at an early age. "In our household the children listened in on everything." At about age twelve, she enthusiastically argued the affirmative in a public school debate on the topic "Should the Government Own the Coal Mines?" Her parents took her regularly to the neighborhood Socialist Sunday night forum. Just after Flynn's fifteenth birthday, her mother suggested she read Edward Bellamy's *Looking Backward.* She then began to read works by Karl Marx and Frederick Engels. She was not yet sixteen when she was invited to give her first speech to the Harlem Socialist Club. With her mother's encouragement, she accepted the offer. "I tried to select a subject upon which my father would not interfere too much," Flynn recalled, "something he did not consider too important. It was 'What Socialism Will Do for Women.'"[14] The speech was her own and its success led to many other invitations to speak. She quickly became a prominent soapbox orator. Because of her many nighttime meetings, however, her grades in school declined dramatically. Flynn ignored the advice of her principal and her mother to concentrate on her studies and dropped out of school, an action she "deeply regretted" in later years.[15] Despite these regrets, she was launched on a career that included periods as a leading labor organizer, civil liberties partisan, and Communist official.[16]

Armand Hammer was born in 1898 into a family of Jewish immigrants on the Lower East Side of New York. As a young person, his father, Julius, had become a steelworker, organized a trade union, and joined the Socialist Labor Party. "Throughout his life, my father was warmly emotional and sentimental, easily moved to anger and pity by the sufferings of the poor and the cruel labors of the underprivileged masses of that time," Hammer recalled.[17] Remaining a socialist, Julius became a small business owner in pharmaceuticals and then a physician with a thriving practice. He achieved a modest prosperity. "He could have made himself many times richer," Armand commented, "if he had insisted on collecting all his bills; or if he could have restrained himself from giving money away," such as paying for his patients' prescriptions.[18]

Concern for the safety of their children led the Hammers to move from the crowded Lower East Side, which had both dangers and a vibrant radical subculture, to the then-sparsely populated Bronx. When the Bronx also became crowded and dangerous, twelve-year-old Armand was sent away to live with family friends in a small Connecticut town. During his four-year stay in Connecticut, he saw and interacted with well-to-do children from the other side of the tracks. He read Horatio Alger stories and the biographies of financiers like Rockefeller, Carnegie, and Vanderbilt. "I began to see plainly that the American system made it possible for individuals to do great things," Hammer recalled, "to create lasting business enterprises which gave employment to millions and improved the living standards of everybody. I was particularly impressed with the charitable endowments of these vastly rich men—the colleges, libraries, art galleries and medical facilities."[19]

Although Hammer adopted a capitalist rather than a socialist vision, he shared some of his father's political views and was influenced by his ethical example. As a fifteen-year-old high-school student back in the Bronx as World War I began, Armand delivered an impassioned speech against the "horror and futility of war." Over seventy years later, Armand wrote, "I could make much the same speech today."[20] Hammer believed the example of his father's "goodness" inspired him to compose what he calls his "personal creed" early in life. "In my bed at night, I would ask to be as good as I could be and give as much help as I could to others. I found that I liked myself best when I was helping other people—and I wanted to like myself."[21] It was this personal creed that led him to regularly give away a large part of his fortune.

Like Hammer, Peggy Dennis was born into a family of Russian Jews in New York City. Her parents had been revolutionaries in Russia, and they immersed themselves in the socialist movement in the United States. When Peggy was three, the family moved from New York to Los Angeles for health reasons. Unlike the Hammers' relocation to the Bronx, the move by the Dennis family produced no separation from a radical subculture. Both of Dennis's parents were socialists, and in her memoirs, she recalled that the revolutionary Jewish subculture was the primary reality of her childhood: "We children grew and played in this self-contained, foreign-born, radical community. We were enrolled in the Socialist Party Sunday school at the Labor Temple at the time we started public school kindergarten, and the former was more important than the latter. Among my early memories are those of being lifted each week onto a table in stark meeting halls and lisping my way through recitations of revolutionary poems by Yiddish writers my parents and their comrades loved so passionately. Papa coached me at home, explaining the pathos and courage and hope of the words I was to recite."[22]

In interactions with the larger world beyond their radical subculture, Dennis's family dramatically asserted its socialist distinctiveness. The children stayed out of school on May Day, proudly stating the reason for their absence. On the other hand, Dennis and her sister attended school on Jewish holidays. During World War I, Peggy refused to buy war savings stamps despite the criticism she received for keeping her class from a "100% patriotism record."[23] As she recalled it: "We were belligerently atheist, internationalist, and anti-imperialist, and the narrow-mindedness of our block, our school, and our community only made us feel special and superior."[24]

Despite the clear sense of a socialist identity, Dennis successfully competed in the academic, extracurricular, and peer-group activities in junior and senior high school in the early 1920s. She won schoolwide elective office, participated in statewide oratorical contests and Shakespearean festivals, won the lead in her senior play, and was editor of her junior- and senior-high newspapers. She "went steady with popular athletes and... belonged to the in-groups noted for being intellectual, service-minded, trend-setting."[25] On evenings and weekends, on the other hand, she was involved in Communist meetings, Marxist discussions, and in organizing a Communist children's group. Dennis kept her school and political lives separate, with the latter remaining "always the more important and real to us."[26]

Their parents encouraged Dennis and her sister to enroll in Teachers College at the University of California so they could become "economically independent from whatever husbands we might someday acquire."[27] Neither completed the course of study. Nevertheless, Peggy concluded: "We were happy, unconflicted, suffered no identity crises, saw no generation gaps. We lived in isolated security among our own kind. The goals and hopes of our parents were ours. We rejected those of society around us; ours was the dream of the Future." Her sister became a garment worker and trade union leader. Dennis became a revolutionary.

Dorothy Healey's childhood was similar to Dennis's. Healey's parents also moved the family to California for health reasons when she was a child. Her parents were Jewish immigrants from Hungary and became socialists in the United States. Born in 1914, Dorothy attended her first socialist meetings "when I was still in diapers."[28] "By the time I was twelve years old," she recalls, "there was no question in my mind what I was going to be when I grew up.... I knew...my life was going to be devoted to the revolution. Along with discussions with my mother, one of the greatest influences on me was reading Upton Sinclair's novels.... I just throbbed with indignation over the unhappiness of the miners and the oil workers and the injustice and cruelty of the bosses."[29]

The views of her peers began to influence Healey when she was in junior high school in Berkeley. She "started feeling terribly self-conscious about all kinds of things about my appearance, especially my clothes. My mother, of course, thought people should ignore such nonsensical bourgeois details as how you looked and what you wore. The important thing was what was in your mind. Besides, we didn't have much money."[30] Her mother made clothes but did so poorly. Healey did not rebel, however. "I was ashamed to say how much those dresses embarrassed me. I never learned the things that other girls were taught while growing up, how to fix your hair, or how to choose clothes."[31]

Although she was not rebellious, Healey did branch out socially in junior high school. Most of her friends were top students who were well-to-do and lived in the Berkeley hills while her family lived in the lowlands. At fourteen, however, she joined the Young Communist League (YCL). "I quickly lost interest in the friends I had made in junior high school," Dorothy recounts. "The parties I had started being invited to up in the hills had never really been fun for me anyway."[32]

Although she shared her mother's political outlook and values, Healey's adolescence was not problem-free. She had found a new social life in the YCL. Her new friends were in their late teens and early twenties. Healey lost interest in school, failed to do her homework, and stopped getting good grades. Two older siblings were both very good students and Healey's indifference to school angered her mother, who placed a high value on education. In 1931 Dorothy dropped out of high school a month before graduating to accept a YCL assignment to go to work in a cannery. Both her brother and sister had gone on to the university and her mother was very disappointed. "In spite of her Communist loyalties, Mama considered the Young Communist League to have been a terrible influence on me. Here I was casually flinging away the chance for the education that she had been denied in her childhood."[33]

Less than a year after Healey became a YCL member, the stock market crashed. Left-wing organizing opportunities expanded greatly and she was involved in organizing unemployed councils and unions, speaking on street corners, and supervising a branch of the Communist children's group, the Young Pioneers. With so many workers needing help and the left-wing movement growing, Healey's vision as a twelve-year-old became a reality. She spent her youth organizing for a variety of left-wing organizations and unions and eventually became a full-time official for the Communist party.

Another California Communist was Rose Chernin, who remembers the thirties as the "golden time of our movement."[34] She recalls that "there was always an excitement," an excitement that was contagious for the children of Communists. Rose's first daughter, Nina, was born in 1929 and, as Rose recalls it,

Her entire life she lived in the movement. When I joined the party and began to organize full time, I always took her with me. I felt I had something to give to this little girl, an understanding to pass on to her. Children were very important in our movement; who else would carry on our struggle?...We knew, when she grows up, she will be joining the Young Communist League. She will be going down to write for the *Daily Worker*.... She was very proud to be a Communist when she was in high school and this pride began when she was a little girl, holding my hand when we walked in the coop in the East Bronx.... She had a gentle nature, very thoughtful and our people loved her. You would look at her and you would think, Here is what a girl will be like under socialism.[35]

Nina's unstressed absorption of her parent's values and political ideology occurred in the context of a strong left-wing subculture that provided security and affirmation for parents and children. Thus the radical youth involved in the 1930s mass student movement saw their activism as an "auxiliary...to the labor movement and its struggle for a more egalitarian social order." Instead of rebelling against their parents, Robert Cohen found, thirties student "activists seemed eager to link their own political activism to some legacy from their parents and siblings."[36] Although the larger society was far from being pro-Communist, opportunities for leftists to find affirmation there as well were numerous. Communists led protests of the unemployed in the early 1930s, became the left wing of the New Deal in the mid-1930s, and joined in the national effort to defeat Nazi Germany and militarist Japan in the 1940s. The larger societal framework turned decidedly hostile, however, with the onset of the cold war in the late 1940s. By the early 1950s, the country was in the grips of anticommunist hysteria. It was an especially difficult time for parents of young children and teenagers.

A memoir that focuses on that difficult time is Carl Bernstein's *Loyalties*. Bernstein, who achieved fame with his colleague Bob Woodward for their exposure of Watergate in the 1970s, recalls his childhood in the 1950s and attempts to come to grip with the meaning of his parents' lives as left-wing activists. His father was a leader of the United Public Workers union and his mother was a leader of the Committee to Save the Rosenbergs. As a child growing up in the nation's capital during the 1950s anticommunist hysteria, Bernstein saw officials, neighbors, and friends turning against his parents. He rebelled: "I'm not sure exactly when the notion of my father being 'different' from other fathers began to tug so strongly, but the sense of shame, of being threatened, of being vulnerable to something over which I had no control, came early. Sometimes I hated him for it, and I articulated my rage through whatever misdemeanor was closest at hand."[37]

Bernstein's rebellion against his parents took such forms as acts of shoplifting, reckless driving, and vandalism that got him in trouble with the law. These acts of what was then called juvenile delinquency greatly troubled his parents as did his failure to apply himself to his studies and his poor grades. Bernstein also rebelled by joining in peer-group activities that involved associations antagonistic to the left-wing subculture in which his parents moved. When the family lived in a District of Columbia neighborhood, ten-year-old Carl's friends were Catholics, and he tried out for a Catholic Youth Organization football team. The Bernsteins were non-religious Jews. His parents accepted positive peer-group activity. For his football tryout, Bernstein's father bought him a uniform costing more than a week's groceries. He made the team, and his father's support included attendance at a father-and-son prayer breakfast prior to the season's opening game.

Bernstein responded not only to peer pressure but to what he perceived as the dominant values of the larger culture. In 1952, at the age of eight, he donned "I Like Ike" and "Ike and Dick" buttons while his parents debated whether to support Adlai Stevenson or Vincent Hallinan of the Progressive Party. In 1954, after a report of his mother's appearance before the House Un-American Activities Committee, some of the Bernstein's friends, neighbors, and relatives cut off contact with them. Bernstein reacted to the family's difficulties by "becoming a patriotic nut."[38] He was class air-raid warden, led the Pledge of Allegiance, read the Bible aloud on Wednesday mornings, and went to St. Columbia's Episcopal Church for optional prayer on Fridays.

When the Bernsteins moved to a Maryland suburb, most of Carl's new friends were Jewish. He joined and became a leader in a religious Jewish fraternity and argued stridently and eventually successfully to have a bar mitzvah. Although they would have preferred he make different choices, his parents supported the positive forms of rebellion. The negative forms of rebellion caused them greater difficulty. After an incident in which Bernstein's driver's license was suspended and he was put on a year's probation for a second time, his father decided he had to do "something constructive." He helped his son get a summer job at the *Washington Star*, and thus began his career in journalism.

Despite his anger, hostility, and rebellion against his parents, young Carl assimilated many of his parents' values. His mother was a leader of the movement to integrate Washington's public accommodations in the early 1950s. In response to the sit-in movement that began in 1960, Bernstein wrote articles in the school newspaper arguing that "Jewish kids, Jews perhaps more than any other people, belonged in the civil rights movement."[39] Advocating a social awareness platform, he then ran and was elected regional president of the Aleph Zadik Aleph (AZA) youth organization. The region stretched from the District of Columbia to North Carolina. When the train to a North Carolina AZA convention stopped for repairs, Bernstein and other AZAers and members of the BBG, a Jewish sorority, refused to leave the black waiting room at the Greensboro station despite threats of arrest. "I announced that anybody who didn't want to get arrested should get back on the train. Everybody stayed and waited." The police did not carry out the threat.[40]

Although as an adult Bernstein has many political disagreements with his parents, he has an underlying respect for their values. In writing *Loyalties*, he particularly focuses on learning the stories of his father's efforts to defend hundreds of federal workers against accusations of disloyalty. He interviews some of the individuals his father defended and learns about his father's role in the campaign to desegregate Washington, an effort he had associated with his mother because as a child he'd participated in the campaign himself alongside his mother. Bernstein quotes his father on the role of the United Public Workers in the early postwar years: "'Everything that happened in Washington, opening up the cafeterias to black people, breaking open the counting rooms, beginning a consumer movement, hiring black bus drivers in the city, setting up the restaurant picket lines—that was our people.'"[41] Although he relies more on instinct in personal and professional matters, Bernstein comments that he's always valued his father's judgment "more highly than anyone else's especially on questions that might be regarded as either moral or political. He has an innate sense of decency that leads him almost unerringly to the proper course.... He arrives at his judgments carefully, yet almost effortlessly, bringing pragmatism to a wellspring of what, in another age, might have been termed humanism."[42]

When Communist party leader Rose Chernin was arrested under the Smith Act in 1951, her daughter Kim was 11 years old. Like Bernstein, Kim's attitude was a mixture of acceptance of her parents' values and rebellion against them. "Since I was a small girl I have been fighting with my mother. When the family was eating dinner some petty disagreement would arise and I'd jump from the table, pick up a plate and smash it against the wall. I'd go running from the room, slamming doors behind me. By the age of thirteen, I insisted that Hegel was right and not Marx. 'The Idea came first,' I cried out from the bathroom, which had the only door in the house that locked. 'The Spirit came before material existence.'"[43]

Kim was greatly affected by the death of her sister Nina in 1945. Her mother "fell apart" and thought about suicide. When the family moved to California, Kim was sent to a boarding school for a time. Then came the cold war onslaught. Fear began to dominate Kim's thinking. "I figured things out. I figured out there was some new danger in the world. The fascists had gone. The concentration camps were gone. The Jews had gone to Israel. Now it was the turn of the Communists. We were Communists, it was our turn."[44] Earlier she had been told to be proud of being Communist, now "I wasn't supposed to tell the kids at school. I shouldn't repeat anything I heard my parents say at home."[45] After her mother's arrest in

1951, the fear dominated her life. Kim's greatest fear was that she would be questioned herself and would inform on her family's friends. "Would they torture my mother in jail? Would they torture me? Would I tell the names I knew?" Nevertheless, Kim participated in the left-wing subculture and hoped to be a revolutionary like her mother.[46]

Peer relations became critical in Kim's development. After her mother's arrest, "old friends drifted away." When Kim spoke up to a teacher on behalf of a black student, she gained the friendship of the black, Mexican, and Asian students. For several years, the minority students were her social world. At one point, however, her rebelliousness won the admiration of even the well-to-do white students. She was invited to the parties of the school's social elite. Despite guilty feelings, she left her black and Mexican friends who had provided her "a protective circle" during her time of difficulties. She even found herself laughing at and telling racist jokes, and making "fun of everything I loved and cherished.... I seemed to have felt that if I lied enough, and made enough racist comments, people would forget that I was a Jew and my parents were Communists."[47]

Kim tried at once to share her parents' values and to rebel against them and all authority. Her rebelliousness, the stresses on the family stemming from the arrest and trials of her mother, and peer pressure prepared the ground for a break with her parents' views. Rather than seeking an independent path to adulthood based on critical reflections on her own experiences, she saw her choices as becoming a professional revolutionary like her mother or rejecting her family's values. Kim chose to become an apolitical poet. For years, her political differences with her mother led to many hurtful arguments. In the course of writing their story, they achieved a mutual respect for each other's different choices. In writing the story of her mother's courageous actions in defense of other radicals threatened with jail and deportation and in criticizing her own racist acts, it is clear that Kim writes not only out of love for her mother but also continues to share many of her parents' values.

Margaret Collingwood Nowak's memoir, *Two Who Were There: A Biography of Stanley Nowak*, recounts the experiences of two of Michigan's leading left-wing activists. Stanley, an immigrant from Poland, was one of the first organizers of the United Automobile Workers and went on to serve for ten years in the Michigan state senate. Despite—or perhaps because of—his prominence in Michigan politics, the federal government twice tried to take away his citizenship, in 1942 and again in 1952. The second attempt, coming during the worst days of McCarthyism, was the more serious. The case came to trial in 1954 and resulted in conviction. Stanley won his case on appeal to the Supreme Court only in 1957.

Two Who Were There focuses on the Nowaks' lifetime of political activities, but it includes a brief discussion of how the family successfully managed to survive the repressive onslaught and remain intact.

Our relationship was a steadying factor. We were in complete agreement on the issues and values that had led to this period in our lives, and we would not have done anything differently even if we could have. The families of dear friends were destroyed in facing similar struggles. Men who had not fully shared their political beliefs and activities with their families saw them alienated by the price demanded in unfavorable publicity, ostracism, and condemnation. Divorces and separations resulted, and children were hurt and bitter. Because Stanley and I fully believed in what we did, were committed, and shared our goals, we were able to weather the difficulties and be supportive of each other. Because we had shared our beliefs and goals with Elissa, without preaching, she also reacted in this spirit and was proud of what her father had done and the principles for which he stood.[48]

The political trials to which Rose Chernin, Stanley Nowak, and numerous others were subjected were among the harshest forms of repression. Many more were called before the House Un-American Activities Committee, as the Bernsteins were, or were fired, blacklisted, or ostracized. It was a decade of suffering and fear for both parents and children. Nevertheless, many children absorbed their parents' values by a kind of "osmosis." Linn Shapiro remembers the political discussions with her parents' adult left-wing friends as "absolutely intoxicating."[49] Another child of the fifties—David Goldring—recalls that "[my] political absorption came from the way my parents lived and dealt with problems more than from any explicit political direction.... Above all, there was a pretty strong, firmly established atmosphere of love in the home. People were dealt with as whole human beings."[50] Although weakened by repression, left-wing Jewish groups continued to run summer camps and *shules,* after-school educational programs to teach Jewish tradition and Yiddish literature, which provided left-wing children of the fifties with important sustenance. The summer camp experience saved many left-wing children from isolation.[51] "My salvation was camp," Debra recalled. "There's no question that I spent ten months of the year counting down the days 'til I could get to the summer."[52] Jeannie grew up in suburban New Jersey and found camp "a total revelation, that there were all these other people who were just like me.... I spent high school, every single weekend, running into New York to see my friends from camp, and discounting that anyone I went to school with could possibly be interesting."[53]

As the repressive climate began to ebb in the late 1950s, new civil rights and peace movements developed and grew into a mass radical upsurge in the 1960s. In both the 1930s and 1960s, millions of people participated in demonstrations, picket lines, and strikes, wrote letters to Congress, campaigned for candidates, and joined organizations. A significant minority of these participants drew radical conclusions from their experiences in movements for social change. While 1930s radicalism centered around organizations and movements led by Communists, there was no such focal point to 1960s radicalism. The institutions and the subcultural world of the left had been shattered by cold war repression. Commentators, historians, and activists themselves labeled the 1960s radicals a *New Left*. The label referred both to the youthfulness of the participants and a perceived discontinuity with the Communist-oriented *Old Left*.

The 1950s victory of anticommunist paranoia led participants and commentators alike to exaggerate the discontinuity between Old Left and New Left. Like Chernin and Bernstein, most children of Communist, left-wing, and ex-Communist families were affected by the shattering of the left in the 1950s and the anticommunist pressures dominating the larger society. In a great many families, both parents and children dropped some left-wing beliefs that had characterized the movement in earlier periods. Nevertheless, a core set of values survived among parents and children alike. With the much more hospitable climate of the 1960s, the children participated in the new radical upsurge and helped to shape it. Many developed a lasting commitment to social-change activism.

Among the young people participating in the radical upsurge were the children of Ethel and Julius Rosenberg. In their moving memoir, *We Are Your Sons*, Robert and Michael describe how they were "shielded from publicity by loving adults" and grew up in a secure and loving environment with Anne and Abel Meeropol, the couple who adopted them. In April 1958, at the age of 10, Robert Meeropol participated in his first peace march and then joined in the early picketing of Woolworth's to protest the store's segregation policy. "I shared the Meeropols' belief in civil rights and human dignity.... I harbored a strong sense of justice, was bothered when someone was picked on and for the most part avoided the teasing that went on in school, thinking how badly I'd feel if I were teased. These feelings spilled over into politics, especially the issue of injustice to minority groups."[54]

It was, of course, the black-led civil rights struggle in the South that started a movement that expanded into the multi-issue radical upsurge of the 1960s. Angela Davis grew up in Birmingham, Alabama, in the 1950s when race-based repression was a daily reality for black southerners. Although her family did not suffer from the anticommunist hysteria, Davis's mother had been a member of the radical Southern Negro Youth Congress in the 1930s, and the Davises were friendly with families who were victims of the cold war purges. As a teenager, Davis attended the alternative high school in New York City run by the American Friends Service Committee where the Meeropols also studied. She joined a Communist youth organization and became one of the early participants in the new radical upsurge.[55]

Citing a survey of participants in two 1980s gatherings of children of Communists and his own interviews, Todd Gitlin comments on these children of the left: "Many took in a powerful moralism. There are rights and wrongs, and it is important to live by the rights."[56] In a study about the origins of the New Left, James P. O'Brien found that children of left families brought to the college campuses "a set of attitudes favorable to peace, civil liberties, and racial tolerance as well as a willingness to act in support of these goals."[57] After interviewing a sample of fifty 1960s Chicago student activists and their parents, Richard Flacks found that "the great majority...are attempting to fulfill and renew the political traditions of their families."[58]

For her influential study on the origins of the women's liberation movement of the 1960s, Sara Evans sought out New Left activists to interview. "Again and again," she writes, "I was surprised to discover a radical family background."[59] Evans notes that "The experience of girls growing up in activist families tended to encourage independence and self-confidence and to place a premium on egalitarian ideals."[60] Commenting on one such woman she interviewed, Evans notes that

her family was infused with a great sense of morality and social concern.... As a very small child she expected herself to defend anyone who was being mistreated. In the first grade she stepped into a circle of children throwing stones at a black child; in the second grade she intervened to stop an Italian child from being beaten; and in the third grade she defended a student against a teacher who was administering corporal punishment. Such an intense sense of identification with the downtrodden coupled with a strong sense of self led her to become active in civil rights, SDS, the anti-war movement, and to provide key leadership in the initial phases of the women's liberation movement.[61]

Although Evans found that activists with radical family backgrounds were a minority among New Leftists, "women with such backgrounds provided much of the key leadership in developing a new feminism.... They...had learned a willingness to question and a deep sense of social justice.... Again and again, when a voice was raised within the new left pointing out male domination...it came from one of these women—these 'red diaper feminists.'"[62]

Although many children of Old Left parents became activists in the 1960s, the institutional structure of the left began to crumble during the repressive 1950s and was not rebuilt in subsequent decades. The post-1960s left-wing movement has no single organizational center comparable to the Socialist party in the period prior to 1920 and the Communist party in the period between the early 1930s and the mid-1950s. Left-wingers participate in a multitude of causes—for peace, solidarity with Latin America, the feminist, civil rights, and environmental movements—but the post-1960s left is fragmented organizationally. It has fewer, smaller, and different geographical centers of concentration than in the past. In the 1930s and 1940s, there were lively centers of left influence in a number of working-class neighborhoods in many major cities. Now, left strongholds are university towns like Cambridge, Massachusetts, and Berkeley, California. Children of left-wing working-class parents have usually become professionals, entered a national job market, and become geographically dispersed. Leftists wishing to transmit their values to their children in the past twenty years often have to travel to visit relatives, find few people in their neighborhoods and workplaces who come from similar backgrounds, and lack the institutional support system of camps, cultural groups, fraternal organizations, and left-led trade unions available in earlier periods.

In 1982 and 1983, when a group of red diaper babies (most of whom grew up in the 1950s) gathered together, a focal point of their concern was how to transmit left-wing values to their children in the absence of the vibrant left subculture they had experienced when they were growing up. For example, Bill regrets that there's no "Sunday school or a camp" for his eight-year-old son to "get any political help" when he's older and is contemplating organizing a "sort of Sunday school for the kids in my neighborhood."[63] Steve, father of ten- and five-year-olds, also is "interested in finding support networks for Left culture for my children. How do you give them the support you know they can't get in the general community?"[64] Molly, the mother of a fourteen-year-old son, commented: "I feel a real vacuum. We [1960s activists] left no institutions or groups or anything for our kids to move into. Now he's out there trying to figure out what to do.... He's not gonna fight. He's not gonna register [for the draft]. I want to make sure that that's his belief and not [just] my belief. How do you teach children to develop their own beliefs so that they're solid?"[65] Elizabeth finds that her five-year-old daughter

needs more support than just my husband and I can provide. She needs to know that there are other people in the culture who have our beliefs. We're vegetarians. We don't eat the same kind of foods. We're not religious. She just can't seem to find any place where she fits in. Who is she like? She's not like her friends.... The problem is that we're so few and far between that I feel like we need some type of institution.... an extended family or an extended culture to take care of the problem of being different, to make her feel she is less different.[66]

One avenue of influence that some parents use is taking children to demonstrations. One parent relates that she takes her daughter to events such as the June 12, 1982, nuclear freeze march "where there are a lot of people and they're singing.... There are things going on; there's excitement. She's really enjoyed herself. She listens to those speeches."[67] Another parent recounted how he took his daughter to the labor movement's 1981 Solidarity Day demonstration: "We set it up so that she did a report for her class. She wanted to make sure there would be leaflets, took pictures with her camera. She went back and convinced her whole class to hate [President] Reagan."[68] Aside from demonstrations, the channels for reinforcement of left ideas are limited. Some parents take their children to one of the small number of progressive camps that remain. One group in Brooklyn has organized a *shule*.[69]

Some of the older children attending the red diaper weekends along with their parents expressed their views on left-wing values and culture. As in earlier generations, these youth of the eighties were picking up their parents' ideas. A Boston University college student commented on his acceptance of his parents' views: "I myself have always been aware of their philosophies and agreed mostly, because that's where I got most of my beliefs from."[70] Niki, a seventeen-year-old, reported that she "relied on them [her parents] for telling me everything that's right and wrong. For a while, if somebody would ask me a question, I would say, 'I can't answer this until I ask my folks.'" She and other children with similar experiences decided they needed to read, study, and think more for themselves. "It's been a real hard thing for me to learn they're not always right, or maybe they are, but I have to develop my own opinions," Niki concluded.[71] Another youth agreed: "Although I still believe in most of what they believe in, I've done a lot more reading and come to conclusions on my own."[72]

Some of the 1980s children of the left are already activists. Maggie Levenstein was born in 1962. Her parents were first-generation radicals active in the Cambridge area. Levenstein and her younger siblings attended a Black Panther Party Liberation school when she was eight or nine. At twelve she became active in the Cambridge Tenants Organizing Committee. "I remember that I stopped watching Saturday morning cartoons when I started going to meetings every Saturday morning."[73] Nevertheless, she felt relatively isolated. Even in Cambridge, Levenstein knew only one other leftist kid. She reported feeling different, ashamed, and "wished my mother looked like other mothers...act[ed] like other mothers."[74] Living in an integrated working-class neighborhood, her parents wanted them to participate and be like the other kids. Levenstein's mother was active in the new feminist movement and she herself reports the "Women's Movement was probably the major influence, in terms of defining myself and who I was." She finds it difficult, however, "to balance the feminist expectations from your family with not so feminist expectations from outside.... Maybe I want to do all these things so boys care about what I look like and that's the worst thing in my mother's mind, something I'm never supposed to do. I think those are hard things to work out when you have your parents' values and you exist in the world and those other values are there."[75] Adding to her difficulties is that she feels "a lack of connectedness between us and past generations" and the absence of "a culture to participate in...so that you feel like you're part of something that has come from someplace."[76]

Children of 1980s Socialists experience many of the same difficulties as the children whose parents were raised as Communists. Commenting on her teenaged children's situation, Barbara Ehrenreich, chair of the Democratic Socialists of America (DSA), reported: "One of the worst things now is that they don't know other kids who are political." Although DSAers Beth and Steve Cagan's oldest daughter was active in an antiapartheid group, Beth noted that their children "tend to feel like oddballs, charting new territory."[77]

Despite the development of broad new mass movements during and after the 1960s, the left subculture has not recovered from the trauma of the 1950s. As in the past, however, children of left-wing parents are absorbing their parents' values and entering into social and political activity. The children are also experiencing the pain of being different, but, unlike their parents, they do not have the extended family networks, social support systems, and subcultural institutions such as camps to sustain them. Left-wing parents are succeeding in raising caring children, but they miss the help and the sense of wholeness of the Communist subculture in which they grew up. The Communist party persists, but it is not central to the vast array of new movements as it was to the progressive movements of the 1930s, 1940s, and 1950s.

The left-wing approach to care can be usefully compared with that of other subcultures to clarify the distinctiveness of the left's view. The value of caring is present to one degree or another in many subcultures, and academic researchers have developed recommendations to help parents, schools, and universities promote caring values among children and youth.[78] The discussion here focuses on a comparison of the left's concept of care with those in the upper class and in non-left working-class families, both white and African American. In *Women of the Upper Class*, Susan Ostrander provides a portrait of upper-class families in a large Midwestern city, paying particular attention to child-rearing practices, values transmission, and volunteer activities. Like left-wing parents, upper-class parents want their children to be happy and to do well in life. The upper-class women interviewed by Ostrander also want their children to become caring adults. What Ostrander's subjects mean by these ideas, however, is distinct from what left-wing families believe. There are also formal similarities between the parenting practices of Ostrander's subjects and the left-wing families described here, but once again the content of the children's upbringing is quite different.

Ostrander found that upper-class parents had "stringent expectations" and expressly "channeled" their children into a specific world.[79] The children are sent to class-segregated schools, participate in debuts, are expected to succeed in careers such as business, medicine, and law, and are expected to make compatible marriages within the upper class. The upper-class women were active volunteers, Ostrander found, and "want

their children to be seen as people who 'contribute to the community.'"
Although they themselves complain about "the pressures of living up to a
family name...[and] the burdensome obligations of being expected to
contribute to the community.... they want their children to carry on as
they have."[80] There are family and class traditions to uphold, a sense of
"noblesse oblige," that in Ostrander's view function "to justify and legitimate their class privilege."[81] Thus the concept of caring in this subculture
involved an emphasis on the difference and superiority of the carer. This
approach is markedly different from the egalitarian and collectivistic
approach to care characteristic of the left subculture.

Although upper-class children are relatively isolated from the larger society, Ostrander found that their parents nevertheless are concerned about
such negative phenomena as use of drugs, poor performance in school, or
inappropriate marriages or career choices. Given their family's economic
resources and their mother's expenditure of time devoted to child rearing,
upper-class children are assisted in overcoming problems at school and
negative peer and societal influences. "Upper-class children," Ostrander
maintains, "including those who are admittedly poor students, are simply
not allowed to fail academically or personally."[82] If poor behavior persists,
the negative sanction of reducing or eliminating the child's access to family
money may be used. As in the left, parental and subcultural influences work
in the same direction, to acculturate children to parental and class values.

The children of the upper class, while sheltered for many years, are
influenced by peers and do come in contact with the larger society. They
may pull away from the narrowly circumscribed path set for them by getting involved in drug use, picking an inappropriate interest such as rock
music, or falling in love with the wrong person. In that larger society,
moreover, upper-class children may have to contend with ideas, attitudes,
and people hostile to the upper class. In contrast to the left's usual experience, however, the larger society also provides a great deal of positive
reinforcement and respect for members of the upper class as the leading
citizens of their community.[83]

Much is expected of children both of the left and of the upper class. The
material advantages enjoyed by the children of the upper class are many
and assist them in successful transitions to adulthood along the lines of
their parents' expectations. On the other hand, the rigid expectations do
lead to difficulties for some of these youth. The independence central to
adulthood is carefully circumscribed in the upper-class world, especially
for women. Caring is seen as a necessary but subsidiary complement to
assuming one's elite status in the world. In many ways, children of the left
face a bumpier road to adulthood. Their path is far less clearly drawn for
them and they tend to be quite independent in their thinking and actions.
Nevertheless, children of the left often assimilate the left's concept of caring in a deep and lasting way. One cares for others who are suffering not

because one is different or superior to them but because one is like them. Leftists see themselves as members of a class or group that is oppressed and exploited and therefore feel a oneness with all people suffering from injustice in the world. Upper-class women who choose to challenge their oppression as women may also feel a oneness with others suffering from injustice. In pursuing such a course, however, such women are seeking to develop a new set of caring values rather than the elite noblesse oblige approach described by Ostrander.

How similar are leftists to non-left members of the working class? Like left-wing working-class families, the working-class families that are the subject of Lillian Breslow Rubin's 1976 study, *Worlds of Pain: Life in the Working Class Family,* have often faced severe economic hardship. Rubin's interview subjects recalled "parents who worked hard, yet never quite made it; homes that were overcrowded; siblings or selves who got into 'trouble.'"[84] Rubin reports few happy memories of childhood among the people she interviewed. They accepted their parents' lack of attention to their emotional needs as an inevitable consequence of their parents' lives of pain and deprivation and do not criticize them for it. These attitudes contrast with those of children of left-wing families who recall many happy times and have both positive things to say about the parental attention they received as well as a number of criticisms.

Since her interviewees were preoccupied with "the daily struggle for survival," Rubin finds that, "in the context of their lives and daily struggles, looking either backward or forward makes little sense; planning for the future seems incongruous."[85] While Rubin's subjects looked neither forward nor backward, having a sense of history is central to the left-wing outlook. "History sat down with them" is the way Vivian Gornick put it in her study of the Communist milieu.[86] "I believe this was the feeling most Communist Party members had," Annette Rubinstein maintains; "history sat down with us. We were a functioning part of history, a small part or a large part depending on our specific contributions, but all part of a tremendous and ultimately victorious movement."[87]

Rubin discusses two major subgroups in her study: "settled-livers" and "hard-livers." The settled-livers had "stable work histories.... were cautious, conservative, church going, and if they drank, they did so with moderation."[88] Settled-livers believed in conforming, were strict with their children, and valued the ethic of hard work and "the American myth that everyone can pull themselves up by their bootstraps." The hard-livers, in contrast, were "the non-conformists—those who cannot or will not accept their allotted social status."[89] The rebellions of the hard-livers take the form of "explosive episodes of drinking and violence, the gambling away of a week's wages...unexplained work absences...and...sudden, angry quittings."[90] The hard-liver's protest is a "personal rebellion," Rubin argues, "rooted in the individualistic ethic of American life." Neither hard-liver nor settled-liver engages in "constructive action directed at changing the social system."[91]

In contrast to the individualism of both the settled-livers and the hard-livers, leftists have a collectivist approach. The left, indeed, orients itself on "constructive action directed at changing the social system." Those of Rubin's subjects who are union members acknowledge some of the benefits of belonging but "more commonly...gripe about it."[92] Left-wingers, by contrast, tend to be active members of their trade unions and have played important roles in strengthening these working-class institutions. Both they and their coworkers have thereby benefitted.[93]

Given their present-mindedness, it is not surprising that interest in school and, indeed, in reading is limited among both the settled-livers and the hard-livers. Left-wing parents typically expect their children to do well in school and many students meet their parents' high expectations. Literacy is emphasized in left-wing families and in the left subculture generally. Somewhat paradoxically, then, members of this collectivist subculture have an important advantage as individuals participating in the market economy. They more readily acquire new skills and are more knowledgeable and sophisticated participants than similarly situated non-left people in the struggle to survive in an increasing complex and crisis-ridden economy.

Ostrander's and Rubin's studies indicate that the values of children of upper-class and non-left white working-class families are quite different from those of the working-class left. Some African American memoirs describe upbringings in non-left families that resemble those of left families in their emphasis on education and on identification with and service to the oppressed group of which one is a member. Angelo Herndon was born in 1913 in Wyoming, Ohio. His father was a miner and his mother was a servant. The family was extremely poor; they often had too little to eat. The Herndon family was highly religious rather than politically radical. Nevertheless, the message that Herndon received from his parents was similar to that of children in left families. Education, his father advised him, "was a powerful weapon with which to fight poverty and the handicaps of racial discrimination. Once he said to me in his soft quiet voice that he and Mother wanted me to become an educated man so that I could be of service to my people."[94]

In her foreword to James P. Comer's *Maggie's American Dream: The Life and Times of a Black Family,* television newscaster Charlayne Hunter-Gault recalled her father's expectations that she would get good grades and her mother's "hands-on involvement in my schoolwork, as well as in my school."[95] Mothers, grandmothers, and teachers supplied children with "a sense of pride in who we were and where we came from and where we were going. As routinely as they continued to raise the pennies, the notion of education as an essential ingredient of my life became a part of my thinking. It never occurred to me that I wouldn't go on to college after high school. Or achieve my goals...Every day was black-history day."[96]

"Church was the center of our family's life," James Comer recalls.[97] Comer's father was active as a deacon in the church. His mother, however, "often privately challenged the message in the church," which led the children to develop a critical mode of thinking. Comer recalled his mother's observation: "'We ought to be talking about getting together to do something about life on these cement streets we live on now rather than golden streets in heaven we don't know nothing about.'"[98] Comer's commitment to formal religion was also shaken by examples of unchristian practices of Christians that he observed: "I became increasingly wary of people who talked a Christian game and played an unchristian game. Gradually we [he and his siblings] moved from our usual seat on the second row to the middle and then to the back of the church."[99]

There was a vibrant intellectual life in the Comer family as the children engaged in after-dinner debates. Maggie Comer listened to her children's clever game and only intervened occasionally. James Comer recalled his mother's troubled reaction to his proposal to scrap the welfare system: "But Jim, how would the poor people take care of themselves?" She was relieved when he replied that "there should be a job for everybody and that the government should provide jobs when there weren't enough to go around."[100] Like children in families affiliated with the left-wing movement, the Comer children were learning both about caring for others and the necessity of social change.

Maggie Comer focused her attention on the development and proper upbringing of her children. "I believe in talking with children, taking time with them, taking them to places of interest, doing things together," she declares. "You explain to the child and they want to learn more."[101] Her son recalled: "Mom and Dad had this notion that there were fine things in life that kids should experience—educational places and activities, successful people going places and achieving great things. They felt that would cause us to strive to do the same."[102] The Comers expected their children to get good grades and to go to college. All did so. James Comer became a Yale University child psychiatrist, and his siblings also received graduate degrees. As is the case in left families, the Comers instilled a social vision in their children as well as a striving for success. Comer has been active with the New Haven public schools in developing projects to help low-income children achieve. "Life in a world changing ever faster because of science and technology is like a relay race with each generation almost desperately passing the baton on to the next. Past and present policies and practices which made it extremely difficult for black Americans to achieve at the level of their ability is like dropping the baton."[103]

The transmission of caring values to children in the Comer, Hunter, and Herndon families resembles the process that takes place in many left-wing

families. Parents show concern for the development of the child, emphasize the value of education and literacy, and expect their children to
achieve in school. At the same time, parents also provide firm moral guidance to their children, emphasizing the importance of acting for justice by
their own example. Finally, parents also set an example and teach their
children to demonstrate concern for other oppressed blacks or working-
class people and for all of humanity. Left-wing parents have a particular
philosophical, political, and historical approach that assists them in transmitting caring values to their children. A broadly similar approach to caring for others is sometimes conveyed by families with a somewhat
different political outlook.

Transmitting the values of caring to children is as challenging and difficult as it is necessary. The left's experience indicates that there are four levels at which the values of each generation are formed. The influence of the
immediate family, of the parents, is most obvious and usually the
strongest factor. Three other principal factors can be identified, but their
significance varies with time, place, and circumstance. The particular subcultural niche in which a family is located is influential. It may, in fact, be
a meeting ground of more than one subculture. Members of the extended
family, neighbors, and members of one's church, social organization,
political group, or trade union all contribute to the shaping of the child's
values.

Often most troubling to parents is the impact of peers. Although parents—left, right, and center—are often negative about the influence of
peers on their children, this is an inevitable part of youth's development.
To become mature adults, children must break free and establish their
own independent identities. They look to their peers because it is among
members of their own generation that they make the attachments that
mark their independent adulthood.

Finally, the larger society influences children and youth through the
state of the economy and such institutions and media as government,
schools, newspapers, television, and film. Such a fundamental reality as
the degree to which decent, well-paying jobs are available reverberates
through family, subcultural life, and peer interactions. For the left, government repression and hostile presentations of the Communists and
Communist ideas in the media also have been enormously important.

For much of the twentieth century, left-wing parents had the support of
a rich subcultural world to assist them in guiding their children into
adopting a radical vision and a caring approach to others. Although societal influences hostile to the left and peer group pressures pulled their
children in different directions, particularly during the 1950s, left-wing
parents often succeeded in transmitting their values to their children.
However, the strength of the left subcultural world appears to have
declined in the past few decades. The left continues to be out of sync with

the dominant political philosophies of our society and has been unable to fully recover from the setbacks suffered during the height of the cold war, when it was most out of sync.

Nevertheless, left-wing parents are managing to transmit caring values to their children. As they go about their separate tasks of overcoming sex and race inequality, preserving the environment, supporting world peace and solidarity with Third World countries, and fighting for jobs and health care for all, they are attempting to rebuild that subcultural world and to achieve the kind of unifying oneness available to their parents' and grandparents' generations. Despite its difficulties, the left persists and continues to seek the development of a society and a world that cares for all people in the belief that "another world is possible."

NOTES

1. Mari Jo Buhle, *Women and American Socialism, 1870–1920* (Urbana: University of Illinois Press, 1983); Sara Evans, *Personal Politics* (New York: Alfred A. Knopf, 1979); Rochelle Gatlin, *American Women Since 1945* (Jackson, Miss.: University Press of Mississippi, 1987); Van Gosse, "'To Organize in Every Neighborhood, in Every Home': The Gender Politics of American Communists between the Wars," *Radical History Review* 50 (1991): 109–41.

2. Barbara Myerhoff, *Number Our Days* (New York: Simon & Schuster, 1979), 117.

3. Elizabeth Gurley Flynn, *The Rebel Girl: An Autobiography; My First Life (1906–1926)* (New York: International Publishers, 1973), 44.

4. Quoted in Elaine Neil Orr, *Tillie Olsen and a Feminist Spiritual Vision* (Jackson, Miss.: University Press of Mississippi, 1987), 154.

5. Ibid., 157–9.

6. Robert Meeropol and Michael Meeropol, *We Are Your Sons: The Legacy of Ethel and Julius Rosenberg* (Boston: Houghton Mifflin, 1975), 165–66.

7. Kim Chernin, *In My Mother's House* (New York: HarperCollins, 1984), 106–7.

8. Vivian Gornick, *The Romance of American Communism* (New York: Basic Books, 1977); Arthur Liebman, *Jews and the Left* (New York: John Wiley and Sons, 1979); Paul C. Mishler, *Raising Reds: The Young Pioneers, Radical Summer Camps, and Communist Political Culture in the United States* (New York: Columbia University Press, 1999); Kenneth Teitelbaum, *Schooling for 'Good Rebels': Socialist Education for Children in the United States* (Philadelphia: Temple University Press, 1993).

9. Flynn, *Rebel Girl*, 23.

10. Ibid., 36.

11. Ibid., 29–30.

12. Ibid., 40.

13. Ibid., 40–1.

14. Ibid., 44–46, 53.

15. Ibid., 64.

16. Ibid., 23–64; Rosalyn F. Baxandall, ed., *Words on Fire: The Life and Writings of Elizabeth Gurley Flynn* (New Brunswick, N.J.: Rutgers University Press, 1987);

Stephen Charles Cole, "Elizabeth Gurley Flynn: A Portrait" (Ph.D. diss., Indiana University, 1991).

17. Armand Hammer with Neil Lyndon, *Hammer* (New York: Putnam, 1987), 13–14, 42–61.

18. Ibid., 54.

19. Ibid., 59.

20. Ibid., 60.

21. Ibid., 55.

22. Peggy Dennis, *The Autobiography of an American Communist* (Westport, Conn.: Hill, 1977), 19–26.

23. Ibid., 21.

24. Ibid.

25. Ibid., 24.

26. Ibid.

27. Ibid., 25.

28. Dorothy Healey and Maurice Isserman, *Dorothy Healey Remembers: A Life in the American Communist Party* (New York: Oxford University Press, 1990), 22.

29. Ibid., 25.

30. Ibid., 24.

31. Ibid.

32. Ibid., 28.

33. Ibid., 36.

34. Chernin, *Mother's House*, 101.

35. Ibid., 100–101, 167.

36. Robert Cohen, *When the Old Left Was Young: Student Radicals and America's First Mass Student Movement, 1929–1941* (New York: Oxford University Press, 1993), 248–49.

37. Carl Bernstein, *Loyalties: A Son's Memoir* (New York: Simon & Schuster, 1989), 15.

38. Ibid., 103–24.

39. Ibid., 151.

40. Ibid., 15, 90–91, 124–26, 136–53, 170.

41. Ibid., 175. See Chapter 5 for a discussion of the role of the United Public Workers union and federal workers' eventually successful effort to win collective bargaining rights.

42. Bernstein, *Loyalties*, 19.

43. Chernin, *Mother's House*, 7.

44. Ibid., 215.

45. Ibid., 216.

46. Ibid., 215–25, 303.

47. Ibid., 226–7, 251–5.

48. Margaret Collingwood Nowak, *Two Who Were There: A Biography of Stanley Nowak* (Detroit: Wayne State University Press, 1989), 237–38.

49. Judy Kaplan and Lin Shapiro, eds., *Red Diaper Babies: Children of the Left: Edited Transcripts of Conferences Held at World Fellowship Center, Conway, New Hampshire, July 31-August 1, 1982, July 9–10, 1983* (Somerville, Mass.: Red Diaper Productions, 1985), 1–2, 28. For additional stories of the experience of growing up in Communist families, see Judy Kaplan and Linn Shapiro, eds., *Red Diapers: Growing Up in the Communist Left* (Urbana: University of Illinois Press, 1998).

50. As quoted in J. Anthony Lukas, *Don't Shoot: We Are Your Children!* (New York: Random House, 1971), 23.

51. Liebman, *Jews and the Left,* 315–24, 555–57. See also Mishler, *Raising Reds.*

52. As quoted in Kaplan and Shapiro, *Red Diaper Babies,* 25.

53. Ibid., 27–28.

54. Meeropol and Meeropol, *We Are Your Sons,* 259–78.

55. Angela Davis, *An Autobiography* (New York: Random House, 1974), 75–113.

56. Todd Gitlin, *The Sixties: Years of Hope Days of Rage* (New York: Bantam Books, 1987), 73.

57. James P. O'Brien, "The Development of a New Left in the United States, 1960–1965," (Ph.D. diss., University of Wisconsin, 1971), 23.

58. Richard Flacks, "The Liberated Generation: An Exploration of the Roots of Student Protest," *Journal of Social Issues* XXIII (1967): 68.

59. Evans, *Personal Politics,* 120 n.

60. Ibid., 121.

61. Ibid.

62. Ibid., 121–4.

63. Kaplan and Shapiro, *Red Diaper Babies,* 63.

64. Ibid., 63–64.

65. Ibid., 64.

66. Ibid., 63–65.

67. Ibid., 69.

68. Ibid.

69. Ibid., 69–73.

70. Ibid., 87.

71. Ibid., 89.

72. Ibid., 87–89.

73. Ibid., 8.

74. Ibid.

75. Ibid., 93.

76. Ibid., 7–8, 88–93.

77. Maxine Phillips, "Family Ties of Parents, Politics, and Progeny," *Democratic Left* ll (1986): 3–5.

78. Ervin Staub, "The Origins of Caring, Helping, and Nonaggression: Parental Socialization, the Family System, Schools, and Cultural Influence," in P.M. Oliner et al., eds., *Embracing the Other: Philosophical, Psychological, and Historical Perspectives on Altruism* (New York and London: New York University Press, 1992).

79. Susan A. Ostrander, *Women of the Upper Class* (Philadelphia: Temple University Press, 1984), 142.

80. Ibid., 77.

81. Ibid., 77, 128–129.

82. Ibid., 84.

83. Ibid., 75–92, 128, 142.

84. Lillian Breslow Rubin, *Worlds of Pain: Life in the Working Class Family* (New York: Basic Books, 1976), 48.

85. Ibid., 39, 48.

86. Gornick, *The Romance of American Communism,* 7.

87. Annette Rubinstein, "The Cultural World of the Communist Party: An Historical Overview," in M.E. Brown, R. Martin, F. Rosengarten, and G. Snedeker,

eds., *New Studies in the Politics and Culture of U.S. Communism* (New York: Monthly Review Press, 1993), 242.

88. Rubin, *Worlds of Pain,* 31.

89. Ibid., 34, 36.

90. Ibid., 34.

91. Ibid.

92. Ibid., 201–2.

93. Roger Keeran, "The Communist Influence on American Labor," In M. E. Brown, R. Martin, F. Rosengarten, and G. Snedeker, eds., *New Studies in the Politics and Culture of U.S. Communism* (New York: Monthly Review Press, 1993), 163–97.

94. Angelo Herndon, *Let Me Live* (New York: Arno Press and the New York Times, 1969), 5–14.

95. James P. Comer, *Maggie's American Dream: The Life and Times of a Black Family* (New York: New American Library, 1988), xiv.

96. Ibid., xv.

97. Ibid., 137.

98. Ibid.

99. Ibid., 139.

100. Ibid., 125.

101. Ibid., 93–94.

102. Ibid., 131.

103. Ibid., 226.

CHAPTER 3

When Henry Met Franklin

In the film *Annie!*, little orphan Annie persuades the obstreperous business tycoon Oliver P. Warbucks to meet with President Franklin Roosevelt. As one of the forgotten people of whom FDR spoke, Annie is a Roosevelt supporter who has been inspired by the president's hopeful message. Due to Annie's presence at the meeting, FDR is able to persuade Warbucks to join in singing the optimistic and humanistic song, *Tomorrow*. The greedy business person is clearly on his way toward a moral transformation. The coupling of Roosevelt's charm and the appeal of the needy, as represented by Annie, is irresistible. Of course, compared with Ebenezer Scrooge, Warbucks suffers little on his way to redemption.

Annie!, of course, is fiction and a fantasy at that. In fact, it's a revisionist fantasy. Harold Gray's comic strip Little Orphan Annie was anti-New Deal. In one strip, for example, the self-reliant Annie says, "I never thought I'd *rather* be in a 'home'...but that was 'fore I knew there could be anybody like Mrs. Bleating-Hart...But I don't want to be a 'public charge' if I can help it! At least here I'm earning my way and not livin' off o' taxpayers!" Sounding very much like Henry Ford, the comic strip's self-made millionaire, individualist Oliver Warbucks, proclaims, "I see nothing so unusual in sharing our profits with our workers—when our business makes money I feel all those connected with it should make money.... I think [our workers]...are entitled to a piece of the profits—the bigger our profits—the bigger their wages." It is of pivotal importance, however, that this generosity emanates from the benevolence and wisdom of the business owner Warbucks, and not from protests by what he characterizes as "sore-headed" workers or their unions or regulations of a caring government. Indeed,

Gray's Oliver Warbucks died in 1944 because he could not continue to live under the New Deal regime. After FDR died, Gray brought Warbucks back to life.[1]

Interestingly, the anti-New Deal comic strip was Henry Ford's favorite.[2] Neither the comic strip Warbucks nor the real-life Henry Ford was likely to be taken in by the collectivistic notion that government should take responsibility for helping the needy to survive and live decent lives when the private economy failed to provide employment at decent wages for all who needed work. Nevertheless, there *was* a real world meeting between Roosevelt and Ford on which some pinned hopes that one or the other of these two famous individuals would be transformed. Five years after FDR assumed office, he had his first meeting as president with the country's most famous industrialist. On April 27, 1938, Ford and Roosevelt met for a two-hour luncheon conference. Attending the meeting with Ford were his son, Edsel, and his publicist, William J. Cameron. Also attending the meeting were G. Hall Roosevelt, the president's brother-in-law, and Marriner S. Eccles, governor of the Federal Reserve Board. Hall Roosevelt, Eleanor Roosevelt's brother and former controller of the city of Detroit when Frank Murphy was mayor, had arranged the meeting. Hall's effectiveness as an intermediary to Ford may have been due to the fact that he was then an employee of the Ford Commercial Credit Co., an auto financing firm.[3] By the summer of 1938, moreover, Hall "had become antagonistic" to Murphy, then Michigan's New Deal governor.[4]

What brought Ford, the antiunion exponent of individualist self-reliance, and Roosevelt, architect of New Deal programs of social responsibility by government and advocate of a new acceptance of trade unionism in American political life, together on April 27, 1938? What were the hopes and fears of observers? What was the significance of the meeting in the context of the overall relationship between these two influential figures?

The FDR-Ford meeting took place after FDR had been substantially weakened by the fight over his proposal to pack the Supreme Court, the formation of an anti-New Deal coalition of Republicans and conservative Democratic in Congress, and, most importantly, the onset of a severe recession. Sales of industrial products slumped dramatically, layoffs mounted, and the unions' bargaining power ebbed. By mid-April 1938, auto employment in the Detroit area had declined from 250,000 to 70,500. The plunge was especially severe at the Ford Motor Company, where employment was down to 11,500 from a normal level of 87,000.[5] The recession created political problems for the Roosevelt administration, which could not escape responsibility for the bad economic news. It threatened to undermine the basis of the administration's popularity.

Although the initial signs of a business downturn were evident as early as August 1937 and a major stock market sell-off occurred in October, the

Roosevelt administration was unsure what actions to take to counteract the situation. Indeed, later analysts attributed a major share of the blame for the recession to a cutback in federal funding as the administration sought to balance the budget. Other factors were a tightening of the money supply by the Federal Reserve and a withdrawal of $2 billion in consumer purchasing power due to the initiation of regressive Social Security tax payments. A common conception at the time was that businesspeople were holding back on investing. Liberals within the administration thought that there was a strike by capital against the administration. The president himself "was convinced that the situation was at least partially the result of a business conspiracy...against him." In a mirror-image version of the latter analysis, Roosevelt's conservative advisors thought the problem underlying the economy was a lack of business confidence and argued for reassuring business by moving toward a balanced budget or returning to the business-government cooperation approach of the National Recovery Administration (NRA) as the road to recovery. Weakened by the Court-packing battle, Roosevelt for several months vacillated between the advice of liberals to increase social spending and attack monopoly practices, and the advice of conservatives to continue with the budget-balancing approach and establish an entente with business.[6]

In the closing days of 1937, administration liberals took the offensive. In a December 26 radio address, Assistant Attorney General Robert Jackson, head of the Justice Department's antitrust division, blamed the recession on monopoly pricing practices. Jackson maintained that there was a "strike of capital" against New Deal reform. In a December 30 national radio network address, Secretary of the Interior Harold Ickes attacked the "big business fascism" of the Fords and others of America's Sixty Families.[7]

The Jackson and Ickes speeches gained extensive press coverage. When a reporter asked Roosevelt on December 31, "Do you agree with what those two gentlemen have been saying?" FDR responded by reciting a parable about how "a President by the name of Theodore Roosevelt" who had called some individuals "'malefactors of great wealth'" and was charged with calling all people of great wealth "malefactors' which, of course," FDR declaimed, "had absolutely nothing to do with what he had actually said." The frustrated reporter's rejoinder, "Mr. Ickes and Mr. Jackson were much more specific, Mr. President," elicited laughter but no follow-up comment from the president. When another reporter tried to pin him down by asking, "Does that mean that you say that Mr. Ford and General Motors and the others who are named are responsible for the Depression?" FDR demurred, "Oh, I think we will leave it to the parable."[8]

At the next Cabinet meeting, FDR jokingly gave the two officials credit for a January 14 meeting with Alfred Sloan of General Motors and Ernest Weir of Bethlehem Steel: "Do you know that this conference would not have been possible if it had not been for the speeches of Bob Jackson and

Harold Ickes? Prior to the speeches, these businessmen refused even to come in to talk to me. After the speeches they were only too glad to come in. One of them said this morning: 'But for God's sake call off that man Ickes.'"[9]

Despite the joking, FDR's meetings with business executives were a response to his conservative advisors' entreaties. In a politically precarious position, he was keeping his options open. Ford was an atypical and idiosyncratic businessperson but one who had a substantial public following. Roosevelt had been able to win all sorts of allies through a combination of his personal charm and the appeal of the power of the presidency. Perhaps even as strange a duck as Henry Ford could be won over.

Prior to the 1938 meeting, Ford had rejected appeals to meet with the president. Although he occasionally had said nice things about FDR and exchanged birthday greetings with him,[10] his criticisms of the president were more frequent. Roosevelt, in turn, offered criticisms of the auto magnate. Ford campaigned for Hoover in 1932; FDR responded by charging that "the Republican campaign management and people like Henry Ford...are guilty of spreading the gospel of fear."[11] Although most business leaders supported the administration's National Recovery Administration, Ford pointedly refused to sign the auto industry code. Ford was worried, unnecessarily to be sure, that Section 7(A) of the National Industrial Recovery Act was a threat to the open shop and that "every detail of our operation can be placed under control of a committee one-third of whom are politicians and one-third of whom are labor leaders." Of the NRA's Blue Eagle emblem, Ford told Ernest Liebold, his personal secretary, "Hell, that Roosevelt buzzard! I wouldn't put it on the car."[12] NRA head Hugh Johnson inaugurated a federal government boycott of Ford cars, a policy which FDR publicly supported. After several months, the federal government relaxed the ban. During the more than yearlong dispute, Charles Edison, son of Ford's friend Thomas Edison, and Senator James Couzens, Ford's former business partner, sought unsuccessfully to arrange a meeting between Ford and FDR to resolve the NRA dispute. Although Ford wrote to Edison that he had "deep respect" for Roosevelt "personally and as President," and believed that FDR had "an earnest and religious desire to do everything possible to ease the situation of this country," he refused to respond to the president's wish that Ford meet "to talk this over with him." Eventually, Edsel and Eleanor Ford visited the president in Warm Springs, Georgia, on November 24, 1934; the elder Ford telegraphed that he and his wife Clara Ford were unable to visit because of the state of her health. Cameron recalled that it was he who "wrote this refusal." Edsel's visit "was just a graceful out for Mr. Ford. For some reason he didn't want to go."[13]

Several important Ford officials noted Ford's essential hostility to Roosevelt. Cameron remembered Ford's very negative reaction to Roosevelt's inaugural address and maintained, "I doubt that he ever trusted Mr. Roosevelt."[14] Liebold commented that Ford disliked the new president's actions in the banking crisis and "had a very personal reaction" to Roosevelt's criticism of "economic royalists." The icing on the cake, according to Liebold's 1951 reminiscences, came "when we found that he [FDR] was of Jewish ancestry."[15] Harry Bennett said simply, "Mr. Ford hated Roosevelt."[16]

Perhaps Ford was willing to meet with Roosevelt in April 1938 because of the president's new political vulnerability and the fact that this was one in a series of meetings in which, as his conservative advisors wished, the president was seeking economic guidance from business leaders. Another factor was that Ford's supporters had waged a nationwide campaign for just such a get-together. This campaign developed in reaction to the attacks on Ford by Ickes and other administration liberals.[17] Early in January 1938, the Ford-Dearborn post of the Veterans of Foreign Wars complained to the president that "their neighbor and benefactor" had been "unduly criticized and defamed by high members" of his administration. The VFW called on the president to eliminate any opposition to the "sound industrial principles and policies of Henry Ford."[18] To assure that their entreaty would receive attention from the president, the group sent copies of their communication to members of Congress and the Dearborn press.

A more extensive campaign on Ford's behalf was organized by the Dearborn Pioneers Club, which described itself as "a noonday luncheon group of 70 members." Motivated by the attacks on Ford by members of FDR's "official family," the club circulated petitions praising Ford as "one of the best friends that the working man has had." The club's petition claimed that attacks on Ford were causing discord and thus slowing the recovery; it called on the president to settle labor-management differences equitably and "stop demoralizing and demolishing propaganda." The club's initiative became a national campaign, with a claimed total of 540,000 signatures from over 7,000 cities and towns. Although the petitions reflected the existence of a substantial pro-Ford sentiment, the president and his wife were sent complaints that in some instances employees were being forced to sign the petition.

When Republican Representative George Dondero asked the president if he would meet with representatives of the club to receive the petitions, he reported that most of the signatures came from businesspeople. When no meeting was forthcoming, the petitions were mailed to the president. In an accompanying letter, club president Arthur Ternes assured the president that neither the Ford Motor Company nor the Republican party was involved in the campaign, and that he and the club secretary had voted Democratic in the last three presidential elections. This campaign received considerable press coverage and culminated with a dedication at a public celebration in Dearborn of Henry and Clara Ford's 50th wedding anniversary. Acknowledging that the attacks on Ford had ceased, Ternes hoped the petitions would help the president "better determine the esteem with which Mr. Ford is held throughout the nation," and he expressed optimism about the forthcoming meeting between Ford and Roosevelt.[19]

Although, when interviewed years later, Cameron pooh-poohed the Dearborn Pioneers Club campaign, he sounded the same themes in an address to a Chamber of Commerce dinner in Bay City, Michigan, on April 19. "Government can help now," he said of the recession, "by keeping still, by putting a gag on Ickes and Jackson, by ceasing to act as God over forces of nature, and by ceasing to pass punitive legislation."[20]

While these specific 1938 events set the stage for Ford's willingness to visit FDR, there is no smoking gun to Ford's thinking. Ford tended to produce verbalizations that were often unclear. He was regarded as "emotional" by his son, Edsel, "inconsistent" by labor advisor Harry Bennett, and as a shy person afraid of his cultural and educational "inferiority" by public relations spokesperson Cameron. "He lived on the fringes of the community all the time," Cameron explained, "physically and intellectually."[21] Because of Ford's penchant for saying peculiar and sometimes incomprehensible things in public, company officials accompanied him when he spoke to reporters and advised reporters on what Ford really meant and what the company preferred be kept out of the papers. Cameron played this role with such frequency that it was said that he seemed able to read Ford's mind.[22]

To the non-mind-reading scholar, there remains an element of uncertainty about what Ford hoped to accomplish in visiting the president. *Detroit News* reporter Jay Hayden had good access to the company but was unsure of Ford's goal. He asked, "Is Ford...coming in the hope of finding a basis for compromise of his differences with the President or will he stand pat and use the White House as a sounding board for accentuating the conflict"?[23] Ford's public comments about his acceptance of Roosevelt's invitation contributed to the doubts about his purpose. Interviewed outside his Wayside Inn in Boston on April 21, Ford said: "I'm going to let him look at somebody who is not coming to tell him how to run the country. I'm not going to give him advice." Referring to the fact that he had known the president when the latter was assistant secretary of the navy, Ford declared: "I'm going to renew an old acquaintanceship of years' standing. I am going to give the President a chance to look at somebody who doesn't want anything."[24]

Although Ford's antagonism to FDR stemmed in large part from the president's labor policies, the company was relying on the courts, not the presidential meeting, for help in this area. Just two days before the FDR-Ford meeting, the company received favorable news on the legal front. After extensive and well-publicized hearings on the company's violation of workers' rights by such actions as the beating of unionists at the Battle of the Overpass, the National Labor Relations Board (NLRB) had found the company guilty of unfair labor practices and ordered it to cease such practices on December 23, 1937. The Supreme Court's decision on April 25, 1938, in the *Morgan v. United States* case, however, gave Ford an opportunity to bring the enforcement process to a standstill for over a year. Although the *Morgan* case involved the Department of Agriculture and the Packers and Stockyards Act, the Court's finding that "Those who are brought into contest with the Government in a quasijudicial proceeding aimed at the control of their activities are entitled to be fairly advised of what the Government proposes and to be heard upon its proposal before it issues its final command" applied equally to the NLRB and the Wagner Act.[25]

Since there had been no intermediate report in the Detroit case, Ford attorney Frederick Wood, representing the litigants in both the *Morgan* and *Schechter Poultry Corp. v. United States* cases, went on the offensive on April 27. He sought a delay in the Circuit Court of Appeals hearing on Ford's appeal of the NLRB decision so that he could take depositions on how the NLRB made its decision and whether the members were influenced in their decision by CIO or Roosevelt administration figures. In response to the Ford offensive, the NLRB retreated on May 2, 1938, asking the Circuit Court of Appeals to allow it to withdraw its decision so that it could issue an intermediate report. The legal maneuvering became increasingly complex. Suffice it to say that a comparable decision and order were finally issued on August 9, 1939, more than 19 months after the initial order.[26]

With the labor policy context in flux in April 1938, there were both hopes and fears about the meeting. CIO unionists, liberals, and leftists were worried. Although industrial unionism had established a base in such leading companies as General Motors, Chrysler, United States Steel, and General Electric in 1937, it was far from clear in 1938 if it would become a permanent part of the American scene. An important section of American industry, including such companies as Bethlehem Steel and Westinghouse as well as Ford, resisted any change from the old order of labor relations in their factories. Henry Ford personally symbolized this antiunionism because of his fame, wealth, and publicly stated determination to never accept unionization by his employees. Ford's anti-Semitic record at a time when fascism was on the march also made him anathema to many. United Automobile Workers (UAW) executive board member Irvan Cary wired the president to call attention to Ford's "absolute refusal to abide by the Wagner Act at his assembly plant at Long Beach, California" and to report that the "entire West Coast labor front is anxiously awaiting outcome of tomorrow's conference." A Detroit Ford employee wrote to FDR that his meeting with Ford "is sure playing with fire.... Every time any of the employees mention anything about Law the big bosses tell them that you are working for the Ford Motor Com[pany] and that Ford makes his own Laws."[27]

Although his antiunion practices made him anathema to industrial unionists and their liberal allies, Henry Ford drew support from anti-New Deal, pro-business Republicans as well as from many other Americans who saw Ford as an antiestablishment figure. The Ford Motor Company's $5 per day wage policy of 1914, Ford's low-price policy, and his conflicts with bankers had won him a significant public following. There had even been a significant Ford-for-President boom in 1923. To Americans untroubled by his recent right-wing and antilabor proclivities, Ford symbolized the small town and rural virtues of individualism, hard work, and piety. While many of Ford's supporters may have been pleased at the prospect of a meeting between their idol and the president, there were also letters and telegrams sent to Ford at the White House "begging Mr. Ford not to be beguiled into surrender of his individualistic ideas."[28]

In the press, there was speculation that FDR might ask Ford to inaugurate an annual wage as a way of contributing to the recovery and renewing the tradition of labor reform established more than twenty years earlier with the $5 a day wage policy. If Ford initiated such a policy, other auto companies might follow suit. General Motors was considering such an innovation because the Social Security Act provided an exemption of the 3 percent payroll tax for employers who guaranteed workers 1,200 hours of work per year.[29] Among those who were hopeful about the annual wage possibility was *Detroit News* correspondent Blair Moody (later appointed to the U.S. Senate by Democratic Governor G. Mennen Williams). Moody wrote: "One of the tragedies of the present situation is that two men with the vision of Roosevelt and Ford—both New Dealers in the best sense of the word—cannot get together on the national problem instead of sticking their tongues out at each other at a distance." Those who were not New Dealers "in the best sense," in Moody's view, were Roosevelt's "one-sided" NLRB and "the high-handed autocracy of Henry's little army."[30]

What actually transpired at the meeting became a source of controversy in the days following the event. Apparently, it was a pleasant lunch. Cameron recalled that Roosevelt "used ... all" his charm "that day," telling Ford, "I'm so glad to see you. My mother was so pleased to know that you were coming. She said, 'Franklin, I'm so glad that you're going to see Mr. Ford because Mr. Ford is not only a great man, he's a good man.'" The principal topic discussed was government economic policy. Roosevelt outlined his pump-priming plans and Eccles explained the logic behind government deficit spending. Ford apparently was unmoved. In parting, Ford told Roosevelt, "You know, Mr. President, before you leave this job, you're not going to have many friends, and then I'll be your friend."[31] Emerging from the meeting, the Ford party adhered to the etiquette of allowing the White House to report on meetings with the president. As an unofficial White House advisor, Hall Roosevelt felt free to make some vague positive remarks: "There was nothing that smacked of commercialism in any way, and very little economics was discussed. In fact, it reminded me very much of a family conversation at Wayside Inn." Stephen Early, FDR's secretary, announced that, "there would be no statement now or later concerning the conference."

Following the White House meeting, the Ford party headed by train to New York where Ford was scheduled to give a speech to the Bureau of Advertising of the American Newspaper Publishers Association. En route to New York, Ford spoke with *Detroit News* reporter Hayden and *Detroit Free Press* reporter Clifford Prevost. Having an early deadline, Prevost took down Ford's words and filed his story. Hayden's later deadline permitted him to get Cameron's interpretation of Ford's words. Cameron went with Hayden to the *New York Times* where Hayden typed up the story. Apparently, Cameron knew Ford's thinking better than Ford knew it. Ford blew up when he read Prevost's account and barred him from the company. Actually, the problem with Prevost's story was that it included some questionable statements by Ford that the latter presumably found embarrassing.[32]

The two news accounts made evident that there was no meeting of the minds between FDR and Ford. Prevost reported that "Ford was obviously of the opinion that President Roosevelt has no plan for solving [the] present depression." Hayden reported Ford as saying: "If finance would get out of government and government would get out of business everything would go again.... If government will just get out of the way and give natural American enterprise a free wing it will do the job." In a similarly conservative formulation, Prevost quoted Ford as saying: "The Government should be the policeman to exercise only that power necessary to maintain an orderly method of living." Ford expressed his opposition to the annual wage idea and to the president's notion that the automobile industry should plan its production to reduce the recessionary impact of big swings in auto sales. He agreed with Roosevelt that decentralization of industry was desirable but saw no role for the government in this process.

According to Hayden, Ford's "praise of Mr. Roosevelt was confined to one point. 'I believe he is entitled to great credit for rousing the people to think.... There is more public interest in national problems today than ever before.'" That this was a dubious compliment was evident when Ford added: "The American people basically are sound and they will right the situation for themselves as soon as they come to understand it." Ford expressed enthusiasm for one politician, the anti-New Deal vice president, John Nance Garner, and repeated his strange idea that "some of the men in Wall Street" were "responsible for much of the labor strife so prevalent in the country," by which he meant that unions were somehow controlled by financiers as part of their effort to gain control of all manufacturing and marketing operations.[33]

The main difference between the two stories is that Prevost reported that "Ford clashed frequently" with Eccles at the meeting and took positions at the meeting for reducing government spending and against increasing the debt.[34] In response to these comments, Roosevelt intimates gave "a broad and amused hint...that...Ford...didn't think up his good speeches until long after he was through visiting President Roosevelt." Noting that Ford's audience "didn't consist of clairvoyants," FDR's unnamed spokespersons said they did not know what was going on in Ford's mind until they read the news accounts of his interview. The president was said to have read Ford's statements "with mingled surprise and amusement." Eccles publicly maintained that "Mr. Ford didn't clash with me. I guess he said he didn't agree, and shook his head in dissent. But I'm not aware of any wordy clash having taken place." Although most news accounts were favorable to Ford, the *New York Post* suggested that "the aged multimillionaire motor maker...seems to have got mixed up about what he actually said and what he thought later he should have said."[35]

A column by Joseph Alsop and Robert Kintner disputed the charge that Ford was thinking up good arguments only after the meeting. Relying on an unnamed source, they reported that the president asked Ford what plans he had to bring about recovery. Ford replied, "I haven't any and I don't think you have either." Ford was said to have disagreed with the president's idea of a quota on auto production and to have asserted that, by aiding the CIO, the president was really aiding the large bankers. The columnists reported that Ford disagreed with Eccles's ideas on deficit spending, among other topics, with statements such as "The less this country spends, the quicker the recovery."[36]

Irritated by the stories putting him in a bad light, Eccles issued a statement on May 3 elaborating on his role in the meeting and criticizing the "uniformly false" reports that he and Ford "discussed and differed" with respect to governmental policy. He insisted that his role in the meeting, apart from "purely incidental conversation," was to provide Edsel Ford and Cameron with two quotations dealing with England's debt in the nineteenth century and the maldistribution of income in the United States in the late 1920s. Henry Ford was "inspecting some of the White House rooms" while Eccles presented the quotations to his companions.[37]

While in New York, Ford met with a large group of reporters at his hotel the day after his meeting with the president. Questioned by several reporters in his hotel room, Ford complained, "People are looking for a leader. They ought to be their own leaders, but they're looking for a leader. And they've got a leader who is putting something over on them, and they deserve it." When reporters sought to pin Ford down on whether he was talking about Roosevelt, the auto magnate refused to say. The *New*

York Times reporter concluded that Ford probably was not talking about FDR because, earlier in the interview, Ford said of the president: "You never heard me say anything against him, did you?" The *New York Times* report of the Ford interview noted that Ford then lowered his voice and said, "'What's the use…What's the use? He's like the rest of us, trying to do the best he can. Don't you think so?'"[38]

That evening Ford attended the newspaper publishers' banquet at the Waldorf-Astoria. Unfortunately for his hosts, he had changed his mind about delivering one of that evening's three speeches. No one who knew Ford would have been surprised. Ford production head Charles Sorensen recalled that Ford "could not make a speech. His few attempts to do so were pitiful." Once when a group of dealers presented him with a windmill, Ford "was called on to make a speech," executive H. C. Doss remembered. "He stood up and said something like 'good morning,' waved his hand to us, and that was all." Sorensen recounts a similar incident in which Ford attempted a spur-of-the-moment speech to plow salespeople: "Mr. Ford didn't say more than a dozen words. He was so confused, no one could understand him. He turned to me, mumbled something, and walked out of the room." After the latter incident, Ford said he'd never try to speak in public again.

Why, then, had Ford accepted the invitation to speak to the newspaper publishers? Perhaps his love of favorable publicity led him to agree to speak, but as the moment drew near, Ford's fear took over. Cameron recalled, "I often wonder how I lived through some of these things. There was always the tension of not knowing what was going to happen.… Finally I induced him to say something." The publishers, Cameron told Ford, "were in the same trouble that he was. They were important." Ford finally agreed, and gave a speech variously reported as twenty-three, twenty-four, twenty-seven, or thirty words: "Mr. Toastmaster, and gentlemen, we are all on the spot. Stick to your guns, and I will help you, with the assistance of my son, all I can. Thank you." When he sat down, the toastmaster remarked that it had been a long time since Ford had given a speech. Ford replied that it would be the last time.[39]

FDR's only comment to the press about his visit with Ford was that he "was interested to see what the press said about it." When he was asked to comment on Ford's speech to the editors, the president replied, as he often did, "I have only read the headlines." The quick reporter's comeback, "That is all there was to it," elicited laughter but no further comment from FDR.[40]

Newspaper commentaries after the meeting, like those before it, were favorably inclined to Ford's position. Labor partisans expressed their dismay. The day after the Ford-FDR meeting, former Ford employee Marjorie Vincent wrote the president: "If the interview you had with Henry Ford is as purported in the newspapers, real New Dealers feel that to have given the prestige to a man such as he is known to be, by having him to a White House conference was a mistake." Vincent credited Senator Couzens, Ford's former partner, for the $5 wage policy and any past "humanitarian motives" in the company. Henry Ford, on the other hand, was "the most selfish, self-centered man alive." Vincent hoped Roosevelt would do something to "offset...the vicious propaganda" resulting from his meeting with Ford.[41]

Confessing his "fears and trepidations that you would accomplish the impossible and make Henry a human being," George Knott passed along the humorous resolution of his United Mine Workers local union:

Whereas the President of the United States met with Henry Ford for the purpose of changing his mind and Whereas this was to all intents and purpose[s] a waste of time, therefor[e] be it resolved That the President of these United States shall in the future, by some scientific means ascertain beforehand whether his guests have a mind.[42]

Pleased that Ford made no move in Roosevelt's direction, conservatives and far-right groups were upbeat in the wake of the meeting. A week after the Ford-FDR meeting, 400 Nazis of the German-American Bund in the Yorkville section of New York City cheered "wildly" when a speaker proposed Ford as a candidate for president. Roosevelt, on the other hand, was ridiculed as the "Charlie McCarthy of the White House."[43]

There was no meeting of the minds between Ford and Roosevelt, no change in their essentially antagonistic positions. Although Roosevelt wanted business support, what he wanted was business support for his leadership, not a 1920s-model business-government partnership in which business needs were the fulcrum of government policy. FDR thus welcomed an April 26, 1938, statement of business leaders pledging cooperation with the administration and continued with his new left-tilt, which involved increasing funds for housing and welfare and a determined campaign to pass a wages and hours bill. Although Roosevelt had made occasional gestures to antilabor critics in 1937 and 1938, he generally offered strong support to the embattled NLRB and expressed a sympathetic attitude to the position of organized labor. Ford, meanwhile, maintained his stance on the opposite side of the political spectrum, which involved both a conservative philosophical framework and a determined policy of blocking unionization of the company.

In retrospect, the failure of the Ford-FDR meeting to produce a significant change in direction by either protagonist seems to be an inevitable result of the two principals' philosophical and class orientations. FDR's orientation toward the working class and poor involved no socialist commitment, to be sure, but it did involve a substantial revision of the U.S. political system to grant a greater stake, and even some power, to the people at the bottom. FDR was a leader of upper-class origin who included service to the needy as part of his vision. Ford was a leader of middle-class origin who became wealthy and thought that pursuing his personal interests would mean personal success for himself and would be good for others.

Although Ford's antagonisms to unionism and FDR were typical of the business community, the depth of the social crisis of the 1930s and the strength of the desire for change by working people led some employers toward new ways of thinking. Interestingly, the need for new business approaches was so great that Ford's only child, Edsel, who became president of the Ford Motor Company in 1918, was among those who wished for a new direction. If Henry Ford, just three months shy of his 75th birthday in April 1938, had stepped aside, the results of the White House get-together likely would have been positive.

The president had a different and warmer relationship with Edsel Ford than with Henry Ford. In 1928, shortly after FDR purchased Warm Springs and established the Warm Springs Foundation, Edsel and Eleanor Ford made a donation of $25,000 to enclose the pool at Warm Springs so that it could be used year-round. FDR wrote to his mother about the *"fine cheque"* Edsel sent him for the foundation and noted: "The Edsel Fords were with the Piersons for a week and I liked them both very much."[44] In 1938, Edsel served as treasurer for the Detroit Committee for the President's Birthday Ball for the Benefit of the Sufferers from Infantile Paralysis.[45] In January 1938, with other auto industry officials, he attended a White House conference with FDR aimed at discouraging "high pressure" selling of autos.[46] Among those with whom Edsel served on the President's Birthday Ball were Michigan Governor Frank Murphy and Abner Larned, head of the Works Progress Administration (WPA) in Michigan. Edsel was present at the farewell party for Murphy after his 1938 electoral defeat and subsequent appointment as U.S. attorney general. After Henry Ford made his statement about building 1,000 planes a day in May 1940, Ickes noted in his diary that Edsel told Secretary of the Treasury Henry Morgenthau "that sometimes his father got 'emotional' and that it was up to him (Edsel) to make good. Morgenthau was satisfied that Edsel Ford wants to cooperate to the fullest extent possible."[47]

Edsel's humanistic and cooperative impulses had little impact on company policy, however. Although Edsel was president of the company, Henry retained control and often overrode his son's decisions to the point of publicly humiliating him.

In the years following the 1938 meeting, the differences between FDR and Ford grew. Ford's foreign policy orientation was isolationist and anti-British, whereas FDR was pro-British and increasingly interventionist. Ford continued to violate the National Labor Relations Act while Roosevelt played a critical role in preventing the act from being crippled by amendments. As the economy improved, organized labor rebuilt and eventually prepared a new campaign to organize Ford Motor Company.

By the time the union campaign got underway, the defense program had reached massive proportions and there were new calls for restricting labor in the name of the defense effort. Ford began to receive large contracts for producing defense items, which the union protested. The union called for a consumer boycott of Ford cars and federal government denial of government contracts to Ford and other labor-law violators, on the grounds that such contracts aided the company in its illegal activities. The union argued, moreover, that Ford was not a reliable producer because it failed to deal equitably with its employees.

The union campaign began to produce results. Sidney Hillman, codirector of the National Defense Advisory Commission and the Office of Production Management, argued the union's case within the councils of government, and FDR himself began to raise the question with other members of the administration. Finally, on April 1, 1941, the union shut down Ford's River Rouge complex, site of two-thirds of Ford's production activity. Ford charged the strike was a Communist plot to disrupt defense production. FDR and Michigan Democratic Governor Van Wagoner gave Ford no aid. Instead, they sought to persuade the company to bargain with the union and agree to an NLRB election. The company capitulated to the pressure. On May 21, 1941, 70 percent of Ford workers voted for the UAW-CIO. One month later, the company and the union signed their first contract. At the last moment, Henry Ford threatened to carry out his early promise to shut down the factory rather than go forward with a new relationship with his employees. His wife threatened to leave him if he pursued this course, and Ford decided to accept the new situation. There was not a fundamental change in his outlook, however. The company's labor relations policies remained chaotic and would be put on a new footing only after Edsel Ford's premature death in 1943 and the cessation of Henry Ford's active involvement in the company following a second stroke. Edsel's son, Henry Ford II, defeated those in the company who would carry on in the old way in 1945.[48]

The New Deal approach to labor relations had become consolidated in major areas of the industrial economy. By then, however, Franklin Roosevelt was dead. Postwar hopes for a resurgent New Deal were dashed by the eruption of the cold war and by a renewed big-business offensive to enact restrictive labor legislation with no FDR in the White House to help stem the tide.

NOTES

1. Robert C. Harvey, *The Art of the Funnies: An Aesthetic History* (Jackson: University of Mississippi Press, 1994), 99–104 (emphasis in original).

2. David L. Lewis, *The Public Image of Henry Ford* (Detroit: Wayne State University Press, 1976), 538 n. 17.

3. Clipping, *Washington Star,* May 2, 1938, Acc. 984, Reel 25, Ford Motor Company Archives, Dearborn, Michigan (hereafter cited as FMCA).

4. *New York Times,* April 28, 1938, 1:8; Sidney Fine, *Frank Murphy: The New Deal Years* (Chicago: University of Chicago, 1979), 486–88.

5. Report of UAW Research Department on Employment in Greater Detroit, April 18–23, 1938, UAW Executive Board Minutes, Addes Coll., Box 6, Archives of Labor History and Urban Affairs, Wayne State University, Detroit.

6. Kenneth S. Davis, *FDR: Into the Storm 1937–1940* (New York: Random House, 1993), 137–42, 206–8.

7. William Leuchtenburg, *Franklin D. Roosevelt and the New Deal* (New York: HarperCollins, 1963), 246–48.

8. Franklin Roosevelt, *Complete Presidential Press Conferences of Franklin D. Roosevelt* (New York: Da Capo Press, 1972), 10:439–41.

9. Harold L. Ickes, *The Secret Diary of Harold L. Ickes: The Inside Struggle, 1936–39* (New York: Simon & Schuster, 1954) II:295.

10. Birthday greetings can be found in Acc. 1, Boxes 3 and 64, and Acc. 23, Box 7, FMCA.

11. *The Public Papers and Addresses of Franklin D. Roosevelt,* vol. 1 (New York, 1932), 795.

12. As quoted in Sidney Fine, "The Ford Motor Company and the N.R.A.," *Business History Review* 32 (Winter 1958): 360–62.

13. Ibid., 362–371; Reminiscences of William J. Cameron, 240, FMCA.

14. Reminiscences of William J. Cameron, 147.

15. Reminiscences of E.G. Liebold, 1337, 1393–94, 1406, FMCA.

16. Harry Bennett, *We Never Called Him Henry* (New York: Fawcett, 1951), 120.

17. Clipping, "Ford Attacks Bring Protest," Federal Mediation and Conciliation Service, Case #199–1461, National Archives.

18. Gordon G. Moore to FDR, January 8, 1938, and attached Resolution, OF 3217, FDR Library.

19. Clipping, "Two Mile Petition—Longest in the World—Honors Henry Ford," dateline April 12, 1938, Acc. 984, Reel 25, FMCA; Arthur A. Ternes to FDR, April 23, 1938, and attached petition, summaries of anonymous letter to president, March 8, 1938, and George A. Dondero to president, March 24, 1938, OF 3217, FDR Library; Clipping, "Ford Attacks Bring Protest," n.d.; Mildred V. Smith to Mrs. Roosevelt, March 18, 1938, Walter Williams to FDR, Wyman Silcox to FDR, April 3, 1938, FMCS, Case #199–1463, National Archives.

20. Clipping, *Detroit Free Press,* April 20, 1938, Ford Clipping File, Acc. 984, Reel 25, FMCA.

21. Reminiscences of William J. Cameron, 115–16, 137, 191.

22. Ibid., 155; Clipping, "The Commentator," *Detroit News,* April 29, 1938, Acc. 984, Reel 25, FMCA.

23. Hayden also expressed uncertainty about whether FDR was seeking to compose his differences with Ford or to put Ford on the spot. Hayden was probably trying to provide a balanced article, raising questions about both sides. There seems little doubt that FDR was not trying to put Ford on the spot. Clipping, *Detroit News,* April 23, 1938, Acc. 984, Reel 25, FMCA.

24. Clippings, dateline April 21, 1938, Acc. 984, Reel 25, FMCA, *Newsweek,* May 2, 1938, 10.

25. Morgan v. U.S., 304 U.S. 1, 19 (1938).

26. In re Ford Motor Co. and UAW, 14 NLRB 346 (1939); James A. Gross, *The Reshaping of the National Labor Relations Board* (Albany: State University of New York Press, 1981), 30–39.

27. Irvan J. Cary to the President, April 26, 1938, Truly Ford Employees to the President, April 25, 1938, OF 3217, FDR Library.

28. *New York Times*, April 28, 1938. See also Reminiscences of William J. Cameron, 151.

29. Clipping, *Detroit Times*, April 25, 1938, Acc. 984, Reel 25, FMCA; Alfred P. Sloan, Jr., *My Years at General Motors* (New York: McFadden-Bartell, 1965), 404.

30. Blair Moody to Laurence Lenhardt, April 6, 1938, Blair Moody Papers, Michigan Historical Collection, Bentley Library, Ann Arbor, Mich.

31. Reminiscences of William J. Cameron, 150–52.

32. Robert Lacey, *Ford, The Men and the Machine* (Boston: Little, Brown, 1986), 384–86.

33. *New York Times*, April 28, 1938; *St. Louis Post-Dispatch*, April 28, 1938; *Detroit Free Press*, April 28, 1938; *Time*, May 9, 1938, 10.

34. *Detroit Free Press*, April 28, 1938.

35. Clippings, *New York News*, April 29, 1938, *New York Post*, April 29, 1938, Acc. 984, Reel 25, FMCA.

36. Clipping, *Washington Star*, May 2, 1938, Acc. 984, Reel 25, FMCA.

37. Clippings, *Baltimore Sun*, May 4, 1938, United Press International (UPI), May 4, 1938, Acc. 984, Reel 25, FMCA.

38. *New York Times*, April 29, 1938, 14:3.

39. Charles Sorensen, *My Forty Years with Ford* (New York: W.W. Norton and Co., 1956), 27–29; Reminiscences of H.C. Doss, 55, FMCA; Reminiscences of William J. Cameron, 153–54; *Time*, May 9, 1938, 10; Clipping, UPI dispatch, April 29, 1938, clipping, *Detroit Times*, April 28, 1938, clipping, *New York News*, April 29, 1938, clipping, *New York Post*, April 29, 1938, Acc. 984, Reel 25, FMCA. After an analysis of the company's extensive clipping books, David L. Lewis concluded that "Ford spoke to groups unfamiliar to him only sixteen times in his life." *Public Image of Henry Ford*, 64.

40. Franklin Roosevelt, *Complete Presidential Press Conferences of Franklin D. Roosevelt* (New York: Da Capo Press, 1972), 11:398–99.

41. Marjorie E. Vincent to FDR, April 28, 1938, OF 3217, FDR Library.

42. George Knott to FDR, May 2, 1938, OF 3217, FDR Library.

43. Clipping, *Yorkville (N.Y.) Advance*, May 5, 1938, Acc. 984, Reel 25, FMCA. Although the Yorkville paper called the participants in this gathering "pro-Nazi," the Bund was a Nazi organization. Ronald H. Bayor, *Neighbors in Conflict*, 2nd. ed. (Urbana: University of Illinois Press, 1988), 60–62. Its leader was Fritz Kuhn, a Ford Motor Company employee from 1928 to 1937. Lewis, *Public Image of Henry Ford*, 152.

44. Nathan Miller, *FDR: An Intimate History* (Garden City, N.Y.: Doubleday, 1983), 212; Edsel Ford to FDR, March 15, 1928, FDR to Mama, March 17, 1928, in Elliot Roosevelt, ed., *F.D.R.: His Personal Letters, 1905–1928* (New York: Duell, Sloan & Pearce, 1948), 634–45.

45. Abner E. Larned to Frank Murphy, December 30, 1937, Frank Murphy Papers, Box 19, Michigan Historical Collection, Bentley Library, Ann Arbor, Mich.

46. *New York Times*, January 22, 1938, 1:2; Clipping, "Magnate Who Has Fought New Deal to Give No Advice," Associated Press dispatch, April 21, 1938, Acc. 984, Reel 25, FMCA.

47. Abner E. Larned to Frank Murphy, December 30, 1937, Frank Murphy Papers; Sidney Fine, *Frank Murphy: The New Deal Years* (Ann Arbor: University of Michigan Press, 1984), 27–28; Ickes, *The Secret Diary*, III:197.

48. Sorensen, *My Forty Years*, 268–71; Allan Nevins and Frank Ernest Hill, *Ford: Decline and Rebirth, 1933–1962* (New York: Charles Scribner's Sons, 1962), 252–69.

CHAPTER 4

"I'm Fighting for Freedom": Coleman Young, HUAC, and the Detroit African American Community

Cold war scholarship has focused a great deal of attention on the effects of repression on various areas of U.S. life. Numerous works have discussed the near destruction of the left-wing movement in Hollywood, the trade unions, the schools, and colleges.[1] Although the persecution of Paul Robeson and W. E. B. DuBois has been chronicled,[2] less attention in the cold war literature has been paid to the effect of repression on the African American community at the local level.[3] A result of this oversight is that the continuing vitality of the African American radical tradition has been poorly understood. Despite many criticisms, Robeson and DuBois retained their stature as national role models for African American activists and intellectuals. Equally important, however, to the survival of the African American radical tradition has been the continuing strength of African American radicalism at the local level.

One of the important local centers for the African American left in the 1930s and 1940s was the city of Detroit. This chapter examines how Detroit African American leftists, their allies, and the Detroit African American community as a whole responded to the anticommunist juggernaut which hit Detroit in 1952. Detroit's left-progressive African American leadership core, it is argued, managed to survive these trying times and hold together a following at the local level. When national conditions became more favorable, these leaders were able to regroup and expand their influence and power.

It was probably concern about just such a possibility that was on Federal Bureau of Investigation (FBI) Director J. Edgar Hoover's mind when, on February 21, 1952, he wired the Detroit FBI to register his approval for the interviewing of an FBI informant by House Un-American Activities Committee (HUAC) investigators. It was just four days before the scheduled opening of HUAC hearings in Detroit on so-called Communist infiltration into defense industries, and Hoover gave this local event his personal attention. Hoover also sanctioned sharing with the HUAC investigators information about "proposed CRC [Civil Rights Congress] picketing and packing HUAC hearings." More ominously, Hoover advised that, to establish that CRC picketing is illegal, "it is necessary to prove that the picketing is with intent to interfere with, obstruct or impede the administration of justice or to influence any judge, juror, witness, or court official in the discharge of his duty."[4]

Although the FBI records released under the Freedom of Information Act do not disclose the identities of its informants, it is likely that the informant referred to by Hoover was Bereneice Baldwin, an African American whose story identifying 28 Detroiters as Communists before the Subversive Activities Control Board in Washington produced banner headlines in the Motor City just 10 days prior to Hoover's wire. A plan to open the Detroit hearings with Baldwin's testimony was dropped, however, because she was being cross-examined in Washington.[5] The idea of leading off with an African American informer was probably no accident since committee investigators knew that its list of witnesses likely to be "unfriendly" included a disproportionate number of prominent African American Detroiters. Moreover, the committee's most visible public opposition came from the Civil Rights Congress, within which African Americans played a prominent role. Indeed, African Americans were often at center stage during the Detroit hearings. Although the committee's general goal was to expose Communists in defense industries, its main Detroit target was Local 600 of the United Automobile Workers, which represented 60,000 workers at the Ford Motor Company's River Rouge complex and was the largest local union in the world. The vast Rouge complex included 16 buildings, each of which had its own full-time union officials. The committee's second target was a group of African American leaders, Communist and non-Communist, who rejected the cold war consensus but retained a good deal of influence within Detroit's African American community. HUAC's purpose in holding local hearings was not to gather information relevant to national security legislation, but rather to arouse public animosity to Communists and their allies and thereby undermine the ability of leftist individuals and organizations to function politically. Committee member Charles E. Potter told the *Detroit News* that the FBI knew the facts, "but this will be the public's first knowledge of what is going on."[6]

In targeting UAW Local 600, HUAC was selecting one of the bulwarks of left-wing influence in the United States. To be sure, HUAC's assumption that Communists dominated the local was inaccurate.[7] However, the left had played a decisive part in the early underground phase of the unionization effort at Ford and in winning unity between African American and white workers. Communists continued to function in the local's progressive caucus, which retained a sizeable following in the local. In the March 1951 local union election, candidates affiliated with the progressive caucus had won three of the four highest offices in the local, the presidencies of several units (buildings), and about half the seats on the local's executive board and general council. The sizeable left and progressive presence in the membership and leadership of Local 600 often led the organization to take controversial stands on both trade union and political matters. Local 600 was one of the few large organizations advocating a cease-fire in Korea in 1951. It spoke out "for international peace and cooperation of all nations" and against "an impending World War III" during the Korean War when such ideas were branded as Communist in the mass media.[8]

Contributing to the orthodox concern with Local 600 was the fact that it served as an important base of support for radicalism within the African American community. This occurred because of the employment of a large number of African Americans, the inclusion of African Americans in leadership at the unit and local levels, and the significant role the local played in community affairs. The Ford Rouge complex became the Detroit area's largest employer of African American workers in the 1920s, and about 12,000 African American workers were employed at the complex in 1952. The highest-ranking African American official, William Hood, the local's recording secretary, served as the president of the National Negro Labor Council (NNLC), a left-led national organization of African American trade unionists.[9]

Although influential in Local 600, the left was also vulnerable there. Anticommunist forces led by Walter Reuther had won control of the UAW's national leadership in November 1947. An opponent of the left, Carl Stellato, was elected president of Local 600 in 1950 and initiated an anticommunist campaign that included a requirement that all 550 elected and appointed local representatives sign a loyalty oath. Stellato attempted to remove five building unit officers from their positions on the grounds that they were Communists and thus not eligible for office under the union's constitution. Substantial opposition to the anticommunist campaign, however, led to the defeat of the purge effort and Stellato's abandonment of his anticommunist campaign. He retained the presidency of the local in a close 1951 election. Although dropped by Local 600's president, HUAC recalled Stellato's charges during its 1952 hearings as did the UAW international leadership when it took action against Local 600 in the wake of the HUAC public relations onslaught.[10]

Among other important organizations that HUAC interrogated in Detroit were the Civil Rights Congress (CRC) and the National Negro Labor Council (NNLC). The Civil Rights Congress was formed in 1946 as a merger of the International Labor Defense and the National Federation for Constitutional Liberties. As an organization whose focus was the defense of democratic rights, the Civil Rights Congress was involved in campaigns for justice for the Martinsville Seven, Willie McGee, and other victims of racist repression. In 1951 Paul Robeson and William Patterson presented to the United Nations the CRC petition, *We Charge Genocide,* which chronicled the violence and denial of African American people's rights taking place in the United States. Although modest in numbers, with 500 to 1,000 members, the Detroit chapter of the CRC had an active staff and broad community support. Anne Shore, the Detroit CRC's director of organization, recalled that the organization "depended on a coalition of labor, white, black, middle class, and intellectual and it had been a very effective organization over the years." African Americans were prominent in the leadership of the Civil Rights Congress, including Detroit's Rev. Charles A. Hill, a national board member, and Arthur C. McPhaul, the full-time executive secretary of the Detroit chapter.[11]

The National Negro Labor Council was founded in 1951 as a black-led organization within the trade union movement. It championed "full freedom" for African American people, focusing on their economic needs, and sought democracy and equality within the trade union movement. As a left-progressive organization, the NNLC was critical of attacks on civil liberties and of the Korean War, but its principal activities revolved around the struggle for jobs for African Americans and fair employment practices legislation. Its approach called for direct action as well as political action. Among the key national leaders of the NNLC along with Hood was another Detroiter, Coleman Young, who acted as executive secretary. Detroit was the organization's national headquarters.[12]

Rev. Charles A. Hill was the most prominent African American leader subpoenaed. Pastor of the Hartford Avenue Baptist Church since 1920, Rev. Hill had long been active in a variety of progressive causes. When most of the African American clergy supported the Ford Motor Company against the UAW in its early organizing efforts, Hill staunchly supported the union. He worked with union leaders to prevent race riots in the 1939 Dodge strike and the 1941 Ford strike. Rev. Hill had served as president of both the Detroit branch of the NAACP and the Baptist Ministerial Alliance. In 1942 Rev. Hill led thousands of African Americans and their white allies in the struggle to retain Sojourner Truth Homes "for those for whom it was built." In 1945 Detroit African American leaders drafted Hill to run for Common Council and he won the endorsement of the Congress of Industrial Organizations (CIO) Political Action Committee. At a time when the African American population was an estimated 210,000, or 12.7 percent of the city total, Rev. Hill received 142,000 votes in the citywide race, finishing 14th (9 were elected) and gaining 29 percent of the vote. Rev. Hill again represented the aspirations for African American representation in city government when he ran in 1947 and again received CIO backing. In 1948 Rev. Hill joined with such prominent national figures as Paul Robeson and W. E. B. DuBois in supporting the Progressive party campaign of Henry Wallace. When Hill was the city council candidate put forward by the African American community in 1949 and 1951, he no longer enjoyed the support of the CIO but still gained over 20 percent of the ballots cast. Then in complete control of the UAW, Walter Reuther saw to it that no union support went to anyone who was willing to work with Communists. Rev. Hill was not one to abandon old friendships and alliances because of changing political circumstances. He continued to stand for a united and militant fight for complete equality for African American people and social progress for all. At the time of the hearings, he was president of the Michigan Peace Council.[13]

Another prominent leader subpoenaed to testify was attorney C. LeBron Simmons. Like Rev. Hill, Simmons had played a prominent role in assisting the UAW during the 1941 Ford strike. As president of the Detroit chapter of the National Negro Congress, he had helped to mobilize broad support in the African American community for the union cause. In 1942 he had served as secretary and legal counsel for the Sojourner Truth Citizens Committee. In 1944 Simmons had received 15,600 votes in a primary contest for Democratic state representative, missing a nomination that was tantamount to election by 900 votes. Simmons also played a leadership role in professional organizations such as the National Lawyers Guild and the Wolverine Bar Association, the organization of Detroit's African American attorneys.[14]

Arthur McPhaul, executive secretary of the Civil Rights Congress, was subpoenaed also. He first became active in the left-wing movement during the depression. As a worker in the Rouge complex's pressed-steel building, where African Americans made up fewer than 10 percent of those employed, he was elected committee member and then vice president of the union's building unit of 10,000 workers. McPhaul was also a key initiator of an African American caucus which sought with some success to increase African American representation in the leadership of the UAW and CIO in the mid-1940s. In 1951 Ford fired McPhaul for giving a speech in the plant lunchroom, even though many other union leaders also gave speeches at the same lunchroom meeting without being dismissed.[15]

Best known today of the subpoenaed witnesses was Coleman Young. Young was called to testify as executive secretary of the National Negro Labor Council along with president Hood. Born in Alabama in 1918, Young had moved to Detroit with his family in 1923. Like a number of other Detroit African American activists, Young had been initiated into politics at the neighborhood barbershop of an African American Marxist named Haywood Maben. It was a scene of lively discussion and a place for political education. Young was an excellent student but was denied a college scholarship because of discrimination. Landing a job at Ford, Young joined the union in the underground days but was fired after, as Young recalled it, he laid out a company "thug" with a pipe. He was also fired from a post-office job because he was organizing for a union. Young worked with Rev. Hill on the Sojourner Truth housing struggle and aided the Ford organizing drive from the outside as a volunteer organizer. As an officer during World War II, Young fought against segregation in the army and, according to Communist party leader James Jackson, wrote articles for African American newspapers exposing the conditions of African American service members under the pseudonym Captain Midnight.[16]

Returning from the army, Young became an international representative with the left-wing United Public Workers Union. In 1947 he was elected as director of organization of the Wayne county (Detroit area) CIO, the first time an African American was elected to a position of such prominence in the Detroit labor movement. One of three full-time elected officials of the county CIO, Young emerged as the principal leader of the organization. He led the group in union organizing drives and protests of police brutality against African Americans. In 1948 Young was state director of the Progressive party of Michigan and ran for State Senate on the party's ticket. In 1951 he was one of the founders of the National Negro Labor Council.[17]

George Crockett was the attorney for Young, Reverend Hill, McPhaul, and many other "unfriendly" witnesses. As an attorney for the Labor Department, Crockett had attracted the attention of the UAW during World War II and was invited by then president R. J. Thomas to function as executive director of the union's new Fair Practices Committee. Crockett gained widespread recognition for his successful effort to win support in many local unions for the principles of equality on the job and in the union. He tackled complaints of discrimination, publicized the union's position to the public, and involved himself in the affairs of the community. Crockett had a regular column in the *Michigan Chronicle,* one of Detroit's two African American newspapers. His relationship with the UAW came to an end, however, when anticommunists took control of the union. In 1949 Crockett appeared as attorney for former New York City Council member Benjamin Davis in the trial of the top leaders of the Communist party accused of violating the Smith Act. For his vigorous defense of his client, Crockett was held in contempt of court; he was awaiting the outcome of his appeal of the contempt citation at the time of the Detroit HUAC hearings.[18]

To understand the threat that the House Un-American Activities Committee hearings represented to these African American leaders, the hysteria of the times must be recalled. As early as 1946, a domestic anticommunist campaign accompanied Truman's initiation of an anti-Soviet foreign policy. Truman established loyalty investigations of all federal employees in 1947. That same year, Congress passed the Taft-Hartley Act with the requirement that trade union officials had to file non-Communist affidavits if their unions were to have access to the National Labor Relations Board. Truman's Justice Department secured indictments against the top leaders of the Communist party under the Smith Act in 1948. The Hiss and Rosenberg cases further created fears that leftists were spies threatening the security of the country. When the United States began fighting Communists in Korea in 1950, the frenzy at home reached a new pitch. That year, Sen. Joseph McCarthy rose to prominence with his charges of Communist infiltration of government, and Congress passed the Internal Security Act with its provisions for deportation, detention, and registration of so-called Communist-front organizations. The Michigan legislature and the Detroit city council passed similar restrictive legislation. Throughout this period, HUAC traversed the country, holding hearings timed to coincide with strikes and NLRB or union elections. The daily newspapers printed screaming headlines and individuals whose names were listed in the paper often faced firings and sometimes violence. The forces responsible for these repressive laws, investigations, media campaigns—and of the accompanying hysteria—had two chief purposes. First, they sought to eliminate any significant dissent to a policy of confrontation with the Soviet Union and extensive intervention elsewhere in the world. Second, they sought to halt any push toward an expanded New Deal by destroying the left-progressive coalition that helped propel the New Deal forward. Left-wing organizations often played initiating roles on both domestic and foreign policy fronts and they were therefore a special target, but anyone who challenged the cold war consensus was subject to attack.[19]

HUAC's visit to Detroit was preceded by "all the ballyhoo of a three-ring circus." FBI and committee investigators began questioning Detroit activists in preparation for the hearings as early as October 1951. Two weeks before the committee arrived, Detroit's newspapers joined in creating an anticommunist climate when they gave front-page banner headlines to Bereneice Baldwin's testimony identifying 28 Detroiters as Communists before the Subversive Activities Control Board hearing in Washington on the question of registering Communists under the Internal Security Act.[20]

Progressives attempted to combat the incipient hysteria. The Civil Rights Congress devoted its full energies to organizing the defense. Local 600 established a defense committee to support its subpoenaed members and protect the local itself. *Ford Facts,* the local's paper, focused an entire issue on an attack on HUAC. The newspaper criticized the reactionary voting records of committee members and several building presidents wrote columns against the committee. The Wolverine Bar Association unanimously deplored the HUAC investigation and expressed support of

its "highly respected" member, C. Lebron Simmons. The Baptist Ministerial Alliance, for its part, gave full backing to Rev. Hill. On the Sunday
before the hearings opened, the ministers group gained broad community
support at a rally it sponsored at Rev. Hill's church. Local 600 held a
protest rally of 500 at the same time.[21]

On February 25, 1952, the opening day of the hearings, a small but spir-
ited picket line of 50 people organized by the Civil Rights Congress
protested the witch-hunt. One picket wore a Ku Klux Klan robe and carried a puppet labeled "Wood," whose hands and legs moved when he
pulled the strings. John Wood, representative from Georgia, was HUAC's
chairperson. The Ku Klux Klan charge stemmed not only from the fact
that Wood was a southerner but also because four of the first six names of
subpoenaed witnesses released to the press included the African American leaders Hill, Young, Simmons, and Hood. Young accused the committee of "singling out Negro leaders." "If chairman Wood of Georgia thinks
the Negro people will be intimidated by his group he is sadly mistaken,"
Young declared. Rev. Hill called the charge of un-Americanism against
him "laughable when you think that I polled more votes in seeking to be
elected to the common council of the City of Detroit than Congressman
Wood polled to be elected Congressman in Georgia because of Georgia's
disfranchisement of the Negro." Wood responded to these charges by
issuing a statement that the committee had no intent to raise "racial
issues."[22]

The Republican members of the committee and the GOP leadership in
the House of Representatives sought unsuccessfully to have the hearings
televised. The Republicans hoped that TV publicity would give a boost to
committee member Charles E. Potter's ambition to unseat Michigan Democratic senator Blair Moody in the fall elections. Potter had lost his legs in
World War II and effectively assumed a patriotic stance. The Democrats
blocked TV coverage, no doubt for similar partisan reasons. With the
newspapers providing sympathetic coverage of the GOP demands and
accusations, the Democrats were on the defensive on this issue. Both
Moody and Democratic governor G. Mennen Williams came out in support of televising the hearings. There was hardly a shortage of publicity,
however. The daily newspapers gave them banner headlines and pages of
stories each day and radio coverage was extensive. It was "like the World
Series," Coleman Young recalled.[23]

The only witness to testify on the first day of the hearings was an FBI
informer. He identified a large number of individuals as Communist party
members, giving the hearings its requisite dramatic beginning, which was
reported in the corresponding sensational manner in the city's newspapers.
On the second day, there was another informer and several unfriendly white
witnesses were called, each of whom took the Fifth Amendment. The concluding witness for the day was Edward Turner, the president of the Michi-

gan and Detroit branches of the NAACP. The committee subpoenaed Turner, whom it expected to be friendly, to counter the charge that it was engaging in a racist attack on African American leaders. Turner responded to a question on the progress of the Communist party among African Americans with a lengthy denunciation of discrimination in Detroit in jobs, housing, education, and public accommodations. Throughout Turner's prepared statement, Chairman Wood "sat grimly champing on a cigar and staring out the window," the *Daily Worker* reported. Turner said that, although the Communists had "demonstrated their willingness" to take up the issue of civil rights, the positive role in the community of such organizations as the NAACP, the Urban League, the CIO, and the Council of Churches had prevented them from gaining a following. Wood thanked Turner for his testimony, but it did not provide the committee with the unqualified backing it sought.[24]

Rev. Hill was the first witness called to testify on the third day of the hearings. He was accompanied by his attorney, George Crockett. When Crockett objected to the committee's procedures, Wood threatened him with expulsion from the committee room. The committee asked Rev. Hill a series of questions about banquets, petitions, and organizations involving Communists. He refused to answer, invoking his privileges under the Fifth Amendment. For more than an hour, the committee sought to "bait, harass, and intimidate" Rev. Hill. Republican representative Donald L. Jackson of California denounced Hill in the strongest terms: "For a minister, for a man of the cloth, to aid or comfort or endorse or lend his assistance to Communists or to the Communist Party is to compound the offense by including God Almighty in his treason." Hill, for his part, told the committee the Bible was his only guide. "I let God lead me wherever there is discrimination or segregation or injustice of anybody, of any kind. I ask nobody their religious or political beliefs.... I have been interested in primarily one thing, and that is discrimination, segregation, the second-class citizenship my people suffer, and as long as I live, until it is eradicated from this American society, I will accept the cooperation of anybody who wants to make America the land of the free and the home of the brave."[25]

Later that same day, C. LeBron Simmons and Arthur McPhaul were called to testify. Both stood up to the committee and refused to answer questions. McPhaul was subpoenaed to bring with him the records of the Civil Rights Congress. He was asked repeatedly if he would produce the records. After claiming his rights under the Fifth Amendment, McPhaul finally said simply, "I will not." He was later cited for contempt of Congress for that statement, and, after a long series of appeals, finally went to jail for several months.[26]

Coleman Young was the lead-off witness the following morning. Young recalled his thoughts prior to the impending interrogation: "I said to myself: Why should I take any shit off a son of a bitch from Georgia? How can he question my Americanism?" In his testimony, Young took the offensive at the outset and maintained it throughout his appearance. He criticized Wood and committee counsel Frank Tavenner, who was from Virginia, on their bigoted pronunciation of the word "Negro" and forced them to apologize and correct themselves. Aware that the committee and the media assumed guilt when a witness took the Fifth Amendment, Young cited the First Amendment as well as the Fifth when he refused to answer the inevitable opening question, "Are you now a member of the Communist Party?" This was a risky course to take because reliance on the First Amendment alone would bring a contempt of Congress citation. However, Young successfully avoided Wood's attempt to trap him into a simple refusal to answer a question.

As executive secretary of the National Negro Labor Council, Young stated that he was quite willing to explain the program of that organization, but he refused to answer questions about other organizations labeled subversive by the committee or the attorney general. Tavenner was, therefore, unsuccessful in his attempt to get Young to affirm his theory that the NNLC was a reactivation of the National Negro Congress, which had been put on the attorney general's list. Although no other unfriendly witness was allowed to read a statement, Young's aggressiveness enabled him to read the NNLC preamble, which contained the organization's statement of purpose.[27]

During his hour and a half of testimony, Young vigorously denounced the racist attacks against African American people. He told Wood: "I happen to know, in Georgia Negro people are prevented from voting by virtue of terror, intimidation, and lynchings. It is my contention you would not be in Congress today if it were not for the legal restrictions on voting on the part of my people." When Representative Jackson asserted that Young could not criticize California on a similar basis, Young cited the recent success of the NNLC's San Francisco branch in breaking down Jim Crow hiring practices on the street railway and at Sears. "You can't tell me that Jim Crow doesn't exist in California. There is a whole lot wrong with California that has got to be straightened out." When Jackson brought up the issue of "freedom," Young interrupted him to declare, "That is the point, Mr. Jackson, I am fighting for freedom myself." In response to Jackson's assertion that African Americans had progressed a lot in 80-odd years, Young interrupted him again and informed him, "We are not going to wait 80 more years, I will tell you that."[28]

When questioned about his introduction of Communist party leader and then New York City Council member Benjamin Davis at a 1948 meeting, Young averred, "I think that any meeting in which the first Negro councilman ever elected to office in the State of New York were to attend would be of interest to a great number of Negroes. It would be to the credit of any party if that Negro were elected under the label of that party."[29]

In a final attempt to put Young on the spot, Potter asked him if he would serve again in the armed forces if the Soviet Union attacked the United States. Young confidently replied: "I am a part of the Negro people. I fought in the last war and I would unhesitatingly take up arms against anybody that attacks this country. In the same manner I am now in the process of fighting discrimination against my people. I am fighting against un-American activities such as lynchings and denial of the vote. I am dedicated to that fight and I don't think I have to apologize or explain it to anybody."

The *Detroit Free Press* was outraged by Young's testimony. The newspaper complained that the committee had loosened the "reins" and Young "took the bit in his mouth and ran wild." To progressives, Young's testimony was the hearings' high point. The *Free Press* observed that other witnesses "pounded (Young) on the back" at the conclusion of his testimony.[30] Young "turned the hearings upside down," the Civil Rights Congress noted, "and acted as accuser for the entire hour and a half he was on the witness stand."[31] In the community, many African American Detroiters took pride in Young's success at standing up to his inquisitors and criticizing racism and discrimination. "I felt like Joe Lewis home from a title fight," Young reminisced. "People called out my name as I walked down the street, and small crowds gathered when I stopped. Guys patted my back in the barbershop."[32] A phonograph record containing his testimony circulated in the African American community. As Young told Studs Terkel: "That single incident endeared me to the hearts of black people. Fightin' back sayin' what they wanted to say all their lives to a southern white."[33] In his autobiography, Young remarked, I had spoken for all of them, and they were standing a little taller."[34]

There was a range of opinion, to be sure, among African American leaders and in the African American press. The *Pittsburgh Courier* called Young "the sharpest witness to appear before the committee" and headlined the apology Young obtained on the pronunciation of "Negro." On the other hand, Rev. Malcolm Dade, pastor of Saint Cyprian's Episcopal Church and a member of the city of Detroit's Loyalty Commission, responded to Rev. Hill's defiance of the committee by submitting a statement to the committee assuring it of the loyalty of African American people and the African American church. Most black ministers, however, continued to support Rev. Hill. A *Michigan Chronicle* columnist called Rev. Hill "naive" on the question of communism but responded to Dade's intervention by declaring "the Negroes need no apologist for their loyalty." In an editorial on the hearings, the *Detroit Tribune* argued that the committee "is not only unconstitutional, but morally wrong." Although conservative leaders continued to retain posts of leadership, the critical approach to the hearings of the African American press was a reflection of the antagonistic attitude toward the witch-hunt present in broad circles of the African American community.[35]

The situation outside the African American community was quite different. The sensational headlines in the press combined with the fears generated by the years of anticommunist propaganda by all the leading forces of society led to violence. At several factories, there were work stoppages and physical attacks against witnesses identified in the hearings. There was a lynch-mob style to these incidents. Many of those victimized were African Americans and their assailants used racist epithets when they attacked. There was no incident at the Ford Rouge complex nor in many other plants, but the spread of the hysteria in several plants concerned union leaders. UAW President Reuther publicly stated that he would not cooperate with HUAC. The UAW issued a statement criticizing the use of violence, but, in typical liberal anticommunist fashion, it said this was a weapon of the "totalitarians themselves." The implication that the UAW leaders agreed with the goals of the vigilantes within the union while disagreeing only with their methods weakened the statement's effectiveness as a plea for tolerance. In an administrative letter to its locals, moreover, the international office acknowledged that it was "understandable that members of our union are resentful" of Communists given the "aggressive war in Korea," but that union members "must not participate in unlawful acts as walking alleged Communist party members out of the plant." Anticommunist activists should use "democratic means for dealing with members of our union who are guilty of conduct detrimental to the best interests of our union," the administrative letter explained. These mixed messages did not stop the hysteria.[36]

The Americans for Democratic Action (ADA) adopted a posture similar to that of the UAW. The ADA released a statement that it was "deeply concerned with the lynching atmosphere created by reactions to the recent hearings," but complained that the positive program against communism was being forgotten and that the committee had " turned up a mixed bag of small-time Communists and alleged Communists" instead of revealing the top command of the Communist party. Indeed, in its internal discussions, the ADA was split three ways between a pro-civil liberties group, a group rejecting civil liberties for what it viewed as a Communist "conspiracy," and a group that "had both feet planted firmly in mid-air."[37] About three months after the peak of the hysteria and unworried about being called subversive, Ford Motor Company vice president and general counsel William T. Gossett made an unqualified critique of the committee's methods in a speech to the Detroit Bar Association. Gossett charged that congressional investigations into "personal conduct...resemble grand juries" but provide witnesses none of the "basic constitutional safeguards" of those proceedings. Gossett called for a "calm reappraisal" of these investigations by the "Bench and the Bar." He acknowledged, however, that, in the meantime, "the rights of individuals are being most grievously assaulted," and predicted that "there will be no solution unless the people are aroused."[38]

Because there were few calm and effective voices against the hysteria, it is not surprising that the witch-hunters achieved many of their goals. Potter, for one, succeeded in his objective of winning a U.S. Senate seat in November 1952. Although Reuther had not taken vigorous action against vigilantism, after the committee concluded the interrogation of about a dozen Ford UAW leaders, he and the UAW executive board acted aggressively against Local 600, placing an administratorship over the local. Five building officials were suspended from office for five or more years, including two African Americans, Dave Moore, vice president of the axle building, and Nelson Davis, vice president of the foundry. When the administratorship came to an end, the anti-Reuther top officials again won leadership in the local, but the influence of the left-wing began to wane. The National Negro Labor Council and the Civil Rights Congress functioned for a few more years before disbanding in 1956 in the face of the legal repression. Recalling the circumstances that led to the demise of the CRC, Anne Shore remarked on people "who walk around you" on the street as if they did not know you. She was evicted from her apartment and followed when she traveled by car or walked on the street. "I don't think we ever felt good," she contended, "there was such oppression that you woke up every day to the attacks that were ahead of you."[39] Crockett and McPhaul both spent some months in jail. Many individuals lost jobs and faced blacklisting.[40] Coleman Young was among those who had to go from job to job in those days. His cousin, Dr. Claud Young, recalled that "he paid a terrible price for being labeled."[41]

Although there were setbacks and much suffering, the left-progressive African American leaders retained a base of support in the community. In a special election in 1955, Rev. Hill ran for the Democratic nomination for Congress and received 7,600 votes to the 12,000 votes for the winner, who had the UAW endorsement. Young won his first election in 1961 as a delegate to the state constitutional convention. In 1962 he missed election as state representative by a handful of votes, but in 1964 he easily won a seat in the state senate. In 1966 George Crockett was elected Recorder's Court Judge.[42]

These African American leaders were able to retain a broad base of support because the McCarthyite hysteria failed to penetrate the African American community to the degree that it did most sections of the white community. "The African American community was an island of sanity in a sea of hysteria," Arthur McPhaul recalled. Although an important section of African American leadership had joined in support of the cold war, some prominent leaders and segments of the African American press remained critical even in the area of foreign policy. The fact that so much of U.S. foreign policy was directed against liberation movements in the colonial world was one important reason for this phenomenon. Not swallowing whole the underlying justification for the hysteria, the African

American community looked more skeptically at its repressive consequences on the domestic scene.[43]

Another important factor in the atypical response of the African American community was the fact that the left-progressive movement had
struck deep roots in the community during the 1930s and 1940s. The Communists had led the unemployed movement in the early 1930s in which
African Americans were numerous as activists and as leaders. Other activities in which the left played a leading part were the campaign to free the
Scottsboro Boys, the Ford organizing drive, and the struggle against fascism. In the UAW, most African American activists supported the left-
wing prior to 1947. The African American membership of the Communist
party in Detroit in the early postwar years was about six hundred.[44]

Although most involved in these early struggles did not retain organizational ties with the much weakened left-wing movement after the 1950s,
many retained the basic values they had learned from their participation
in the struggles of the 1930s and 1940s. When opportunities for new political struggles opened, many of these seasoned activists provided guidance
and support to the new protest movements of the 1960s and, in some
cases, emerged as leading Detroit officials in the 1960s, 1970s, and 1980s.
After fourteen years as a judge of the Detroit Recorders Court, Crockett
was elected a member of the U.S. House of Representatives in 1980, where
he served 10 years. Erma Henderson, elected a member of the Detroit City
Council in 1972 and city council president in 1977, was outspoken on
behalf of many progressive causes. Like Young, she had been a leader of
the Progressive party in the early cold war years. After serving nine years
as a state senator, Coleman Young was elected as Detroit's first African
American mayor in 1973. For twenty years, Young served as Detroit's
mayor and headed a powerful political coalition that was a force to be
reckoned with in state and national politics. Many left-wingers were critical of some of Young's stances, such as his criticism of Jesse Jackson's candidacy for president in 1984 and his concessions to the auto corporations
as he attempted to address the severe economic difficulties faced by the
city of Detroit. Nevertheless, few would deny that Young remained an
effective practitioner of the art of coalition politics. By his lights, Young
continued "fighting for freedom" during a period of new opportunities
and new problems for African Americans. Recalling the 1993 reunion of
the National Negro Labor Council in his recent autobiography, Young
commented: "It transported us back to the invigorating days when black
and white people damned the odds and the feds and the conservative
unions by laboring together on behalf of the disadvantaged worker. That's
the attitude this country needs right now."[45]

The radical impact on Detroiters of the left-wing leadership tradition
was evident when African National Congress (ANC) leader Nelson Mandela toured the United States to thank his supporters after his release from

prison in 1990. Young was one of the hosts for Mandela's visit and pledged that the city of Detroit would contribute one million dollars to the ANC. Fifty thousand people cheered Mandela in Detroit's Tiger Stadium. Making the appeal for donations at the stadium was Rev. Charles Addams, Hill's successor as pastor of the Hartford Avenue Baptist Church. Mandela visited the Dearborn Assembly Plant at the Rouge complex where the workers shut down production for 18 minutes in his honor. UAW President Owen Bieber presented Mandela an honorary UAW membership card and a UAW jacket and cap. Mandela told the Ford Rouge workers, "I am your flesh and blood. I am your comrade."[46]

An examination of the repressive drive against left-wing African American leaders and organizations in Detroit shows that, while nearly all the left-wing organizations were destroyed, a left-progressive leadership trend retained a base of support in the community and weathered the storm. Including the story of the repression and survival of Detroit's African American left in the reexamination of the period of McCarthyite repression should lead to a more differentiated approach to that era. The drive was not always as successful as the inquisitors wished; left-wingers retained an influence in some areas, an influence which grew when new social movements emerged in a new political period.

NOTES

1. David Caute, *The Great Fear: The Anti-Communist Purge Under Truman and Eisenhower* (New York: Simon & Schuster, 1978); Larry Ceplair and Steve Englund, *The Inquisition in Hollywood: Politics in the Film Community, 1930–1960* (Garden City, N.Y.: Anchor Press/Doubleday, 1980); Martin Halpern, *UAW Politics in the Cold War Era* (Albany: State University of New York Press, 1988); Ellen W. Schrecker, *No Ivory Tower: McCarthyism and the Universities* (New York: Oxford University Press, 1986).

2. Charles Wright, *Paul Robeson: Labor's Forgotten Champion* (Detroit: Balamp, 1976); Gerald Horne, *Black and Red: W.E.B. Du Bois and the Afro-American Response to the Cold War, 1944–1963* (Albany: State University of New York Press, 1986); Manning Marable, "Peace and Black Liberation: The Contributions of W.E.B. DuBois," *Science and Society* XLVII (Winter 1983–84): 385–405; Charles W. Cheng, "The Cold War: Its Impact on the Black Liberation Struggle within the United States," in Ernest Kaiser, ed., *A Freedomways Reader: Afro-America in the Seventies* (New York: International Publishers, 1977), 292–306. See also Gerald Horne, *Black Liberation/Red Scare: Ben Davis and the Communist Party* (Newark, Del.: University of Delaware Press, 1994).

3. An important effort to tell many of the local stories within the framework of a national study is Gerald Horne, *Communist Front? The Civil Rights Congress, 1946–1956* (Rutherford, N.J.: Farleigh Dickinson University Press, 1988). Wright's *Robeson* discusses repression of African American trade unionists. There is a brief discussion of the issue of cold war repression of African Americans in Detroit in Wilbur C. Rich, *Coleman Young and Detroit Politics: From Social Activist to Power Bro-*

ker (Detroit: Wayne State University Press, 1989). Ann Fagan Ginger and David Christiano, eds., *The Cold War Against Labor* (Berkeley: Meiklejohn Civil Liberties Institute, 1987) is an anthology of short secondary and primary accounts of cold war repression, a number of which concern the African American community. Relevant national studies that touch on the impact of cold war repression on African Americans are Philip S. Foner, *Organized Labor and the Black Worker, 1619–1981,* 2nd ed. (New York: Praeger, 1982); Manning Marable, *Race, Reform, and Rebellion: The Second Reconstruction in Black America, 1945–1990,* 2nd ed. (Jackson: University of Mississippi Press, 1991); and Mindy Thompson, *The National Negro Labor Council: A History* (New York: AIMS, 1978). See also Ernest Thompson and Mindy Thompson, *Homeboy Came to Orange: A Story of People's Power* (Newark, N.J.: Bridgebuilder Press, 1976) and Coleman Young and Lonnie Wheeler, *Hard Stuff: The Autobiography of Coleman Young* (New York: Penguin, 1994).

4. D.M. Ladd to FBI Director Hoover, January 29, 1952, Hoover to Communications Section, February 21, 1952, FBI Doc. # 61–7582–1787, FBI Papers, Series 3, HUAC, Box 5, Marquette University, Milwaukee, Wis. Donald Appell, the HUAC investigator in charge of the hearings, was in "almost daily liaison" with Detroit FBI agents during the hearings. Memo SAC Detroit to Director, April 11, 1952, no. 1809, FBI Papers, Marquette University, Milwaukee, Wis., cited in Kenneth O'Reilly, *Hoover and the Un-Americans: The FBI, HUAC and the Red Menace* (Philadelphia: Temple University Press, 1983), 246.

5. *Detroit Times,* February 13, 1952; *Detroit News,* February 13, 24, 1952.

6. *Detroit News,* February 24, 1952.

7. Andrew provides a critique of the charge that Local 600 was "Communist-dominated." William D. Andrew, "Factionalism and Anti-Communism: Ford Local 600," *Labor History* 20 (Spring 1979): 227–55.

8. *Ford Facts,* June 2, 1951; *Fortune* 44 (August 1951): 44; Letter, Carl Stellato et al., to Walter Reuther, March 13, 1952, Nat Ganley Collection, Box 6, Archives of Labor History and Urban Affairs, Wayne State University, Detroit (hereafter cited as WSU). *Fortune* commented that in backing Sen. Edwin C. Johnson's (D-Colorado) cease-fire proposal, Local 600 was endorsing "a program of ending the Korean war that had received virtually no labor support outside the party-line unions." "Mutiny at Ford," *Fortune* 44 (August 1951): 44.

9. Halpern, *UAW Politics,* 257–62. According to a UAW survey in February and March 1947, African Americans were 21.5 percent of 74,500 workers in four Detroit-area Ford plants. The percentage of African Americans at the Rouge complex was certainly higher since plants outside the Rouge had relatively few African American employees. In 1952 employment of union members at the Rouge complex was about 60,000. Memorandum, J.H. Wishart to Walter Reuther, April 11, 1947, and attached UAW Research Department, Employment Survey—February–March 1947, Walter Reuther Collection, Box 33; *Proceedings of the Thirteenth Convention of the UAW-CIO, April 1–6, 1951,* Cleveland, Ohio, 470.

10. Andrew, "Factionalism and Anti-Communism: Ford Local 600," 239–55; Halpern, *UAW Politics,* 259–60.

11. Horne, *Communist Front?,* 71; Art McPhaul Statement, Civil Rights Congress Coll., Box 41, WSU; Interview with Art McPhaul, October 6, 1984; William L. Patterson, ed., *We Charge Genocide: The Historic Petition to the United Nations for Relief from a Crime of the United States Government against the Negro People* (New

York: International Publishers, 1951); William L. Patterson, *The Man Who Cried Genocide: An Autobiography* (New York: International Publishers, 1971), 146–208; Oral history interview with Anne Shore, 1982, Oral History of the American Left, Tamiment Library, New York University.

12. Thompson, *National Negro Labor Council.*

13. Dominic J. Capeci, Jr., *Race Relations in Wartime Detroit: The Sojourner Truth Housing Controversy of 1942* (Philadelphia: Temple University Press, 1984); Gloster B. Current, "The Detroit Elections: Problem in Reconversion," *The Crisis* 52 (November 1945), 319–25; *Detroit News,* January 28, 1946; *Detroit Free Press,* November 8, 1945, November 6, 1947, November 10, 1949, November 8, 1951; Wayne County CIO Council Press Release, October 20, 1947, Merle Hendrickson Coll., Box 2, WSU; Arthur D. Kahn, *Speak Out! America Wants Peace* (New York, 1951), 30.

14. Capeci, *Race Relations,* 83, 130; Martin Halpern, "The 1941 Strike at the Ford Motor Company;" *Michigan Manual, 1945–46,* 243–44.

15. Interview with Art McPhaul.

16. Interview with Shelton Tappes, June 3, 1984; Studs Terkel, *American Dreams Lost and Found* (New York: Pantheon, 1980), 355–68; Young, *Hard Stuff,* 29–42; Interview with James Jackson, October 23, 1983; Halpern, *UAW Politics,* 218.

17. Interview with James Jackson; Interview with Shelton Tappes; Terkel, *American Dreams,* 355–68; Minutes of Wayne County Council, June 16, 1948, UAW Local 51 Coll., WSU; Progressive party of Michigan news release, October 25, 1948, copy in author's possession; County of Wayne Official Statement of Votes Cast in the General Election, November 2, 1948, James Couser Coll., WSU; U.S. Congress, House Committee on Un-American Activities, Hearings, *Communism in the Detroit Area,* 82nd. Cong., 2d. Sess., 1952, 2878–2891; Thompson, *National Negro Labor Council,* 10.

18. Halpern, *UAW Politics,* 214, 237; Interview with Shelton Tappes. Crockett lost his appeal and served four months for contempt of court. Interview with George Crockett, September 15, 1985; Stanley I. Kutler, *The American Inquisition: Justice and Injustice in the Cold War* (New York: Hill and Wang, 1982), 158, 164; George Crockett, "Paul Robeson; True Revolutionary," *Freedomways* 13 #1 (1973): 10–13.

19. Robert Justin Goldstein, *Political Repression in Modern America* (Cambridge, Mass.: Schenkman, 1978), 287–334; James Truett Selcraig, *The Red Scare in the Midwest, 1945–55* (Ann Arbor, Mich.: UMI Research Press, 1982), 4–15; Wright, *Robeson,* 70–82; Caute, *Great Fear,* 88–95, 358–64.

20. "Jobs Not Witch-Hunts," *Michigan Worker* flyer, copy in author's possession; Thompson, *National Negro Labor Council,* 30–31; *Detroit Times,* February 13, 1952; *Detroit News,* February 13, 1952.

21. *Daily Worker,* February 27, 1952; *Ford Facts,* February 10, 1952; *Detroit News,* February 24, 25, 1952.

22. *Detroit News,* February 19, 25, 1952; *Daily Worker,* February 22, 26, 1952.

23. *Detroit News,* February 25, 27, 1952; Terkel, *American Dreams,* 355–68. See also Young, *Hard Stuff,* 121.

24. HUAC, *Communism in Detroit,* 2713–2817; *Daily Worker,* February 27, 1952.

25. HUAC, *Communism in Detroit,* 2819–2833.

26. Ibid., 2865–2876; Interview with Art McPhaul, Oral History Interview with Anne Shore.

27. Terkel, *American Dreams*, 355–68; HUAC, *Communism in Detroit*, 2878–2892.

28. HUAC, *Communism in Detroit*, 2878–2892.

29. Ibid. Davis was actually the second African American council member elected in New York City, succeeding Adam Clayton Powell, who left the position for a successful bid for the U.S. Congress. John Henrik Clarke, "The Early Years of Adam Powell," *Freedomways* 7 (Summer 1967): 199–213.

30. *Detroit Free Press*, February 29, 1952.

31. CRC newsletter, February 29, 1952, Detroit Civil Rights Congress Coll., Box 41, WSU.

32. Young, *Hard Stuff*, 132.

33. Terkel, *American Dreams*, 363.

34. Young, *Hard Stuff*, 132.

35. *Michigan Chronicle*, March 8, 1952, *Pittsburgh Courier*, March 8, 1952, *Detroit Tribune*, March 1, 1952; Interview with Art McPhaul.

36. B.J. Widick, *Detroit, City of Race and Class Violence* (Chicago: Quadrangle, 1972), 127–36; UAW Local 7, "Local 7 Members, Important!" CRC statement, March 7, ; Carl Haessler, "Detroit Red Hunt Fails to Panic Unions," *Federated Press* Central Bureau release, March 1, 1952, CRC Coll., Box 41, WSU; *Sunday Worker* (Michigan Edition), February 24, 1952; *Ford Facts,* March 8, 1952.

37. ADA Detroit Chapter Statement, March 9, 1952, Orville Linck to Vilet Gunther, April 6, 1952, Americans for Democratic Action Papers, Series III, no. 60, State Historical Society of Wisconsin, microfilm edition.

38. Address by William T. Gossett, Ford News Bureau Release, June 4, 1952, Nat Ganley Collection, Box 27, folder 41, WSU.

39. Oral history interview with Anne Shore.

40. Anne Shore to Aubrey Grossman, March 3, 1952, microfilm edition of the papers of the Civil Rights Congress, Part II, Reel 27; Interview with Art McPhaul. See note 18 above.

41. *Detroit Free Press*, January 6, 1974.

42. "1955 Lessons of 15th C.D. Race," Ganley Coll., Box 7, WSU; Rich, *Coleman Young,* 80–5.

43. Interview with Art McPhaul; Mark Solomon, "Black Critics of Colonialism and the Cold War," in Thomas G. Paterson, *Cold War Critics: Alternatives to American Foreign Policy in the Truman Years* (Chicago: Quadrangle, 1971), 205–39; Cheng, "The Cold War: Its Impact on the Black Liberation Struggle." African American, Third World, and Communist criticism of the discrepancy between U.S. government leaders' democratic claims and the discrimination against African Americans at home contributed to civil rights advances here.

44. Halpern, "The 1941 Ford Strike"; Interview with Art McPhaul; Interview with Christopher Alston, August 18, 1984; Notes on report of Christopher Alston, 1946, Ganley Coll., Box 3, WSU.

45. Elaine Latzman Moon, *Untold Tales, Unsung Heroes: An Oral History of Detroit's African American Community, 1918–1967* (Detroit: Wayne State University Press, 1994), 197; Young, *Hard Stuff*, 330.

46. *Detroit Free Press,* June 26, 29, 1990.

CHAPTER 5

"From the Top Down or from the Bottom Up?" John F. Kennedy, Executive Order 10988, and the Rise of Public Employee Unionism

On January 17, 1962, President John F. Kennedy issued Executive Order 10988 granting a form of limited collective bargaining rights to most civilian employees of the federal government. The president was acting on the basis of a recommendation of the Task Force on Employee-Management Relations in the Federal Service that he had appointed the previous June. Task force studies indicated that 762,000 persons, or 33 percent of federal employees and an especially impressive 84 percent of postal workers, were already union members in 1961, but only a few thousand workers were covered by collective bargaining agreements. Kennedy and his task force hoped that providing for recognition of employee organizations would lead to more cooperation between federal workers and managers and better service for the public. By 1966, 620,000 postal workers, 90 percent of the total, and 299,000 other federal workers, 18.5 percent of the total, were covered by union contracts.[1] Since Congress still set pay levels and established classification systems, these first contracts gave federal workers only a limited say over their work lives. Nevertheless, union recognition gave federal workers a new sense of dignity, pride, and power.

Despite the emphasis on labor-management cooperation in the task force deliberations, federal workers, gaining limited collective bargaining rights, gradually abandoned the association-type organizations that emphasized cooperation with management and turned to militant trade unionist approaches. The biggest advances came in 1970 when 200,000 postal workers conducted an unauthorized and illegal strike and thereby gained substantial increases in wages and something tantamount to real collective bargaining. The legal prohibition against federal workers' strikes remained in effect, however, making it difficult for other unions to emulate the postal workers' example and achieve similar gains. Nevertheless, there were some improvements on Kennedy's initial grant of collective bargaining rights in a new executive order issued by President Richard Nixon in 1971, and these rights were incorporated into law in the 1978 Civil Service Act under President Jimmy Carter.

The federal workers' story is closely intertwined with the simultaneous rise of unionism among state and local public employees. Kennedy was responding both to ferment among federal employees and to a growing militancy among state and municipal workers, particularly in large cities. Prior to Executive Order 10988, only Wisconsin had adopted, and just in 1961, legislation providing for a union recognition vote by state or local employees. With state and local employment ballooning and workers' grievances over low wages and poor conditions piling up in the 1950s, union membership jumped from just 307,000 in 1960, or 5.0 percent, to 1.6 million in 1962 and then to 2 million in 1966, about 25 percent of all employees. The rise in union membership, workers' militant actions, including strikes, and the example of Kennedy's executive order led a number of states to revise their laws to provide for union recognition and collective bargaining. Significantly less likely to be union members than their counterparts in private employment prior to the 1960s, public workers in the space of a few years achieved a unionization rate comparable to that of private sector workers. With the erosion and decline of unionism in the private sector since the mid-1970s, public sector workers in the year 2000 were more than four times as likely to be union members as were private sector workers, 37.5 percent as compared with 9.0 percent. A relatively weak and marginal component of organized labor in January 1962 when Kennedy took his supportive action, public workers' unions were a central component of the movement 40 years later, encompassing over 7 million members and 43.7 percent of total union membership.[2]

In issuing Executive Order 10988, Kennedy responded to a simmering grassroots movement among public employees and in turn brought that movement to a rapid boil. A variety of forces acted on the Kennedy administration on this issue, but its pro-union and liberal tilt led the administration to fully consider and take account of the views of the AFL-CIO and its affiliates. The left was much weakened due to cold war repression and the shaping of the order at the highest level stemmed from the work of anticommunist liberals. Nevertheless, radical influences at the grass roots were a vital factor in drawing the administration's attention to the issue. A turning point in the unionization of public employees, union recognition and limited collective bargaining for most public employees stemmed from a Democratic president, a grassroots movement, and complex coalition politics in which the role of the left was attenuated but still present.

Before turning to the grassroots upsurge that began in the 1950s and the acquisition of new rights by public employees in the 1960s, four points merit consideration. First, public employees' history prior to the 1950s included militant actions, successful pressure on the government to improve their conditions, and the development of a wide array of unions and associations. Second, public employees contended with substantial restrictions on their political activity and severe sanctions against militant actions, particularly strikes. Third, liberal Democrats who wanted to improve public workers' conditions had to contend with the legacy of Franklin Roosevelt's opposition to collective bargaining for public workers on the grounds that it would interfere with governmental sovereignty. Fourth, left-wing unionists had become an important presence among public employees in the 1930s and, while they faced firings and jail during the cold war, they persisted as activists and leaders in a variety of public work settings and unions.

As early as 1836, artisans and laborers in the Philadelphia Navy Yard conducted a successful strike for the 10-hour day won earlier by workers in the city's private sector. With local labor parties influential in numerous cities, President Martin Van Buren signed an executive order in 1840 extending the 10-hour day to all federal workers. In 1866 government printers in Washington, D.C., conducted a successful strike to win the 8-hour day that their union had won in the private sector, establishing the principle of comparability for themselves. In 1868 Congress enacted legislation providing all federal "laborers, workmen, and mechanics" the 8-hour day. [3] The metal trades unions succeeded by strike action and lobbying to get a legislative ban in 1915 on timing federal workers with stopwatches, an effective ban on the Taylor system. Continued union strength in the army arsenals and navy yards contributed to emergence of the wage board system for determining blue-collar workers' wages based on the area *prevailing wage.* In 1961 blue-collar workers covered by the wage-board system constituted 660,000 full-time workers, or 28 percent of civilian federal employees. [4]

Unions arose among other federal employees, especially postal workers, after the enactment of the Civil Service Act in 1883 lessened the role of political patronage and made it possible for workers to see their jobs as permanent. Letter carriers joined the Knights of Labor beginning in 1886, won legislation, thanks to the Knights, providing for the 8-hour day in 1888, and formed the National Association of Letter Carriers (NALC) in 1890. Several organizations developed among postal clerks, which, like the NALC, focused on legislative lobbying. [5] As William Macy, chair of the Civil Service Commission during the Kennedy administration, noted, legislators were "sensitive to public opinion and accessible to representatives of ever larger groups" on issues such as salary and hours of work, leave time and insurance benefits. [6]

Although they achieved important gains, unionists in the public sector faced special obstacles. In 1909 Nicholas Murray Butler, president of Columbia University, in an influential essay, opposed union membership by government employees and articulated the concept that the government employer was a sovereign and could not negotiate with employee unions without diminishing that sovereignty.[7] Presidents Theodore Roosevelt and William Howard Taft issued executive orders forbidding public employees' lobbying activities. Postal workers' organizations and the AFL successfully lobbied against these gag orders and the restrictions were overturned by the Lloyd-LaFollette Act of 1912. The act gave postal workers the right to join or refrain from joining unions, the right to petition Congress, and the right to affiliate with the labor movement as long as there were no obligation or assistance to strike action by federal employees.[8]

A World War I-era upsurge in public employee unionism came to an end with the breaking of the Boston police strike in 1919, which was caused by city reprisals against members of the Boston Police Union for its affiliation with the AFL. This was a significant blow to the movement linking public employees with the organized labor movement and to public worker militancy. Although surviving public employee unions emphasized their commitment to avoiding strikes, courts routinely enjoined not only police officers and firefighters from joining unions but other public employees as well on the grounds of the alleged threat to public safety. This was the case even if the union in question had a no-strike provision in its constitution since such provisions might be changed.[9]

Federal employees suffered a new political setback in 1939 with the passage of the Hatch Act prohibiting them from active participation in partisan political campaigns. Franklin Roosevelt signed the act and in 1940 supported amendments that further undermined federal workers' political activism by authorizing the Civil Service Commission to govern these restrictions, and, in addition, extended the restrictions to state and local employees receiving federal funds.[10] When public employees, especially teachers, participated in the national strike movement following World War II and won significant wage concessions, state legislatures responded by passing new antistrike laws. At the federal level, fears about potential strike action by the left-wing United Public Workers of America (UPWA) led Congress to enact a rider to an appropriation bill depriving federal employees of their salaries if they belonged to unions that proclaimed the right to strike and requiring employees to file affidavits declaring they had no such affiliations. The Taft-Hartley Act of 1947 made strike action by federal workers illegal with immediate dismissal among the penalties. Public Law 330 in 1955 made it a felony for federal workers to strike, assert the right to strike, or belong to an organization that asserts such rights.[11]

Liberal Democrats in the 1950s and 1960s seeking to aid public employee unions were mindful of the legacy of Franklin Roosevelt. Most trade unionists had strongly supported Roosevelt's New Deal, but public employee unionists were excluded from the charter of rights established under the 1935 Wagner Act and later suffered from Roosevelt's support of the Hatch Act restrictions. Despite the absence of supportive legislation, public employee unionists were encouraged by Roosevelt's pro-labor stance and they increased their organizing activities. Indeed, while he opposed militant tactics being employed by new federal employee unions, Roosevelt encouraged trade union membership among public employees. Most importantly, however, Roosevelt publicly embraced the government-as-sovereign concept in 1937. Using the occasion of declining a speaking invitation, Roosevelt wrote a highly publicized letter to Luther C. Steward, president of the moderate National Federation of Federal Employees (NFFE), to "forestall" anti–collective bargaining legislation that would diminish "the Administration's control over personnel policy."[12] Roosevelt's letter balanced praise for employee organization with an emphasis on the limits on unions' roles. Employee organizations had a "logical place in governmental affairs," Roosevelt wrote, but "government employees should realize that the process of collective bargaining, as usually understood, cannot be transplanted into the federal service.... The very nature and purposes of government make it impossible to bind the employer in mutual discussions with employee organizations."[13] Although FDR applauded Tennessee Valley Authority collective bargaining agreements as examples of "collective bargaining and efficiency" proceeding "hand in hand" when he dedicated the Chickamaugua Dam on Labor Day in 1940,[14] his 1937 statement emphasizing governmental sovereignty was far more influential and was regularly included in an official "personnel handbook" indicating that "collective bargaining in the federal service was 'impossible.'"[15] Opponents of collective bargaining for public employees continued to cite Roosevelt's statement in the 1950s and 1960s.

Although most public workers made no important gains toward collective bargaining rights during the 1930s New Deal, many did begin to turn to left-wing unions in that decade. In large cities, postal substitutes, who were provisional civil service workers, found their pay dropping to as little as six dollars weekly because of the decline in mail business. The postal subs formed their own militant organization, many regular postal employees formed a movement for an industrial union of all postal employees, and there were picket lines and demonstrations by other public workers as well. Out of this ferment, two left-wing CIO unions emerged, the United Federal Workers of America (UFWA) and the State, County, and Municipal Workers of America (SCMA). The UFWA was the only federal union to challenge FDR's 1937 cutbacks and, with the help of the CIO, it launched an ultimately unsuccessful constitutional challenge of the Hatch Act.[16] Both the UFWA and the SCMA sought collective bargaining and, like other left-wing unions, emphasized rank-and-file activism and interracial solidarity. In 1944 the UFWA was the first national union in over 40 years to elect a woman, Eleanor Nelson, as its president. In April 1946 the two unions merged to form the UPWA. A resolution at the merger convention specifying strike procedures provoked an antistrike congressional rider, leading the union to emphasize that it opposed strikes against the federal government.[17]

The UPWA's pragmatic response to congressional sanctions proved insufficient once the cold war red scare began. President Truman's June 1947 loyalty program forced it to focus all its activities at the federal level on defending accused members.[18] Adding to the UPWA's woes was expulsion from the CIO in 1950. Across the country, hundreds of UPWA members were fired while several leaders and activists faced jail.[19] Unable to survive as a national organization, the UPWA did manage to endure in Hawaii where the left-wing International Longshoremen's and Warehousemen's Union continued as a major force in the islands' political life. In New York City, the Teachers Union dropped its affiliation with the UPWA in 1953 and continued to function as an independent left-wing union despite firings and other repressive actions against many members and leaders.[20] A number of UPWA locals in California affiliated with the Service Employees International Union and became "the core of the militant locals that…dominate the public employee scene in California," Jack Stieber reported in 1973.[21] In a variety of other places as well, left-wing organizers and activists managed to find new roles to play in the other public employee unions as the labor movement entered a new stage in the mid-1950s.

Although the merger of the AFL and CIO in late 1955 brought most union members into a single federation and reduced jurisdictional conflicts, there was little increase in efforts to organize in new fields such as public employment. Instead, as AFL-CIO President George Meany explained it to the public in a *New York Times Magazine* article, the AFL-CIO would seek to "break new ground" in the area of labor-management relations. A new interdependence was possible, Meany argued, because the "unalterable opposition of the American labor movement to communism provides basic security for American business." Public workers were so little on Meany's mind that he went out of his way to reassure business that their fears that labor was interested in *"'big government' or socialism"* were misplaced by asserting that U.S. unions had no interest since "it is impossible to bargain collectively with the Government."[22] After a number of off-the-record interviews with union leaders, Sterling Spero and John Capozzola reported that the AFL-CIO "rendered inconsequential financial support to public employee unions until the late 1960's" and "preferred, with the exception of the teachers, a hands-off policy."[23]

Although the 1950s was in political terms a conservative period, the decade witnessed a rising militancy among public employees in large cities. This was particularly notable in New York City, where the expansion of city government services contributed to a 17.5 percent increase in overall public employment in the city in that decade but not corresponding improvements in wages or working conditions. Prior to the 1950s, a few groups of New York City employees, most notably the Teamsters-affiliated sanitation workers, had secured concessions through political connections with mayors, other city officials, and Tammany Hall. The Transport Workers Union had collective bargaining in the transit system when it was in private hands in the 1930s and retained a significant power base which enabled it to win concessions. During the mid and late 1950s, organized laborers, motor vehicle operators, case workers, teachers, police officers, firefighters, and clerical workers expressed their discontent by conducting numerous protest demonstrations and a few strikes. After winning election in 1953 in a campaign that included a pledge to improve city workers' conditions, Robert Wagner, Jr., initiated three important changes in the city's labor relations policy the next year. He created the Career and Salary Plan for the classification of employees, pressured the Transit Authority to conduct a representation election and to sign a contract with the Transport Workers Union, and issued an interim order offering workers under his supervision "full freedom of association...to negotiate the terms and conditions of employment." When the Parks Department's autocratic Robert Moses ignored the interim order, Jerry Wurf, a 1930s Socialist who headed AFSCME Council 37, effectively publicized the issue. An embarrassed Wagner forced Moses to conduct a representation election, which AFSCME won overwhelmingly, but it was unable at first to secure a contract. The interim order did not lead to collective bargaining, but unions were pleased when in 1956 Wagner approved a dues check-off for city unions.[24]

Wagner made an important personnel move when he asked Ida Klaus, solicitor of the National Labor Relations Board (NLRB), to join his administration as his labor advisor in 1954. Though Klaus lacked political connections, Wagner went to see Tammany Hall leader Carmine DeSapio and told him, "I have to have somebody who knows labor relations. I'm surrounded by politicians in this field who don't know anything. Don't ask for political clearance for her because I can't get it. I haven't got any. And I have to have her." DeSapio went along, telling Wagner, "If she's that good, you ought to pay her more money."[25]

Klaus was anxious to leave the NLRB because Eisenhower's election "cast a pall over all of us." The first Republican president in 20 years, Eisenhower "was just as coldblooded as he could be," Klaus recalled. "He wanted to get rid of everybody."[26]

In going to work for Wagner, Klaus was returning to her roots in New York City. She grew up in the 1910s in the Brownsville section of Brooklyn where there were strong Socialist and trade union movements. Her parents owned a grocery store and Klaus remembers giving credit to strikers and going with her mother on a "great mission" to strike headquarters to make a contribution. There were Socialists in her family and her cousin married David Dubinsky, who later became president of the International Ladies Garment Workers Union (ILGWU). As one of three college students waiting tables in Saratoga Springs, Klaus organized a union and acted as the workers' spokesperson. Perhaps the strongest influence on Klaus, however, was Judaism. She graduated from the Teachers Institute of the Jewish Theological Seminary of America, taught Hebrew, and was influenced especially by the Biblical "prophets of social justice."[27]

A relatively conservative figure in the 1930s NLRB, which had a significant Communist group, Klaus took a moral vision and a pro-labor sensibility to the Wagner administration. Klaus was at first shocked by the atmosphere at city hall. "I was working in a real sewer in City Hall—I mean, moral, ethical sewer," she recalled. "And a very low cultural level.... I did not like that environment at all." In the mayor's office, she "was surrounded by politicians of the crudest kind." Wagner, when not paying attention to her proposal for a comprehensive labor relations program for public employees, reminded her of "kids I used to teach in Hebrew school when the World Series was on!" Only when she suggested that "we could...call it 'The Little Wagner Act'" did he respond and suggest she write up her idea. Klaus delivered a book-length policy study to Wagner in 1956. The program was issued as Executive Order 49 in 1958 as a response to union pressure for a wage increase. The city would certify unions as exclusive bargaining agents for particular groups of workers. As Klaus recalled it, "the brilliant thought" came to budget director Abe Beame "that they could take Ida Klaus's order and give them these rights, and they wouldn't have to give them money."[28]

Executive Order 49 provided a structure for certification of bargaining agents and negotiation of contracts. Compared with the Wagner Act which bore his father's name, Mayor Wagner's executive order had significant limitations. The scope of bargaining was not defined and the order gave the mayor's administration discretion in deciding on the bargaining unit, which allowed it to promote unions more likely to collaborate with the administration. Nevertheless, New York City public employee unionists viewed the order as a "Magna Charta." The autocratic Uniformed Sanitationmen's Association, a Teamsters affiliate, was the first to be certified in 1958 and to win a contract. Two years later, this conservative machine-controlled union conducted a one-day strike. As a nonfavored union, AFSCME District Council 37 held a massive protest demonstration that resulted in the closure of some city offices in 1959 and conducted long strikes among zookeepers in the spring of 1961 and among motor vehicle operators in November 1962. AFSCME won recognition and contracts. In the motor vehicle operators strike, united support from the labor movement for the drivers forced Wagner to rescind the firing of 16 workers.[29]

Police officers were not covered by Executive Order 49 and repression had stopped a 1951 CIO drive in the police department, but officers elected a militant as president of the Patrolman's Benevolent Association in 1958, gained a dues check-off and "de facto collective bargaining" in 1959, and won a 15 percent wage increase in 1961.[30] Former UPWA members founded a new left-wing union, the Social Service Employees Union (SSEU) in 1961. The union included older black and Jewish caseworkers who had begun their careers during the 1930s and young college graduates, including some civil rights activists, "looking for a socially relevant career outside the business world." The SSEU promoted solidarity with welfare recipients and emphasized rank-and-file participation and job actions.[31]

As employees of the board of education, New York City's 45,000 teachers were not covered by Wagner's executive order, but new possibilities opened up for them as well. The New York teachers' achievement of union recognition and a union contract proved to be a critical turning point. The publicity stemming from the dramatic circumstances of their victory and the size of the bargaining unit sparked a national surge of union activism among teachers, one of the largest groups of public employees.

Prior to the 1950s, the Communist-oriented Teachers Union (TU) had the largest membership among New York City teachers and had been active in promoting progressive legislation, defending academic freedom, and in promoting increased hiring of black teachers, improvements in black schools, school integration, and a black-history curriculum. Weakening the Teachers Union was a 1930s split and the resulting rivalry with the Socialist-oriented Teachers Guild which retained the affiliation with the American Federation of Teachers (AFT) of the AFL. Cold war red scare firings thinned the ranks of the TU and the board of education excluded the TU in 1950 from the right to confer and use school buildings that was accorded to other teacher organizations. Under these circumstances, most new teachers and some former members sought new vehicles to challenge the board of education. Although teachers were divided into more than 100 different organizations based on ethnicity, religion, location, and grade level and subject taught, resentment grew over being treated like children by their principals, teaching large classes, and receiving low pay. A *New York Times* editorial in 1955, "Teach or Wash Cars?" asked why anyone would take a teaching job at $66 a week when washing cars paid $72.35.[32]

The independent High School Teachers Association, led by former TU member Samuel Hochberg and Roger Parente, the son of a building trades unionist, organized boycotts of extracurricular activities and then in Feb-

ruary 1959 conducted a successful strike of evening classes. Some Socialists, especially David Selden, a former Michigan autoworker who acted as
the AFT representative in New York, and Ely Trachtenberg, a Teachers
Guild board member, departed from past factionalism and supported the
evening teachers strike. Members of the HSTA (now renamed Secondary
School Teachers Association) merged with the Teachers Guild to form
Local 2, United Federation of Teachers (UFT), which retained its affiliation
with the AFT. The UFT called a strike the day before the November 1960
election. The union had canceled a May strike plan when the superintendent promised action on their demands but set the new date because nothing had come of those promises. UFT President Charles Cogen and AFT
President Carl Megel opposed the strike, but a militant group within the
UFT, led by Parante and Hochberg, insisted that relying on the "good
graces of elected officials" would accomplish less than militant action.[33]
The militants selected the November 7 date with the thought that officials
of the Democratic city would hesitate to take action against striking teach-
ers "for fear of alienating potential Democratic voters."[34] Prior to the
strike, UFT leaders and Selden met with Megel, George Meany, and New
York City Central Labor Council President Harry Van Arsdale. When Van
Arsdale asked Megel, "Don't they have to get permission from the International?" Selden recalled, Megel replied that locals had autonomy in the
AFT. Selden reported Meany took "a heavy puff on his cigar and "blurts,
'For Christ's sake, Harry. Can't somebody blow the whistle on these
guys?'"[35]

About 5,000 teachers struck. Some strikers were disappointed that so
few joined the strike. The UFT agreed to a truce during which Mayor Wagner would appoint a fact-finding committee, consisting of Van Arsdale,
Dubinsky, and Jacob Potofksy, the president of the Amalgamated Clothing
Workers (ACW). The appointment of a committee composed of three
labor leaders was a significant concession, but even more important was
the fact that the UFT had succeeded in conducting a bold action and
escaping punishment. According to a leader of the TU, which opposed the
strike, "Even among many who had opposed the strike, there were many
who were elated that teachers had been able to defy the Board of Education. The threat of reprisals by the Superintendent brought protest not
only from the UFT and the Teachers Union, but from school faculties.
Teachers began to look to the UFT for leadership."[36] The labor committee's
recommendations eventually led to an election in May 1961 in which
teachers voted for collective bargaining by three to one. In a December
1961 election supervised by Klaus, teachers voted for the UFT by a wide
margin over an NEA-affiliated group and the TU. The UFT had proved
itself to be capable of leading teachers' struggles, and it had significant
financial help from the AFL-CIO's Industrial Union Department headed
by Walter Reuther, and from the UAW, ILGWU, and ACW. While the NEA

was by far the larger national organization and threw significant resources into the campaign, it had a small New York membership and was disadvantaged by the fact that it had opposed the initial vote on collective bargaining. The TU vote was limited to its core supporters.

Wanting a contract with substantial gains in pay, working conditions, and a dues check-off, rather than promises that could be forgotten once the heat was off, the UFT militant faction succeeded in winning a close membership vote for immediate strike action on April 10, 1962, overriding the executive board's proposal to delay action for a week while fact-finding proceeded. Both factions united to pull off an effective strike by 20,000 teachers on April 11, 1962. The board threatened to fire all the strikers under terms of New York's antistrike Condon-Wadlin Law and succeeded in getting an injunction, which the UFT executive board voted to obey by a 32–12 vote. Before the board decision, Governor Nelson Rockefeller had sent telegrams calling all the principals to a meeting. Rockefeller made available an additional $13 million to the city so that teachers would receive an across the board raise of $995, which was $295 more than the board's pre-strike offer. There would be no reprisals against strikers and Rockefeller agreed to look into finding an alternative to the Condon-Wadlin Law. The parties reached final settlement terms on the first teacher contract in September 1962.[37]

The determination of a growing minority of New York City teachers to conduct two strikes and risk being fired was the key to the establishment of collective bargaining and a strong union. The strikes ended quickly with modest concessions because of the role of intermediaries who wanted to help the teachers but also strongly opposed strike action because of fear of negative political consequences for Democrats. Secretary of Labor Arthur Goldberg intervened after teachers approved the concept of collective bargaining with a proposal to the UFT for a separate vote for junior high teachers and later separate balloting for elementary and high school teachers. The union rejected the idea in favor of its own preference for an immediate systemwide vote, thinking this was a better way to foster teacher unity and defeat the NEA. In intervening to bring an end to the first UFT strike, Van Arsdale announced the strike's termination and made a public declaration that "there will be no recurrence" before the union's delegate assembly had met to consider the strike-ending proposal.[38] When the second strike took place, most labor leaders were silent except for Morris Iushewitz, who served alongside Van Arsdale as secretary of the Central Labor Council. Iushewitz, a school board member, called the strike "an unmitigated disaster" and said he was "appalled by the recklessness and irresponsibility" but opposed the injunction.[39] Goldberg was "adamantly opposed to public employee strikes," Marjorie Murphy notes, and quotes the labor secretary's warning the UFT "to resolve your difference by means other than strikes."[40] Pressure from union lead-

ers contributed to the UFT executive board's decision to obey the injunction in the 1962 strike. On the other hand, in the context of a pro-labor voting public and an upcoming gubernatorial contest between Rockefeller
and Wagner, the teachers' display of militancy led to quick action in their
favor. Teacher unionists everywhere drew inspiration from the New York-
ers' audacity.

On January 12, 1963, AFT President Megel wrote to the AFL-CIO to
request organizational help because it was "impossible for us to keep up
with the requests that are coming in daily from teachers who want to organize a local of the American Federation of Teachers."[41] AFT membership
rose from 70,821 at the time of its May 1962 convention to 100,109 two
years later.[42] The surge in teacher interest in unionism would continue and
eventually cause the NEA, initially a professional association that
included administrators, to shift toward a positive approach toward collective bargaining.[43]

The left-influenced militancy evident among New York trade unionists
was also developing among federal workers. Most importantly, the Progressive Feds movement arose within the National Federation of Post
Office Clerks. The Progressives sought an industrial union of all postal
workers, an end to dual black and white locals, proportional representation at union conventions, and election of national officers by referendum.
The Progressives drew their strength from big city locals with thousands
of members whose clout in the national convention was limited to 10
votes, the same as a local with 10 members. Formed in 1946, the Progressive Feds continued to function despite internal security act suspensions
of nine New York activists, including six local officers. One of those suspended in December 1955 and subject to a loyalty investigation, Moe
Biller, would play a key role in the 1970 postal strike. Biller grew up on the
Lower East Side of New York in an orthodox Jewish and working-class
family. Like many others who became leaders of the postal union movement, he took a post office job after graduating from college in the 1930s.
Although he was a Democrat and not a leftist by background, Biller was
radicalized by his experience as a postal substitute contending with a
company union. When he was called to testify before the Internal Security
Board in 1956, Biller had to contend with the question, "Do you know
Julius and Ethel Rosenberg?" Although he did not know them, Biller did
live in the apartment building where the Rosenbergs had resided before
their arrest. By 1956, however, the red scare hysteria was beginning to sub-
side and the Supreme Court ruled that the Eisenhower administration had
cast a wider security net than Congress intended in including all positions
and departments under a new standard for dismissing employees if there
were "reasonable grounds" to do so. Returned to their jobs, the New York-
ers two years later participated in the Progressives walkout from the 1958
convention of the National Federation and then in the founding of the

National Postal Union (NPU) in 1959. Its initial membership was 26,000, but it soon grew to 80,000. The Manhattan-Bronx Postal Union (MBPU), the largest NPU affiliate, grew to 20,000.[44]

Elite institutions also began to respond to the ferment among public workers. In 1955 the Committee on Labor Relations of the American Bar Association issued a report calling on the government "to deal with its public servants in a reasonably similar basis" to that imposed on private sector employers.[45] The federal Civil Service Commission began consulting more frequently with the union leaders over issues like the Merit Promotion Program. In June 1958, moreover, Rocco C. Siciliano, special assistant to the president for personnel management, issued from the White House a request to all federal departments and agencies that they regularly solicit the views of employee organizations. Wisconsin was the first state to enact favorable legislation, establishing a "declaration of rights" in 1959 and a machinery for conducting elections and authorizing collective bargaining in 1961.[46]

With a rising rank-and-file militancy and a somewhat more favorable attitude by important institutions, unions began a significant campaign to secure legislation to give federal employees collective bargaining rights, an effort supported by John Kennedy. In 1956 Kennedy testified in favor of a Senate bill before the Committee on Post Office and Civil Service. During the 1960 election campaign, Kennedy wrote to a post office union leader that he had "always believed that the right of Federal employees to deal collectively with the Federal departments and agencies in which they are employed should be protected." He asserted, moreover, that a Democratic Congress "with Democratic leadership from the White House could deal effectively with a proposal of this nature."[47]

Supporters of federal workers' unions introduced 26 bills in the 87th Congress. Most important was the Rhodes-Johnston bill, versions of which had been introduced in Congress since 1952. Under the bill filed by Representative George Rhodes on January 3, 1961, agencies would be required to bargain collectively with unions of government employees and unions would collect dues via a check-off procedure. Managers who interfered with union efforts to represent their members would be punished, grievances could be submitted to binding arbitration, and disputes could be referred to a government labor relations panel appointed by the president.[48] Although Kennedy was on record as supporting the earlier legislation, there was opposition from important federal agencies.

When the Civil Service Commission staff prepared a draft executive order as an alternative to legislation on February 10, 1961, it was willing to concede to unions representing the majority of employees in an "occupational segment" the right to be consulted exclusively but not to bargain collectively.[49] In response to the House Post Office and Civil Service Committee's consideration of the Rhodes bill, Cyrus Vance, then general counsel of the Department of Defense, sent to budget director David Bell a draft "opposition report" on March 22, 1961. Vance noted, however, that it "would be strengthened measurably if it were possible to state definitely" that the president planned to issue an executive order on the subject.[50] Meanwhile, Leon Wheeless, director of the Civilian Personnel Division at the Department of Defense, sent a communication to the AFL-CIO Metal Trades Department, asking for its comment on a "proposed unilateral order" for defense department employees. The Metal Trades Department preferred a presidential order, Andrew Biemiller, director of the AFL-CIO Department of Legislation, told labor secretary Arthur Goldberg on April 19, 1961. Biemiller, appointed by AFL-CIO President George Meany to coordinate the activities of affiliated government employee unions, forwarded to Goldberg a draft of the AFL-CIO's own proposal for an executive order, which "we understand the Administration is contemplating issuing."[51] Frederick Dutton, special assistant to the president and cabinet secretary, stepped in to coordinate responses to the defense department initiative and told Goldberg that President Kennedy wanted him to head an "informal study group" that included Bell, a designee of the Department of Defense, and Civil Service Commissioner John Macy to make recommendations on policy on the recognition of federal employee unions. Dutton indicated to Goldberg a sense of urgency because of the "several pieces of pending legislation and some criticism of the many years in which the Executive Branch has failed to provide guidance."[52] A White House staff commentary on the Rhodes bill was harshly negative: "Any such sweeping legislation would be distinctly adverse to the public interest and completely inconsistent with the substantial impositions of responsibility and authority under which our Government was created and must operate. It would constitute an unthinkable invasion of executive authority and responsibility."[53] Goldberg's challenge would be to develop an approach to collective bargaining for federal workers that avoided the negative reaction that many within the administration had to the Rhodes bill provisions.

Goldberg was an ideal choice to lead the high-level informal group and the task force that was to follow. Goldberg had been chief counsel of the CIO and of the Steelworkers Union, succeeding the left-winger Lee Pressman in both positions in 1948 when the CIO embraced anticommunism. Goldberg had been the architect of the merger of the AFL and CIO. He had developed a working relationship with John Kennedy during the hearings on the Landrum-Griffin bill in 1959 and had the president's strong support. Goldberg selected his key assistants in the Department of Labor and the staff for the task force. With a wealth of negotiating experience, Goldberg was skilled at finding compromises. Teacher union militants might reject some of his proposals and federal unionists would find shortcomings in the executive process Goldberg led, but the labor secretary kept the focus on a speedy process that would achieve the goal of establishing collective bargaining in the federal service.[54]

Why was there a quick shift from the legislative front to executive action? What might have happened if Kennedy's pro-labor advisers had prevailed upon him to support the Rhodes bill or to submit a legislative proposal of his own? In an influential early study, Wilson R. Hart, labor relations director for the Defense Supply Agency, asserted, "The Executive Order pulled the rug from under the government unions just as they were about to pluck the golden apple. It not only deprived them of the prize but made them like it!"[55] Hart cites no evidence to support his colorful language or his implication that labor leaders were not sophisticated. Douglas Schoen's generalization is closer to the mark: "The memorandum represented an attempt by the White House to circumvent Congress on the issue; there a solid body of opinion was decidedly hostile to giving federal employees the right to organize and bargain collectively."[56] The House was split about 180–180 between liberal and conservative members with the remaining members in a swing group. An early test showed the Chamber of Commerce and the National Association of Manufacturers were better able to persuade the swing group on a purely labor issue. Despite support from both the House and Senate government operations committees, Republican as well as Democratic NLRB members, and the Republican-appointed NLRB general counsel, Kennedy's Plan No. 5 to reorganize the NLRB to speed the handling of unfair labor practices cases was defeated on the House floor by a 231–179 vote.[57] The defeat of the NLRB measure probably reflected the clout of private business interests, but the House showed no less hostility to federal unions. In 1962, "in reprisal for Executive Order 10988," a Department of Labor official noted in a confidential memorandum that the House adopted the Ashbrooke amendment to the federal employees' Welfare and Pension Plan placing restrictions on AFL-CIO members. The amendment was "knocked out in conference,"[58] but the Senate's attentiveness to labor interests was also doubtful. Senator Hubert Humphrey complained after the 1962 elections that "not a single Democratic Senator" applied to be a member of the Senate Labor and Public Welfare Committee.[59] The Congress showed no interest in the task force's recommendation for legislation to authorize a dues check-off for federal employee organizations, which President Kennedy formally proposed on April 19, 1962. Supporting the president's executive initiative was pragmatic, not foolish.[60]

Responding to the recommendation of the Goldberg group, President Kennedy issued a memorandum creating the Task Force on Employee-Management Relations in the Federal Service on June 22, 1961. Chaired by Goldberg, the task force also included Secretary of Defense Robert McNamara, Day, Bell, Macy, and Ted Sorenson, special counsel to the president. Since "participation" of employees in developing personnel policies "con-

tributes to the effective conduct of public business," Kennedy called on
the task force to make recommendations on the "broad range of issues" in
"federal employee-management relations" including "standards for
recognition" and grievance and appeal procedures.[61]

Although Kennedy advised consultation with employee organizations,
he put two limits on the recognition process. He cited equal employment
policy as a basis for denying recognition to any organizations that discriminated on the basis of race, color, religion, or national origin. Citing no
particular policy basis, the president likewise excluded organizations
"which assert the right to strike against or advocate the overthrow of the
government of the United States." Kennedy needed no policy basis
because there were numerous laws on the books against revolutionary
advocacy and the 1955 statute against federal employees joining organizations that advocated the right to strike. By including restrictions against
the right and the left in his guidance, Kennedy was steering a course consistent with the concept of vital center liberalism articulated at the dawn
of the cold war red scare by Arthur Schlesinger, Jr., an advisor to the president. There were few critics of these restrictions at the time, but the arrest
and conviction in 1961 of Archie Brown, a local official of the International
Longshoremen's and Warehousemen's Union, for serving as a union officer while a member of the Communist party was overturned as an unconstitutional bill of attainder by the Supreme Court in 1965. By the late 1960s,
moreover, some unions and many rank-and-file workers would launch a
major challenge to the restriction on strike advocacy. In 1961 federal workers and trade unionists were grateful that a movement toward collective
bargaining was at last beginning and civil rights advocates welcomed the
emphasis on nondiscrimination. Secretary Goldberg advised federal
department and agency heads that the two limitations on what organizations management should consult were effective immediately.[62]

The staff director for the task force was Daniel P. Moynihan. Then a
young professor at Syracuse University, Moynihan was an active Democrat who had worked for former New York Governor Averill Harriman.
Goldberg also recruited Ida Klaus to serve as a consultant to the task force.
New York City's new labor relations policy designed by Klaus was an
important model for the task force.[63] The task force quickly gathered information from over 80 associations and unions, half of them AFL-CIO affiliates, with membership in the federal workforce.[64] The task force held
hearings in Washington, D.C., and six other cities to give input to
employee organizations and the public into the process of developing its
recommendations.

During the course of the task force deliberations, opposition to collective bargaining from the Defense Department and the Civil Service Commission diminished. Both McNamara and Macy supported the new
direction.

Most unions responded very favorably to the creation of the task force. Some local unions, such as a Meridien, Mississippi, local of IRS employees who were members of Lodge 1694 of the American Federation of Government Employees, hoped they could get immediate help with a rigid management. Several unions, such as the National Postal Union (NPU), emphasized that they truly adhered to the nondiscrimination requirement of the president's equal employment policy. Some unions, including the NPU and the Metal Trades Council of the AFL-CIO in Massachusetts, indicated that they preferred legislation to an executive order but nevertheless would work within the task force framework. James Landgren, the operations director of the AFL-CIO Government Employees Council, suggested appointing Meany or his representative to the task force and urged the president to support the Rhodes and Johnston bills.[65]

Kennedy's policy of limiting consultation to organizations that did not discriminate based on race had a salutary impact on efforts of civil rights advocates to promote interracialism within the union movement. A number of unions had racially segregated local unions. Moynihan reported that the Letter Carriers "ordered all such [locals] to merge on pain of losing their charters."[66]

Moynihan biographer Douglas Schoen commented that when Moynihan and Goldberg met with Kennedy late in 1961 to discuss the task force report, the president "showed little interest in the subject and seemed not to remember that six months earlier he had agreed to provide for union recognition." Although Moynihan's recollection, the basis for Schoen's comment, is probably accurate, it may indicate not so much Kennedy's indifference but rather his concentration on issues that were more politically controversial. At the time of the meeting, Kennedy was focused on an attack on his brother Ted's candidacy for the president's old Senate seat.[67]

Although Kennedy gave priority to foreign policy, he also had a strong commitment to carrying out the liberal Democratic agenda that congressional Democrats had developed in the late 1950s. In a 1960 Labor Day message, Kennedy appealed to voters to elect a Democratic Congress to carry out a liberal reform program. He was sensitive to labor issues as a result of his 14 years of service on the House and Senate labor committees. During 1959 hearings that led to the Landrum-Griffin Act, Kennedy was embarrassed when AFL-CIO President George Meany responded to his comment that friends of labor saw no problems with a particular provision with the exclamation, "God save us from our friends." Arthur Goldberg recalled that Kennedy never forgave the AFL-CIO staffer who wrote Meany's testimony. In the wake of this incident, however, Kennedy shifted from relying on his congressional staff members, the true target of Meany's barb, to becoming personally acquainted with union leaders and getting their perspective on issues directly. Kennedy spoke clearly as an

ally of labor when he opposed "so-called 'right-to-work' laws," delays in
NLRB certification proceedings, and "legislation designed to repress
labor" in a speech in Milwaukee, Wisconsin, on April 3, 1960. Directly
challenging a central theme of the antilabor campaign of the 1950s,
Kennedy remarked: "There are those in America today who say that labor
is too big—that it has grown too strong. But I say that the size of organized
labor is a blessing—and its strength is a powerful force for the good of all
America."[68] Kennedy was acutely aware of labor support for his candidacy in 1960 and credited key union officials for their work on his behalf.
At the ceremony at which Goldberg was sworn in as labor secretary,
Kennedy told F. Nordy Hoffman of the Steelworkers, "I never went to a
city in the United States that the Steelworkers weren't out there to meet
me at the airport. I know that's your doing, and I appreciate it."[69] As president, Kennedy continued the practice of listening carefully to labor people. Esther Peterson, a staff member for the Amalgamated Clothing
Workers before her appointment as assistant secretary of labor and director of the Women's Bureau, had lobbied Kennedy in Congress and
recalled that "he listened...if you went to him with a good outline of
arguments he would use it."[70] Peterson recalled Kennedy remarking in a
White House meeting, "I can't make up my mind until I know what
Esther says."[71]

Kennedy was a cold warrior and went along with McCarthyism, but he
wanted the best advice he could get and drew many liberals who had
doubts about him into his administration. Paul Samuelson, a Stevenson
supporter, recalled being asked to advise the Kennedy campaign: "I
finally decided that whatever John F. Kennedy or Robert's roles had been
in the McCarthy congressional days, John had cast his lot with the liberal
cause and would be an effective president." John Kenneth Galbraith
recalled that Kennedy was a student of Russ Nixon, the left-wing economist at Harvard and sought an in-depth understanding of economic
issues. "Remember, I'm pretty good at this; I was a student of Russ
Nixon," Kennedy wrote on one memo. On the other hand, while Kennedy
could express pride in having learned from a left-wing intellectual, he
pressured Martin Luther King, Jr., to dispense with the advice of two individuals, Stanley Levison and Jack O'Dell, who the FBI claimed had ties to
the Communist party. Given the administration's support for civil rights,
Kennedy told King, these connections could have a disastrous impact on
its political position as well as that of the movement. Kennedy apparently
was unworried about his own association with Nixon who had left Harvard to become an official of the left-wing United Electrical Workers, a
leader of the Progressive party of Henry Wallace, and managing editor of
the National Guardian in the 1960s.[72]

Kennedy appointed two strongly pro-labor figures to the NLRB, who,
along with one Eisenhower-appointed pro-labor Democrat, reversed the

pro-management direction of the NLRB under the Republicans. The Kennedy-Johnson-era NLRB, James A. Gross commented, "came as close to full and effective implementation of a national labor policy encouraging unionization and collective bargaining as the Wagner Act Board chaired by J. Warren Madden did in the two years after the Supreme Court ruled the law constitutional." During the Madden era, pro-CIO Communists had played central roles on the NLRB staff and pro-labor Socialists were among the more conservative figures working for the agency. The purging of the left in the NLRB in 1940 and in the federal government generally during the post–World War II red scare precluded Communist-oriented leftists from obtaining positions on the Kennedy era NLRB, but board chair Frank McCulloch set a distinctly pro-labor tone in the 1960s. The son of a Chicago suffragist, McCulloch had served as industrial relations secretary for the Council for Social Action of the Congregational-Christian Churches of America, director of the labor education program at Roosevelt University, and staffer to Senator Paul Douglas, who served on the Senate Labor Committee with Kennedy. Among other innovations, McCulloch Board rulings expanded the scope of collective bargaining into decisions such as subcontracting for economic reasons that employers had previously considered a matter of exclusive management rights.[73]

Although labor issues were not Kennedy's top priority, he understood labor issues, consulted closely with top labor officials, and appointed progressive pro-labor people to key positions in his administration. He saw labor as a key part of his political base and cared about the issues important to this constituency.

The task force made its report to the president as scheduled on November 30, 1961. The task force responded to the rising union sentiment among federal and other public workers but also responded to the views of a diverse array of organizations among federal employees and to the views of federal government managers. It attempted to strike a compromise, incorporating some of the ideas from the Wagner Act but also concepts from the administration-guided procedures established in New York City and more conservative pro-management ideas as well. "Wherever any considerable number of employees have organized for the purpose of collective dealing," the task force recommended, "the attitude of the Government should be that of an affirmative willingness to enter such relations." On the other hand, the task force stated its "emphatic opinion that the union shop and the closed shop are contrary to the civil service concept...and are completely inappropriate to the Federal service."[74]

Kennedy signed Executive Order 10988, embodying the task force's recommendations, at a White House ceremony attended by task force members, union leaders, and three members of Congress from the civil service committees. As the president mentioned when he appointed the task force, the order excluded employee organizations that asserted the right to strike, advocated the "overthrow" of the government, or discriminated based on "race, color, creed, or national origin." The order established three levels of recognition for federal employee organizations: informal, formal, and exclusive. In units where a majority of employees selected a particular organization and that organization had at least "a substantial and stable membership" of 10 percent, that union would act as the exclusive agent for all employees in the unit. If there were no exclusive representative, management would provide formal recognition to organizations meeting the 10 percent membership standard. Under formal recognition, management would consult with recognized organizations as it formulated and implemented personnel policies. Informal recognition meant the organization could present "its views on matters of concern to its members," but management had no obligation to consult such groups. The order specified similar rights to all employees to present views "on matters of personal concerns" to officials and to select their own grievance representatives.

The three forms of recognition provided the opportunity for a variety of employee organizations with distinct goals, philosophies, and constituencies to continue to function. Responding to the concerns of several professional organizations, the order specified that units would not combine professional and nonprofessional employees unless the majority of professionals voted for such inclusion. Following private sector practice, organizations winning exclusive recognition had a duty to bargain for nonmembers as well as members. Significantly weakening the sphere for union action, the order specified that all agreements were subordinate to Federal Personnel Manual and agency regulations and had to include an airtight management rights clause. The order provided for arbitration of grievances, but of concern to unions was that the finding of the arbitrator was only advisory to the agency rather than binding as in the private sector. Also troubling to unions was a provision forbidding membership recruiting, dues collection, or other internal union business during duty hours. The FBI and CIA were specifically excluded from terms of the order and other intelligence and security agencies could choose, at the discretion of their heads, to be excluded. Lastly, the order provided for a temporary implementation committee which would report to the president on proposed standards for the conduct of employee organizations and a code of fair labor practices. The president issued a companion executive order at the same time, Executive Order 10987, which established a new grievance procedure throughout the federal service.

Union reaction to the new Employee-Management Cooperation (EMC) program was notably positive because of the big advance in opening the door to exclusive representation and the negotiation of collective bargaining agreements. The most innovative idea was the provision for three different levels of recognition. Problematical, however, were the many limitations on union rights compared with the private sector, most notably the right to strike, the severe limitations on bargainable issues, and control of the recognition process by management. In a cogent and broad-ranging critique of the task force's recommendations, the American Federation of Government Employees pointed out that the "constant repetition of the 'right to refrain from joining' may be construed to mean…there is still some question as to whether the employees should."[75] Indeed, the EMC was influenced not only by the positive ideas of the Wagner Act but also by the antiunion and individualist concepts in the Taft-Hartley and Landrum-Griffin acts. The order implicitly excluded the union security options of the union shop and the closed shop that the task force had rejected.[76]

On the floor of the Senate, Senator Johnston said he was "personally delighted because the executive order appears to embody many of those principles which I have fought to establish legislatively over the years." Although he was "confident" that the order was "a long step in the right direction," he promised that the Senate committee would review the order and propose legislation to rectify "any omissions or shortcomings."[77] Senator Humphrey joined in affirming support for legislative action if necessary. Although the senators may have been displeased about being upstaged, neither senator mentioned the fact that any subsequent president could withdraw what President Kennedy established nor did either suggest immediate action to make permanent a good first step. Indeed, it would be 16 years before Congress acted on the issue.

About a month after Kennedy issued the executive order, managers gathered to discuss how they would implement the EMC program. Teresa Wren told the managers that the labor department had found that "well *over half*" of the provisions in industry contracts were matters that could be negotiated in government. She warned them to "be careful not to undercut the union's rights. This is an entirely different relationship than you have had in the past—not consultative but equal." On the other hand, Wren said that management would be determining bargaining units (subject to review by the Department of Labor), management could continue to run employee councils, and managers would be benefiting from the Kennedy administration's pay reform, which emphasized that higher level classifications were most in need of pay increases.[78]

Some agencies wanted to continue established antiunion practices. International Association of Machinists President A.J. Hayes complained to Goldberg that the navy department was discouraging employees from signing authorization cards for the Metal Trades Council because other "'employee organizations'" were not ready to organize as yet. This "unstated preference for the 'company union' type of organization violated the executive order," Hayes maintained. The order would have "little value" unless industrial relations managers administered it "in the spirit in which it was formulated."[79]

The management of the Post Office also aroused union concerns by its actions in implementing the order. Fear of a new type of management domination was the concern of NPU President John MacKay. Assistant Postmaster General Richard Murphy told a meeting of union representatives that supervisors and managers "could serve as national officers of employee unions." MacKay told Goldberg this was "unconscionable" because postal unions had in the past included supervisors only for fringe benefit purposes and attempted to give them "neither legislative nor grievance representation."[80] The United Federation of Postal Clerks voiced strenuous objections to Murphy's declaration that a union would have to win a majority among eligible voters to be granted exclusive representation, not a majority of those casting votes as was the practice in NLRB and railway elections. Claiming over 51 percent of the clerks were dues-paying members, union President E.C. Hallbeck nevertheless suggested it would be "exceedingly difficult to get many" to vote since they were scattered in 15,000 post offices and sometimes were the only clerical employee at the office. Persuaded by Hallbeck's objections, the Temporary Committee on Implementation of the Employee Management Relations Program, chaired by Goldberg, persuaded the Post Office to follow the "generally applicable" rule of going by a majority of those voting "provided that a representative number of those eligible to vote actually participated in the election."[81] Moe Biller, president of the MBPU, wrote President Kennedy to complain that postal management was banning the 50-year-old "practice of collecting organization dues 'on-the-clock'" in the New York post office and thereby causing the union "exceptional and undue hardship." With the National Postal Union, with which the MBPU was affiliated, and the president both seeking legislation for a dues check-off, Biller asked that the operative provision of E.O. 10988 against on-the-job dues collection "not be effectuated" until Congress established the dues check-off. Pressure from the unions succeeded in getting postal management to back off enforcement of the ban.[82]

When the Defense Department established a rule that 60 percent of the employees had to vote in a representation election for the selection of an exclusive agent to be valid, the AFL-CIO objected. Sixty percent participation seemed eminently reasonable to Labor Department staff and the decision was allowed to stand. "What on earth are they worried about[?]" Moynihan asked.[83] Other agencies adopted the 60 percent rule. Three years later, unions were still complaining about the rule as a labor department review found that many elections fell below the 60 percent participation threshold with some agencies going "out of their way to advise employees that they are not required to vote."[84] A related problem was a policy not to conduct run-offs when no union won a majority. In both instances, unions objected to policies that erected obstacles to the selection of collective bargaining agents not present in NLRB procedures. The Civil

Service Commission resisted a change to the runoff rule, a Department of Labor participant in negotiations observed: "Apparently [it] is fearful that one concession to the Metal Trades will simply open the door to further and...more serious concessions."[85]

Despite these obstacles, federal unions entered into a "period of intense organizational activity" and achieved considerable results, Willard Wirtz reported to the president after one year of the EMC program. Wirtz had replaced Goldberg as secretary of labor when Kennedy appointed the latter to the Supreme Court. The Post Office conducted representation elections in June 1962 that resulted in six craft unions winning "nationwide recognition right for 464,504 in their respective crafts."[86] As of December 1962, 17 other organizations won the right to exclusive representation for nearly 50,000 employees in other agencies. Nearly 70 percent of the latter group were in the navy units. Wirtz did not mention the local success of the MBPU in winning exclusive representation for 25,000 workers in New York. In the second year of the program's operation, the number of non-postal employees in units covered by exclusive recognition increased to 180,000.[87]

Unions won most of these early victories, but some associations also gained exclusive recognition in some bargaining units. Some associations sought lesser forms of recognition. The NFFE, after first welcoming the task force process, opposed the results. It was troubled by the notion that dual locals meant de facto segregation and wished to continue such locals and simply adopt a requirement that no one be denied membership in any local. It objected to the exclusion of supervisors from bargaining units with their subordinates and opposed exclusive recognition as leading to an adversarial relationship between employer and employee.[88] NFFE President Vaux Owen charged that recognizing a union that included non-federal employees as members weakens presidential "control and turns the course of the state toward anarchy."[89] An NFFE lawsuit against the executive order was unsuccessful and in 1964 the NFFE convention elected a new president who turned the organization to a policy of working within the framework of the order.[90]

The National Alliance of Postal Employees, a predominately black independent industrial union with 25,000 members, was also unhappy with the prospect of craft unions winning national exclusive recognition in the Post Office. Railway postal clerks had established the alliance in 1913, two years after the Railway Mail Association barred blacks. Delegates to the organization's national convention protested against "throwing their working lives into indifferent if not hostile hands." Craft unions were "at best doubtful instruments for the protection of the rights of minority group employees," President Ashby Smith argued, since they had removed racial barriers and abolished segregated locals only because of the threat of nonrecognition.[91] The alliance received formal recognition under the executive order and continued to defend black employees against what it saw as management and craft union harassment and loss of jobs by relocating postal facilities away from urban areas.[92]

Employee organizations saw gaining a dues check-off as a vital step in stabilizing their organizations. The implementation group was sympathetic to this aim. Initially, President Kennedy followed the task force recommendation and proposed legislation to institute the dues check-off, but a legal opinion in January 1963 by the comptroller general that the executive branch had the authority under existing law to permit such deductions led him to establish the procedure by a directive to the Civil Service Commission on May 21, 1963, with January 1, 1964, set as the date for the new policy to go into effect. Concerned about a Cleveland newspaper strike and the railway labor situation, Kennedy waited until these matters were resolved before issuing the pro-union order. As a "counter-balance for the checkoff," the president at the same time approved the implementation committee's recommended Standards of Conduct for Employee Organizations and Code of Fair Labor Practices.[93]

Under the standards of conduct, employee organizations had to maintain democratic procedures, fiscal integrity, and exclude from office "persons affiliated with Communist or other totalitarian movements and persons identified with corrupt influences." Under the fair practices code, management was prohibited from interfering with workers' rights under the order, discouraging membership, or sponsoring or assisting employee organizations. There were restrictions on union "coercion" of employees and agencies, strikes and slowdowns. The most controversial issue was picketing. The implementation committee's initial language would have prohibited any picketing on labor-management issues. Revised language, cleared with Meany, prohibited picketing "engaged in as a substitute" for a strike or slowdown.[94]

Limitations on the right to strike, congressional control of many aspects of personnel policy, and the strong management rights requirements of the executive order all influenced the first round of negotiations under the EMC. B. A. Gritta, head of the AFL-CIO Metal Trades Department, complained that many agencies had adopted a "'take it or leave it' position at the bargaining table."[95] In some cases, unions contented themselves with contracts that were little more than a statement of agency policy or "agreements to agree." In other cases unions won beneficial contract clauses on substantive matters. In the national postal negotiations signed on March 20, 1963, for example, unions won some important concessions such as on disciplinary procedure.[96]

The November 1963 AFL-CIO convention saw the issuance of the executive order as opening a "new era" in labor-management relations in the federal service and expressed "sincere gratitude" to the president for both the executive order and the dues check-off directive. The convention took positive note of several other developments affecting federal employees, including a congressionally mandated pay increase of more than 10 percent, establishment of the principle of "comparability" of federal employee pay with that in the private sector, and liberalization of the Hatch Act's restriction on political activities. On the other hand, the convention addressed several problems with the EMC program. It called on the president to end the 60 percent rule and the blocking of runoff elections. The convention recommended the executive order be revised to authorize "binding arbitration as agreed to by the parties" to resolve disputes over negotiations and charges of either unfair labor practices or violations of the standards or fair practice codes.[97]

Although the federal government was ahead of almost all states in the initial establishment of limited collective bargaining following Kennedy's executive order, many states quickly moved beyond the federal approach to full collective bargaining. Michael Goldfield notes that states with "high percentages of private sector employees organized were most likely" to pass pro-union public sector bargaining laws and that teacher collective bargaining legislation in particular tended to follow large-scale teacher unionization.[98] By the mid-1970s, 24 states had passed legislation providing for mandatory bargaining for all state and local employees while 6 additional states provided these rights for some groups. Six states provided for a limited right to strike.[99]

The growth of union membership among public workers at federal, state, and local levels led to a burst of strike activity after 1965. Between 1966 and 1974, an average of 174,000 public workers struck each year with an average of 1,431,767 workdays lost. Local government workers conducted a large majority of these strikes, which usually led to significant gains for workers.[100] Particularly important was the 1968 sanitation workers' strike in Memphis. The assassination in Memphis of civil rights leader Dr. Martin Luther King, Jr., who was helping to galvanize community support for the workers' uphill struggle, brought increased attention and support to the strike and helped the workers to achieve a decisive victory. AFSMCE leader William Lucy commented that the Memphis strike led to "a new kind of respect and a new kind of recognition" for municipal sanitation workers nationally.[101]

Federal workers became increasingly discontented as they compared their limited gains under the executive order with the increasing and more substantial progress of municipal workers in large cities. Federal workers' unions began to campaign for legislative redress in 1965 and members of Congress introduced pro-labor bills and resolutions. International Association of Machinists District 44 President William H. Ryan characterized the executive order in 1966 as "an armless, legless, mindless, toothless monstrosity—it's helpless and hopeless."[102] Increasing militancy among public employees led previously cautious professional and federal unions to revise long-standing no-strike policies. The NEA dropped its no-strike position in 1967. The American Nurses Association, the United Federation of Postal Clerks, the National Postal Union, and the National Association of Government Employees followed suit in 1968. A number of small work stoppages by federal workers took place in 1968 and 1969, most notably by the Professional Air Traffic Controllers Organization and by rank-and-file postal workers in New York City.[103]

President Johnson responded to the federal workers' criticisms by creating a Review Committee in September 1967 to assess the EMC program. The structure of the Review Committee was identical to that of the original task force, but the new committee was assisted by an outside advisory panel of labor relations academics. The final report of the committee included some recommendations favored by unions such as arbitration, the creation of a federal labor relations panel, and a 12-months dues' deduction for exclusive representatives. Two members of the committee, Secretary of Defense Clark Clifford and Joseph Califano, special assistant to President Johnson, refused to sign the report, however. With the country increasingly opposed to the Vietnam War, Clifford raised national security concerns with the president, stating he could "foresee" developments that he "would be powerless to control."[104] Having decided not to run for reelection, with a divided administration and party, Johnson focused on the Vietnam War crisis, refused to publish the committee's report, and took no action to amend the Kennedy order.

Johnson's failure to act led to the review process continuing under President Richard Nixon. A Nixon study committee made recommendations that were similar but more conservative than those of the Johnson review committee. Nixon issued Executive Order 11491 on October 29, 1969, revising the EMC program along the lines recommended by his study committee. Although the "Nixon program rankled many union leaders because it failed to make the substantive changes they deemed necessary," Nesbitt concludes that the order, nevertheless, "achieved several long overdue reforms."[105] The Nixon order created a Federal Labor Relations Council composed of executive officers to supervise the program and a Federal Services Impasse Panel to settle deadlocked negotiations. Although the council was not the independent agency that the unions wanted, the expansion of the scope of bargaining, the inclusion of binding arbitration, and the abolition of the 10 percent membership and 60 percent participation in voting requirements were responses to union demands for improving the EMC program.[106] The base of power that federal unions had won under the Kennedy order was such that a Republican administration facing a Democratic Congress felt obliged to respond to that institutionalized strength rather than dismantle the program.

Of all federal workers, the postal workers took the biggest leap toward full collective bargaining as a result of their dramatic strike action. Dissatisfaction among postal workers and their high level of unionization had played a significant part in the movement resulting in partial federal collective bargaining. Discontent about low pay in particular, which remained a congressional prerogative, led Congress to adopt the Federal Salary Reform Act in 1962. Although the reform measure provided that federal workers' pay should be comparable to that of private sector workers, the federal government failed to deliver on the promise because of concerns about Post Office deficits and inflation. Postal management responded to the fiscal crisis by measures, such as the introduction of letter-sorting machines, hiring temporary workers, and limiting overtime, that angered permanent workers and created a crisis in the quality of service. Postal workers also were furious that their wages failed to keep up with inflation while members of Congress doubled the president's pay in 1970 and increased their own salaries by 41 percent. Responding to the fiscal crisis, President Nixon proposed a plan to change the postal service into a self-supporting nonprofit public corporation in which employees would have collective bargaining rights comparable to those in the private sector. Although Post Office director Blount specifically excluded the right to strike from the list of rights employees would have under Nixon's proposal, the repetition by administration officials of the idea that the postal workers would fall under the Wagner Act contributed to the growing strike sentiment among rank-and-file workers.[107]

Postal workers in New York and other large cities had watched nonfederal public employees conduct illegal strikes and achieve large wage increases without being punished in the mid and late 1960s. A rank-and-file movement in Branch 36 of the NALC in Manhattan and the Bronx voted to strike on March 17, 1970, and was immediately backed by the leaders of Brooklyn Branch 41 and by Moe Biller of the independent MBPU, whose members then honored the letter carriers' picket lines. When a mass meeting of 6,500 MBPU members took place the next day, radical activists pushed for an immediate voice vote to strike and the crowd shouted "Power to the People." Biller insisted on a secret ballot before leaving the chaotic meeting. The members voted to strike by about a nine-to-one margin. The strike spread to large and small cities throughout the country. Workers ignored court injunctions to return to work and initially refused to return to work despite promises that direct bargaining over wages would finally take place. Nixon's declaration of a national emergency and the sending of 25,000 National Guard and Army Reserve troops to New York City to take over postal workers' jobs led many to go back to work but did not end the strike. With NALC leaders and members of Congress announcing a wide-ranging agreement meeting the workers' key demands, strikers voted to return to work at a mass meeting on March 25. Although the announcement had exaggerated administration concessions, the workers did win a 14 percent wage increase and collective bargaining rights.[108] In August 1970 President Nixon signed the Postal Reorganization Act, establishing the U.S. Postal Service as an independent agency within the federal government. Although initially opposed to the downgrading of the Post Office from departmental rank, postal unions won significant wage and legal concessions as part of the change in the postal system. Most importantly, the NLRB would henceforth supervise representation elections and handle unfair labor practices complaints for postal workers. Although the postal workers did not win the right to strike, the act provided for binding arbitration if bargaining reached an impasse.[109]

Vincent Sombrero, a leader of the rank and file, was elected president of Branch 36 by the end of 1970 and president of the NALC in 1978. The one postal union leader who had supported the strike, Moe Biller of the MBPU, became president of the American Postal Workers Union (APWU) in 1980, a new union formed in 1971 by the merger of five postal unions. The NALC, with the aid of the American Civil Liberties Union, also won an important court victory in 1969, nullifying the antistrike affidavits and the prohibition against asserting the right to strike on the basis that they were unconstitutional restrictions on free speech. The United Federation of Postal Clerks, one of the five unions forming the APWU, was unsuccessful, however, in challenging the most fundamental restriction on federal employee unionism, the prohibition on strikes. The Supreme Court in 1971 rejected the union argument that the ban was a violation of workers' constitutional right to strike.[110]

Despite this important setback, public employee unions had by then consolidated their place in the U.S. social order. Managers in the public sector no longer could run public workplaces by fiat but often had to contend with employees backed by feisty independent unions. The unionization of a significant component of the public workforce was assisted by improvements in public policy but came primarily from a burgeoning grassroots movement. Sparked by militants and radicals, that movement reached its highest and most successful peaks when workers developed a substantial degree of organization and unity and found the courage to take strike action. A favorable political and economic context was also important as public officials combined antistrike measures with a willingness to negotiate with union officials, who ranged from militants seeking to extract the maximum concessions possible to more moderate leaders who sought more limited gains and a quick end to strike action.

For employees outside the postal service, there were some improvements in the EMC program under two additional executive orders until legislation was enacted under President Jimmy Carter. The Civil Service Reform Act of 1978 sponsored by Carter had increased efficiency as its focus, but it also "widened the scope of bargaining and enhanced the role of the neutral interpretative agency."[111] Congress still retained sole authority over wage- and fringe-benefit determination. Despite the limited scope of bargaining in nonpostal unions, federal unions' political lobbying on workers' behalf and the provision of on-the-job protection have allowed federal employees to retain the enlarged membership base they won in the wake of the enthusiastic embrace of the right to select collective bargaining agents provided by Kennedy's executive order. Membership in public sector unions at the federal, state, and local levels continued to grow in absolute terms and as a proportion of all eligible employees.

At the same time that public employees were seeking to establish their right to equal treatment as workers in the nation's system of labor relations, the campaigns of minorities and women to end their second-class status reached new heights. Several of the most crucial political and legal developments in the modern civil rights and feminist movements occurred during the Kennedy and Johnson administrations. Nelson Lichtenstein has argued that one reason for the public workers' union successes in a time of declining fortunes for unions generally was that their campaigns to advance workers' rights in civil service systems effectively drew on the developing "rights culture" of the 1960s and 1970s.[112] The intertwining of the struggles of public workers with the civil rights struggle began in the 1940s with the campaigns of the UPWA to desegregate Washington, D.C., and of the Teachers Union to promote African American history. In the 1960s and early 1970s, the militancy of African Americans contributed to many of the most important public workers' strikes in the nation's largest cities. All of the Memphis sanitation workers in 1968 were African American, as were two-thirds of the postal strikers in 1970.

The black community was one of the most important political allies for public workers' struggles. The 1968 strike of the UFT against community control of the schools in Ocean Hill-Brownsville, however, weakened the alliance between the teachers and the African American community in New York. Although the NEA responded more slowly to the civil rights movement than did the AFT, it moved to end segregation in its state associations, merged in 1966 with an association of black teachers with which it had long cooperated, and nominated Elizabeth Koontz as its first black president in 1967. Although the NEA president served only a one-year term and real power lay with the executive director, even a symbolic selection was important and the NEA had a strong integrationist group whose influence grew over the years. As it shifted toward a more trade unionist orientation, the NEA's greater sensitivity on racial issues helped it to win the dominant position among teachers nationally.[113]

The relationship between public workers' struggles and women's struggle for equality is more complex. Although women had predominated in the leadership of the AFT in the 1920s and 1930s and the left-wing unions included women in prominent roles, by the 1950s and 1960s males dominated the leadership of public employee unions. Contrast the scene at the signing of Executive Order 10988 in 1962, where Ida Klaus is the only woman present, to that when President Kennedy in 1963 signed the Equal Pay Act, establishing the right of women to equal pay for equal work, where women predominated. In many of the successful struggles for union gains, moreover, male teachers, postal workers, and sanitation workers emphasized that they were seeking respect as males. The influence of the signing of the Equal Pay Act, and even more profoundly of the Civil Rights Act of 1964 with its bar to discrimination in employment based on sex as well as race, the founding of the National Organization for Women in 1966, and the rise of the women's liberation movement led to new job opportunities and a growing militancy among women public workers. Masculinist rhetoric in male public workers' expressions of their union goals waned as the women's movement expanded and affirmative action led to the inclusion of women in such previously predominately male work areas as carrying the mail, police work, and fire fighting. Resistance to women persisted most in fields such as fire fighting with its historic emphasis on an "expressive, fraternal masculinity." As Mark Wilkens notes in his study of Tampa, Florida, firefighters, "the subtle resistance of men helps to ensure that any woman who is too distinctly assertive and outspoken will abandon the profession or modify her behavior."[114] Despite these difficulties, the breakdown of all-male occupational preserves was an important step toward the development of a broader sense of class identity among working people.

African American grassroots militancy eventually led to local leadership and then inclusion in higher levels of union leadership of public workers' unions. Women's rise into leadership positions took place a bit more slowly but was notable, especially at the local level, by the 1980s.[115] Inclusion of minorities and women in leadership has helped the trade union movement to focus more attention on the problems of the most oppressed workers.

A relatively high level of women's and minority participation is one of several ways in which public employee unions have contributed to the overall strength of the trade union movement and to its role as a force for social progress. Most obviously, public employee unions have became a central component of overall trade union membership. Public employee unions have contributed in substantial ways to the recent efforts at revitalizing the labor movement. Public workers readily understand the importance of political decisions in shaping their own work lives. They have entered into the political arena, however, not merely on their own behalf but with a generally progressive vision to help the poor and advance the cause of social justice.

Public employee unions became a great source of institutional strength to the trade union movement. The prime cause of this development was the grassroots militancy of public employees themselves. Aiding the public workers in their campaign was a strong and politically influential trade union movement in the private sector, a Democratic president responsive to labor and liberal appeals, and a diverse grouping of left-wing activists. Finding a path through the rocky terrain of the crisis in American political and economic life that emerged in the 1970s, however, was a challenge to labor, its progressive allies, and the first post–Vietnam War Democratic president, Jimmy Carter.

NOTES

1. Task Force on Employee-Management Relations in the Federal Service, "A Policy for Employee-Management Cooperation in the Federal Service," in Harold S. Roberts, *Labor Management Relations in the Public Service* ([Honolulu]: University of Hawaii Industrial Relations Center, 1968), Part 1: 8–10; Roberts, "Negotiated Agreements," Ibid., Part 5: 542–3.

2. The source for the estimate of state and local unionization is Leo Troy and Sheflin, *U.S. Union Sourcebook: Membership, Structure, Finance, Directory* (West Orange, N.J.: Industrial Relations Data and Information Service, 1985), 3–20, A–2, which uses data from union and association financial reports and provides a somewhat lower figure for federal union membership than is contained in the task force documents. *Statistical Abstract of the United States, 2001*, Table No. 637.

3. Sterling D. Spero, *Government as Employer* (Carbondale: Southern Illinois Press, 1972), 81–88; Murray B. Nesbitt, *Labor Relations in the Federal Government Service* (Washington, D.C.: Bureau of National Affairs, 1976), 90–99.

4. Spero, *Government as Employer*, 96–101; Nesbitt, *Labor Relations*, 26–30, 92–95; "Federal Wage Board Systems," Staff Paper No. 10, in Staff Report I, Task Force on Employee-Management Relations in the Federal Service, Records of Secretary of Labor Arthur Goldberg, Box 41, RG 174, National Archives (hereafter cited as NA); Daniel Moynihan, "An Impression of the Possible Course of Employee Management Relations in the Federal Service in the Light of Proposals Presented at the Public Hearings and in the Employee Organization Questionnaires," For Use by Task Force on Employee-Management Relations in the Federal Service, n.d., Daniel P. Moynihan Papers, Box 4, Library of Congress.

5. Spero, *Government as Employer*, 106–117; Nesbitt, *Labor Relations*, 35–40.

6. John W. Macy, Jr., "The Role of Bargaining in the Public Service," in Sam Zagoria, ed., *Public Workers and Public Unions* (Englewood Cliffs, N.J.: Prentice Hall, 1972), 9.

7. Spero, *Government as Employer*, 2–3.

8. Sterling D. Spero and John M. Capozzola, *The Urban Community and Its Unionized Bureaucracies: Pressure Politics in Local Government Labor Relations* (New York: Dunnellen Publishing Company, 1973), 4–5, 16, 313; Mansour Ahmed Mansour, "The Legal Rights of Federal Employees to Unionize, Bargain Collectively, and Strike" (Ph.D. diss., Ohio State University, 1969), 28–29. As this law was put into effect, other federal workers gained the same rights.

9. Joseph Slater, "Public Workers: Labor and the Boston Police Strike of 1919," *Labor History* 38 (Winter 1996–97): 7–27; Joseph E. Slater, "The Court Does Not Know 'What a Labor Union Is': How State Structures and Judicial (Mis)constructions Deformed Public Sector Labor Law," 79 *Oregon Law Review* 981 (2000).

Unions, Radicals, and Democratic Presidents

10. Gilbert J. Gall, "They May Vote in Silence: The Roosevelt Court and the United Federal Workers Challenge of the Hatch Act," paper presented at North American Labor History Conference, October 1992, 39.

11. Marvin J. Levine and Eugene C. Hagburg, *Public Sector Labor Relations* (St. Paul, Minn.: West Publishing, 1979), 15; Marjorie Murphy, *Blackboard Unions: The AFT and the NEA, 1900–1980* (Ithaca, N.Y.: Cornell University Press, 1990), 182–95; Spero, *Government as Employer*, 199–201, 332–34; Rhonda Hanson, "United Public Workers: A Real Union Organizes," Ann Fagan Ginger and David Christiano, eds., *Cold War Against Labor* (Berkeley, Calif.: Meiklejohn Civil Liberties Institute, 1987), 1:176–77.

12. Nesbitt, *Labor Relations*, 10–11. See also Spero, *Government as Employer*, 345.

13. Nesbitt, *Labor Relations*, 10–11; Spero, *Government as Employer*, 346.

14. Spero, *Government as Employer*, 346.

15. Nesbitt, *Labor Relations*, 11. Only a few thousand workers gained collective bargaining rights during the New Deal era in the TVA and several agencies of the Department of Interior. "Bargaining Procedures in the Department of Interior," Staff Paper No. 13, in Staff Report I, Task Force on Employee-Management Relations in the Federal Service, Records of Secretary of Labor Goldberg, Box 41, NA.

16. Spero, *Government as Employer*, 156–64, 191–97; Gall, "They May Vote in Silence."

17. Spero, *Government as Employer*, 194–95, 216–26. Hanson, "United Public Workers: A Real Union Organizes," 172–85; Philip Foner, *Women and the American Labor Movement* (New York: The Free Press, 1980), 2:366. See Chapter 2 for a discussion of the role of the UPWA in promoting desegregation in Washington, D.C.

18. Griffin Fariello, *Red Scare: Memories of the American Inquisition: An Oral History* (New York: Avon Books, 1996), 141–43. The Atomic Energy Commission "ordered the University of Chicago to break its contract with UPWA workers at the Argonne National Laboratories." Ellen W. Schrecker, "McCarthyism and the Labor Movement: The Role of the State," in Steve Rosswurm, *The CIO's Left-led Unions* (New Brunswick, N.J.: Rutgers University Press, 1992), 146.

19. Rhoda Hanson, "United Public Workers: The Conscience of the Capitol," in Ginger and Christiano, *Cold War*, 2:389–98. Sachs is quoted in Fariello, *Red Scare*, 390–95.

20. *New York Times*, February 14, 1953, 4; March 1, 1957, 29; February 22. 1984, A10.

21. Jack Stieber, *Public Employee Unionism: Structure, Growth, Policy* (Washington, D.C.: Brookings Institution, 1973), 32.

22. George Meany, "Meany Looks into Labor's Future," *New York Times*, December 4, 1955, SM11(emphasis in original).

23. Spero and Capozzola, *Urban Community*, 14.

24. Joshua Freeman, *Working Class New York* (New York: New Press, 2000), 201–3; Joshua Freeman, *In Transit: The Transport Workers Union in New York City, 1933–1966* (New York: Oxford University Press, 1989), 325–26; Jewel Bellush and Bernard Bellush, *Union Power and New York* (New York: Praeger, 1984), 29–30, 63–64; Mark H. Maier, *City Unions: Managing Discontent in New York City* (New Brunswick, N.J.: Rutgers University Press, 1987), 44–47, 96, 112–14.

25. Interview with Ida Klaus by David C. Berliner, 1976, Jewish Women of Achievement Collection, New York Public Library, 202–3.

26. Ibid., 197–8.

27. Ibid., 74–86; Nick Ravo, "Ida Klaus Obituary," *New York Times,* May 20, 1994, 10.

28. Klaus interview, 146–8, 204–6.

29. Freeman, *In Transit,* 325–6; Maier, *City Unions,* 44–52; Bellush and Bellush, *Union Power,* 29–30, 63–69.

30. Maier, *City Unions,* 92–95.

31. Ibid., 60–68.

32. Celia Lewis Zitron, *The New York City Teachers Union, 1916–1964* (New York: Humanities Press, 1968); "Class Struggle: The UFT Story," Parts 1 and 2, *New York Teacher,* February 19, March 4, 1996, <http://www.uft.org/?fid=65&tf=139>, <http://www.uft.org/?fid=65&tf=140>, (accessed December 1, 2002); *New York Times,* January 26, 1955, 24.

33. Maier, *City Unions,* 108–16.

34. David Selden, *The Teacher Rebellion* (Washington, D.C.: Howard University Press, 1985), 44.

35. Ibid., 46–47.

36. Zitron, *Teachers Union,* 47–48.

37. *New York Times,* April 12, 1962, 1; Maier, *City Unions,* 108; "Class Struggle: The UFT Story," Part 7, <http://www.uft.org/?fid-65&tf=145>, (accessed December 1, 2002); Murphy, *Blackboard Unions,* 217.

38. Selden, *Teacher Rebellion,* 45–64.

39. *New York Times,* April 12, 1962, 30.

40. Murphy, *Blackboard Unions,* 216.

41. Carl Megel to John Livingston, January 12, 1963, AFT Papers, Series I Box 1, Archives of Labor History and Urban Affairs, Wayne State University, Detroit (hereafter WSU).

42. Report of Carl Magel and administrative staff to 1962 AFT convention, 43, AFT Series III Box 19, WSU Address of Carl Megel to 48th AFT Convention, August 18, 1964, AFT Papers, Series III Box 25, WSU.

43. Murphy, *Blackboard Unions,* 236–31.

44. John Walsh and Garth Mangum, *Labor Struggle in the Post Office: From Selective Lobbying to Collective Bargaining* (Armonk, N.Y.: M.E. Sharpe, 1992), 57–69, 142–61.

45. Nesbitt, *Labor Relations,* 15.

46. Rocco C. Siciliano, "To the Heads of Executive Departments and Agencies," June 3, 1958, Harold Leich, "Where We Stand on Union-Management Relations in the Federal Service," March 21, 1961, Union-Management Relations in the Federal Service Background Papers, Records of Secretary of Labor Goldberg, Box 42, NA; Spero and Capozzola, *Urban Community,* 57.

47. Irving Bernstein, *Promises Kept: John F. Kennedy's New Frontier* (New York: Oxford University Press, 1991), 211; Nesbitt, *Labor Relations,* 18–19; John F. Kennedy to John W. Ames, October 31, 1960, Daniel P. Moynihan Papers, Box 75, Library of Congress. A similar Kennedy letter to the postal union is cited in, Mansour, "Legal Rights," 37.

48. *Congressional Record,* 87th Cong., 1st sess., January 3, 1961, 35; "H.R. 12 (Rhodes), 87th Congress, Summary of Major Provisions," Moynihan Papers, Box 75, Library of Congress.

49. "Employee-Management Bills—87th Congress, Staff Paper No. 5," Staff Paper No. 10, in Staff Report I, Task Force on Employee-Management Relations in the Federal Service, Records of Secretary of Labor Goldberg, Box 41, NA; Draft Executive Order, February 10, 1961, Records of Secretary of Labor Goldberg, Box 42, NA.

50. Cyrus Vance to David E. Bell, March 22, 1961, Meyer Feldman Papers, Box 11, John F. Kennedy Library, Boston (hereafter cited as JFK Library).

51. Andrew J. Biemiller to Arthur Goldberg, April 19, 1961, Records of Secretary of Labor Goldberg, Box 19, NA.

52. Frederick G. Dutton memorandum for William Carey, April 21, 1961, Kennedy Papers, White House Central Files, Box 491, JFK Library; Dutton memorandum for Arthur Goldberg, April 29, 1961, Records of Secretary of Labor Goldberg, Box 24, NA.

53. Memorandum on House Post Office and Civil Service Committee Activities, 87th Cong., 1st sess., Part III—Employee Matters, 5, November 1961, Kennedy Papers, President's Office Files, Legislative Files, Box 50, JFK Library.

54. David L. Stebenne, *Arthur J. Goldberg: New Deal Liberal* (New York: Oxford University Press), 64–65, 120–25, 174 ; Oral History Interview of Esther Peterson by Ann Campbell, January 20, 1970, 39, JFK Library.

55. Wilson R. Hart, "The U.S. Civil Service Learns to Live with Executive Order 10,988: An Interim Appraisal," *Industrial and Labor Relations Review* 17 (January 1964): 205.

56. Douglas Schoen, *Pat: A Biography of Daniel Patrick Moynihan* (New York: HarperCollins, 1979), 70.

57. For the 180–180 estimate, see Oral History Interview with Andrew Biemiller by Sheldon Stern, May 24, 1979, 25, JFK Library; James A. Gross, *Broken Promise: The Subversion of U.S. Labor Relations Policy, 1947–1994* (Philadelphia: Temple University Press, 1995), 156–59.

58. E.T. Herrick, Confidential Memorandum to James T. Reynolds, December 6, 1962, Moynihan Papers, Box 75, Library of Congress.

59. Hubert Humphrey to John Bailey, February 16, 1963, Kennedy Papers, White House Central Files, Box 191.

60. John F. Kennedy, "Letter to the President of the Senate and the Speaker of the House on Withholding of Federal Employee Organizations Dues," April 19, 1962, *Public Papers of the Presidents, John F. Kennedy, 1962*, (Washington, D.C.: GPO, 1963), 340. House staff members did make the helpful suggestion that recently enacted payroll legislation was "broad enough" that the executive branch could proceed on its own with the check-off. The administration was soon to pursue this course. See below. E.T. Herrick, Confidential Memorandum to James T. Reynolds, December 6, 1962, Moynihan Papers, Box 75, Library of Congress.

61. Arthur Goldberg Memorandum for Myer Feldman, June 7, 1961, and attached draft Presidential Memorandum, June 1, 1961, Records of the Secretary of Labor Goldberg, Box 73, NA; John Kennedy, "Memorandum on Employee-Management Relations in the Federal Service," June 22, 1961, *Public Papers of the Presidents, John Kennedy 1961* (Washington, D.C.: GPO, 1962), 469–70.

62. Ann Fagan Ginger and David Christiano, "ILWU Communist Slays the Son of Taft-Hartley," in Ginger and Christiano, *Cold War*, 2:707–8; United States v. Brown, 381 U.S. 437 (1965); Arthur Goldberg to Department and Agency Heads, July 14, 1961, Records of Secretary of Labor Goldberg, Box 42, NA.

63. Klaus interview, 208–9.

64. Goldberg to M.C. Coutto, August 3, 1961, Records of Secretary of Labor Goldberg, Box 41, NA.

65. Charles E. Harrison to Arthur Goldberg, July 1, 1961, John W. MacKay to Goldberg, July 4, 1961, Records of Secretary of Labor Goldberg, Box 42, NA; James Langen to John Kennedy, June 16, 1961, AFL-CIO microfilmed records, JFK Library.

66. Daniel P. Moynihan Memorandum for Secretary Goldberg, July 27, 1961, Daniel P. Moynihan Papers, Box 75, Library of Congress.

67. Schoen, *Pat*, 71.

68. Interview of Arthur Goldberg by Frank Cormier and William Eaton, Cormier and Eaton Papers, JFK Library; Oral History Interview of George Meany by Arthur Goldberg, July 17, 1964, and August 18, 1964, JFK Library; John F. Kennedy, 1960 Labor Day Message, UAW President Walter P. Reuther Coll., Box 367, WSU; Remarks of Senator John F. Kennedy, Milwaukee, Wisconsin, April 3, 1960, "Labor—The Source of American Strength," Moynihan Papers, Box 380, Library of Congress.

69. Oral History Interview of F. Nordy Hoffman by Donald Ritchie, August 4, 1988, 120, Senate Historical Office, Senate Oral History Program, <http://www. senate.gov/learning/learn_history_oralhist_hoffmann3.html.> (accessed November 2, 2002).

70. Oral History Interview of Esther Peterson, 31.

71. Gerald S. Strober and Deborah H. Strober, eds., *"Let Us Begin Anew": An Oral History of the Kennedy Presidency* (New York: HarperPerennial, 1993), 155–56.

72. Strober and Strober, *"Let Us Begin Anew"*, 69, 245; Taylor Branch, *Parting the Waters: American in the King Years* (New York: Simon & Schuster, 1988), 833–45.

73. Gross, *Broken Promise*, 147–91; James A. Gross, *The Reshaping of the National Labor Relations Board* (Albany: State University of New York Press, 1981).

74. Task Force on Employee-Management Relations in the Federal Service, "A Policy," 15, 29.

75. "Comments of the American Federation of Government Employees to Secretary of Labor Arthur J. Goldberg on the Report of the President's Task Force on Employee-Management Relations in the Federal Service," December 28, 1961, Records of Secretary of Labor Goldberg, Box 41, NA.

76. Nesbitt, *Labor Relations*, 134–40.

77. Copy of *Congressional Record*, January 18, 1962, 380, Moynihan Papers, Box 75, Library of Congress.

78. Federal Conference on Employee-Management Relations, February 27, 1962, Moynihan Papers, Box 74, Library of Congress (emphasis in original). Kennedy thought that the "paramount personnel problems" were achieving "comparability" and ending the "compression in the salary scales" of those in the "upper career ranks." John Kennedy to Nicholas Kelley, May 2, 1962, Kennedy Papers, President's Office File, Box 72, JFK Library. The AFL-CIO was critical of Kennedy's pay proposal for ignoring the needs of lower pay workers. *New York Times*, July 30, 1962, 21.

79. Goldberg advised Hayes to appeal through Navy channels. A.J. Hayes to Arthur Goldberg, March 23, 1962, Temporary Implementation Committee, "Position Paper on Item Four," April 5, 1962, Goldberg to Hayes, April 10, 1962, Records of Secretary of Labor Goldberg, Box 43, NA.

80. John MacKay to Arthur Goldberg, March 27, 1962, Records of Secretary of Labor Goldberg, Box 43, NA.

81. E.C. Hallbeck to Goldberg, April 6, 1962, Goldberg to Hallbeck, May 2, 1962, Records of Secretary of Labor Goldberg, Box 43, NA.

82. Moe Biller to John Kennedy, December 7, 1962, H.T. Herrick to Secretary Wirtz, February 14, 1963, Records of Secretary of Labor Willard Wirtz, Box 63, RG 174, NA.

83. H.T. Herrick to Daniel Moynihan, June 11, 1962, with Moynihan's hand-written note, Moynihan Papers, Box 75, Library of Congress.

84. Louis S. Wallerstein to James J. Reynolds, August 27, 1965, Willard Wirtz Papers, Box 2, JFK Library.

85. Nelson M. Bortz to James Reynolds, (handwritten: John Donovan, Attn. Mr. Wirtz), December 18, 1963, Records of Secretary of Labor Wirtz, Box 62, NA. For a metal trades complaint, see B.A. Gritta to Willard Wirtz, June 7, 1963, Records of Secretary of Labor Wirtz, Box 62, NA.

86. Willard Wirtz to John Kennedy, January 25, 1963, Records of Secretary of Labor Wirtz, Box 63, NA.

87. Ibid.; John W. Macy to the President, January 17, 1964; Records of Secretary of Labor Wirtz, Box 63, NA.

88. NFFE Press release, no date, Records of Secretary of Labor Goldberg, Box 43, NA; Vaux Owen to Arthur Goldberg, October 13, 1961, Records of Secretary of Labor Goldberg, Box 41, NA; Nesbitt, *Labor Relations*, 105–6.

89. Vaux Owen to John Kennedy, April 2, 1963, Records of Secretary of Labor Wirtz, Box 62, NA.

90. Nesbitt, *Labor Relations*, 71–72.

91. Ashby Smith to J. Edward Day, March 20, 1962, Kennedy Papers, White House Central Files, Box 466; Sterling D. Spero and Abram L. Harris, *The Black Worker* (New York: Atheneum, 1968), 123. The membership figure is as of January 1968, Nesbitt, *Labor Relations*, 318 n.

92. Spero, *Government*, 164; Nesbitt, *Labor Relations*, 54, 320.

93. Nesbitt, *Labor Relations*, 210. The quote is from H.T. Herrick to W. Wirtz, April 4, 1963, Willard Wirtz Papers, Box 2, JFK Library; John F. Kennedy memo-randum for the Chairman, Civil Service Commission, May 21, 1963, White House press release, May 21, 1963, Records of Secretary of Labor Wirtz, Box 62, NA.

94. For the text of the two documents, see Ronald A. Wykstra and Eleanour V. Stevens, *Labor Law and Public Policy* (New York: Odyssey Press, 1970), 410–15; Charles Donahue Memorandum for the Secretary of Labor, November 27, 1962, Willard Wirtz Papers, 1994 accession, Box 2, JFK Library; Willard Wirtz to Tempo-rary Committee, January 11, 1963, Lee White Papers, Box 5, JFK Library.

95. *Proceedings of the Fifth Constitutional Convention AFL-CIO, November 14–20, 1963, New York, New York*, 1:564.

96. Nesbitt, *Labor Relations*, 171–77, 318–22.

97. *Proceedings of the Fifth Constitutional Convention AFL-CIO*, 1:325, 556–66; 2:216.

98. Michael Goldfield, "Public Sector Union Growth and Public Policy," *Policy Studies Journal* 18 (1989–90): 414.

99. George Meany, "Union Leaders and Public Sector Labor Unions," in A. Lawrence Chickering, ed., *Public Employee Unions: A Study of the Crisis in Public Sec-tor Labor Relations* (San Francisco: Institute for Contemporary Studies, 1977), 167–8.

100. David Lewin, "Collective Bargaining and the Right to Strike," in Chickering, *Public Employee Unions*, 148–9.

101. Michael Honey, "Martin Luther King, Jr., the Crisis of the Black Working Class, and the Memphis Sanitation Strike," in Robert H. Zieger, ed., *Southern Labor in Transition, 1940–1995* (Knoxville: University of Tennessee Press, 1997), 166–68.

102. Albert A. Blum and I.B. Helburn, "Federal Labor-Management Relations: The Beginning," *Journal of Collective Negotiations* 26 (1997): 259.

103. Nesbitt, *Labor Relations*, 374–86.

104. Ibid., 271.

105. Ibid., 111.

106. Informal recognition ended and local formal recognition was phased out. Nesbitt, *Labor Relations*, 132, 158–164, 182, 447–52.

107. Aaron Brenner, "Striking Against the State: The Postal Wildcat of 1970," *Labor's Heritage* VII, No. 4 (Spring 1996): 4–27.

108. Ibid.; Nesbitt, *Labor Relations*, 386–95; Walsh and Magnum, *Labor Struggle*, 17–37.

109. Nesbitt, *Labor Relations*, 341–45.

110. Brenner, "Striking Against the State," 22; Nesbitt, *Labor Relations*, 391–95; Walsh and Magnum, *Labor Struggle*, 161–62.

111. Sar A. Levitan and Alexandra B. Noden, *Working for the Sovereign: Employee Relations in the Federal Government* (Baltimore: Johns Hopkins University Press, 1983), 5–6.

112. Nelson Lichtenstein, *State of the Union: A Century of American Labor* (Princeton, N.J.: Princeton University Press, 2002), 185.

113. Murphy, *Blackboard Unions*, 196–206, 229–31.

114. Mark Wilkens, "Gender, Race, Work Culture, and the Building of the Fire Fighters Union in Tampa, Florida, 1943–1985," in Zieger, *Southern Labor*, 194–95.

115. Deborah E. Bell, "Women and the Rise of Public-Sector Unionism Since the 1960s, in Eileen Boris and Nelson Lichtenstein, eds., *Major Problems in the History of American Workers* (Lexington, Mass.: Heath, 1991), 621–33. There were few women in the national leadership of most public sector unions in the 1970s. Norma M. Riccucci, *Women, Minorities, and Unions in the Public Sector* (New York: Greenwood Press, 1990), 23–28.

CHAPTER 6

Jimmy Carter and the UAW: Failure of an Alliance

In the aftermath of Watergate and Richard Nixon's resignation, a large number of Democrats sought their party's presidential nomination and the chance to run against the vulnerable Republican Gerald Ford in 1976. Expecting a deadlocked convention, the United Automobile Workers (UAW) and eight other liberal unions in the Labor Coalition Clearinghouse focused on electing substantial numbers of convention delegates from their unions and thereby gaining a significant voice in the selection of the nominee at the convention.[1]

In the UAW, each council of the UAW Citizens Action Program (CAP), the union's political action arm, made its own decision on the presidential primary or caucus. In the very first presidential contest on January 19, 1976, the influential Iowa CAP Council supported Jimmy Carter in that state's Democratic caucuses. Doug Fraser, then director of the Michigan CAP Council and a supporter of the liberal Morris Udall, was surprised by the Iowa action. When Fraser asked Soapy Owens, the director of the Iowa council, about the decision, Owens explained that he had talked with all the candidates and Carter was "the most impressive." Carter's ability to impress people in one-on-one and small-group settings was an important feature of his campaign successes. Carter won substantial national publicity in the Iowa caucuses with his second-place finish behind a slate of uncommitted delegates. Carter then went on to win 30 percent of the New Hampshire vote on February 24, enough for a first-place finish in the highly publicized first primary.[2]

As the campaign developed, UAW leaders watched the candidates and assessed membership attitudes. In a survey of its Indiana members conducted by a polling organization around the time of the New Hampshire primary, the union found that a plurality of members (37 percent) had voted for Nixon in 1972. Only 28 percent reported that they had voted for George McGovern.[3] For the 1976 nomination, 35 percent supported Indiana's own Senator Birch Bayh, a liberal. Alabama Governor George Wallace, whose campaign mixed racist, antiradical, and antiestablishment appeals, was the choice of 22 percent of union members surveyed. Carter had 15 percent and Senator Henry Jackson, best known for his hawkish views on foreign and defense policy, had 12 percent. Most troubling to the surveyors was the gloomy outlook for the general election. The survey found Bayh leading Gerald Ford among the UAW membership by only a 47 percent to 39 percent margin. A majority of those supporting Carter, Jackson, and Wallace for the Democratic nomination favored Ford over Bayh in the general election.[4] Some UAW leaders were concluding that a strong liberal could not win the 1976 general election.[5]

Although the UAW had backed McGovern in 1972 and was one of the most politically liberal unions, its liberalism was qualified by a heavy dose of pragmatism about real-world politics and the opinions of union members. Concern about Wallace led UAW President Leonard Woodcock to make a first tentative move in Carter's direction. "My relationship with Carter begins in '72 because George Wallace whipped us in [the] Michigan [Democratic primary]," Woodcock recalled in 1990. Wallace had "tens of thousands of honest good UAW members in his pocket." As the 1976 primaries were about to begin, Woodcock commented that Wallace tapped a "deep vein of discontent...not just the racist thing—you're getting the whole business on taxes, too."[6]

Woodcock looked for someone "who could do to Wallace in Florida what was done to Muskie" in New Hampshire in 1972, pull him below the vote expected of him by the press.[7] As a southern candidate from the neighboring state of Georgia, Carter was able to persuade the liberal presidential candidates to stay out of the Florida primary so the anti-Wallace vote would not be split.[8] The UAW's regional director and Florida CAP Council were happy about Woodcock's proposal to work for Carter in the Florida primary. To help out, Woodcock visited Florida and spoke before the union's retired workers councils, declaring that Carter might best serve the interests of organized labor.[9] As UAW representative John Barnett, a Carter supporter, put it, the Woodcock visit "had a helluva effect.... Of course, President Woodcock didn't endorse Jimmy but he didn't not endorse him either."[10] In the March 9 primary contest, Carter led the field with 34 percent of the vote, topping Wallace by 3 percentage points and seriously wounding his candidacy. Carter was strongest in the middle part of the state, which was also the concentration point for the UAW campaign.[11]

The road from support for Carter in one primary to full endorsement began when Woodcock first met Carter the day after the UAW leader's

speech to southwest Florida retirees. Uninvited, Carter dropped by Woodcock's motel room and the two chatted for an hour as TV reporters waited
outside. Woodcock was impressed by Carter, "by the keenness of his intel-
lect," and by his "very honest approaches to...questions." Although he
did not endorse him, Woodcock accepted Carter's invitation to appear
with him at a fundraising dinner.[12]

Woodcock had sought Georgia Representative Andrew Young's advice
on his Florida strategy and was urged to go ahead. After the Florida primary, Woodcock had dinner with Young in Washington. Young, a prominent African American civil rights leader, predicted Carter would win the
nomination. "If people like you don't get close to him early enough to be
able to talk to him," Young advised Woodcock, "it could be a bad scene."
Young recommended that Woodcock "stop being coy" and endorse
Carter. To convince other board members, Woodcock cited Young's rea-
soning and argued that the Georgian was the only candidate who could
beat Ford. Woodcock maintained that, on issues, "after discussion," Carter
"seemed to come down on the right side." It was, however, "outside
events" rather than the strength of Woodcock's arguments that won the
majority over to Carter. Although Carter came in a poor fourth in the New
York primary, the press treated him as the front-runner because of his victories in North Carolina, Illinois, and Wisconsin.[13]

As Carter gained a commanding lead, Fraser told Woodcock "if Carter
won Pennsylvania...I was prepared to move to Carter" in the Michigan
primary. "If we did not," Fraser felt, "people might charge labor was using
its influence disproportionately."[14] After Carter's Pennsylvania victory on
April 27, the Carter bandwagon appeared unstoppable and the UAW was
ready to get on board.[15]

UAW officials and Carter staffers had already laid the groundwork for
the union's endorsement. Carter staffer Stuart Eizenstat recalled that
national health insurance (NHI) was the key issue, a condition of the
UAW's support. UAW and Carter people worked together on Carter's
April 16, 1976, speech to the National Student Medical Association outlining his support for NHI. The union was flexible on the specifics, but
Eizenstat remembers, it had some "litmus tests" of a minimum program—
"universality, comprehensiveness, [and a] mandatory system." Carter
proposed a nationwide mandatory health insurance program financed
through employer and payroll taxes as well as general tax revenues. The
Carter plan would provide for setting of institutional rates and doctor
fees, uniform benefits, uniform standards of care, and freedom to choose
one's physician. The *New York Times* reported that Carter's proposal
"seemed almost identical" to the Kennedy-Corman bill to establish a single payer national health system except that Carter indicated in response
to a question that there might be private administration of part of the program.[16] The next day, when a delegate told Carter he had given a great

speech on NHI, Carter replied, "It should be. Leonard Woodcock wrote it."[17]

Two UAW vice presidents and the six UAW regional directors in Michigan formally endorsed Carter on May 6 and the union released funds for use on Carter's behalf in the May 18 Michigan primary. Woodcock added his personal endorsement the next day, commenting: "If a political genius had offered to produce a candidate who could carry the working class as well as the crucial black, moderate, and liberal votes in the North, and at the same time defeat the strident segregationists of the South, he would have been called a dreamer. And yet that is what Jimmy Carter has done." Woodcock later recalled that there was "amazing rank and file support for Carter in our membership...because we have...tens of thousands of ex-hillbillies or children of people who came up from the South in the auto plants." Carter won a narrow victory in Michigan. Polling data showed that members of other unions supported Udall by 50 percent to 35 percent while UAW members backed Carter by a 53 percent to 35 percent margin. With Frank Church winning the Nebraska primary the previous week and Jerry Brown winning the Maryland primary by a landslide on the day of the Michigan primary, Woodcock recalled, "it would have been curtains" for Carter if he had lost in Michigan, too. Carter called Woodcock the next day and said, "I know why I'm still a candidate. I will never forget it."[18]

Despite some additional bumps in the road, Carter continued to pile up delegates and was able to assure his nomination before the Democratic convention opened. Hoping to win in November, Democrats rallied around the Carter candidacy. Carter staffers secured a platform that avoided controversial issues or specific commitments but adhered to traditional Democratic positions. Carter negotiated effectively with women and African American delegates and reassured liberals and labor when, as Woodcock recommended, he selected Senator Walter Mondale, a liberal, as his running mate. A united and enthusiastic convention resulted.[19]

The close relationship Carter and Woodcock had established during the primary season continued during a difficult general election campaign. The UAW's substantial campaign activities included the organization of phone banks in 12 states and the distribution of more than 30 million leaflets, buttons, stickers, and peanuts in the month of October. A UAW-CAP registration drive claimed close to 250,000 new voters. The UAW also participated in the electoral activities of the Clearinghouse, Operation Big Vote, and the Labor Council for Latin American Advancement.[20] The UAW played a significant part in Carter's narrow victory in the general election.[21]

The UAW leadership had reason to be optimistic. Carter's campaign had emphasized some liberal themes and the president-elect had great respect for UAW leaders and pledged to consult them often. Although Carter's electoral margin was slim, the Democrats had decisive majorities in both houses of Congress.[22]

Carter consulted with Woodcock during the transition process on his Cabinet selections. The UAW was invited to have a representative on the Carter transition team. In turning down this offer, Stephen Schlossberg, Director of Government and Public Affairs for the UAW, told Landon Butler, Carter's labor liaison, "I think we would be more content to maintain [a] regular institutional lunch once a week between you and me and regular telephone contact rather than send someone over."[23] Woodcock, who was required to step down as UAW president at the UAW's upcoming spring 1977 convention because of his age, was expected to be named secretary of Health, Education, and Welfare (HEW). He decided to remove himself from consideration for that position because he thought it might magnify widespread cynicism about the political process. He did not want anyone to think his early support for Carter had been motivated by a desire to further his own career. Nevertheless, Woodcock personally and the UAW institutionally were in on the ground floor of the new administration. After retiring as UAW president, Woodcock in May 1977 accepted a position as U.S. emissary to the People's Republic of China.[24]

In the first few weeks of his administration, Carter ran into problems with the labor movement on economic policy, the minimum wage, and common site picketing. In April, AFL-CIO Secretary Treasurer Lane Kirkland charged that Carter was failing to keep his promises to working people.[25] The language of UAW leaders was more temperate. On a "Meet the Press" broadcast on May 29, 10 days after he succeeded Leonard Woodcock as UAW president, Douglas Fraser made a few mild criticisms of the president but said he was encouraged by Carter's speech to the union's convention affirming that he would introduce NHI legislation early in 1978.[26]

Carter responded to pressure from labor and the civil rights community united in the Coalition for a Fair Minimum Wage, and the two sides reached a compromise in July. AFL-CIO leaders remained quite critical, however, of the administration's decision to put priority on balancing the budget rather than job creation.[27] For the UAW, labor law reform and national health insurance were the two key issues that would determine the value of its alliance with Jimmy Carter. Labor law reform was the first priority: "If we can't win this issue in the months immediately ahead, then we didn't win the election last November, it's that simple," Fraser told the Democratic Socialist Organizing Committee.[28]

During the spring of 1977, the AFL-CIO drafted a comprehensive labor law reform bill. Commenting on the AFL-CIO proposal as it was taking shape, Carter advisers Stu Eizenstat and Bill Johnston wrote to the president: "We can greatly help ourselves with labor by sending a Message and taking a leadership role on at least *some* (not all)" of the proposed changes. Why not all? Eizenstat and Johnston identified several provisions that they regarded as "controversial." Most important was section 14B of the

Taft-Hartley Act, which allows states to outlaw the union shop. "Our active support for the bill will be made more difficult if the AFL-CIO retains the most controversial aspects through mark-up, especially [the repeal of section] 14B."[29] During the campaign, Carter had promised to sign a repeal measure if it passed the Congress but also had said he would not advocate repeal. Although the trade unions viewed repeal of 14B as highly important, reforms addressing the process of union certification and securing of first contracts now loomed more important. "You've got to have a union in the plant before you can have a union shop," said Leonard Woodcock.[30]

After several rounds of negotiations with the Labor Department, the AFL-CIO agreed to drop repeal of 14B, a provision that would have required employers taking over a business to honor the existing union contract, and a provision to allow some certifications of bargaining agents via a card-check process. Eizenstat advised Carter that "the AFL-CIO accepted these major compromises, along with a number of lesser ones, because they *very much* want Administration backing for their bill." Eizenstat outlined three courses of action: (1) neutrality, "The unions would consider this tantamount to opposition"; (2) a labor law reform message outlining general concepts; (3) a message together with an administration bill. Eizenstat, Vice President Mondale, and Secretary of Labor Ray Marshall all favored an administration bill. The UAW's Stephen Schlossberg expressed "how very important it is for us—and you folks—...that it be a *bill FROM THE ADMINISTRATION.*" Schlossberg noted that a bill could "repair relations which, as you know, need repairs." He also argued that an administration bill could be a "vehicle which can help get the UAW back into the AFL-CIO, which result can work to the long term good not only of labor and the country but also of the Carter Administration." Knowing that Eizenstat favored an administration bill, Schlossberg declared, "I hope you win this one for *everybody!*"[31]

Eizenstat outlined the reforms agreed upon by the Labor Department and the AFL-CIO and told Carter: "If you agree with most of these reforms...an Administration bill is the option with the most political benefit. It is difficult to overestimate the importance of this matter in terms of our future relationship with organized labor. Because of budget constraints and fiscal considerations, we will be unable to satisfy their desires in many areas requiring expenditure of government funds. This is an issue without adverse budget considerations, which the unions very much want. I think it can help cement our relations for a good while."[32]

In supporting Eizenstat's recommendation, Mondale commented that the reforms were "relatively modest" and that "labor representatives have been moderate and constructive."[33] Hamilton Jordan, Carter's chief political adviser, supported an administration bill and stressed that the bill's focus on the removal of inequities in the execution of the law was consistent with the administration's general approach. In contrast with the "narrow special interest" labor issues with which the administration had so far dealt, Jordan argued, labor law reform had "strong *broad* support, particularly from the 'progressive' unions—the UAW, the Machinists, CWA, etc. *These unions represent our real base of support in labor—it is important that we honor their priorities.*" Jordan also noted that a unified labor reform endeavor would aid the effort of UAW leaders to convince its membership to reaffiliate with the AFL-CIO and thereby "bring fresh, progressive and reasonable ideas into an organization (the AFL-CIO) which is now stale and obstreperous."[34]

Carter carefully reviewed the proposed reforms and affirmed support for most of them. He questioned 6 of 13 proposals, however, among them "equal assured opportunity" to unions to address employees. Carter noted that "property rights can kill [the] entire bill" and that "this will be the postcard campaign theme" of bill opponents. Carter also questioned a proposal "to allow workers involved in a *first strike* over economic issues to displace" replacement workers, a provision subsequently dropped from the bill. Carter turned aside the recommendation for an administration bill, preferring a message endorsing "concepts and principles."[35]

On July 18, the president sent his labor law reform message to Congress. He outlined three main goals of the reform: making National Labor Relations Board (NLRB) procedures "fairer, prompter, and more predictable," protecting the "rights of labor and management by strengthening NLRB sanctions against those who break the law," and preserving "the integrity of the federal contracting process by withholding federal contracts from firms that willfully violated orders from the NLRB and the courts." That day, Secretary Marshall held a press conference to explain the proposed legislation in more detail than was contained in the president's message. In his opening statement, Marshall said "the President will send legislation to Congress today on labor law reform." Later in the conference, Marshall realized his error: "Let me correct an impression. I erroneously referred to the President's message as a bill. But the bill, of course, will have to come from Congress. There is no bill."[36] In reality, there *was* an administration-negotiated bill, but Carter's *personal stake* in the measure was a limited one.

In the 11 months between the issuance of his message and the eventual failure to break the Senate filibuster against the bill, Carter made no public addresses on the issue. On the few occasions when he commented on the bill, he provided little help to the cause. Three days after sending his message to Congress, Carter attended a dedication ceremony for a new gymnasium in Yazoo City, Mississippi. At a public question-and-answer session following the meeting, carried live by the Public Broadcasting Service, he was asked why he supported changes "which will have the effect of making it much easier for big labor to organize in the South." Carter's initial response to the question was confused and defensive and accepted the use of the term "big labor" so resented by trade unionists: "I am not sure that the purpose of the legislation," the president stated, "would lead to heavier organization by big labor in the South." Contrast Carter's statement with that of John Kennedy in response to the "big labor" accusation in 1960: "The size of organized labor is a blessing—and its strength is a powerful force for the good of all America." Carter did succeed in getting across a principal goal of the legislation: "If...workers in a plant vote to organize," he explained, "then the new proposal would make sure that management has to comply with the law." Carter passed up an opportunity to make a clear-cut pro-labor statement in the kind of setting where such leadership was most needed. Instead, he concluded: "I don't think that the legislation would lead to more rapid establishment of union workers in the South. There is a heavy emphasis now on unionizing some of our plants in the South. I don't think this legislation would affect it one way or the other in any material way."[37]

In an October telephone interview with members of the National Newspaper Association, Carter told a questioner who criticized the legislation as one-sided that it was "much more moderate or conservative or much more inclined toward the employer's position than it was in its original form because I have the same concern that you do." As he warmed to the subject, Carter did make some positive comments about the bill, but his preference for a neutral approach remained and he continued to show a weak grasp of the specifics of the bill.[38]

Although Carter's public advocacy was weak, his staff and the AFL-CIO worked effectively with the House of Representatives. In addition to lobbying in Congress, the AFL-CIO conducted a major public relations and grassroots campaign with the help of funds generated by a special assessment. It received support from allies such as the National Organization for Women, the NAACP, the United States Catholic Conference, and a coalition of environmentalist organizations. Perhaps most helpful to picking up moderate support for the bill was the congressional testimony in support of the bill offered by John Dunlop on behalf of all former secretaries of labor in both Republican and Democratic administrations. The House passed the labor law reform bill on October 6, 1977, by a margin of 257–163.[39]

After the House passed the bill, the AFL-CIO attempted but was unsuccessful in getting the Senate to move toward immediate consideration. The delay until January 1978 of the Senate Human Resource subcommittee's review led to a loss of momentum and gave business the opportunity to organize a powerful campaign against the legislation. The Senate committee reported out a somewhat weakened bill on January 25, 1978, but the AFL-CIO's wish for immediate consideration was again turned aside. The Carter administration wanted full Senate consideration delayed until

after the Panama Canal treaties were debated and passed. When he outlined "crucial votes" coming up in this session of Congress at the January
30 cabinet meeting, Carter mentioned the Panama Canal treaties and the
national energy plan but not labor law reform.[40]

Once the Panama Canal treaties were passed on April 18, 1978, the
administration and the Senate were ready to turn their attention to labor
law reform. With the Senate debate finally scheduled to begin on May 15,
Carter met for breakfast on May 9 with labor and congressional leaders.
He pledged to continue his support in what would be a "long and bitter
battle" in the Senate. Later that day, Marshall suggested that Carter meet
with "victims of labor law violations to let you hear first hand what these
workers have to say." Marshall also suggested he begin a press conference
with a statement on labor law reform "from the perspective of a business-
man." Eizenstat opposed both a meeting with workers and a press conference statement. In his view, the "battle...has now narrowed to a half
dozen Senators. Their votes won't be affected by Presidential publicity." In
Eizenstat's view, it was the administration's "willingness to use maximum
pressure to help stop the filibuster" that would win more goodwill from
the AFL-CIO. "And from a national political standpoint the less visible
you are on this issue, the better."[41] Carter met with no "victims" and made
no press conference statement.

When Senate debate on the measure opened, conservative senators
launched the expected filibuster. By this time, the business campaign
against the bill was in high gear. The story of the coordinated campaign
against the bill by all of the country's business groups—from the Fortune
500 companies in the Business Roundtable to the National Federation of
Independent Business—has been described well in the literature. "Between
January and May," David Vogel notes, "senators received more than eight
million pieces of mail and were visited by thousands of their constituents."
Senator Jennings Randolph told Secretary Marshall that the opposition
campaign was the most powerful he had seen in his 45-year Senate career.
White House aides Moore and Thomson called it "the most expensive and
powerful lobby ever mounted against a bill in the nation's history."[42]

The AFL-CIO labor law reform task force and the Americans for Justice
on the Job, a coalition of 200 organizations with 80 million members,
attempted to counter the business campaign. Actions by the bill's supporters included a postcard campaign, a lobbying effort by 1,000 steel
workers, and visits to senators and their aides by victims of law violations
from 20 unions. With far fewer resources and channels of communication,
the mobilization by labor supporters failed to match that of the bill's
opponents. In keeping with George Meany's long-standing opposition to
mass demonstrations, the AFL-CIO leadership rejected a proposal by the
task force and several unions to hold a march on Washington of 200,000 to
300,000.[43]

While the bill was being debated in the Senate, Carter met with Senate Majority Leader Robert Byrd (D-WV), bill sponsors Senators Harrison Williams (D-NJ) and Jacob Javits (R-NY), and Secretary Marshall on June 5. The president told reporters he called the meeting "to reaffirm my own commitment to passing labor law reform." The bill was "both needed and moderate," Carter said. When questioned about the bill on other occasions, however, Carter indicated he was ready to see it further weakened. On May 26, a Republican state senator told Carter that the bill was "one of the most dangerous and disastrous pieces of legislation for our free enterprise system" and asked why Carter supported the provision for "blacklisting businesses" which violated the act. Carter effectively defended that provision but then suggested that giving unions access to the employers' property "bothers a lot of Americans." He reassured his questioner "that some of the things of concern to you might very well be changed." Then, on June 9, Carter responded to a reporter's query about the likelihood that labor law reform would be passed with the comment "with those amendments to be offered to remove the more difficult political aspects of the bill...it will be passed."[44]

The administration's congressional lobbyists worked hard to get the votes to break the filibuster, but after the fifth cloture vote on June 15, the bill's supporters were still two votes short of the 60 needed to end debate. On June 16 and 17, Carter visited Panama for a treaty-signing ceremony. After he returned to the White House, Carter was informed by Eizenstat and Johnston: "It appears that it will be more difficult to get the additional two Senators needed to invoke cloture than had been originally thought." This was "an unusual opportunity to show the depth of our commitment to labor." They reported labor to be "very satisfied with our efforts thus far" but that "your own standing with the AFL-CIO and other unions would be greatly enhanced if, at this critical juncture, you publicly became more involved in the effort to get cloture." Accordingly, they recommended a consultative call to Meany or Kirkland and individual meetings with Senators John Sparkman (D-AL), Russell Long (D-LA), Dale L. Bumpers (D-AR), and Edward Zorinsky (D-NE) to attempt to win their votes.[45]

Les Francis, assistant to congressional liaison Frank Moore, opposed immediate meetings with the senators named by Eizenstat and Johnston because contacts were in progress with all four. "Any involvement by the President with any Senators should be at the behest of Bob Thomson or the Vice President," he maintained. Carter noted on Eizenstat's memo that he called Senators Bumpers, Hollings, and Byrd and also phoned Meany and Marshall. The president's daily diary indicates he did not complete the call to Hollings, spoke with Meany for 1 minute, Byrd for 3 minutes, Marshall for 6 minutes, and with Bumpers for 11 minutes. He met with no senators. He did spend 34 minutes that afternoon attending a demonstration of the presentation of Census Bureau information using NASA technology. He also spent over an hour at the White House bowling alley that evening. Thomson's status report on the day's events concluded: "We are still one vote short. We may ask you on short notice to meet with any or all" of three targeted senators during "the next 48 hours." There was no inclination to wheel and deal to get the bill passed. Thomson commented: "If concessions are made on the bill, they should be made by labor in bargaining sessions with the target senators. Our role should remain that of a catalyst." He noted that, if someone asked for something unrelated to the bill, "We must...be prepared to consider [these] requests," hardly an indication that the president or his staff regarded labor law reform as must legislation for which they needed to use their political capital. The bill was sent back to committee on June 22 and died there.[46]

In contrast with his approach and effort on the Panama Canal treaties, Carter did not take the initiative to fight for labor law reform as his own issue. Secretary Marshall had to ask Carter about his "willingness to contact and meet with Senators" on labor law reform. On the Panama Canal treaties, "the President invited hundreds of opinion-leaders to the White House; answered questions regarding the treaties at various town meetings; and dispatched...top officials around the country for lectures and other forums defending the treaties.... President Carter personally made eighty-seven phone calls to senators in the two weeks before the vote on the first treaty." Among those Carter mobilized to help win treaty ratification was none other than Doug Fraser, who called five senators at Carter's request![47]

Trade union leaders were greatly disappointed with the failure to pass the labor law reform bill. A quarter century later, the significance of that defeat looms large. Carter was an ally in the fight to pass the bill, but defeats often lead to recriminations. Landon Butler concluded that "most rank-and-file labor leaders blamed the labor law reform loss on the Administration, and the leadership did little to discourage that view."[48] Eizenstat acknowledged in 1993 that "to this day they [the unions] feel that if Carter only really wanted it," labor law reform "somehow would have happened, which is not true. Carter did want it. We put an enormous amount of time into it." Eizenstat considered the failure to call the bill an "administration bill" unimportant. On the question of presidential publicity, Eizenstat commented that labor law reform, while "a very important political issue...it's hardly the kind of issue which the president takes to the country.... Labor has a certain limited constituency.... Can you imagine a president getting in the Oval Office and having a nationwide address on labor law reform?"[49] Even Carter's most liberal advisers looked upon the labor movement as a politically important interest group rather than a social movement whose cause was just.

UAW leaders, for their part, put the blame on business and the undemocratic 60-vote Senate rule rather than on presidential shortcomings. On August 11, 1978, Doug Fraser wrote to the president to "convey to you my personal and sincere thanks, and those of the UAW, for the great effort you made on this lost cause. No one can fault you, Secretary Marshall, or your staff for failure of will. We just couldn't make it."[50]

Despite those generous comments, the defeat of labor law reform weakened the UAW's ties to the administration. On July 19, 1978, Fraser publicly resigned from the Labor Management Group, blasting "leaders of the business community" for waging a "one-sided class war...against working people, the unemployed, the poor, the minorities, the very young and the very old, and even many in the middle class of our society." He charged that business leaders had "broken and discarded the fragile, unwritten compact" under which "the business elite 'gave' a little bit— enabling government or interest groups to better conditions somewhat" for the have-nots of American society. Fraser characterized the business community's fight against labor law reform as "the most vicious, unfair attack upon the labor movement in more than 30 years."[51]

Citing General Motors' southern strategy as a case in point, Fraser contended: "Where industry once yearned for subservient unions, it now wants no unions at all." Fraser said he saw "no point to continue sitting down at Labor-Management Group meetings...seeking unity with the leaders of American industry, while they try to destroy us and ruin the lives of the people I represent." To respond to this situation, Fraser said the UAW intended to "reforge the links with those who believe in struggle" by "making new alliances and forming new coalitions."[52]

In a press conference discussing his withdrawal, Fraser was asked, "To what degree are you withdrawing your support to President Carter?" The UAW President responded, "Well, I don't think he is involved in this situation, except.... The problem is that it's an ineffective Administration, and therefore you can't come to grips with the problems of the American people." Fraser acknowledged that factors such as the war in Vietnam and Watergate meant that any president would be confronted with a shift in power from the executive branch to the Congress. "I could say that's a product of history or I could say it's because of the man's personality. But we're at a point in history [where] it doesn't make any difference." Although he stressed Congress's failure to enact administrative proposals and the party irresponsibility of 17 Senate Democrats voting against cloture on the labor law reform bill, he thought the administration "has to learn the difference between compromise and capitulation." When asked about the 1980 elections, Fraser implied some regret about the UAW's role in 1976, contending that the primary system meant people were "asked to endorse and support a candidate who you don't know." Although he could support Carter for reelection in 1980, it was too early to comment on the presidential primaries.[53]

Already weakened, the UAW-Carter alliance came apart over Carter's failure to carry out his promise to the UAW to introduce legislation for national health insurance. This had been the condition of the union's initial endorsement of Carter and it was a failure the UAW could not accept.

The UAW had long championed the goal of national health insurance. In a 1968 address to the American Public Health Association, Walter Reuther announced the formation of a Committee of 100 for National Health Insurance. This organization became the labor-based Committee for National Health Insurance (CNHI). The UAW supplied about one-quarter of the funding for CNHI. Reuther served as chair of the organization, as did Woodcock and Fraser as they succeeded to the UAW presidency.[54]

As the UAW's first legislative conference of the Carter administration was about to open on the last day of February 1977, Douglas Fraser declared: "But first things first, and I would put national health insurance at the very top of the list. We have to start getting things in place right now to enact a comprehensive national health security bill." When Carter spoke before the UAW convention on May 17, 1977, he reiterated his support for the issue to loud applause and said the administration was "aiming to submit legislative proposals early next year." Given his fiscal conservatism, however, Carter's health care focus in 1977 was on legislation to control hospital costs. Only if fiscal prudence were established first would it be sensible to move forward and spend money on a new program, Carter thought. Fiscal prudence found few supporters and many enemies and the legislation did not pass. The UAW repeatedly pushed Carter to take action on national health insurance, which, unlike narrowly focused cost containment, had a broad national constituency. With a national system, costs could be controlled, the UAW argued.[55]

Carter responded to the UAW's strong entreaties with delaying tactics. In April 1977, HEW Secretary Joseph Califano established an advisory committee on the issue with the CNHI, the UAW, and other labor unions represented along with such opponents of NHI as Carter economic and budget advisors Charles Schultz, Robert Strauss, James McIntyre, and Michael Blumenthal. The UAW kept pressing for action.[56]

On February 6, 1978, Carter directed that the NHI policy be developed through his new Domestic Policy Review Process. Under this process, a coordinating committee would analyze options for the president's decision memorandum. This was supposed to be ready at the end of March so the president could "announce his principles" in April and move toward legislation that summer. On March 2, 1978, Carter discussed the timing of the legislation with key cabinet and staff members. Secretaries Califano and Blumenthal advocated a delay in legislative action until 1979. Hamilton Jordan argued for immediate action: "The President has a political commitment to the UAW, and the UAW is the best political organization in the country and the most powerful. At a time when our public opinion polls are down, we've got to stay close to powerful organizations like this.... The UAW wants to go to every congressman in the country and offer to help them in their campaigns if they will support NHI. That's the way to get the bill passed." Califano recalled that Carter at first was moved by Jordan's remarks but then accepted Califano's recommendation to announce principles in April and delay legislation until 1979.[57]

When Carter met with Fraser, Meany, Senator Edward Kennedy (D-MA), and other key health care players on April 6, he told them, "I have a standard procedure to involve Cabinet officers in basic decisions and that process will take a month or a month and a half.... This must be done *within* our Administration." The truth was, it had already been in the cabinet review process for two months. So far, the HEW had produced a first draft of the decision memorandum. More important than the bureaucratic delay, in the UAW and Kennedy view, was that the HEW draft had distorted the UAW proposal so that it appeared to be a budget-buster. In reality, the UAW and Kennedy were being flexible and pragmatic in crafting a proposal whose first-year costs would be no more than $30 billion. In contrast to its approach on labor law reform, the Carter administration held the UAW and AFL-CIO at arm's length on NHI. Carter rejected Kennedy's suggestion to establish a working group that would include the labor experts. When Fraser told Carter, "Our point of view could get lost in the shuffle," the president replied, "You will be fully involved at the right time."[58]

In its attempt to secure Carter's support, the UAW and Kennedy had moved away from the concept of a single public system to one in which private health plans would compete for subscribers. When the members of the CNHI and its political action arm, the Health Security Action Coalition, heard about the new proposal at an April 18 conference, "all hell broke lo[o]se," a UAW staffer reported. "Almost to a person, all speakers expressed profound concern about having the insurance carriers participate in a National Health Plan." There was little prospect for mobilizing grassroots backing behind a proposal that was too conservative for health care activists but too liberal for the president.[59]

Carter's promised legislative proposal was still far off when he made public at the end of July the principles that he believed should underlie a national health insurance program. Carter proposed phased-in health reform, with progress to the next phase dependent on the state of the economy. Fraser was "saddened and disappointed." The UAW did not oppose a phased-in plan but insisted that "such phasing must be in the context of a full and comprehensive plan to go to Congress *as a single entity.*" Fraser concluded that "the Administration is unwilling or unable to make the necessary commitment to the major elements of a national health insurance program." Kennedy, Meany, Kirkland, and leaders of several health, senior citizen, consumer, and church groups protested the Carter policy at a Washington press conference. Kirkland noted that the pro-NHI groups had tried their best to accommodate the president, but the situation had "gone beyond the point where we any longer feel we have a clear mutual understanding or agreement on either the tactical methods of pursuing this bill or its contents."[60]

The UAW, the CNHI, and Kennedy worked together to develop a new compromise proposal. Without presidential leadership, however, there was little chance to enact NHI. Fraser declared it "an absolute tragedy" that "after all the years of hard work by so many people on behalf of national health insurance...his Administration came forth with a program we could not support." The union feared that the opportunity to develop a national health care program might be lost for a generation. The UAW's sense of loss was, indeed, profound. Carter had proved to be an unreliable ally.[61]

Carter's ineffectiveness on labor law reform and his breach of promise on health care were the decisive factors in causing the break with the UAW. Was there a personal element to Carter's failure to maintain his alliance with the UAW? Carter's style, Gary Fink has commented, his "peculiar combination of social liberalism, fiscal conservatism, and self-righteous moralism," contributed to communication problems with labor leaders. Fink argues that many labor leaders had anti-southern prejudices and that George Meany, in particular, made the mistake of continuing a rigid confrontational style he had developed during the Nixon and Ford years.[62] Journalist Haynes Johnson quoted an anonymous labor official's early remark about Carter: "'We noted that captivating smile that stopped at the eyes.'"[63]

Whatever personal animosity some labor leaders may have felt, candidate Carter developed good rapport with UAW President Woodcock. Woodcock recalled that, at his first meeting with Carter, he was "very much attracted to the man...one on one he's very impressive, he's an intelligent man, well read."[64] Woodcock and Carter developed an intimate relationship during the 1976 campaign, but the personal element became less important when Fraser succeeded Woodcock as UAW president. Fraser recalled, however, that Carter as president had an "open door policy" with the UAW. Fraser developed a good personal relationship with Carter and regarded him as "a very nice man." Although Fraser was critical of Carter's style and "resent[ed] people wearing their religion on their sleeve," he describes Carter as "a good man, sincere and honest, a man of great integrity." Carter's view of the UAW was similarly favorable. Eizenstat recalled that Carter felt the UAW was the most "broad-spirited" of all the unions and he "liked their leadership."[65]

It was not anyone's personality but Carter's philosophical orientation that led him into actions that disrupted his alliance with the UAW. Carter had decided to pursue the presidency when he met the contenders for the 1972 Democratic nomination and concluded, "Hell, I'm as good as they are." Carter's presidential goal, in Woodcock's view, was "honest, clean government." Woodcock was "never aware" that Carter "had any mission in mind either specific or general."[66] In the view of political scientist Charles Jones, Carter's vision was that he would function as a "trustee" for the nation. He would absorb the information from various experts and then act on behalf of the entire country. His ability to engage in effective negotiation and compromise with congressional leaders and representatives of key constituencies was weakened by this vision of the presidency.[67]

Carter, influenced by his Naval Academy education and his seven years as a naval officer, believed that his role was to represent the nation as a whole and especially focus on foreign and defense policy issues. Carter told the cabinet that, "because of his background, he is interested in keeping in close touch with the military in various ways, including frequent meetings with the Joint Chiefs and visits on aircraft, nuclear submarines, etc." Both Carter's memoirs and those of Rosalynn Carter focus heavily on foreign affairs.[68]

Eizenstat characterizes Carter's overall political position as "moderate" and even "moderate-conservative" on fiscal matters, issues on which the unions were "very liberal." In terms of establishing a sound, working relationship with union leaders, moreover, Eizenstat believes Carter was handicapped by his lack of experience with union leaders. Eizenstat characterizes Carter's philosophy as "populist," by which he means that Carter had an "innate distrust of large institutions."[69] Given Carter's sense that his goal was to represent the general public interest, he lacked an ability to listen well to the views of labor leaders.

Carter's technocratic approach to the presidency, the absence, in Hamilton Jordan's words, of "a unifying philosophy in the White House," led to an inability on Carter's part to lead public opinion. "At some point during that first year," Mondale recalled, "Carter lost confidence in his ability to lead public opinion. He told me once that people no longer listened to what he had to say."[70] Mondale complained: "I never understood how Carter's political mind worked. He had been a loner for so many years that he was in many ways unpredictable, stubborn, often reclusive. He did not get out many times and fight for an issue. He had no confidence in his ability to do that. He wanted to lead the country through hard gifted work. He wanted to persuade the country, like every good engineer does, with numbers and figures, not passion and eloquence."[71]

No longer willing to rely on Carter, the UAW voiced frequent criticisms of the administration's overall course and sought another channel to express its political aspirations. Its alternative political strategy included the initiation of a new coalition of progressive organizations, a protest against Carter's budget priorities at the Democratic party midterm conference, and support for Kennedy's campaign to replace Carter as the Democratic nominee. Although there was no longer a working alliance,

UAW leaders still maintained "friendly contact" with the administration. The UAW continued to support Carter on a variety of issues, including the Camp David accords, hospital cost containment, and the SALT treaty.[72] For his part, Carter continued to provide help to the UAW on issues of immediate concern to it. We "never requested a meeting that wasn't granted," Fraser recalled. On the Chrysler loan guarantee issue, the UAW and Carter each made an "independent judgment" and came out in "the same place." Fraser credited Carter with being "in there with both feet." Eizenstat asked Treasury Secretary Miller to keep Fraser and Detroit Mayor Coleman Young "fully informed" about the Chrysler situation and advised him: "They are both very close to the President."[73]

As a follow-up to his resignation from the Labor Management Group, Fraser issued a call to progressive organizations for a one-day conference to form a new alliance that could wage "a vigorous counterattack against the right wing corporate forces and the political system they dominate." About a hundred organizations representing 20 million people came together at the October 17, 1978, founding meeting of the Progressive Alliance, including many national unions, civil rights, women's, environmental, consumer, and liberal organizations. The UAW's goal was to unite several streams of progressivism into a river of left pressure to counter the ocean of pressure from the right on the political system. "We thought we're so goddam fragmented... if we get all these progressive voices together we could really organize in one very substantial and powerful group," Fraser recalled. The Progressive Alliance program of activity was rather limited, however, so that the streams never really quite came together.[74]

Alliance activities were educational and preparatory, such as holding conferences on the problem of plant shutdowns and commissioning and publishing studies on issues such as stagflation and the impact of corporate money on the political process. Alliance leaders rejected a proposal to organize a march on Washington to protest Carter budget cuts and discouraged attempts to form local branches of the coalition. As a result, there was only a very limited grassroots component to the coalition; it ended up being little more than a letterhead organization.[75]

If the decision to refrain from grassroots organizing was the Progressive Alliance's fatal flaw, how can this decision be explained? Seeing recent defeats as stemming in large part from the failure of Democratic office-holders in the White House and the Congress to implement their party's platform, the main strategy was to bring about party reform and the main tactic to work within the Democratic party. Thus Fraser and other Progressive Alliance members supported the efforts of two liberal Democratic groups, the Democratic Conference and the Democratic Agenda, to reform party procedures and protest Carter administration policies at the Democratic party midterm conference in December 1978.[76] Fraser led a protest against Carter budget priorities of increasing defense spending while reducing expenditures for social programs. A rousing speech by Senator Kennedy highlighted the differences between the liberal wing of the party and the administration. To defeat the challenge, Carter's forces "pulled out all the stops" and carried the day. With the votes of 40 percent of the delegates, however, the liberals won a public relations victory. Jody Powell, Carter's press secretary, complained that the "analysis on the networks and in print was that Carter might have 'controlled' the organization, but Kennedy had won the 'cheers' and 'hearts' of the delegates."[77]

Despite the favorable media attention, the Alliance had not changed the direction of the Democratic party nor had it mobilized its constituent elements into a mass movement. Working within the Democratic party structure had limited appeal. As Stan Weir commented at the time: "It may well be that millions of American workers vote the Democratic Party ticket, but it is not an arena that a mass of people can get into."[78]

Aside from the Alliance's narrow strategy, an additional factor in the shift of the UAW away from the militant progressivism voiced at the Alliance's founding was the threatening bankruptcy of the Chrysler Corporation in 1979 and the subsequent economic difficulties of the auto industry as a whole. Increasingly, the union leadership turned its attention to the immediate economic problems of autoworkers. Describing the union's response to the industry's economic difficulties, a Ford Local 900 bargaining committee representative observed: "Our priority is keeping as many people employed as we can and preserving preferred jobs for the older, higher-seniority workers." As the quadrennial contest for the presidency drew near, however, the possibilities of mobilizing union members and changing the direction of the Democratic party and the country reappeared.[79]

On February 13, 1979, the UAW Executive Board decided to maintain neutrality in the presidential race. This stance was reaffirmed the next month. Despite the neutrality policy, UAW regional directors for the Illinois-Iowa and Missouri regions joined a movement to draft Kennedy in June and July.[80] Fraser hesitated to join this effort because he was focusing on gaining administration support for Chrysler. On the same day that Carter decided to support loan guarantees for Chrysler, he asked Fraser to keep the UAW from campaigning for Kennedy in the Iowa presidential caucus. Kennedy formally announced his candidacy in November 1979. Eight days after Carter signed the Chrysler Corporation Loan Guarantee Act on January 7, 1980, Fraser endorsed Kennedy. While the UAW campaigned hard for Kennedy in Iowa and other states, Carter retained a base of support within the union. Of 800 delegates attending a CAP Council meeting in Washington, 120 attended a reception for Carter-Mondale supporters at which the president dropped by.[81]

As the leading figure in the liberal wing of the Democratic party, Kennedy gained the support of those unionists, such as William W. Winpisinger, president of the International Association of Machinists, who were most dissatisfied with Carter's failure to adhere to a consistently liberal course. Kennedy gained support also from those who felt close to the Kennedy family because of its role in the liberal gains of the 1960s and because of the assassinations of John and Robert Kennedy. To another group of labor leaders, however, Carter's record on general labor issues and on the specific problems of their unions was sufficient to warrant their continued support of the president. Among the Carter supporters was J.C. Turner of the Operating Engineers, a member of the Progressive Alliance executive committee. A third group of unionists and the AFL-CIO Executive Council took a neutral position. The AFL-CIO leadership was pleased when the Carter administration in 1979 demonstrated increased recognition of the importance of the trade union movement when it negotiated a National Accord with the AFL-CIO to "provide for American labor's involvement and cooperation with the Administration on important national issues."[82]

Kennedy led Carter in early opinion polls by 2 to 1 when his potential candidacy drew the support of the many Democrats dissatisfied with Carter's performance. Once he declared his candidacy, however, Kennedy's support began to erode. The additional scrutiny that candidates generally receive once they declare was a factor, as was the onset of the hostage crisis. In a system in which the focus is on the individual candidate as a person rather than as leader of a party, Kennedy was a flawed personal figure. Chappaquidick was "Kennedy's albatross," Doug Fraser said, adding, "It [Chappaquidick] bothered me. Wives of some of my best friends and liberal allies would not vote for him."[83]

The UAW leadership stood with Kennedy in 1980 because of its longstanding relationship with him, their close partnership on the issue of health care reform, and his popularity with large sections of the union membership. When it was clear that Kennedy's candidacy was going to be unsuccessful, however, Fraser publicly called on him to get out of the race, angering Kennedy's campaign people. Disappointed as Fraser was with the Carter presidency, an ultra-right Ronald Reagan as president looked far worse. The UAW endorsed Carter for reelection and worked hard on his behalf, as did most other unions. Dissatisfaction over the state of the economy and the hostage crisis, however, ultimately led the voters to repudiate Carter.[84]

In election day balloting, Carter's support declined from the 50 percent he had received in 1976 to 41 percent. Low turnout by those who preferred Carter was a factor, but polling data indicate he would have lost to Reagan by a 5-point instead of 10-point margin if all adults had voted. Carter's support among voters in union families declined from 59 percent to 47 percent while his support among liberals declined from 70 percent to 57 percent. Only African American voters among core Democratic-leaning groups supported Carter at the same rate (82 percent) as they had in 1976. Voters from union households gave 5 percent more support to Reagan in 1980 than they had given to Ford in 1976 while 7 percent supported John Anderson. Although Anderson, a Republican congress member, had challenged Reagan in the Republican primaries, he drew his greatest support from liberal independents (15 percent), liberal Democrats (13 percent), and Jewish voters (14 percent).[85] "The labor movement, the Democratic Party, progressive forces generally have not dealt with the fundamental problems facing society," commented Jerry Wurf, president of the American Federation of State, County, and Municipal Employees. "For workers the perception of America the beautiful and the dream of upward mobility has been turning sour."[86] The progressive campaign of environmentalist Barry Commoner of the newly founded Citizens party received little media attention and recorded only 234,294 votes.[87] Two decades later, Ralph Nader's campaign as the candidate of the established Green party would provide a more visible and meaningful alternative to disaffected liberals and independents.

Were there roads not taken in the UAW-Carter relationship? Greater personal involvement and more forceful leadership by Carter on labor law reform and early action along the lines of his initial commitment to the UAW on health care would have kept the union at Carter's side. While suggesting that the Carter administration and the president personally did all they could to secure the passage of labor law reform, Marshall acknowledges that, "if we had gone into the Senate and put that bill up shortly after it passed the House, it would have passed the Senate."[88] The "fundamental mistake we made was not pushing for national health insurance in 1977...as our first initiative," Eizenstat believes. "We would have gotten at least pieces of it passed and we would have had the UAW on our side in four years and Kennedy blocked from running."[89]

Taylor Dark views labor support for Kennedy in 1980 as an attempt to revitalize the New Deal political order but argues that "New Deal liberalism...had decayed beyond any easy or forthright repair." Dark maintains that, even had Kennedy won the nomination and the presidency, he, too, would have faced unmanageable economic problems and a Congress in which business influence was growing while labor's was declining.[90] Like Dark, Gary Fink believes that Fraser's support for the Kennedy challenge was a "quixotic effort." He argues, moreover, that the Kennedy challenge "contributed to the growing public perception of a failed presidency." Union leaders were excessively critical of Carter, Fink contends, recognizing his many pro-labor accomplishments only when faced with the "odious alternatives of Ronald Reagan and John Anderson."[91]

Fraser himself later wondered if "we were too harsh" toward Carter and mistaken in supporting Kennedy. "Certainly it made it more difficult to reelect Carter," Fraser stated. "I shudder at the thought that we might have been responsible for Reagan."[92]

Given the disastrous impact of the Reagan and Bush administrations on the labor movement and, as Fraser puts it, Carter's role as "an absolutely great ex-president," second thoughts on the Carter presidency are to be expected. However, although other unions may have been contentious in their approach to Carter, the UAW was eminently practical, reasonable, and respectful toward the president when the alliance was strong and even after it came apart. It seems unlikely, moreover, that a more conciliatory course by Fraser and other labor leaders would have helped Carter's reelection bid. By the midpoint of his presidency, Carter had already alienated the liberal wing of the Democratic party and he moved further right in the last two years of his presidency: He continued to shift funds from domestic social programs to the military and approved the development of the MX missile system. In response to Soviet intervention in Afghanistan, Carter pulled the SALT treaty from the Senate, canceled U.S. participation in the Moscow Olympics, embargoed grain shipments to the Soviet Union, and reinstituted registration for the draft. Kennedy challenged Carter precisely because his presidency was perceived as failing, especially by core Democratic party constituencies. If anything, the Kennedy challenge caused the Carter administration to pay more attention to organized labor and may have somewhat slowed Carter's rightward shift. Liberals, labor, and feminists secured additions to the 1980 Democratic platform that Carter, for the most part, accepted.[93]

If the Kennedy insurgency was not the cause of the Democratic debacle in 1980, its liberal fruits were modest. The Progressive Alliance produced even fewer results. When Fraser resigned from the Labor Management Group, he noted that, historically, the "business elite 'gave' a little bit.... only after sustained struggle, such as that waged by the labor movement in the 1930's and the civil rights movement in the 1960's." Fraser's bold call to "reforge the links with those who believe in struggle" and the initiation of the Progressive Alliance signaled to many radicals a return to the politics of the popular front of the New Deal period.[94] Perhaps if the Progressive Alliance had pursued a strategy of organizing issue-oriented grassroots local coalitions and conducting mass protest activities, it might have begun a process of rebuilding the popular base of the frayed New Deal coalition. The Alliance would have faced the challenge of confronting new problems, such as stagflation, plant closings, and budget crises connected with the decline of the post–World War II hegemony of the United States. It also would have had to unify Democratic constituencies often divided on race relations, women's rights, and the environment.

Missing in the late 1970s were crucial elements connected with the success of the popular front and the New Deal, among them an effective liberal president, a left-influenced grassroots upsurge from below, and a labor leadership strategy more visionary than working within the Democratic party. As a result, the UAW and its allies in the Progressive Alliance were defeated by an activized business-right alliance that gained the political initiative during the Carter years and then captured the presidency in 1980.[95]

NOTES

1. William Crotty, *Party Reform* (New York: Longman, 1983), 131–33; Graham K. Wilson, *Unions in American National Politics* (New York: St. Martin's Press, 1979), 33–34, 48–50; Andrew Battista, "Political Divisions in Organized Labor, 1968–1988," *Polity* XXIV No. 2 (Winter 1991): 181–82.

2. Interview with Douglas Fraser, March 1, 1990; Betty Glad, *Jimmy Carter, In Search of the Great White House* (New York: W.W. Norton, 1980), 233, 238–41; Earl Black and Merle Black, *The Vital South: How Presidents Are Elected* (Cambridge, Mass.: Harvard University Press, 1992), 251; Hamilton Jordan, Discussant, "The Elections of 1976 and 1980," in Herbert D. Rosenbaum and Alexej Ugrinsky, eds., *Presidency and Domestic Politics of Jimmy Carter* (Westport, Conn.: Greenwood Press, 1994), 163.

3. Ten percent voted for other candidates or were not sure how they voted, 19 percent did not vote, and 6 percent were not sure if they voted.

4. Ford also led Bayh among skilled and white-collar workers, and among members under 35 years of age. Peter D. Hart Research Associates, A Survey of Opinions and Attitudes of UAW Regions 3 Members in Indiana, February 1976, President Woodcock Coll., Box 66, Archives of Labor History and Urban Affairs, Wayne State University, Detroit (hereafter cited as WSU).

5. Woodcock's view of Mo Udall in 1976 was that, while Udall would make a good president, he would be a "poor candidate" who would be "badly defeated." Interview with Leonard Woodcock, February 16, 1990.

6. Interview with Leonard Woodcock, February 16, 1990; *Ann Arbor Sun*, December 31, 1975/January 1, 1976.

7. Interview with Leonard Woodcock, February 16, 1990.

8. Jackson competed in Florida and came in third. Glad, *Jimmy Carter*, 231–32.

9. Clipping, *Fort Myers News Press*, March 3, 1976, President Woodcock Coll., Box 245, folder 5, WSU.

10. *Detroit News*, March 11, 1976.

11. Memorandum, Steve Protulis to Hank Lacayo, March 12, 1976, President Woodcock Coll., Box 11, folder 5, WSU.

12. Interview with Leonard Woodcock, February 16, 1990. Transcript of Meet the Press interview with Woodcock, September 5, 1976, 4, President Woodcock Coll., Box 243, WSU. Although Carter and Woodcock were both members of the Trilateral Commission, Woodcock recalled that they did not meet there. Woodcock also had no recollection of meeting Carter during a 1974 Democratic party fundraiser as cited in Dudley W. Buffa, *Union Power and American Democracy: The UAW and the Democratic Party* (Ann Arbor: University of Michigan Press, 1984), 147.

13. Interview with Leonard Woodcock, February 16, 1990. Glad, *Jimmy Carter*, 247–48.

14. Interview with Douglas Fraser, March 1, 1990.

15. Glad, *Jimmy Carter*, 248–53.

16. Interview with Stuart Eizenstat, July 16, 1993; *New York Times*, April 17, 1976, 1:1; Erwin C. Hargrove, *Jimmy Carter as President* (Baton Rouge: Louisiana State University Press, 1988), 34–35.

17. Interview with Leonard Woodcock, February 16, 1990.

18. *Washington Post*, May 8, 1976, 4:7; Glad, *Jimmy Carter*, 323; *New York Times*, May 7, 1976, I, 1:2, May 8, 1976, 10:4, May 20, 1976, 29:3; Interview with Leonard Woodcock, February 16, 1990.

19. Glad, *Jimmy Carter*, 273–80; Kandy Stroud, *How Jimmy Won: The Victory Campaign From Plains to the White House* (New York: William Morrow, 1977), 324–29; Ronald W. Walters, *Black Presidential Politics in America: A Strategic Approach* (Albany: State University of New York Press, 1988), 76–77; Interview with Leonard Woodcock, February 16, 1990.

20. Transcript of *Meet the Press* Interview with Woodcock, September 5, 1976, 11, President Woodcock Coll., Box 243, WSU; Memorandum, Hank Lacayo to International Executive Board, December 8, 1976, and attached report, "Basic Elements—UAW-CAP Campaign 1976 National Elections," President Woodcock Coll., Box 11, WSU.

21. Glad, *Jimmy Carter*, 400–3.

22. Many of those Democrats were labor-endorsed candidates. Of 336 House candidates endorsed by UAW-CAP, 255, or 76 percent, were victorious. Among 31 UAW-CAP endorsed Senate candidates, 19, or 61 percent, were elected. Memorandum, Hank Lacayo to International Executive Board, December 8, 1976, and attached report, "Basic Elements—UAW-CAP Campaign 1976 National Elections," President Woodcock Coll., Box 11, WSU.

23. Memorandum, Stephen Schlossberg to Landon Butler, December 3, 1976, Memorandum, Steve Schlossberg to Leonard Woodcock, December 9, 1976, Douglas Fraser (Personal) Coll., Box 17, WSU.

24. Interview with Leonard Woodcock, February 16, 1990; *New York Times*, May 13, 1977.

25. Burton I. Kaufman, *The Presidency of James Earl Carter Jr.*, (Lawrence: University Press of Kansas, 1992), 29.

26. Fraser criticized the president's withdrawal of a $50 tax rebate proposal and his "too low" minimum wage proposal and was "not completely satisfied" with the administration's approach to stimulating the economy, particularly in the area of youth unemployment. Transcript of interview with Douglas A. Fraser, *Meet the Press*, Vol. 21 No. 22 (May 29, 1977), Martin Catherwood Library, Cornell University School of Industrial and Labor Relations. For Carter's speech to the UAW convention, see *Public Papers of the Presidents of the United States, Jimmy Carter, 1977* (Washington: Government Printing Office, 1977), I:887–94.

27. Gary Fink, "Fragile Alliance: Jimmy Carter and the American Labor Movement," in Rosenbaum and Ugrinsky, *Presidency and Domestic Politics*, 786–88; Archie Robinson, *George Meany and His Times* (New York: Simon & Schuster, 1981), 358–72.

28. *Ypsilanti Press*, June 29, 1977.

29. Eizenstat and Johnston to the President, April 6, 1977, Eizenstat Papers, Box 231 [OIA 6342], Jimmy Carter Library (hereafter cited as JCL) (emphasis in the original).

30. *Detroit Free Press*, March 4, 7, 1977.

31. Steve [Schlossberg] to Stu Eizenstat, Personal and Confidential, circa June 29, 1977, Labor Law Reform folder [OIA 6342] [3], Eizenstat Papers, Box 232, JCL.

32. Eizenstat to Carter, June 30, 1977, Labor Law Reform [OIA 6342] [3], Eizenstat Papers, Box 232, JCL.

33. Mondale to Carter, June 30, 1977, copy attached to Eizenstat to Carter, June 30, 1977, Labor Law Reform folder [OIA 6342] [3], Eizenstat Papers, Box 232, JCL.

34. Hamilton Jordan to President Carter, June 29, 1977, Hamilton Jordan Papers, Labor Law Reform Bill folder, Box 35, JCL (Emphasis in original).

35. Carter also questioned proposals to compensate employees for loss of benefits due to an "unfair delay" in reaching a first contract, to require the Board to seek preliminary injunctions against companies in certain circumstances, to bring American-owned foreign-flag ships under the jurisdiction of the Board and to allow guards and guard unions to join or affiliate with non-guard unions. The foreign-flag ship provision was also dropped from the bill. Memo, Stu Eizenstat to the President, June 30, 1977 with Carter handwritten comments, "Labor Law Reform [OIA 6342] [3]," Eizenstat Papers, Box 232, JCL (emphasis in original).

36. *Public Papers of the Presidents, 1977*, II:1277–79; White House Press Briefing by Secretary of Labor Marshall and Carin Ann Clauss, Solicitor of the Secretary of Labor, July 18, 1977, "Labor Law Reform [OIA 6342] [3]," Eizenstat Papers, Box 232, JCL.

37. *Public Papers of the Presidents, 1977*, II:1332–33. Carter's misuse of labor terminology at Yazoo City makes one wonder how well he understood the provisions of the bill he had so carefully reviewed. He asserted that the legislation "also provides for a quicker determination of labor disputes. It also does protect workers who are injured in violation of the Federal law." The proposed legislation had nothing to do with work injuries and little to do with settlement of contract disputes, the province of the Federal Mediation and Conciliation Service, not the National Labor Relations Board. Carter was more articulate in discussing race relations at Yazoo City. See Donald Cunnigen, "Jimmy Carter as Spokesman of Southern Liberalism," in Rosenbaum and Ugrinsky, *Presidency and Domestic Politics*, 48–49. For Kennedy's statement, see chapter 5, p. 96.

38. Implying that the bill addressed a problem of limited scope rather than widespread abuses occurring throughout the country, Carter argued: "I don't think any worker should be punished through immediate discharge who tries to seek the rights that are applicable in almost all parts of the country for workers." *Public Papers of the Presidents, 1977*, II:1924–25.

39. Barbara Townley, *Labor Law Reform in US Industrial Relations* (Brookfield, Vt.: Gower, 1886), 168–76; *AFL-CIO News*, January 14, 1978. Former Labor Secretary Willard Wirtz also testified. U.S. Congress, House of Representatives, Committee on Education and Labor, *Hearings Before the Subcommittee on Labor-Management Relations, Labor Reform Act of 1977* (Washington, D.C., 1978), 1:320–57, 454–61; 2:202–18, 464–74, 916.

40. Early in January, AFL-CIO Legislative Representative Ray Denison said it was his understanding that "the Panama Canal issue will not precede us." When Carter met with Meany on January 13, 1978, however he was advised to "*not give* Mr. Meany a commitment" on the question of putting labor law reform ahead of the canal treaties "in light of the bitter partisan debate on both issues." *AFL-CIO*

News, January 14, 1978; Memorandum, Landon Butler and Bill Johnston to the President, January 13, 1978, Eizenstat Papers, Box 136 [OIA 6245], JCL; *Congressional Quarterly Almanac,* 1978, 285; Minutes of the Cabinet Meeting, January 30, 1978, folder: "White House—General (Watson, Jack), Secretary Marshall Papers, Box 125, Records of the Department of Labor, RG 174, National Archives (hereafter cited as NA).

41. *New York Times,* May 10, 28:1; Letter, Anne Zimmerman to Ray Marshall, May 11, 1978, folder: "White House—President May 1978," Secretary Marshall Papers, Box 123, Records of the Department of Labor, RG 174, NA; Memo, Ray Marshall for the President, May 9, 1978, Memo, Jack Watson for the President, May 13, 1978 (handwritten "Jack has not seen", 5/12/78 6:00 pm CWS), Memo, Stu Eizenstat for the President, May 11, 1978, "Labor Law Reform [OIA 6342] [3]," Eizenstat Papers, Box 232, JCL.

42. David Vogel, *Fluctuating Fortunes: The Political Power of Business in America* (New York: Basic Books, 1989), 150–59; Townley, *Labor Law Reform,* 139–67, 172–78; *Congressional Quarterly Almanac,* 1978, 284; Ray Marshall, Discussant, "Labor and Politics," in Rosenbaum and Ugrinsky, *Presidency and Domestic Politics,* 814; Memorandum, Frank Moore and Bob Thomson to the President, June 19, 1978, "Labor Law Reform [OIA 6342] [4]," Eizenstat Papers, Box 232, JCL.

43. *AFL-CIO News,* January 7, 1978, February 11, 25, 1978, June 10, 17, 1978.

44. Ibid., June 10, 1978; *Washington Post,* June 6, 1978, 3:2. In his meeting with Illinois legislators, Carter was asked about the bill by a Democratic state representative who favored it because Illinois had lost jobs "due to nonunion wages that are prevalent in the Sunbelt." Although Carter commented on the positive role of the National Labor Relations Act as the basis for labor-management "harmony" and "higher productivity," he focused on the regional issue as a southern rather than national leader. The president recounted his experience as a southern governor "recruiting investments" for his state, asserted that the North-South wage gap had narrowed, and said "I still favor the legislation" even though it might "eliminate some advantages the South does have." *Public Papers of the Presidents of the United States, Jimmy Carter, 1978,* I:990–94, 1070, 1079–80. Carter did make a strong and coherent speech in favor of labor law reform three months after the bill's defeat. At the United Steelworkers convention, he said on September 20, 1978: "Our labor law reform bill is not a grab for power by the unions, but it's a reach for justice, justice for American working men and women which is long overdue.... It's a reasonable and responsible piece of legislation. Its purpose is to prevent a small minority of employers from flagrantly continuing to violate the law." Carter pledged the bill would be at the top of his priority list in 1979. *Public Papers of the Presidents of the United States, Jimmy Carter, 1978,* II:1547. Given the results of the 1978 congressional elections, however, the AFL-CIO decided not to seek a new test of the measure. Robinson, *George Meany,* 387.

45. *Public Papers of the Presidents of the United States, Jimmy Carter, 1978,* I:1118–27; Memo, Stu Eizenstat and Bill Johnston to the President, June 19, 1978, "Labor Law Reform [OIA 6342] [4]," Eizenstat Papers, Box 232, JCL.

46. Memo, Frank Moore by Les Francis to the President, June 19, 1978, Frank Moore and Bob Thomson to the President, June 19, 1978, "Labor Law Reform [OIA 6342] [4]," Eizenstat Papers, Box 232, JCL; President's Daily Diary, June 19, 1978, 2–3, Appointments/Diary File, Box PD-33, Presidential Diary Office, JCL. Russell

Long had promised to be the 60th vote if the administration secured a 59th vote, Eizenstat recalled, but it failed to do so. Eizenstat expected Senator Dale Bumpers of Arkansas to be the 59th vote but recalls that Bumpers decided that the state was not ready to support labor law reform after Governor David Pryor defeated Representative Jim Guy Tucker in the Arkansas Democratic primary on June 13. Pryor criticized Tucker for voting for labor law reform and siding with northern liberals in Congress. Interview with Stuart Eizenstat, July 16, 1993; *New York Times,* June 15, 1978, 10:3; *Congressional Quarterly Almanac,* 1978, 286–87; Townley, *Labor Law Reform,* 178–87. See chapter 7.

47. Memo, Ray Marshall for the President, May 9, 1978, "Labor Law Reform [OIA 6342] [3]," Eizenstat Papers, Box 232, JCL; Tinsley E. Yarborough, "Carter and the Congress" in M. Glenn Abernathy, Dilys M. Hill, and Phil Williams, *The Carter Years: The President and Policy Making* (New York: St. Martin's Press, 1984), 169; Interview with Douglas Fraser, March 1, 1990. In a handwritten note thanking Fraser, Carter wrote: "Without your personal help, approval of the treaties would not have been possible." Carter to Fraser, May 1, 1978, White House Central File, Name File, Fraser, JCL.

48. Taylor Dark, "Organized Labor and the Carter Administration," in Rosenbaum and Ugrinsky, *Presidency and Domestic Politics,* 767.

49. Interview with Stuart Eizenstat, July 16, 1993. George Paulin, executive vice president of the International Association of Machinists remarked in July 1978: "I don't think Carter was [as] forceful on labor law reform as he should have been— as he was on the Panama Canal treaties, for example. He didn't speak about labor law reform once when it was out on the floor." *Washington Star,* July 20, 1978, clipping, in Labor- General [OIA 6245] [4], Eizenstat Papers, Box 231, JCL. IAM President Winpisinger later characterized Carter's performance on the issue as "misfeasance." William W. Winpisinger, *Reclaiming Our Future: An Agenda for American Labor* (Boulder, Colo.: Westview Press, 1989), 35.

50. Letter, Fraser to the President, August 11, 1978, UAW President Douglas Fraser Coll., Box 13, WSU.

51. UAW Press Release, July 19, 1978, President Fraser Coll., Box 2, WSU.

52. Ibid.

53. Transcript of Press Conference, July 19, 1978, President Fraser Coll., Box 2, WSU.

54. David Carroll Jacobs, "The United Auto Workers and the Campaign for National Health Insurance: A Case Study of Labor in Politics" (Ph.D. diss., Cornell University, 1983), 29, 44–48. For earlier efforts, see Edmund F. Wehrle, "'For A Health America': Labor's Struggle for National Health Insurance, 1943–1949," *Labor's Heritage* V (Summer 1993): 28–45.

55. *Detroit Free Press,* February 28, 1977; *Public Papers of the Presidents of the United States, Jimmy Carter, 1977,* I:887–94; Memorandum, Melvin Glasser to Doug Fraser, November 3, 1977, and attachment "Organized Labor's Views on Essential Minimum for a National Health Insurance Program," President Fraser Coll., Box 1, WSU; Memorandum, Stu Eizenstat to the President, February 8, 1978, "Appointments," Presidents Diary, Box PD-24, JCL; Notes on White House Meeting on National Health, [April 6, 1978], President Fraser Coll., Box 1, WSU; *Congressional Quarterly Almanac,* 1977, 499–507; Kaufman, *Presidency of James Earl Carter,* 101–3.

56. Jacobs, "The United Auto Workers and the Campaign for National Health Insurance," 54–57; Joseph A. Califano, Jr., *Governing America: An Insider's Report from the White House and Cabinet* (New York: Simon & Schuster, 1981), 94–95; Memorandum, Melvin Glasser to Doug Fraser, November 3, 1977, President Fraser Coll., Box 1, WSU; Mailgram, Stephen Schlossberg to Landon Butler, December 2, 1977, President Fraser Coll., Box 14, WSU.

57. Memorandum, Stu Eizenstat to Secretary of HEW et al, February 6, 1978, Secretary Ray Marshall Papers, Box 121, folder "1978—White House Gen. (St. Eizenstat)," RG 174, NA; Califano, *Governing America*, 102–3.

58. Meeting with Senator Kennedy and Organized Labor on NHI from Stu Eizenstat and Joe Onek, April 6, 1978, Appointments/Diary File, Box PD-28, JCL; Memorandum, Steve Schlossberg to Doug Fraser, April 5, 1978, Notes on White House Meeting on National Health, [April 6, 1978], President Fraser Coll., Box 1, WSU; Califano, *Governing America*, 104–6.

59. Paul Starr, *The Social Transformation of American Medicine* (New York: Basic Books, 1982), 412–14; Jacobs, "The United Auto Workers and National Health Insurance," 44–48; Memorandum, Joe Magone to Hank Lacayo, April 21, 1978, President Fraser Coll., Box 1, WSU.

60. *New York Times*, July 29, 20:2, July 30, 1978, 14:3; UAW Press Release, July 28, 1978, President Fraser Coll., Box 1, WSU; Notes on White House Meeting on National Health, [April 6, 1978], President Fraser Coll., Box 1; Jacobs, "The United Auto Workers and the Campaign for National Health Insurance," 54–57; *AFL-CIO News*, August 5, 1978.

61. UAW Press Release, July 28, 1978, President Fraser Coll., Box 1, WSU; Jacobs, "The United Auto Workers and the Campaign for National Health Insurance," 54–57; Douglas Fraser to UAW International Executive Board with attached Health Care for All Americans Act of 1979, October 24, 1978, President Fraser Coll., Box 17, WSU. In shifting to a plan that included a central role for private insurance companies, the UAW and Kennedy lost the support of Representative James C. Corman, chief House sponsor of the Kennedy-Corman bill. Corman and Representative Ronald Dellums proposed all public health plans. James C. Corman to Douglas Fraser, December 20, 1978, President Fraser Coll., Box 1, WSU; *Congressional Quarterly Almanac*, 1979, 536–40.

62. Gary Fink, "Fragile Alliance," 783–84, 793.

63. Haynes Johnson, *In the Absence of Power* (New York: Viking Press, 1980), 100–101.

64. Interview with Leonard Woodcock, February 16, 1990.

65. Interview with Stuart Eizenstat, July 16, 1993.

66. Interview with Leonard Woodcock, February 16, 1990.

67. Charles O. Jones, *The Trusteeship Presidency: Jimmy Carter and the United States Presidency* (Baton Rouge: Louisiana University Press, 1988).

68. Glad, *Jimmy Carter*, 58–86; Minutes of the Cabinet Meeting, January 30, 1978, folder: "White House—General (Watson, Jack), Secretary Marshall Papers, Box 125, Records of the Department of Labor, RG 174, NA; Jimmy Carter, *Keeping Faith* (New York: Bantam Books, 1982); Rosalynn Carter, *First Lady From Plains* (Boston: Houghton Mifflin, 1984).

69. Interview with Stuart Eizenstat, July 16, 1993.

70. Steven M. Gillon, *The Democrats' Dilemma: Walter F. Mondale and the Liberal Legacy* (New York: Columbia University Press, 1992), 201–3.

71. Ibid., 201–2.

72. Telegrams, Fraser to Carter, September 9, 1978, March 5, 1979, June 18, 1979, White House Central File, Name File, Fraser, JCL.

73. Interview with Douglas Fraser, March 1, 1990; Memorandum for G. William Miller from Stuart Eizenstat, October 3, 1979, White House Central File, Name File, Fraser, JCL.

74. *Detroit News*, October 18, 1978; Douglas Fraser to Dear :, September 19, 1978, President Fraser Coll., Box 20, WSU; Interview with Douglas Fraser, March 1, 1990.

75. Progressive Alliance newsletter, March 1980, President Fraser Coll., Box 3, WSU; Letter, Marcus Raskin to Douglas Fraser, December 28, 1978, Memorandum, Steve Schlossberg to Doug Fraser, January 2, 1979, Memorandum, Don Stillman to Doug Fraser, February 9, 1979, Typescript, Don Ephlin, February 26, President Fraser Coll., Box 30, WSU; Hank Lacayo to Doug Fraser, September 5, 1979, President Fraser Coll., Box 3, WSU; Andrew Battista, "Labor and Coalition Politics: The Progressive Alliance," *Labor History* Vol. 32 No. 3 (Summer 1991): 401–21.

76. Doug Fraser to UAW Delegates to Mid-Term Democratic Conference, November 17, 1978, President Fraser Coll., Box 6, WSU.

77. The first quote is from Leon Shull to Douglas Fraser, December 11, 1978, President Fraser Coll., Box 5, WSU; Gillon, *The Democrats' Dilemma*, 206–9; Jody Powell, *The Other Side of the Story* (New York: Morrow, 1984); 188–9; Clifton McKleskey and Pierce McKleskey, "Jimmy Carter and the Democratic Party," in Abernathy, Hill, and Williams, *Carter Years*, 35.

78. Weir also argues that autoworkers' criticism of union leaders over the failure to act on working conditions meant that they would not join an issue-oriented grassroots movement either. This seems a more dubious proposition. Stan Weir, "Doug Fraser's Middle Class Coalition," *Radical America* (January–February 1989): 19–29.

79. Andrew Battista, "Labor and Coalition Politics: The Progressive Alliance," 401–21; Kim Moody, *An Injury to All* (London: Verso, 1988), 152–56, 165–69; Robert B. Reich and John D. Donahue, *New Deals: The Chrysler Revival and the American System* (New York: Times Books, 1985), 90–100, 124–31; Larry Poole is quoted in Richard Feldman and Michael Betzold, eds., *End of the Line: Auto Workers and the American Dream* (New York: Wedenfeld and Nicholson, 1988), 184.

80. Memorandum, Doug Fraser to Officers and Board Members, April 3, 1979, Telecopy to Steve Portulis, Transcript of [*Post-Dispatch*] Newspaper Article, July 12, 1979, Clipping, *Chicago Sun-Times*, June 21, 1979, President Fraser Coll., Box 19, WSU.

81. Reich and Donahue, *New Deals*, 129–130; *New York Times*, January 15, 1980, IV, 15:3, January 16, 1980, 19:4, April 28, 1980, IV, 11:2, May 6, 1980, IV, 19:4; *Congressional Quarterly Almanac*, 1979, 285; Memorandum for the President from Landon Butler, January 14, 1980, White House Central File, Name File, Fraser, JCL.

82. *New York Times*, Feb, 22, 1979, July 31, 1979, 13:1, August 12, 1979, IV 1:1, November 18, 1979, 30:1; Winpisinger, *Reclaiming Our Future*, 15, 35; Memorandum, Hamilton Jordan to President Carter, May 3, 1979, and attached Memorandum Landon Butler to Hamilton Jordan, May 1, 1979, "1980 Campaign File;

Labor—Political," Hamilton Jordan Coll., Box 79, JCL; Memorandum, Landon Butler to Hamilton Jordan, April 18, 1980, "Labor Issues," Hamilton Jordan Coll., Box 79, JCL; Dark, "Organized Labor and the Carter Administration," 770–74; Ray Marshall, Discussant, "Labor and Politics," 813–15; Gary Fink, "F. Ray Marshall: Jimmy Carter's Ambassador to Organized Labor," Paper presented to Fifteenth Annual North American Labor History Conference, Wayne State University, October 14–16, 1993, 17–22; Robert J. Flanagan, "The National Accord as a Social Contract," *Industrial and Labor Relations Review* 34 (October 1980): 35–50.

83. McKleskey and McKleskey, "Jimmy Carter and the Democratic Party," in Abernathy, Hill, and Williams, *The Carter Years*, 135–38; Interview with Douglas Fraser, March 1, 1990.

84. Interview with Leonard Woodcock, February 16, 1990; Interview with Douglas Fraser, March 1, 1990; Memorandum, Landon Butler to Phil Wise, June 19, 1980, White House Central File, PL/Carter, Box PL-4, JCL; Elizabeth Drew, *Portrait of an Election* (New York: Simon & Schuster, 1981), 290–91.

85. *New York Times*, November 9, 1980, 28, November 16, 1980, 1.

86. Ibid., November 11, 1980, B8.

87. Micah Sifry, *Spoiling for a Fight: Third Party Politics in America* (New York: Routledge, 2002), 226.

88. Ray Marshall, Discussant, "Labor and Politics," 814.

89. Interview with Stuart Eizenstat, July 16, 1993.

90. Dark, "Organized Labor and the Carter Administration," 777.

91. Fink, "Fragile Alliance," 800.

92. Letter, Douglas Fraser to author, n.d. [December 1993].

93. Ibid.; *New York Times*, August 13, 1980, 1:6, August 14, 1980, II, 1:1; Kaufman, *The Presidency of James Earl Carter*, 133–34, 154, 163–65; Michael J. Malbin, "The Conventions, the Platforms, and Issue Activists," in Austin Ranney, ed., *The American Elections of 1980* (Washington: American Enterprise Institute for Public Policy Research, 1981), 116–32.

94. For example, a leader of UAW retirees wrote Fraser: "Come on, Doug, a few more intelligent blasts, such as the one delivered in Washington and millions of underprivileged people will surely respond in the US and throughout the world." Dave Miller to Douglas Fraser, August 7, 1978, President Fraser Coll., Box 1, WSU.

95. UAW Press Release, July 19, 1978, President Fraser Coll., Box 2, WSU.

Women's Trade Union League Convention, 1915. Leonora O'Reilly and Rose Schneiderman are in the front row, fifth and sixth from the left. Credit: Chicago Historical Society, ICHi-14399.

Crowd listening to Franklin Roosevelt speak outside of Detroit City Hall, October 15, 1936. Credit: Walter P. Reuther Library, Wayne State University.

Ford workers with newspapers proclaiming the end of the Ford strike, April 1941.
Credit: Walter P. Reuther Library, Wayne State University.

Paul Robeson receiving an award from children at Camp Kinderland, 1949. Credit: Fay Itzkowitz.

Coleman Young, left, and his attorney, George Crockett, at the 1952 House Un-American Activities Committee hearings in Detroit. Credit: Walter P. Reuther Library, Wayne State University.

President John F. Kennedy signing Executive Order 10988, January 17, 1962. Ida Klaus is fourth from the left and Secretary of Labor Arthur Goldberg in on the president's left. Credit: Photo No. AR6484B in the John F. Kennedy Library.

President John F. Kennedy signing Equal Pay Act, 1963. Esther Peterson is fifth from the left. Credit: Photo No. AR7965F in the John F. Kennedy Library.

President Jimmy Carter with former UAW president Leonard Woodcock, whom he appointed first emissary and then ambassador to the People's Republic of China. Credit: Jimmy Carter Library.

Moe Biller and New York postal workers voting to end strike and return to work, March 25, 1970. Credit: New York Metro Area Postal Workers Union, Robert F. Wagner Labor Archives, New York University.

UAW strikers picket Champion Auto Rebuilders in Hope, Arkansas, but face permanent replacement, September 1991. Credit: Arkansas Democrat-Gazette.

Bill Clinton signing workplace fairness petition presented by Arkansas AFL-CIO President Bill Becker at Labor Day Picnic, September 1991. Credit: Arkansas Democrat-Gazette.

John Sweeney (*right*), Richard Trumka, and Linda Chavez-Thompson, New Voices leadership team campaigning in Detroit in support of newspaper strikers, 1995. Credit: Jim West.

Seattle demonstration against the World Trade Organization, December 1999. Credit: Jim Levitt/ImpactDigitals.com.

Ralph Nader campaigning for president in Detroit, 2000. Credit: Jim West.

Al Gore supporters at Detroit campaign rally, 2000. Credit: Jim West.

CHAPTER 7

Arkansas and the Defeat of Labor Law Reform in 1978 and 1994

The Republican advantage in presidential politics in the past three decades has been attributed by scholars to a variety of factors: the rise of the New Right and single-issue conservative political groups, the new strength of Republicans among white voters in the South, the increased role of money and business in politics, the decline of the trade union movement, and the significant fissures within the Democratic party, particularly on race and foreign policy. Even when Democrats have won the presidency, these trends have undermined their ability to govern. Thus, Democrats capable of winning the presidency have found it difficult to maintain a viable political coalition while in office. Jimmy Carter in 1976 and Bill Clinton in 1992 each won election due to a combination of support from the Democratic party's core constituencies and the return of part of the South from its recent Republican leaning.

Each of these Democratic presidents struggled with the problem of satisfying both the Democratic party's core constituencies and those swing southern voters. Although Clinton won reelection, both he and Carter failed to seize the opportunity before them to help reverse the conservative trends and expand their southern base at the same time. Labor law reform was that key opportunity to both help organized labor and to strengthen progressive forces in the South. Instead of dynamically seizing and giving leadership to the battle for labor law reform in a way that galvanized and drew low-income voters to them, each was a reluctant partner of organized labor. The Labor Law Reform Bill and the Workplace Fairness Bill thus failed to pass.

As a number of scholars have argued, the South is becoming more like the rest of the country.[1] The effort to win the support of southern members of Congress for reforming the nation's labor laws was far from hopeless. Looking at the process—and the opportunities missed—in Arkansas is especially interesting. Senator Dale Bumpers' was the critical vote lost by the bill's supporters at the last moment in 1978, and both Bumpers and Senator David Pryor voted against cloture on the Workplace Fairness Bill in 1994 despite the fact that their fellow Arkansan in the White House supported the bill. This chapter will chronicle Arkansas's role in these two labor defeats, point to what ultimately tipped Arkansas's senators to vote against labor in the absence of strong presidential leadership to vote for labor, and explain the reasons that both Carter and Clinton chose to provide only weak support for these initiatives.

Although Bill Clinton gave Americans a new awareness of Arkansas, the state has had an unusual number of well-known politicians. Despite Arkansas's small population, Senators Joe T. Robinson, John McClellan, and J. William Fulbright and Representative Wilbur Mills achieved power on the national stage due to Arkansas's character as a one-party state and the congressional seniority system. Governor Orval Faubus earned notoriety for himself and the state in 1957 by his actions against the desegregation of Central High School, thus weakening significantly the state's reputation for racial moderation. The opposition by the civil rights movement, by moderates and liberals, including the leadership of the AFL-CIO and the state's leading newspaper, the *Arkansas Gazette*, to Faubus's segregationist stance, however, prepared the ground for a new politics in Arkansas and the rise to prominence of a new group of "moderate to liberal" politicians in the state.[2]

The key event leading to a change in Arkansas politics was the successful 1964 initiative campaign to repeal the state poll tax. The AFL-CIO, three women's organizations, the Arkansas Education Association (AEA), and a Republican party then led by the moderate Winthrop Rockefeller campaigned together to put the issue on the ballot and won the support of 56 percent of those voting.[3] The AFL-CIO was instrumental in securing Governor Faubus's endorsement of the initiative and it in turn endorsed Faubus's reelection. The AFL-CIO also contributed funds to voter registration drives by black organizations. By 1964 Faubus was "patching up some of his differences with the NAACP and appointing some blacks to state boards and commissions." In that year, in the last election under the poll-tax system, Faubus defeated a significant challenge from Rockefeller by a 57 percent to 43 percent margin.[4]

Elimination of the poll tax transformed Arkansas politics, not only because of the increase in the number of voters but because under the old system local leaders had purchased poll taxes and recorded votes as they wished. One example will suffice. When Brooks Hays was running for governor in 1928, he expressed concern to the Boone County political leader about the vote from his county and wanted the vote called in as soon as it was tabulated. The local leader explained they did not have a telephone or, in response to Hays' inquiry, a telegraph office. "Look here, Brooks, if you're that anxious I could tell you what the vote's going to be and we could just write it down now."[5]

Although Arkansas politics became more honest, open, inclusive, and modern in the 1960s, some old patterns were unchanged or continued in muted form. Large-scale businesses such as Tyson Foods and Wal-Mart, farm interests, and banking and utility companies remained powerful. Despite some Republican victories in statewide and federal elections, Arkansas retained its character as a one-party state. Populist criticism of elites and monopolies such as the utility companies had a continuing appeal to significant groups of voters. The roles of African Americans and women increased considerably, but white males continued to dominate politics. Among many, a state and regional consciousness continued, along with a distrust of outsiders. Personal, one-on-one campaigning was still expected by Arkansas voters.

The innovations in Arkansas politics in the 1960s led the labor movement to hope for both progressive change and increased influence. Since the mid-1970s, however, Arkansas unions, like those elsewhere in the country, have experienced a precipitous decline in membership. Union membership in Arkansas has dropped from about 17.5 percent of the labor force in 1970 to 7.8 percent in 1995. Labor still has an important ally in the African American community, whose share of the electorate stands at about 14 percent.[6]

When Governor Faubus decided not to seek reelection in 1966, the Republican Rockefeller won election as the progressive alternative to a strident segregationist, and he was reelected in 1968 over a Faubus ally. The first Democrat to succeed at the new, more open politics was Dale Bumpers, who emerged from obscurity to win the governorship in 1970.

Bumpers was prominent in the small Ozark town of Charleston, serving as city attorney, president of the school board, and president of the chamber of commerce, but he was little known elsewhere when he entered the Democratic primary race for governor at the age of 44. Bumpers proposed progressive programs to improve education, health care, and prison conditions. He was charismatic both in personal appearances and over television. Bumpers managed to win second place in the Democratic primary with 20 percent of the vote to 36 percent for Faubus, who was once again turning to racist themes in an attempt to return to the governor's mansion. Bumpers picked up support from the enlarged black voting bloc and from organized labor, from liberals and moderates, from the *Arkansas Gazette*, and from Senator Fulbright, and he decisively defeated Faubus in the runoff and then Rockefeller in the general election.[7]

As governor, Bumpers succeeded in increasing state revenues by making the income tax more progressive, increasing teachers' salaries, establishing a state-supported kindergarten program, increasing funding of community and four-year colleges, and improving services for elderly, handicapped, and mentally retarded citizens. In 1974 Bumpers challenged Fulbright's bid for a sixth Senate term. Liberals within the Arkansas labor movement supported Fulbright because of his leadership in the effort to end the Vietnam War, but Fulbright had a consistently antilabor record and the AFL-CIO was neutral in the race. Bumpers was clearly the more populist candidate, blaming big oil for the energy crisis while Fulbright had defended the industry from that charge, advocated higher energy prices, and retained support from Witt Stephens and other energy company owners. As the campaign developed, Fulbright, whose voting record on nonlabor domestic issues had become increasingly liberal, moved to the right to fend off the liberal Bumpers. Bumpers won the primary by a 65 percent to 35 percent margin and won an easy victory in the general election.[8] As senator, Bumpers's voting record during his first term was a liberal one. To understand why Bumpers had a difficult time with the relatively modest labor reform bill in 1978, the story of Arkansas's right-to-work law must be told.

Arkansas first adopted a right-to-work law in 1944 as a result of an initiative to amend the Arkansas constitution sponsored by the Arkansas Free Enterprise Association, a coalition of businesspeople and large landowners who feared that the CIO would organize black tenant farmers. Trade union membership stood at about 25,000 in 1939 but had increased to 43,000, or 17 percent of the workforce, by 1944 due to growth of unions in war industry. The measure was adopted by a 55 percent to 45 percent margin. Areas of the state with war industry were most strongly against the measure.[9]

In 1976 the Arkansas labor movement made a significant effort to repeal the state right-to-work law.[10] A coalition of the state's unions united the AFL-CIO with the then-independent United Automobile Workers, United Mine Workers, and Teamsters unions. The unions kicked off the campaign with a series of rallies around the state in February. To support the repeal effort, leaders from the Arkansas Council of Churches, Arkansas Farmers Union, ACORN, Arkansas Jaycees, NAACP, the Arkansas Women's Political Caucus, and other prominent educational, religious, and civic leaders joined together to form Arkansans for Progress.[11] These coalition efforts succeeded in obtaining nearly 150,000 signatures to place repeal on the ballot. The campaign then sought to win over the electorate with the economic argument that the right-to-work law contributed to Arkansas's status as one of the country's most impoverished states. Representative Andrew Young spoke at a dinner sponsored by supporters of the petition drive and maintained: "The only reason for the law is to keep wages low and keep people poor."[12] A number of clergy focused on the moral implications of free-rider behavior. Bishop Andrew McDonald of the Catholic

Diocese of Little Rock, for example, characterized the right-to-work law as "morally reprehensible to its very core."[13]

To broaden the base of support for the campaign, unions negotiated if-and-when agreements with such large employers as Kroger, Safeway, Reynolds Aluminum, and Southwestern Bell Telephone. These employers agreed to union shop arrangements if and when the law forbidding them was amended. AFL-CIO President Bill Becker maintained, "Enlightened corporate executives do not want the State of Arkansas to use the power of government to keep trade unions weak."[14] To answer opposition charges about compulsory unionism, moreover, the amendment included a provision for a vote by the employees prior to the negotiation of a union shop agreement.

Despite important successes in gaining allies, labor found some of the leading moderate-to-liberal voices in Arkansas politics neutral or opposed to repeal. Senator Bumpers and Governor Pryor both took neutral positions. The *Arkansas Gazette* opposed repeal, arguing that "classical liberals do not look favorably upon compulsion to join or pay fees to any private organization, whether it be a labor union or the Chamber of Commerce."[15] Bill Clinton, who had been strongly supported by labor in a 1974 race for Congress, opposed the repeal effort as he began his campaign for election as state attorney general. Wilbur Mills was supportive, but his support was of little value as he had become a laughingstock due to episodes connected with his drinking.[16]

An even bigger problem for the repeal effort was a well-funded opposition campaign conducted by the Chamber of Commerce, the Associated Industries of Arkansas, and the Freedom to Work Committee. The antiunion advertising campaign emphasized the simple theme that one should not have to pay to work.[17] With the opposition gaining ground with its appeal to individual freedom, Amendment 59 supporters shifted from their economic argument to defensive responses to the opposition criticism:

The BIG BOYS ARE Running a Slick Advertising Campaign to Sell You on Something That Just Isn't True! Your freedom to join or not join a union is GUARANTEED by federal law. Amendment 59 will not change that.

What it amends is a state law which forces local unions to give away their services to non-members....

Amendment 59 applies ONLY to places which already have a local union. If a majority of these workers want a union shop and the employer agrees, the most that can be required of the non-member is a tender of the equivalent of a fee for services rendered.[18]

These convoluted arguments failed to confront head-on the antiunion attack on "compulsory unionism." While it was true that one was free to "not join" a union, that individual freedom amounted to the freedom to quit if the employer and union had negotiated a union shop agreement.

Moreover, to assert that "the most that can be required" of the nonmember is a fee for services correctly characterized agency shop agreements that would be permitted under Amendment 59 but not the union shop provisions it was also designed to sanction. In the November balloting, the proposal went down to a decisive defeat, receiving only 36 percent of the total vote. Though the labor movement spent about $500,000 on the campaign, Becker recalled, "[W]e couldn't adequately explain the issue.... The employers kept the issue very simple and refused to debate."[19]

The right-to-work campaign showed that labor and its allies were a significant minority in the state but had less clout than the business community and its allies. Business was able to shape the broad middle of Arkansas public opinion into thinking of the issue as one of individual freedom. In the wake of the repeal's defeat, politicians had to wonder if they would become targets of business opposition if they identified with trade union efforts to reform labor law.

Although discouraged by the defeat of their effort to eliminate the right-to-work law, Arkansas trade unionists joined in the national effort to mobilize support for a labor law reform bill after Jimmy Carter was inaugurated president. The AFL-CIO and the United Automobile Workers (UAW) negotiated with the Carter administration on the provisions of a moderate bill focused on speeding up NLRB election procedures, giving unions a chance to counter employers' antiunion campaigning at the workplace, and discouraging employers from firing workers seeking to organize unions and from engaging in other unfair labor practices. Labor leaders agreed to drop repeal of the right-to-work provision of the Taft-Hartley Act and several other measures from the reform bill.[20] The AFL-CIO, the UAW, and their allies in the coalition, Americans for Justice on the Job, developed a grassroots campaign to pass the bill. In September 1977 the Arkansas AFL-CIO held rallies in each congressional district. In a few weeks time, about 8,000 postcards urging passage of the law were delivered to Arkansas House members.[21] In the House of Representatives, the three Democratic members from Arkansas voted for the measure while the one Republican voted against it. In the South as a whole, only 31 percent of House members and 41 percent of House Democrats voted for the bill.[22]

Although labor achieved a quick victory in the House, where the bill passed by a margin of 257–163 on October 6, 1977, it was unsuccessful in getting rapid action on the bill in the Senate. The Carter administration put passage of the Panama Canal treaty as its priority for Senate action in 1978, and action on labor law reform was stalled until the treaties were adopted on April 18, 1978. During the seven months from House passage to the opening of the Senate debate on May 15, 1978, the nation's senators were subject to what observers characterized as the most intense lobbying campaign against a piece of legislation in the country's history. The bill's supporters also conducted an active campaign of letter writing, phone calling, and visiting with senators.[23] With a Senate filibuster certain, the bill's backers needed to gain 60 votes to end debate. As in 1976, the bill's supporters found the *Arkansas Gazette* opposed to the labor law initiative.[24] Arkansas's two senators were initially undecided. The strongly antilabor McClellan died in 1977; Governor Pryor appointed Kaneaster Hodges, Jr., to replace McClellan in December. Hodges, who under Arkansas law was ineligible to run in 1978 for the seat to which he was appointed, was a lawyer, a farmer, and a member of the Arkansas Farm Bureau and the Cattlemen's Association. He had served as a legislative secretary to Pryor in 1975.[25] Given his background, Hodges was unlikely to be supportive of a labor bill. Business was more effective in getting its message to Hodges than was labor. When he met with Bill Becker and a labor delegation on January 5, 1978, Hodges "was non committal" but told the labor representatives about the mail he was getting against the bill. Becker's impression was that Hodges "had an open mind and might be helpful." Hodges gave a clear hint on how to win his support when he told the labor people that "as a 'lame duck' senator the only power he had to bring benefits (pork) to Arkansas was by trading votes." Becker communicated this information to AFL-CIO legislative director Andrew Biemiller.[26] It was the Carter administration that was in a position to offer such deals, not the AFL-CIO, but it was disinclined to do so.

Becker pursued another avenue, asking a Machinists union staff representative "to see Governor Pryor to ask him to lean on Hodges for a favorable vote." Becker was told that "Pryor said he would do so." It is unlikely that Pryor ever did so. In a 1997 interview, Pryor could not recall any conversation with Hodges on the issue. On February 2, 1978, Hodges's aide told a steelworker representative that "it is up to Becker and Prior [sic]" and that Becker "was key to his vote." Perhaps Pryor was seeking labor support for his upcoming run for the Senate seat. A few days later, friends of Hodges told labor people that Pryor "is going to run to the right of Jim Guy Tucker [in the Democratic Senate primary] and doesn't want anything to do with pro-labor support. He [Pryor] is having problems with Becker and there is nothing to be gained by supporting the bill."[27] In any event, Hodges soon came out publicly against the labor reform bill. Acknowledging that it was "reprehensible when employers fire an employee for union organizing," Hodges argued that facilitating union organizing was not in the best interest of either business or working people in the South. He maintained that senators from outside the South "made clear that the reason they are for it is to retard the movement of industry to the South."[28]

Given Bumpers's liberal record and his history of voting for cloture, bill supporters focused their attention on him. As Paperworkers Vice President Wayne Glenn explained in a letter to Bumpers, "I have said many times you were the best Chief Executive Arkansas has ever had. You spoke up for the downtrodden and mistreated and you did what you knew to be the right thing."[29] Bumpers acknowledged he was feeling the pressure from his constituents, noting he had heard far more on the labor law issue than on any other, including the Panama Canal treaty. "I've heard practically nothing else."[30] Both sides were encouraging massive letter-writing campaigns. Among business corporations, Tyson Foods was particularly active in encouraging its employees to write.[31]

In a two-page "Dear Friend" letter to constituents, Bumpers attempted to straddle the fence. He praised provisions of the bill that would streamline NLRB procedures and "correct some unnecessary delays that a few employers had taken advantage of because they know that in some instances delay can be less costly than complying with the law." Bumpers predicted that the bill would pass. On the other hand, Bumpers expressed specific concerns about provisions of the law calling for an abbreviated time period before NLRB elections and union use of employer property to address employees, noting that there were "other...provisions...[that] could be improved." He indicated his own vote would depend "on the extent to which the bill has been amended." Bumpers made a point of stressing that constituents who were expressing concern about a threat to Arkansas's right-to-work law were mistaken. "These rights are fully protected and will remain intact and I support them. The people of Arkansas have spoken clearly on this issue by their overwhelming vote to retain the right-to-work law."[32]

While he continued to hold onto the fence, Bumpers made clear on February 16, 1978, that he did not like the bill as it stood but would take a wait-and-see attitude regarding cloture. "In the final analysis," he told a *Gazette* reporter, "I think the law is reasonably fair right now. Last year labor won half and lost half. I am not disposed to vote for a bill that would tilt that scale." On cloture, Bumpers stated, "That will be a very critical vote on this bill and I'll wait and see how it looks at the time."[33] As the last-minute pressure mounted, Bumpers led bill supporters to believe that he would vote for cloture. "Bumpers promised us he would be OK," Becker recalled. "I still remember meeting with the guy like it was yesterday. A group of us went to see him and asked him about the cloture vote and he said, well, I always vote for cloture." Gordon Brehm, Glenn's administrative assistant, recalls that Bumpers also had told Glenn, now Paperworkers president, that he would vote for cloture. Stuart Eizenstat, domestic policy advisor for the Carter administration, likewise fully expected Bumpers to vote with the administration. Russell Long had promised that his would be the 60th vote if the administration could get 59 votes; the administration believed the count had reached 59.[34] In a recent interview, Bumpers recalled, "I gave very serious consideration to voting for that bill." Recalling his meeting with Becker, he noted that he "never promised" he would vote for cloture but told Becker "[I]t had been my custom to vote for cloture." Although Bumpers disputed Becker's subsequent criticism of him for breaking a "promise," the two recollections are quite similar. It seems apparent that Bumpers intended to vote for cloture but changed his mind. Electoral politics intervened.

As the Senate debated the labor law reform bill, Arkansans weighed the merits of several of the state's politicians in the Democratic primary. Bumpers was not facing the voters, but Governor Pryor, the leading candidate to win the nomination for the open Senate seat, encountered stiff competition from House members Jim Guy Tucker and Ray Thornton. Although Pryor was attempting to follow Bumpers's path in moving from the governor's mansion to the Senate, his career thus far had followed a very different trajectory. From a political family in Camden in southern Arkansas, Pryor and his wife published a weekly newspaper after they graduated college. At the age of 26, Pryor campaigned for state representative in 1960. Camden was the site of a large unionized International Paper mill. "I realized that to succeed in our county in an election," Pryor recalled, "I had to know a little about this labor union business." He familiarized himself with the issues and met labor leaders. Most important, he and his wife went "house by house" in the area around the mill and "established a personal rapport with almost each household." Pryor defeated an incumbent with a pro-labor but also pro-Faubus voting record. A reform-minded Young Turk in the legislature, Pryor served for six years there and then sought election to the U.S. Congress. Pryor's pro-labor record helped him to victory as unionists from his state house district passed the word, "He'll listen to you." He then compiled a liberal and 100 percent pro-labor record as a member of Congress from 1967 until he challenged McClellan's bid for a sixth term in the Senate in 1972. Strongly supported by labor and liberals, Pryor forced McClellan into a runoff.[35]

Looking back on the 1972 campaign a quarter century later, Pryor mused, "I probably got too much labor support." McClellan "sold this message very effectively...big labor bosses and big labor unions [are] coming in here...is our Senate seat for sale?" Pryor's campaign was weakened also by a statement which he made and then "tried to retract," in which he was supportive of amnesty for young men who left the country to avoid being drafted to serve in Vietnam. Pryor maintained that his supporters were "a lot of little labor families that work hard for their money, reaching into their cookie jar[s] to help me out." Listing checks to Pryor's campaign from unions, McClellan successfully belittled Pryor's defense. Pryor countered by questioning contributions to McClellan's campaign "from First National Bank, from Arkansas Power and Light Company, from utilities, Wit Stephenses...[the] big fat cats" but McClellan's aggressive attack on Pryor's independence enabled him to retain his seat with a 52 percent victory.[36]

Stung by the charges and by the defeat, Pryor resolved to move to the right. Returning to the House after the primary loss, Pryor voted against a bill to increase the minimum wage. "Pryor shocked everybody. He was our guy," Becker recalled, noting Pryor "said the reason he did it was to show his independence of labor."[37] Despite this straw in the wind, the AFL-CIO endorsed Pryor's successful bid for governor in 1974 and his reelection effort in 1976.[38] Pryor's gubernatorial policies disappointed both the AFL-CIO and the AEA. His calling out of the National Guard in a Fire Fighters strike in Pine Bluff was especially disturbing. The Fire Fighters would have returned to work if they had received such a request from the governor, Bill Becker recalled, but he made no contact with labor representatives. "I can't remember if I asked them to go back or not," Pryor commented in a recent interview. "I was accused of being a strike breaker," Pryor recalled. Attending an AFL-CIO convention even though he was told he would not be welcome, Pryor explained that his actions were based on the need to preserve public safety. "They treated me pretty roughly, saying [you] turned your back on us." Pryor's effort to move to the Senate found both the AFL-CIO and the AEA strongly opposed to their former ally. The AFL-CIO praised Thornton but endorsed Tucker in the primary contest. The AEA likewise endorsed Tucker. Thornton, for his part, had the support of the powerful Stephens family, as he was Wit Stephens's nephew. Both Tucker and Thornton were endorsed by the *Gazette*, which commented that Pryor's record as governor was "eminently forgettable even as he has moved steadily to the right.... His rhetoric sounds increasingly Republican in tone."[39]

Pryor came in first with a surprisingly low 34 percent. Tucker, with 32.5 percent, nosed out Thornton, who had 31.9 percent.[40] Pryor defended his shift away from a pro-labor position by arguing that he had matured. More importantly, he went on the offensive, attacking Tucker's vote for labor law reform. Recalling his opposition to the labor law reform bill, Pryor commented in a recent interview: "It may have been a pure political decision...could have been a philosophical concern but it could have been political. What am I going to get out of this?" Given union criticism of him, Pryor decided he "had to fight fire with fire." In Pryor's view, the 1978 campaign was "the defining moment of an independence from organized labor" that helped him to victory. Pryor launched a frontal assault on Tucker's overall liberal record, asserting that "almost three quarters of the time, Jim Guy Tucker disagreed with his fellow southerners and voted with northern liberals. I am proud to report that the rest of our Arkansas delegation voted with us." Pryor argued that Tucker was a candidate "packaged for home consumption" who "appears to stand up for private enterprise, for limited government, for fiscal responsibility, for a balanced budget and for all those values we treasure in Arkansas," but who voted in Washington with northern liberals against balancing the budget and for reducing defense spending "on needed projects to keep our country strong." The *Arkansas Gazette* expressed its disgust with Pryor's "appeal to prejudice...against organized labor...against outsiders...and particularly—would you believe it?—prejudice against Northerners. The state is now told that Jim Guy Tucker votes in Congress like a damyankee."[41]

Tucker went on the attack, too, raising questions about the intervention by Pryor's campaign manager in a pending rate case involving the Stephenses' gas interests. Tucker speculated about a deal to trade support for Pryor in the runoff for a utility rate increase. Stephens had supported his nephew, Thornton, in the first round of balloting. In the final round of voting on June 13, Pryor won with 55 percent of the votes. Most of the Thornton votes had apparently gone to Pryor.[42] Additional bad news for labor was the victory for the antilabor Beryl Anthony over Winston Bryant for the Fourth Congressional District seat vacated by Thornton. Although a pro-labor candidate won in Tucker's Second District, he ended up losing to a Republican in November.[43]

Victory for Pryor's labor-baiting campaign was another blow to the Arkansas labor movement and apparently led Bumpers to change his mind about voting for cloture. "Bumpers took it as a signal that the state was opposed to labor law reform," Eizenstat remembered. When interviewed 20 years later, Bumpers recalled that, "I knew that voting for the Panama Canal treaties and labor law reform back-to-back would have been political suicide."[44] On the day before the vote, Bumpers put a call in to the Paperworkers President Glenn, presumably to tell him about his change of heart. Glenn was not in the office to take the call and Bumpers joked to Melba Fiser, who took the call, that "he's probably playing golf and I'd like to change places with him." Fiser assured the senator that Glenn was out of the office on business and remarked, "Trust me on this, Senator, he'd like to change places with *you*." Bumpers may have wondered if someone would do to him in 1980 what Pryor had just done to Tucker. Indeed, it might have been Bill Clinton, who won the primary for governor that spring with 60 percent of the vote in the first round of balloting. Bumpers later recalled that, when he first heard Clinton speak in 1974, he thought, "If this guy is elected to the House of Representatives, six years from now he is probably going to come after me. Absolutely! I had no relish for that."[45]

The most crucial of six cloture votes came on June 13, 14, and 15, when 54, 58, and 58 votes were cast in favor of ending debate.[46] Although the bill's supporters offered a compromise proposal that addressed several of Bumpers's concerns, he voted against cloture and offered 11 amendments of his own. He made no commitment to vote for cloture even if his amendments were adopted. With Bumpers' vote gone, there was no reason for Long to vote for cloture and the effort ended two votes short.[47]

What were the opportunities missed? If the Carter administration had pressed for early action on the bill by the Senate, the votes for cloture might have been won before the business campaign had crested. If Carter had embraced the cause of labor reform as a just cause crucial to the South's as well as the nation's progress, he might have spent more time trying to win the votes of southern members of Congress. He might have made one or more speeches on the issue to educate the public. His primary theme, of course, would have been that helping workers to secure their right to self-organization was a matter of simple fairness. As a president from the South, he could have explained that the growth of unionism in the South would be good for the country in general and the South in particular. Carter's approach to the effort was compartmentalized; his support for the bill was in a "do something for labor compartment," his southern identity was in another compartment. This was evident in the way he struggled with a hostile question about the bill at a gymnasium dedication in Yazoo City, Mississippi: "I am not sure that the purpose of the legislation would lead to heavier organization by big labor in the South.... I don't think that the legislation would lead to more rapid establishment of union workers in the South. There is a heavy emphasis now on unionizing some of our plants in the South. I don't think this legislation would affect it one way or the other in any material way."[48]

If the president of the United States had been speaking publicly about southerners' stake in labor law reform, the anti-northern and antilabor arguments might have carried less weight with Arkansas voters and southern senators. In spending more time with southern Democratic senators, he might have made some promises and won the votes of Hodges and some others. A strong and early personal appeal to Bumpers that he should at a minimum maintain his record of voting for cloture might have tipped the balance. Carter "asked Senator Hollings and me to come over to the White House and play tennis, which we did," Bumpers recalled. "I assume that he was inviting us over to lobby us on the tennis court, but it never came up." Carter spoke on the phone with Bumpers for 11 minutes on June 19, presumably about the labor law reform issue, but that was after the Democratic primary and it was only on the phone.[49] Carter's style of "personal, face-to-face campaigning" had been the "centerpiece of Carter's approach" to electoral success in 1976, and he had used personal meetings effectively to win ratification of the Panama Canal treaties.[50] Carter was capable of effective personal lobbying, but, as AFL-CIO leader Lane Kirkland put it, "I don't think Carter was particularly personally interested in labor-law reform. He had no real commitment to it.... He was going along with labor-law reform as an accommodation to us." Bumpers commented: "I got the impression he was not as committed as he led labor to believe he was."[51]

The defeat of labor law reform meant that management's new aggressive tactics against unions would continue and expand. The situation became far worse when a president too weak in his support of trade unions was succeeded in 1981 by one who was positively hostile, and the Senate was captured by Republicans. Ronald Reagan's firing of striking air traffic controllers set the tone for labor relations in the 1980s. Employers in the private sector adopted the tactic of permanently replacing striking workers with greater frequency. Republican appointment of antilabor figures to the courts, the National Labor Relations Board, and other agencies dealing with unions added to labor's difficulties. The number of strikes declined and the proportion of the workforce in unions dropped by 20 percent between 1978 and 1992.[52] On the other hand, there was a new level of activism by the AFL-CIO under President Kirkland. Over 300,000 trade unionists and their supporters traveled to Washington for a Solidarity Day demonstration on September 19, 1981.[53] With the Democrats in control of the Senate after 1986, the AFL-CIO was able to secure passage of legislation under Reagan to require prior notification to workers of a plant closing and under George H. W. Bush to increase the minimum wage.

In 1990 the AFL-CIO Industrial Union Department (IUD) launched a drive for legislation to outlaw the business tactic of permanently replacing striking workers. National publicity over such action by Eastern Airlines and Greyhound led to public sympathy for the workers and opposition to the permanent replacement tactic. A public opinion poll by *Time* and the Cable News Network in March 1990 found a 57–31 percent majority favoring requiring Greyhound to rehire striking workers. Polls by Penn and Schoen Associates in January and June found a 65–26 percent majority opposed to employers having the right to permanently replace striking workers.[54]

Amending the nation's labor laws to prevent such actions found a sympathetic public response. The IUD asked international unions to send in organizers to targeted states such as Arkansas with potential swing congressional votes. The Paperworkers sent Melba Fiser to Arkansas to organize the campaign. Fiser had worked for the Paperworkers in Arkansas for a number of years and had a wide range of labor contacts. She galvanized a grassroots campaign among Arkansas trade unionists and among other supporters of social justice. Two hundred trade union leaders attended an organizing meeting in December 1990 to kick off the campaign. There were "thousands and thousands and thousands" of petition signatures, "thousands" of letters written, and numerous rallies held.[55] Over 200 workers from the Fourth Congressional District met with Representative Beryl Anthony for an hour and a half in February 1991.[56]

Fiser contacted nonlabor leaders and sought their support. One result was the formation of the Arkansas Religious Committee for Workplace Fairness, chaired by the Reverend Bryan Fulwider, president of the Arkansas Interfaith Conference. The Religious Committee emphasized "that it is morally wrong for workers in a free society such as ours to be fired for exercising their right to engage in a legal strike." It drew support from both black and white churches, from Methodists, Presbyterians, Episcopalians, Catholics, Baptists, the Christian Church, Jews, and Muslims.[57] Members of the committee lobbied Congress members, held press conferences, wrote articles in their church papers, spoke to members of their congregations, and published ads in major newspapers. "Politics and religion came together" on April 20, 1992, the *Arkansas Democrat-Gazette* reported, "as leaders from several faiths mixed prayers and hymns with a call for federal legislation to protect striking workers from being fired." Juanita Landmesser, who participated in the service as a representative of replaced striking workers in Hope, Arkansas, wrote that it "was one of the most beautiful and moving experiences of my life."[58]

Another activist coalition Fiser initiated was the Arkansas Women for Workplace Fairness. This group included several women legislators, leaders of the National Organization for Women, the Coalition of Labor Union Women, the Women's Project, the Arkansas Women's Political Caucus, the Arkansas Education Association, and several Democratic party groups. Pamela Walker, the Arkansas Women for Workplace Fairness chairperson, told Senator Pryor: "To have one's *right* to strike taken away is to have one's *right* to bargain taken away. Just ask any of the large number of women who have lost their jobs at Morrilton Plastics in Morrilton or at Champion Auto Rebuilders in Hope."[59] In addition to labor, religious, and women's groups, the Arkansas for Workplace Fairness campaign included the Arkansas Black Leadership Committee for Workplace Fairness. Senior citizen organizations, especially Arkansas Seniors Organized for Progress, were also very active in writing letters, circulating petitions, and attending rallies. In contrast to the 1976 and 1978 labor efforts, the workplace fairness campaign found the *Arkansas Gazette* strongly supportive.[60]

Two of Arkansas's four U.S. representatives, Democrats Bill Alexander and Ray Thornton, voted for the striker replacement bill. The third Democrat, Representative Beryl Anthony, ignored the constituent pressure he had received and joined Republican John Paul Hammerschmidt in voting against the bill. Labor was successful in gaining the support of then-governor Bill Clinton. At a Labor Day picnic on the state capitol grounds that had become a Clinton tradition, Clinton signed a petition asking Bumpers and Pryor to support the bill presented to him by AFL-CIO president Bill Becker. "If you give workers the right to organize and form a union, you can't take it away," Clinton said. "I haven't read the bill, but my instinct is that's what the law was supposed to be all along." Becker expressed the hope that, "If the governor is for this, then maybe Pryor and Bumpers may listen." There was good press coverage of Clinton's signing of the petition and of Becker's views on the issue. The two statewide Arkansas papers also reported on the fact that many of the participants at the picnic had attended the Solidarity Day march on Washington. Much attention was focused on the fact that Clinton was "considering a presidential bid despite his promise that he would remain governor for four years." In explaining why he might abandon his pledge, Clinton told the picnickers, "This country will be in a world of hurt unless someone who understands basic issues like education, insurance coverage and health care takes control."[61]

Senator Bumpers met with representatives from the Arkansas for Workplace Fairness on a number of occasions. On Saturday, March 7, 1992, he met with the Arkansas Religious Committee for Workplace Fairness. According to Fiser's account of the meeting, committee member Jo Ann Bemrich of the Catholic Diocese made an "eloquent and moving appeal," and Hope striker Landmesser made a "strong and emotional plea for his support." Among those attempting to persuade Bumpers was Dr. Jim Argue of the United Methodist Church, a personal friend of the senator. In final comments, the Reverend Fulwider stressed that the group was not "a lobbying group" in the sense it had something to gain from the legislation but that people in "the religious community" were working on the issue "because it is fair, just and moral and we hope the Senator will do the right thing." According to Fiser's recollection, the religious leaders "begged him to do the right thing," but Bumpers's response was "arrogant" and included inappropriate comments toward the Muslim members of the group such as: "[Y]ou fellows are a little out of place here, aren't you[?]" and "What do you think when politicians get up and say we are a Christian country?"[62]

The workplace fairness campaign drew into activity workers who had never been active before. Steve Kelley, a Pine Bluff hourly worker, decided to become active in politics for the first time, he told Representative Beryl Anthony, "when you sold me and all my fellow hourly workers down the river. I'm not any big money special interest group. I'm just a 38 year old married man, father of two boys, work by the hour, sweat all day, bust my butt, good old country boy. I'm trying to raise my sons like I was raised, with simple beliefs, the ones that count, like belief in God and country, respect the flag and stick to your guns when you know you're right.... I'm just one man with one vote but partner I've got a whole bunch of huntin' and fishin' buddies and I've a truck load of friends and I'm going to do everything in my power to try to swing their votes away from you."[63] The sentiments expressed by Kelley were shared by many workers in Anthony's district. A political study committee was formed by trade unionists in the area. The committee picketed Anthony's speaking engagements, conducted sit-ins at his public hearings, and backed an opponent in the 1992 Democratic primary.[64]

In addition to focusing on the congressional workplace fairness legislation, the Arkansas workplace fairness campaign became active in supporting two groups of Arkansas strikers who were permanently replaced. On September 4, 1991, 330 members of UAW Local 1091 at Champion

Parts Rebuilders in Hope went on strike over a proposed reduction in their health benefits. The company moved immediately to permanently replace them. Arkansans for Workplace Fairness mobilized supporters for large rallies in Hope on September 13, 1991, and October 24, 1991. On the latter occasion, nearly 1,000 people participated as Jesse Jackson came to Hope to support the workers and toured Arkansas, speaking to another rally of 500 in Little Rock. On December 14, 1991, the AFL-CIO and Arkansans for Workplace Fairness held a large Christmas Rally of 600 in Little Rock and collected over $5,000 to purchase toys for the children of the Hope strikers and UAW strikers permanently replaced by Morrilton Plastics in 1990.[65]

In their lobbying efforts, the focus of the workplace fairness committee's pressure was once again on Bumpers because Pryor suffered a heart attack in 1991.[66] The moral and social pressure on Bumpers brought by the workplace fairness campaign was immense. His meeting with 21 students, who were members of the Future Voters of America Club, in Newport on March 17, 1992, included heartfelt pleas from students whose parents were professionals, businesspeople, and workers. The students were well-versed in the issue and made effective emotional pleas. Blair Rodgers, the son of an attorney, told Bumpers: "I have known and called you Uncle Dale, all my life. Our families have been friends forever.... You have been my mentor since I was old enough to say the word Democrat.... If we allow this loop hole to continue to grow, soon the very foundation of the Country, the Working people, will fall through." Carla Moore made an appeal as the daughter of parents who were permanently replaced when they went on strike at Morrilton Plastics. "Today, my father earns $4.75 an hour. My mom cleans houses. We live with my grandparents in a three bedroom house. My parents do not sleep together. My mother shares a room with me. My father and brother share the other room." Still proud of her parents, Carla quoted her father: "You can't destroy us, we are indestructible. We will keep coming until you make way for us. We will keep talking until you hear us. We will keep fighting until we win." The senator's comments at the meeting indicated he was not listening very well, asserting that the students were confused on the issue, but they were able to give effective rejoinders to these put-downs. The breadth of the workplace fairness movement in Newport organized by coordinator Marie McClusky was remarkable. In addition to the student group, McClusky organized a Physicians Committee for Workplace Fairness and even inspired 34 property managers and a building contractor to write to Bumpers and Pryor on the issue.[67]

In a recent interview, Bumpers had no recollection of meeting with the high school students. He did recall adjusting his schedule to arrange for a meeting with the workplace fairness group in Newport prior to a scheduled banquet and being "shocked" and "a little put off" when he was

greeted by 20 "people...with placards...kind of a picketing affair."
Bumpers saw this as an "effort to intimidate me." Bumpers did recall
meeting with the religious leaders and noted that he had "immense
respect" for Dr. Argue. Especially impressive to Bumpers was the campaign of labor unionists themselves. "It was very intense," Bumpers
recalled. "It wasn't just here [in Arkansas]. Lord, I'm telling you, they
were walking through the door in Washington. Every time I looked up
there was a labor group coming in." Bumpers felt Fiser was "very acerbic
in her comments to the press about me...she was really at times down-
right rude. I was never rude back." Recalling his negative reaction to incidents in which he was criticized, Bumpers commented that "some of these
people are not very sophisticated in the art of lobbying." Bumpers met frequently with labor groups and "understood precisely what their problem
was and how emotional they were about it [but] as a representative of the
people I have a duty to see both sides."[68]

The workplace fairness campaign's foray into electoral politics had one
major success in the Democratic primary. Anthony was forced into a
runoff and then was defeated by Secretary of State Bill McKuen, a supporter of the bill campaigning with labor's backing. Unfortunately for
labor, McKuen proved vulnerable to media criticism and lost to a conservative Republican, Jay Dickey, in the general election. Bumpers, still undecided on workplace fairness, defeated State Auditor Julia Hughes Jones,
who supported the bill. The AFL-CIO remained neutral in the Bumpers-
Jones race, which Bumpers won easily.[69]

To pick up the extra votes they needed to end cloture, the AFL-CIO
offered an amendment for submitting disputes to fact-finding, under
which the employer could hire permanent replacements if the union
rejected the mediator's proposal but would be barred from doing so if the
union accepted. Kirkland went to see Bumpers, whose compromise idea
was a "small business exemption." When Bumpers indicated his definition of a small business was 500 employees, Kirkland "didn't buy it"
because Bumpers "was playing games." Bumpers recalled suggesting the
500 figure, basing it on the Small Business Administration's criteria for
defining small business.[70] There appeared to be no breakthroughs to get
the extra votes, but the Arkansas workplace fairness campaign had out-
mobilized the opposition. Pryor's office told Fiser on the day before the
vote, "If he goes the way that we're getting the overwhelming word from
home, then he'll be with you." Fiser was especially optimistic about
Bumpers' vote. Fiser recalled: "The last time I saw him at some function
before the vote, he hugged me, he says, oh, you won't be disappointed."
Bumpers maintained, however, "I'm quite sure that never happened."
Fiser was "furious," when she watched from the gallery as Bumpers gave
what she thought was a thumbs-down gesture when he voted against cloture. In an interview with the author, Bumpers demonstrated how he ges-

tured with his index finger as he does when he votes no on a bill. The implication "that I was contemptuous of the issue" was false, Bumpers commented.[71] The final vote was 57–42 for cloture with all 40 northern Democrats in favor. Although Bumpers and Pryor voted against cloture, the vote for southern Democrats as a whole was 12 to 5 in favor of cloture.[72]

Bumpers's explanation of his vote was that it "would have tilted the scales too far." He noted that the sponsors were unwilling to consider a small-business exemption and said there was "little time to evaluate" the last-minute compromise that was offered.[73] In explaining his vote, Pryor argued that the legislation would give strikers "a disproportionate advantage in delicate labor-management negotiations" and "would have substantially reduced if not totally eliminated" the risk and the last resort "aspect of striking." Pryor's only concession was to promise that Congress would act "if the use of permanent replacements continues to increase, thereby eroding the strike as a legal tool of labor." Mary Poppins would call this a "pie-crust promise," easily made, easily broken. After all, a General Accounting Office study estimated that the number of strikes declined by 53 percent in the 1980s and that in the late 1980s employers announced they would hire permanent replacements in 35 percent of strikes and did so in 17 percent of strikes. Four percent of striking workers were permanently replaced. Unions' ability to use the strike weapon already had been seriously eroded.[74] Looking back on the issue in 1997, Pryor commented that his opposition to the legislation was "philosophical...I think it would have unevened the playing field." In Pryor's view, the dramatic decline in labor union membership over the previous two decades stemmed not from a playing field tipped unfairly toward business but from corporations "offering as many benefits as the labor unions...in some instances greater benefits than the labor union shops." Having moved away from the pro-union approach of his early career, Pryor connected his opposition to striker replacement with his general criticism of labor's approach to political action: "There were a lot of David Pryors out there who got burned with their local labor people.... There was a period where you could vote nine times for labor and one time for business and you were on their out list, you were blacklisted. They were extremely unreasonable."[75] Bumpers recalled that "Senator Pryor and I were in constant discussion., we were torn about it." They decided "about forty-eight hours before the vote. [W]e talked about how an economic strike can bankrupt small businesses." In Bumpers' view, "we are mostly small business [in Arkansas]. Labor with workplace fairness...they have a very heavy tool."[76]

Becker acknowledged that concerns about business needs were on the minds of Arkansas's two senators, but he believed that it was large not small businesses which carried the greatest weight: "From time to time they've got to just show the power structure, the business community who come up with the big bucks to help fund the campaigns that they're independent of labor." Bumpers recalled that Tyson Foods was "very much opposed" to the striker replacement bill. "Every major company in Arkansas was opposed to that bill," Bumpers added. "Tyson's always been a strong supporter [of mine but].... You don't vote that way.... If it's an even situation, you might give a little more weight to people who have been supportive of you than the people who have not.... Tyson will tell you I voted against their position as often as I voted for it." Bumpers commented on his lack of support from labor: "Labor's a little more volatile.... I don't think labor gave me a nickel in 1992. I'm not sure they did in '86 either or '80. I've just not had any labor money—really ever."[77]

Most of the issues of concern to the AFL-CIO were general social reform issues on which both Bumpers and Pryor had fairly liberal records. Pure union issues reached the floor of Congress only infrequently, but on those occasions unions were usually quite determined that those they supported vote their way. To the unions, all that was required to support labor law reform and workplace fairness was a recognition that unions had a right to exist and needed some help from government. The pressures of Arkansas's political environment prevented Bumpers and Pryor from adopting such an uncomplicated pro-union stance.

By the time of the workplace fairness vote, the nation's attention was increasingly focused on the presidential race and Bill Clinton. Clinton's campaign for the presidency faced many bumps, among them Bill Becker's criticism of his labor record. Not only had Clinton opposed the repeal of the right-to-work amendment in 1976, but as governor he had facilitated a grant to Morrilton Plastics during the UAW strike there in 1990. The AFL-CIO had held up its endorsement of Clinton for governor that year "until we got word...that [the] strike had been settled; it turned out it wasn't," Becker recalled. In a report on Clinton's record prepared at the AFL-CIO's request, Becker found Clinton on labor's side only 30 percent of the time. In the 1992 campaign, however, Clinton was endorsing the workplace fairness bill and he had ideas about job creation, health care, and education that unionists liked. As the campaign unfolded, Clinton seemed to most AFL-CIO leaders to be "our best bet." Becker was "severely criticized." Becker himself ended up speaking out on Clinton's behalf.[78] Nevertheless, labor received no help from candidate Clinton during the Senate showdown on the bill. Doubts about Clinton in labor circles grew in the wake of the votes by Bumpers and Pryor. Avis Lavelle, a Clinton campaign spokesperson maintained that Clinton had talked to the two senators but "was unable to sway them." Becker faxed John Perkins, COPE director: "For what it's worth, Senator Pryor told me that Clinton did *not* talk to him about S. 55, Workplace Fairness. Bumpers also told me that Clinton did *not* talk to him about S. 55. Bumpers seemed surprised when I mentioned to him that we had received word that Clinton had spoken to he [sic] and Pryor and that they had agreed to vote favorably."[79]

Whatever doubts trade unionists had about Clinton, he looked far better than George H.W. Bush or Ross Perot. The trade unions played an important role in Clinton's electoral victory, and they looked forward to a more activist government that would be fairer to working people in general and unions in particular. During the economic summit conference conducted by Clinton in Little Rock during the transition period after his election, AFL-CIO secretary-treasurer Tom Donahue made an eloquent plea on the issue of workers' economic insecurity, noting that workers "see a system of labor law which simply doesn't work, which is destructive of their rights, which frustrates any of their efforts to organize together and to work together, and they see that if they are forced to go out on strike they will be replaced and the law will say that's a fine result." Instead of reaffirming support for the striker replacement legislation as a matter of basic fairness, of giving workers a sense that they belong and have a place at the table in this new globalized economy, Clinton responded: "I think when we define security in the 1990s and beyond, it will probably never be the way it was in the '50s. We'll have to figure out a different definition of what it means to be a secure American, if you're willing to work hard and work smart."[80]

A few weeks after the inauguration, Secretary of Labor Robert Reich met with Kirkland and Donahue to discuss the administration's agenda. Although Reich assured the labor leaders that the president supported workplace fairness, he was privately doubtful, given that the issue had not even made it onto Clinton's "long list" of priorities.[81] Clinton was willing to see the workplace fairness bill brought up again in the new Congress. Representative Pat Williams, chair of the House Education and Labor Subcommittee on Labor-Management Relations, scheduled hearings on March 30, 1993, only after he had assurances from the Department of Labor that the White House wanted the bill. "I never got the impression this was a live-or-die bill for President Clinton or candidate Clinton, but it is high on his workers' rights agenda," Williams said. Reich appeared before House and Senate subcommittees on the same day to explain the legislation and affirm that the president backed it. Pryor said, "I am willing to look at it again."[82]

The House of Representatives adopted the workplace fairness bill early in the session, on June 15, 1993, by a 239–190 margin. Support was again strongest among northern Democrats (169–1). Southern Democrats favored the bill by a 52–32 margin while the Republican vote was 17–157. There were eight fewer votes for the bill than in 1991 because eight of nine northern seats the Democrats lost in the 1992 election went to Republicans who voted against the bill. As was the case in 1977 and 1991, action in the

Senate was delayed despite a May 5, 1993, vote by the Senate Labor and Human Resources Committee to back the legislation.[83]

The trade unions were pleased with many of the president's initiatives but adamantly opposed to his efforts to pass the North American Free Trade Agreement (NAFTA). Initiated under the Bush administration, trade unions viewed NAFTA as a threat to jobs and labor standards. There was an extensive grassroots mobilization by trade unions that helped convince most Democrats in Congress to vote against the measure. With a solid base of support among Republicans, however, President Clinton was able to win enough Democratic votes to pass the bill. NAFTA was Clinton's Panama Canal treaty. He pulled out all the stops, wheeling and dealing to get the bill passed. During the course of the campaign, he lashed out at labor unions for threatening political retaliation against members of Congress who voted for NAFTA, calling that "real roughshod, muscle-bound tactics." In some labor circles, Lane Kirkland recalled, buttons proclaiming "Bill Becker was right," popped up.[84] Despite the strong words and emotions, NAFTA did not cause a permanent break between Clinton and the trade unions. The dispute came early in Clinton's presidency. He would be president for at least another three years. The next electoral test would be in the 1994 congressional elections, not a presidential contest. There were many other issues on which the two agreed. Both sides, therefore, attended to repairing the rift.[85]

Like Carter, Clinton made no public addresses on the workplace fairness bill. Kirkland credits Clinton with being "considerably more sophisticated than Jimmy Carter" on labor issues. Nonetheless, on the one occasion when he was asked about the bill—by a concerned employer of 30 workers at a town meeting on July 4, 1993, in Eldridge, Iowa—Clinton sounded a lot like Jimmy Carter in Yazoo City:

A lot of small businesses believe that maybe they'd be more of a target for a union if people thought they could strike over wages and benefits. I personally doubt that very much because of the relationships most people have with their employees in small businesses....

The people who are for it in the congress...have no interest in trying to make it either easier or harder than it is right now for people to organize themselves into unions. The question is whether that once the workers vote to join a union, the bargaining process plays out in a fair and balanced way.

Clinton indicated that he had no idea "whether it can pass the Senate" but that "they don't have the votes yet, and we're talking about whether they can get some sort of compromise to deal with the balance issue."[86] Although Clinton explained that, prior to the 1980s, "no strikes were just broken and people...run off on that account," like Carter in Yazoo City, Clinton backed away from an explicit identification with unionism comparable to John Kennedy's. Clinton failed to criticize the permanent replacement tactic, affirm workers' historic right to strike, or explain how the Wagner Act's protection against the unfair labor practice of being fired for going on strike was undermined by the fiction that there is a difference between being permanently replaced and being fired. If the ideological approaches of Clinton and Carter appear similar, it should be pointed out Clinton did far less than Carter. For example, Clinton made no effort comparable to Carter's meeting with the labor law reform bill's supporters during the Senate filibuster. In his memoir, Secretary of Labor Reich recalls Clinton's anger at finding a meeting with labor leaders on his schedule. "Who the hell set this up? Why do I need to be yelled at about striker replacement? I can't ask senators to give me this one when I need them on health care, damn it." Reich recalled his response to Clinton: "What bugs them isn't that you didn't *deliver* striker replacement.... They're angry because they think you didn't *try*." Reich records that Clinton recovered his composure, charmed the union presidents, and promised "I'm gonna try to make this happen."[87] There appears to have been little follow-through on this promise, however, even after the defeat of the health care initiative. The first attempt to secure cloture on the workplace fairness bill came on July 12, 1994, with Clinton just returning home from a weeklong trip to Europe. The second and final try came on July 13.[88]

As the Senate finally moved to consider the bill in mid-1994, a group of Arkansas trade unionists took a 20-hour bus ride to Washington to participate in a press conference with bill sponsor Senator Howard Metzenbaum and to lobby Bumpers and Pryor. Paperworkers leader Alan Hughes recalled that the meeting with the two senators lasted about 20 minutes: "They told us at that time...if I vote for this I really get nothing in return. What they meant by that was your labor votes aren't turning out like they ought to be.... If I vote for this...there's gonna be this group, they're going to come after me with everything they got and can y'all protect me." Publicly, Pryor commented: "I haven't seen any alternative I can support," while Bumpers stated: "I can't see anything that has changed." Metzenbaum said that he had "twisted their arms,...poked them in the eye with a pencil on this" and that the president had lobbied the two Arkansas senators. Neither would comment on discussions with Clinton. In 1997 Pryor recalled no specific discussion with Clinton but "maybe someone from the White House said, 'Is there any way you can change your position?'" Bumpers recalled that Clinton "did lobby me on workplace fairness and he lobbied pretty hard. I don't think we got into the merits or the demerits of the bill. He just wanted me to vote for it." There were some last-minute efforts at compromise, but in the end the vote for cloture fell seven votes short, with Bumpers and Pryor once again voting against it.[89]

An analysis of the votes on the three labor reform efforts shows some significant changes occurring between the Senate votes in 1978 and 1992.

There was a decline in northern GOP support (nine votes) for labor reform and an increase in southern Democratic support (nine votes). The decline in GOP support may be attributed to the growing conservative strength within the GOP and the influence of the Bush administration's hostility to the legislation. Why the gain in southern Democratic support? The southern political alignment was growing more like that of the rest of the country—GOP strength had grown in the South, southern Democrats had fewer conservative supporters than in the past, and labor's 1992 campaign was more effective in the South than the corresponding campaign in 1978.

Between 1992 and 1994, despite a sympathetic Democratic president in the White House, there was an erosion rather than an increase in support for the workplace fairness bill. The vote on cloture was 53–47 compared with the 57–42 of 1992. Two Republicans (Ted Stevens of Alaska and Bob Packwood of Oregon) and one southern Democrat (Sam Nunn of Georgia) who voted for cloture in 1992 opposed it in 1994. Although supporters picked up two votes due to 1992 Democratic gains in California and Wisconsin, they lost a vote due to a 1992 Republican victory in Georgia. In addition, votes for cloture were lost due to Lloyd Bentsen's appointment as secretary of the treasury and his replacement by Republican Kay Bailey Hutchinson in a special election and the appointment of Democrat Harlan Matthews to replace Vice President Al Gore in Tennessee. *Congressional Quarterly Almanac* reported that President Clinton "supported the bill...with less enthusiasm than advocates had hoped for. Union officials said they were angry that the administration had not made the bill a greater priority. Ron Carey, president of the International Brotherhood of Teamsters, expressed disappointment that Clinton had not made the same effort on striker replacement that he made in 1993 on the North American Free Trade Agreement." As the *New York Times* reported, the bill "never inspired the midnight phone calls and political arm twisting that the White House has lavished on other difficult political issues like" NAFTA or the 1993 budget. Reich made a similar comparison in his memoirs and commented: "If he didn't get Dale Bumpers and David Pryor, how hard could he have tried?" Indeed, Reich's own efforts on the bill were modest, as his own priority was in training programs for skilled jobs of the future.[90]

On the other hand, it appears that labor's effort had diminished as well between 1992 and 1994. After the defeat of the workplace fairness bill in 1992, the labor movement focused its energies on the election of Clinton and a Democratic Congress. In 1993 the labor movement was energized in the battle against NAFTA. With the loss of a couple of votes due to elections, Kirkland felt the "votes weren't there." It was "an exercise we had to go through." Kirkland recalled that he "swung a couple of Southerners" in 1992, including Sam Nunn. After Wynch Fowler lost in Georgia, however, Nunn told Kirkland, "I can't do it."[91] In the aftermath of the defeat of the bill, the Clinton administration finally took action with the issuance of an executive order excluding those who employed permanent replacements from bidding on federal contracts. Business interests successfully contested in the courts the attempt to use presidential powers to accomplish what they had prevented the Congress from doing. Nevertheless, Clinton's efforts in this regard, coupled with his standing up to the new Republican majority in the Congress, helped to reduce discontent within labor's ranks.[92]

If the workplace fairness bill had been high on Clinton's priority list, he might have left Bentsen in the Senate and worked to convince Matthews, Nunn, Oklahoma's David Boren, Bumpers, Pryor and Hollings to vote for cloture if not the bill. He could have made a pitch to the country on the issue of the undemocratic Senate rule which permits a minority of 41 to prevent action on needed social measures supported by the majority of the country and the majority of the Congress. As Bill Becker put it, "[I]f he had asked Pryor and Bumpers to vote for cloture and really meant it and was damn serious about and wanted their votes, he would have gotten them. You don't turn a president down on an issue that he's strung out on." Although Kirkland is doubtful about the possibility of winning Bumpers's and Pryor's votes, he speculated that Lyndon Johnson-style persuasion might have won some votes.[93]

The similarities between Clinton and Carter's performance on these two labor law reform measures are notable. Both presidents viewed their political role as a centrist one, adhering to Democratic traditions but moving away from a stance too close to the liberal wing of the party. Although trade unions were a significant organized interest group whose concerns one had to respond to, union issues were at best a subsidiary matter. Carter saw his role as a trustee for the nation who combined religious values, a concern for social justice, and the fiscal conservatism of the businessperson. Clinton saw his role as a visionary who could respond to the concerns of core Democratic constituencies with sophistication and balance and reach out to the broad middle of American public opinion with sensible and cost-effective reforms on issues such as welfare and crime manipulated in the past by Republican conservatives. Clinton believed, moreover, that he could move the country as a whole forward by focusing on U.S. international leadership, global competitiveness, strengthening human resource development through expanding and improving education, and nurturing children. Preserving his personal political capital so that he could put his vision into place appeared to subordinate all other concerns. Although Clinton endorsed the trade union position, his actions were of marginal benefit to the workplace-fairness cause.

The commitment of trade union officials and grassroots labor activists to secure change beneficial to working people was evident in both the 1970s and 1990s. Although the Arkansas labor movement has significant influence, the clout of the Arkansas business community has proved greater whenever the issue is strengthening the organized labor movement. Business organizations mobilize pro-business elements whenever this threat appears and have the resources to appeal to nonbusiness elements in the name of individualist values. Even some populist and liberal elements desert the banner of labor collectivism when business is able to frame the issue as one of individual freedom from coercion, as happened in 1976. Politicians concerned about political survival face the certainty of business opposition if they support specifically pro-union measures. Business interests and conservatives continue to participate in Democratic primaries as the only game in town in a still predominately Democratic state. Nevertheless, the "Big Three" of recent Arkansas politics—Clinton, Pryor, and Bumpers—have exhibited a philosophy of "progressive populism" in Diane Blair's view. Pryor himself characterizes his philosophy as populist while Bumpers sees himself as a "social liberal" but "fiscal conservative." Bumpers and Pryor have irritated some specific business groups by their criticism, but pro-union action would result in a general business hostility. Instead, both senators and their spouses found themselves the guests of honor on inauguration day in 1993 at a Washington breakfast buffet for 1,200 Arkansans hosted by Don Tyson of Tyson Foods.[94] Although both senators have done many good things for the downtrodden, they do these things as moral and civic-minded, comfortably well-off people. It may be that the ultimately deciding factor is that their day-to-day frame of reference is the world of the Don Tysons, who feel so deeply that unions have no place, instead of the world of the permanently replaced and now poverty-stricken strikers of Hope and Morrilton. We do not know how Bumpers and Pryor might have responded if their fellow Arkansan in the White House had provided a Rooseveltian vision of being a little to the left of center, standing up for unions as a necessary democratic counterweight to the power of business in the private economy, and advancing the idea that: "The test of our progress is not whether we add more to the abundance of those who have much; it is whether we provide enough for those who have too little."[95]

NOTES

1. Dewey W. Grantham, *The South in Modern America: A Region at Odds* (New York: HarperCollins, 1994); Earl Black and Merle Black, *The Vital South: How Presidents Are Elected* (Cambridge: Harvard University Press, 1992).

2. The phrase "moderate to liberal" is borrowed from J. Bill Becker, former president of the Arkansas AFL-CIO, who used the phrase to describe leading Arkansas politicians. Interview, December 17, 1996. In his classic study of southern politics, Key said Arkansas had "the one-party system in its most undefiled and undiluted form." V.O. Key, Jr., *Southern Politics* (New York: Vintage Books, 1949), 183.

3. The Twenty-Fourth Amendment had outlawed the poll tax in federal elections.

4. The three women's groups were the League of Women Voters, the American Association of University Women, and the State Federation of Business and Professional Women. In the six years following the adoption of the amendment, the number of registered voters increased by 23 percent. The Voting Rights Act of 1965 was not applied in Arkansas since registration of African Americans was above the 50 percent trigger point in 1965. Calvin R. Ledbetter, Jr., "Arkansas Amendment for Voter Registration without Poll Tax Payment," *Arkansas Historical Quarterly* LIV (Summer 1995): 138, 151–58, 162; Alan Draper, *Conflict of Interests: Organized Labor and the Civil Rights Movement in the South 1954–1968* (Ithaca, N.Y.: ILR Press, 1994), 96. The quotation is from Diane D. Blair, *Arkansas Politics and Government* (Lincoln: University of Nebraska Press, 1988), 52–53.

5. Blair, *Arkansas Politics and Government*, 42.

6. *Statistical Abstract of the United States*, 1980, Table No. 715, 1996, Table No. 683; Blair, *Arkansas Politics and Government*, 80.

7. Timothy P. Donovan and Willard B. Gatewood, Jr., *The Governors of Arkansas: Essays in Political Biography* (Fayetteville: University of Arkansas Press, 1981), 235–41; Interview with Dale Bumpers, February 17, 1998.

8. Bumpers later commented that he had "always wanted to go to Congress" and Fulbright appeared vulnerable. Timothy P. Donovan and Willard B. Gatewood, Jr., *The Governors of Arkansas: Essays in Political Biography* (Fayetteville: University of Arkansas Press, 1981), 235–41; Randall Bennet Woods, *Fulbright: A Biography* (Cambridge, England: Cambridge University Press, 1995), 653–70; Interview with J. Bill Becker, December 16, 1996.

9. The same year, Florida adopted a right-to-work law by a similar margin while California defeated one by a 59 to 41 percent vote. Gilbert J. Gall, "Southern Industrial Workers and Anti-Union Sentiment: Arkansas and Florida in 1944," in Robert H. Zieger, ed., *Organized Labor in the Twentieth Century South* (Knoxville: University of Tennessee Press, 1991), 228–31.

10. Technically, it was a proposal to amend the constitutional right-to-work amendment rather than repeal it. If the majority of a collective bargaining unit agreed, union and management could negotiate a union security agreement. *Arkansas Gazette*, November 4, 1976.

11. *Arkansas Union Labor Bulletin*, February 15, May 15, 1976.

12. Ibid., May 15, 1976.

13. *Arkansas Gazette*, November 4, 1976, 1A:4.

14. *Arkansas Union Labor Bulletin*, March 15, 1976.

15. *Arkansas Gazette*, November 8, 1976.

16. Ibid., April 17, 20, 25, May 30, 1976; Interview with J. Bill Becker, December 17, 1996; Meredith Oakley, *On the Make: The Rise of Bill Clinton* (Washington, D.C.: Regnery Publishing, Inc., 1994), 154–57; *Almanac of American Politics*, 1976, 40.

17. *Arkansas Gazette*, November 4, 1976; Interview with J. Bill Becker, December 17, 1996.

18. *Arkansas Union Labor Bulletin*, November 1, 1976.

19. *Arkansas Gazette*, November 4, 5, 1976; Interview with J. Bill Becker, December 17, 1996. Gilbert Gall interviewed Becker in 1986 and writes that Becker said that funding for the campaign was spotty. Gilbert J. Gall, *The Politics of Right to Work: The Labor Federations as Special Interests, 1943–1979* (New York: Greenwood Press, 1988), 197.

20. See Chapter 6.

21. J. Bill Becker to Affiliates, Re: Rallies—Labor Law Reform, September 16, 1977, Clipping, "Labor Bill Backed," *Jonesboro Sun*, September 27, 1977, Becker to All Affiliates, October 19, 1977, Arkansas AFL-CIO Files, Labor Law Reform, Local Correspondence.

22. Notes of Labor Law Reform Bill in 13 Southern States for IWA Speech, August 4, 1978, Files of the Arkansas AFL-CIO, Labor Law Reform, Local Union Correspondence; *Congressional Quarterly Almanac*, 1977, 172-H.

23. See Chapter 5.

24. AFL-CIO President Bill Becker wondered, "Could it be because your very own ox is being gored?" Becker noted that the *Gazette* management had used delaying tactics to thwart a union campaign at the paper in 1974–75. After a 17-month process, the election was lost on a 30–30 tie vote. *Arkansas Gazette*, February 25, 1978, 14A.

25. *Historical Report of the Secretary of State*, 1978, 1:81.

26. J. Bill Becker to Andrew Biemiller, January 9, 1978, Arkansas AFL-CIO Files, Labor Law Reform, National Correspondence.

27. J. Bill Becker to Andrew Biemiller, January 9, 1978, Notes on Senator Kaneaster Hodges, n.d., Arkansas AFL-CIO Files, Labor Law Reform, National Correspondence; Interview with David Pryor, July 7, 1997.

28. Clipping, "Hodges Opposes Labor Measure, Believes It Would Hurt Arkansas," *Arkansas Gazette*, February 11, 1978, Arkansas AFL-CIO Files, Labor Law Reform, Local Correspondence.

29. Wayne Glenn to Dale Bumpers, February 27, 1978, Arkansas AFL-CIO Files, Labor Law Reform, Local Correspondence.

30. *Arkansas Gazette*, February 17, 1978.

31. H.D. Baird to the President, February 8, 1978, Bob Roberts to Dale Bumpers, February 7, 1978, Public Reaction, Labor Law Reform Proposal, Secretary of Labor Ray Marshall Papers, Box 96, Records of the Department of Labor, RG 174, National Archives (hereafter cited as NA).

32. Dale Bumpers to Dear Friend, n.d., Arkansas AFL-CIO Files, Labor Law Reform, Local Correspondence.

33. *Arkansas Gazette*, February 17, 1978, 1A.

34. Becker notes that Bumpers disputes that he made any pledge but "people who were with me agree that he said what I just described to you." In the wake of the dispute over the pledge, "our relationship hasn't been the same since." Interview with J. Bill Becker, December 17, 1996; Interview with Stuart Eizenstat, July 16, 1993; Interview with Melba [Fiser] Collins and Gordon Brehm, December 30, 1996.

35. Interview with David Pryor, July 7, 1997.

36. Calculated from the data in *Historical Report of the Secretary of State*, 1986, 207.

37. Interview with J. Bill Becker, December 30, 1996. Becker's recollection is confirmed by the record. *Congress and the Nation*, 1969–72, III:720, 46ab.

38. Interview with J. Bill Becker, December 30, 1996.

39. Ibid., December 30, 1996; Interview with David Pryor, July 7, 1997; *Arkansas Gazette*, May 16, 1978.

40. Calculated from the data in *Historical Report of the Secretary of State*, 1986, 207.

41. *Arkansas Gazette,* June 3, 8, 11, 1978.

42. Ibid., June 11, 1978.

43. Ibid., June 11, 14, 1978; *Historical Report of the Secretary of State,* 238.

44. Interview with Dale Bumpers, February 17, 1998.

45. Interview with J. Bill Becker, December 17, 1996; Interview with Melba [Fiser] Collins, December 30, 1996; Interview of Stuart Eizenstat, July 16, 1993; *New York Times,* March 27, 1993, 9:3. Recent news articles have highlighted Clinton's role in supporting Pryor in the 1978 primary and the part played by Clinton adviser Dick Morris.

46. *Congressional Quarterly Almanac,* 1978, 284–87, 28-S.

47. *Arkansas Gazette,* June 17, 1978.

48. *Public Papers of the Presidents, Jimmy Carter, 1977,* II:1332–33.

49. President's Daily Diary, June 19, 1978, 2–3, Appointments/Diary File, Box PD-33, Presidential Diary Office, Jimmy Carter Library; Interview with Dale Bumpers, February 17, 1998.

50. "Arkansas voters still expect, indeed demand, the human supplement to the televised appeals and will punish those who never appear personally in their vicinity." Blair, *Arkansas Politics and Government,* 59; Black and Black, *The Vital South,* 251.

51. Interview with Lane Kirkland, November 14, 1996; Interview with Dale Bumpers, February 17, 1998.

52. Computed from *Statistical Abstract,* 1996, Table No. 681, and *Statistical Abstract,* 1980, Table No. 714. On the decline in the number of strikes and the use of permanent replacements, see U.S. General Accounting Office, *Strikes and the Use of Permanent Replacements in the 1970s and 1980s* (GAO/HRD91–92, January 18, 1991).

53. Interview with Lane Kirkland, November 14, 1996.

54. Committee for Workplace Fairness, "Polls Show Public Strongly Opposes Firing of Striking Workers," Files of Melba [Fiser] Collins, copy in author's possession.

55. Interview with Melba [Fiser] Collins, December 30, 1996.

56. Ibid.

57. "We Believe in Workplace Fairness!" *Arkansas Democrat-Gazette* ad, April 12, 1992, Files of Melba [Fiser] Collins, copy in author's possession.

58. *Arkansas Democrat-Gazette,* April 21 1992; Arkansas Religious Committee Interfaith Service Program, "A Call for Justice in the Workplace, April 20, 1992, Juanita Landmasser to Arkansas Religious Committee, April 25, 1992, Files of Melba Fiser Collins, copy in author's possession.

59. Pamela D. Walker to David Pryor, January 22, 1992, Files of Melba [Fiser] Collins, copy in author's possession.

60. Rev. Ellihue Gaylord to All NAACP Branch Presidents, January 21, 1992, Melba Fiser, Brief Report of the Arkansans for Workplace Fairness Grassroots Campaign, September 1990–May 1992, Clippings, *Arkansas Gazette,* May 7, June 2, July 16, 30, August 28, 1991, Arkansas AFL-CIO Files, Workplace Fairness. By this point the *Gazette* was in a circulation war with the *Arkansas Democrat* and it sold out to the *Democrat* in the course of the campaign.

61. Clippings, *Arkansas Democrat,* September 3, 1991, *Arkansas Gazette,* September 3, 1991, files of Melba [Fiser] Collins, copies in author's possession.

62. Melba Fiser, Report on Meeting of Arkansas Religious Committee for Workplace Fairness Meeting with Senator Dale Bumpers, March 7, 1992, Files of Melba [Fiser] Collins, copy in author's possession; Interview with Melba [Fiser] Collins, December 30, 1996.

63. Steve Kelley to Beryl Anthony, n.d., Files of Melba [Fiser] Collins, copy in author's possession.

64. Melba Fiser, Brief Report of the Arkansans for Workplace Fairness Grass-roots Campaign, September 1990–May 1992, Files of Melba [Fiser] Collins, copy in author's possession; Interview with Alan Hughes, September 16, 1996; interview with Melba [Fiser] Collins, December 30, 1996.

65. Clippings, *Texarkana Gazette,* September 6, 1991, *Hope Star,* September 16, 1991, October 25, 1991, *Arkansas Democrat-Gazette,* October 23, 25, 1991, Arkansans for Workplace Fairness, Press Release, December 12, 1991, Memo, B. Demczuk to Rev. Jackson, October 21, 1991. The National AFL-CIO contributed $2,500. Bill Becker to Thomas Donahue, December 16, 1991, Arkansas AFL-CIO Files.

66. Interview with Melba [Fiser] Collins, December 30, 1996.

67. Questions and Comments for Meting with Senator Bumpers, March 17, 1992, Roger L. Green, M.D., statement, n.d., "Bumpers Speaks on 'Striker Replacement' Bill," Clipping, *Newport Daily Independent,* June 17, 1991, Letters, Marie [McCloskey] to Melba [Fiser], with attached letters to Senator [Bumpers], Arkansas AFL-CIO Files; Interview with Melba [Fiser] Collins, December 30, 1996.

68. Interview with Dale Bumpers, February 17, 1998.

69. *Arkansas Times,* July 2, 1992, Arkansas AFL-CIO Files, Workplace Fairness. Jones later switched to the Republican party.

70. Interview with Lane Kirkland, November 14, 1996; Interview with Dale Bumpers, February 17, 1998.

71. Interview with Melba [Fiser] Collins, December 30, 1996.

72. *Congressional Quarterly Almanac,* 1992, 17-S.

73. *Arkansas Times,* July 2, 1992, Arkansas AFL-CIO Files, Workplace Fairness.

74. David Pryor to Tim Brewer, July 10, 1992, Arkansas AFL-CIO Files, Workplace Fairness; U.S. General Accounting Office, *Strikes and the Use of Permanent Replacements in the 1970s and 1980s* (GAO/HRD91–92, January 18, 1991).

75. Interview with David Pryor, July 7, 1997.

76. Interview with Dale Bumpers, February 17, 1998.

77. Interview with Bill Becker, December 17, 1996, Interview with Dale Bumpers, February 17, 1998.

78. Interview with J. Bill Becker, December 17, 1996; *Arkansas Democrat-Gazette,* January 15, 16, 17, 1992, March 15, 1992, May 2, 1993; Interview with Alan Hughes, September 16, 1996.

79. *Congressional Quarterly Almanac,* 1993, 396; *Congressional Quarterly Weekly Report,* April 3, 1993, 841; Clipping, Jill Lawrence, "Unions, Minorities Sticking with Clinton Despite Doubts," *Arkansas Democrat-Gazette,* June 22, 1992, Arkansas AFL-CIO Files, Workplace Fairness; Bill Becker to John Perkins, June 22, 1992, Arkansas AFL-CIO Files, Workplace Fairness (emphasis in original).

80. Bill Clinton, *Economic Conference (1992: Little Rock: Ark), President Clinton's New Beginning* (New York: Donald I Fine, n.d.), 95–97.

81. Robert B. Reich, *Locked in the Cabinet* (New York: Alfred A. Knopf, 1997), 66–67.

82. *Congressional Quarterly Almanac,* 1993, 396; *Congressional Quarterly Weekly Report,* April 3, 1993, 841.

83. *Congressional Quarterly Almanac,* 1991, 313–15, 52–53-H; *Congressional Quarterly Almanac,* 1993, 396–97, 54–55-H.

84. *Public Papers of the Presidents, Bill Clinton, 1993,* II:1920; Elizabeth Drew, *On the Edge: The Clinton Presidency* (New York: Simon & Schuster, 194), 338–46; Interview with Lane Kirkland, November 14, 1996.

85. Interview with Lane Kirkland, November 14, 1996.

86. Ibid.; *Public Papers of the Presidents, 1993,* I:1005–6.

87. Reich, *Locked in the Cabinet,* 175–76.

88. *Public Papers of the Presidents,* 1994, I:1367–68; *Congressional Quarterly Weekly Report,* July 16, 1994, 1936.

89. *Arkansas Democrat-Gazette,* June 15, 1994; *Congressional Quarterly Weekly Report,* July 16, 1994; Interview with Alan Hughes, September 16, 1996; Interview with David Pryor, July 7, 1997; Interview with Dale Bumpers, February 17, 1998.

90. *Congressional Quarterly Almanac,* 1994, 403; *New York Times,* July 13, 1994, D, 18:5; Reich, *Locked in the Cabinet,* 149, 175.

91. Interview with Lane Kirkland, November 14, 1996.

92. *New York Times,* February 3, 1996.

93. Interview with J. Bill Becker, December 17, 1996; Interview with Dale Kirkland, November 14, 1996.

94. Diane D. Blair, "The Big Three of Late Twentieth Century Arkansas Politics: Dale Bumpers, Bill Clinton, and David Pryor," *Arkansas Historical Quarterly* LIV (Spring 1995): 69; Interview with David Pryor, July 7, 1997; Interview with Dale Bumpers, February 17, 1998; *Arkansas Democrat-Gazette,* January 21, 1993.

95. Frank Roosevelt, Second Inaugural Address, in Philip S. Foner, ed., *Franklin Delano Roosevelt: Selections from His Writings* (New York: International Publishers, 1947), 25.

CHAPTER 8

The Crisis of the Labor Movement in the United States and the Search for a New Vision in Domestic and Foreign Affairs

The labor movement in the United States has entered a period of dramatic change. After decades of relative decline in union membership, the AFL-CIO has a more progressive leadership committed to organizing the unorganized, enhancing labor's political clout, revitalizing the movement, and increasing international labor solidarity. My goals in this chapter are to examine the causes of union decline and to evaluate the search by the labor movement for a new vision to guide both its domestic and foreign policy.

The proportion of union members in the U.S. nonagricultural labor force (union density) peaked in 1953 at 32.5 percent. Union density declined gradually to 28.9 percent in 1975. Between 1975 and 1987, the rate declined precipitously, reaching 17.0 percent. The decline has since continued, but at a somewhat slower pace, falling to 13.5 percent in 2000. The drop has been especially dramatic in the private sector where union density for nonagricultural workers is 9.1 percent, lower than the level in 1930.[1]

There are several factors involved in this decline. The decrease in employment in the highly unionized manufacturing and mining industries, the employers' shifting of jobs toward the more conservative southern states, and the growth of the service sector in which employers rely on the use of part-time employees provide part of the explanation. More fundamental, however, are the move by private employers, in the context of an increasingly globalized economy, to aggressive antiunion policies, the internal political weaknesses of the labor movement, and an unfavorable legal environment.

The majority of employers in the United States have been extreme in their antiunion animus throughout most of the history of the country. Prior to the 1930s, workers were able to effectively combat this hostility and establish union power only in specific local and regional labor markets. Unions were able to develop power as national collective bargaining agents during the 1930s due to a militant labor upsurge and radical changes in the nation's labor law. It is important to understand the 1930s transformation and the subsequent reversal of both U.S. labor law and internal union politics in order to understand labor's present dilemma.

The U.S. labor movement in the 1920s was weak, crippled by court injunctions, and dominated internally by conservatives. With the onset of the Great Depression, the Communist party led a strong protest movement against unemployment and strengthened its base among the working class. Strikes were few during the first three years of the depression, but the American Federation of Labor (AFL) achieved an important victory against the crippling antiunion injunction tool with the passage of the Norris-LaGuardia Act in 1932. With the onset of Franklin Roosevelt's New Deal in 1933, there was both broadened left activism by a number of left parties and organizations and the growth of old and new trade unions. The synergy between grassroots activism and the New Deal led in 1935 to a radical revision in labor law and the founding of a powerful new labor movement, the Congress of Industrial Organizations (CIO), in which leftists played important roles in the leadership and at the grass roots. The Wagner Act outlawed company unions and other management "unfair labor practices" that interfered with the self-organization of workers. For the first time, the law required the employer to bargain in good faith with a union chosen by a majority of workers as their sole collective bargaining agency. With the favorable political context of Franklin Roosevelt's reelection as president and Frank Murphy's election as governor of Michigan in 1936, autoworkers succeeded in compelling General Motors to sign a contract while corporation appeals of the constitutionality of the Wagner Act were pending. The combination of a grassroots movement, sympathetic politicians, and a favorable law led to an increase from 14.2 percent union density in 1936 to 22.5 percent in 1940. Although Roosevelt replaced the National Labor Relations Board's (NLRB) original progressives with moderates, the wartime employment boom and a pro-union stance by the National War Labor Board helped unions to increase union density to 30.4 percent in 1945. Not only had the trade unions increased their membership nearly fourfold during Roosevelt's tenure in office, they dramatically increased their political clout in Washington and in local communities.

The passage of the Taft-Hartley Act in 1947 and the purging of the left in the trade union movement were the decisive events in weakening the trade union movement in the United States. Although trade union membership stabilized at about 32 percent of the labor force between 1947 and

1955, the new law limited the possibilities for advances by labor and the purging of the left took much of the vision out of a movement that relies on volunteerism, the spirit of caring and self-sacrifice, and radical spark-plugs and policies to make progress. The Taft-Hartley Act outlawed many forms of labor solidarity and banned access to the NLRB by unions with Communist officials, thereby putting up new barriers to trade union growth. The southern organizing drives by the AFL and CIO were both defeated. All southern and some western states passed right-to-work laws banning the union shop as they were permitted to do by Section 14b of the Taft-Hartley Act.[2]

The gradual decline in union density from 31.8 percent at the time of the AFL-CIO merger in 1955 to 28.9 in 1975 did not bother federation President George Meany. After all, Meany came from the old conservative AFL with its emphasis on control of local markets by skilled workers rather than the national bargaining by industrial unions of the CIO. Opposition to radicalism had long been the hallmark of the AFL. The merged AFL-CIO's commitment to anticommunism brought it significant resources as it acted as a key vehicle for the U.S. government's cold war operations.[3] American workers gained few benefits from such operations and the new resources were not applied to organizing the unorganized. Despite the AFL-CIO's conservatism, moreover, new right-wing attacks on unions in the late 1950s led to the passage of the Landrum-Griffith Act in 1959 and a new level of government supervision of trade unions. Even in the 1950s, however, grassroots movements among working people persisted, most importantly among public employees.

The 1960s brought some forward steps for working people. Public employee protests culminated in the 1960s in rapid union growth and changes in public policy by the federal government and many state governments to provide for recognition of unions and collective bargaining. The John F. Kennedy and Lyndon B. Johnson administrations also witnessed other advances of benefit to working people such as the Civil Rights Act of 1964, the enactment of the Medicare program, and increases in minimum-wage rates. On the other hand, in spite of concerted efforts by the AFL-CIO, Congress did not repeal of the right-to-work provision of the Taft-Hartley Act. Moreover, the substantial numerical growth of unions in the 1960s boom, particularly in the public sector, was less rapid than the growth in the labor force as a whole.

In 1969, in the wake of divisions in Democratic constituencies over the Vietnam War and race relations, the pro-labor administration of Lyndon B. Johnson was replaced by the antilabor administration of Richard Nixon. The advent of economic crisis in 1969 added to labor's troubles. By the mid-1970s, with the United States facing grave new economic difficulties connected with the Vietnam War, excessive military spending, and loss of international competitiveness, private employers launched an antiunion offensive in the economic arena and greatly expanded their activity in the political arena. A dramatic decline in union density began.

When the Watergate scandal and the continuing poor performance of the economy led to Democrat Jimmy Carter's election in 1976, unions made a significant effort to enact a labor law reform bill. Unions sought legislation which would have speeded up NLRB election procedures, increased the penalties on employers who fired workers trying to organize a union, denied federal contracts to labor law violators, allowed unions to have equal access to workplaces to speak to workers, compensated employees for an unfair delay in reaching a first contract, and allowed workers involved in a strike for a first contract to displace replacement workers. To obtain Carter's support, the unions agreed to drop from the bill provisions to repeal 14b and for a card-check process for union recognition. Although the bill passed the House by a wide margin and 58 members of the Senate voted for it, supporters fell 2 votes short of the 60 votes needed to end the filibuster by antilabor senators. Unions gained some help from the Carter administration, but Carter's support of the moderate labor law bill was weak and he betrayed his promise to seek national health insurance legislation.[4]

The Carter administration's failures in economic and foreign policy led to the advent of 12 years of Republican rule. President Ronald Reagan set a new antilabor tone in 1981 with the firing of striking air traffic controllers and the hiring of replacement workers. Unions faced two overwhelming problems during these Republican years. The widespread use by business of the replacement tactic initiated by Reagan made strikes significantly more hazardous. There was a dramatic decline in both the number of strikes and union bargaining clout. In addition, the continuing unfavorable labor law situation and the business offensive were compounded by the appointment of antilabor partisans to the NLRB. Organizing new workplaces became even more difficult. Not only did unions' role in the economy decline, but, not surprisingly, the gap between the rich and the rest of the population widened dramatically and the real income of working people declined or stagnated.

Just prior to the arrival of Reagan in the White House, Lane Kirkland assumed the presidency of the AFL-CIO. Kirkland continued Meany's emphasis on cold war foreign policies but did initiate changes in two important areas. Kirkland agreed to sanction AFL-CIO sponsorship of mass protests against Reagan's policies. He also worked successfully to regain affiliation by the UAW, the Teamsters, and the United Mine Workers to the AFL-CIO. Toward the end of 1980s, moreover, the AFL-CIO was scoring some political victories such as the passage of legislation requiring employers to provide notification prior to plant shutdowns. Support from a Democratic Congress provided unions with a means to maintain a basic floor of social protection for the nation's working people. To counter the business striker replacement tactic, the AFL-CIO Industrial Union Department launched a significant campaign for a Workplace Fairness Bill to ban the practice. The bill passed the House of Representatives in 1991 but once again the effort in the Senate in 1992 fell short of ending a filibuster, this time by a 57–42 margin. The bill would have been vetoed by President George H. W. Bush, but by this time the campaign for the presidency was at the top of public attention.[5]

Bill Clinton, a supporter of workplace fairness, won the presidency. The Workplace Fairness Bill once again passed the House in 1993 but received only 53 votes of the necessary 60 in the Senate in 1994. Clinton offered only minimal assistance to the workplace fairness effort. His administration focused greater attention on the Dunlop Commission's review of existing labor law. While most members were pro-union and the commission made a number of recommendations similar to those in the 1978 labor law reform bill, the commission's attempt, in accord with its mandate from the secretaries of Labor and Commerce, to promote labor-management cooperation by weakening the Wagner Act's sanctions against company unions greatly troubled labor leaders. Unions were most upset, however, with Clinton's pushing of NAFTA through the Congress and attacking unions while doing so. Although Clinton's appointments pleased labor leaders and they supported his stance on health care, by 1994 Clinton's record of achievement on the two key issues of his campaign was abysmal. He retreated on his job creation program immediately and then lost even the small program that he was seeking. The health care proposal that drew great support during the campaign became an impossibly complicated mess that would have increased the domineering role of private insurance companies. With the health care proposal defeated, the 1994 midterm election gave Republicans control of Congress for the first time in 40 years.[6]

The advent of the aggressive Newt Gingrich-led Congress led to an upheaval in labor leadership. As long as the AFL-CIO had a good working relationship with the Congressional leadership, backward steps could be minimized and some gains could be made even when a Republican was in the White House. The 1994 election results led the majority of labor leaders to take a new look at the crisis facing unions and to develop a new strategy. A movement arose within the AFL-CIO executive council to replace Dale Kirkland as president.

The insurgency was led by Gerald McEntee, president of the American Federation of State, County, and Municipal Employees (AFSCME), and John Sweeney, president of the Service Employees International Union (SEIU), and drew support from leaders of most of the large industrial unions. The critics charged the Kirkland administration with indifference to the declining union membership base and inactivity in the face of the conservative offensive. Although Kirkland had majority support in the council, where each member had one vote, leaders of unions with a majority of the federation's membership supported the insurgency. The insurgents, calling themselves New Voices, mounted a public campaign for federation leadership. The movement's slogan, "America Needs A Raise," emphasized a new mission to reduce the rising inequality in the United States. New Voices called for devoting a third of the AFL-CIO budget to organizing and for creating an "independent political action program based on mobilizing members." The New Voices slate consisted of Sweeney for president, Richard Trumka of the United Mine Workers for secretary-treasurer, and Linda Chavez-Thompson, an AFSCME vice president, for a new position of executive vice president. Chavez-Thompson, a Mexican American, would be the first person of color and the first woman in the top leadership ranks of the AFL-CIO, thereby emphasizing another New Voices theme, the need for a leadership inclusive of minorities and women. At the AFL-CIO convention in October 1995, Sweeney and Trumka won election with 56 percent of the vote; Chavez-Thompson was then elected by acclamation. The executive council was expanded from 35 to 54 members with the New Voices slate and its opponents agreeing on a joint slate. The New Voices slate took care to prevent a split from developing, and at the same time increased significantly, the representation of minorities and women in the council.[7]

Aware of the deep crisis facing the labor movement, the Sweeney administration has attempted to craft a new vision in both domestic and foreign policy. The Sweeney administration set organizing the unorganized as its number-one priority. Not far behind is a program of independent political action. In addition it has attempted to democratize and revitalize the labor movement, gain new public support for unions and enhance the practice of coalition politics, and modernize the federation's foreign policy and promote international labor solidarity. Given the Republican majority in the Congress, changing labor law was not on the immediate agenda, but the Sweeney administration has made notable accomplishments.

As president of the SEIU, Sweeney had emphasized organizing the unorganized. Under his leadership, SEIU grew from 625,000 members in 1980 to 1.1 million in 1995. Although much of this growth came as a result of mergers, it also stemmed from attention to organizing. The independent women's organization 9 to 5 joined SEIU to get support for its organizing activities among clerical workers. Under Sweeney, one-third of the union's budget was devoted to organizing. As AFL-CIO president, Sweeney hoped to improve the climate for organizing by making the labor movement a visible leader in the struggle to improve the lives of all working people. The new AFL-CIO leadership encouraged its affiliates to increase their organizing budgets. Although the AFL-CIO "doesn't do organizing," it has trained 150 organizers a year at its Organizing Institute and it has supported "multi-union organizing campaigns that target whole industries." Several AFL-CIO central labor councils coordinated joint campaigns in their communities with the aid of the federation. In addition, the federation has sponsored the Union Summer program to provide public visibility and support to specific labor campaigns with the aid of college student activists.[8]

Several unions have increased their organizing activities, and the biggest joint campaign is that of the building trades unions in Las Vegas. "From organizing unrepresented workers to mobilizing and motivating our members in the political process, to reaching out to our communities, we have become the new Building Trades," declared Robert Georgine, president of the AFL-CIO Building and Construction Trade Department.[9]

In 1994, the last year of the Kirkland presidency, union membership grew by 142,000 while union density dropped from 15.8 percent to 15.5 percent. The pattern of modest growth that does not keep up with the rate of growth in the economy has continued under the Sweeney administration. In 1998, unions recruited 373,000 members, but the net gain in membership was only 101,000 and union density dropped to 13.9 percent. The discrepancy between private and public sector unionization grew larger with union density in the private sector dropping 0.2 percent to 9.5 percent contrasting with a rise of 0.3 percent to 37.5 percent in the public sector.[10] The continuing strong opposition of business and the weakness of labor law are factors in the AFL-CIO's failure to reverse the declining trend, but there have also been problems with the federation's approach. After decades in which organizing did not occur, the number of trade unionists who knew how to do it became smaller and smaller. The emphasis has been on the professional organizer rather than on mobilizing the rank and file. Organizers are trained and then sent out to do the job. In the summer, a large number of college students are enrolled in the Union Summer program, trained, and then sent to designated Union Cities for a publicity campaign. Although the Union Summer campaign has educated a significant number of young people in trade unionism and has gained favorable media attention, organizing gains have been modest. Even the activities of experienced organizers have often been of the hit-and-run variety. Instead of forming a rank-and-file committee that builds a base among the workers, the tendency has been to rely on the work of the outside organizers who distribute leaflets, run meetings, collect signatures, and file for an NLRB election. In the rare instances where such a campaign succeeds, the question arises how strong the resulting union will be in terms of getting a first contract or obtaining improvements in workers' situations and surviving.

An example of the problems with the recent approach to organizing is illustrated by the AFL-CIO's most recent major success. SEIU organized 75,000 minimum-wage home-care workers in Los Angeles County. Each worker worked for a single client. To win the employers' acquiescence to a representation election, the union agreed to a no-strike clause in a yet-to-be negotiated contract, the continued right of the client to hire and fire, and to file no grievances against the clients. The organizing campaign was conducted by 22 full-time SEIU organizers with assistance from 75 other organizers from other local unions and from SEIU campaigns around the country. In a story highlighting the campaign's importance, journalist Harold Myerson noted that the last local campaign which organized such a large body of workers was the United Automobile Workers' 1941 unionization campaign at the Ford Motor Company. In the Ford drive there were 40 full-time organizers, but there were also more than 1,000 volunteer organizers among the Ford workers themselves.[11] The vast resources employed by the union in the Ford drive provided a context, but the critical organizing was done by the workers themselves. In contrast, in the L.A. home-care workers drive, the key figure was David Rolf, "a first-class political finagler," according to Myerson, and the campaign was "from its inception as reliant on amassing political clout as it was on actually organizing workers" because of the "dependence on both state and county government."[12] Will authority now shift to the workers in SEIU Local 434B or will it remain with staff who are sophisticated in the ways of lobbying with the politicians who can make the necessary appropriations to improve the workers' conditions? Will the union be able to maintain the workers' initial enthusiasm for change given the numerous concessions over working conditions accepted by the union before the first contract was negotiated? For predictive purposes, the experience of SEIU Local 399 in Los Angeles is not encouraging. SEIU Local 399 led the union's Justice for Janitors campaign in the city and organized thousands of new members. The staff-led local model entered a crisis, however, as a rank-and-file reform slate won a majority of the executive board. Disputes between the president, who the reformers did not challenge, and the board led SEIU to put the local into trusteeship.[13]

Although emphasis on the mobile organizer is the dominant approach, some unions have been experimenting with a membership-based organizing approach. A number of local unions, particularly in the Teamsters, the Communication Workers of America, and the Hotel and Restaurant Employees (HERE), have developed a "culture of organizing." Rank-and-file workers are involved in organizing workers who do similar jobs or live in their neighborhoods. According to a study done for the AFL-CIO, "unions won representation elections in 73 percent of the union drives conducted by ordinary members, but only 27 percent of those organized by professional organizers."[14]

The Sweeney administration responded to the aggressive right turn in the nation's politics by greatly intensifying the union's political action program. In the 1996 elections, the unions increased their contributions to Democratic candidates and the Democratic party. More importantly, the

AFL-CIO established a special $35 million political fund for its own independent radio and television advertising and employment of 131 political coordinators for campaigns by union volunteers in key Congressional districts. The AFL-CIO "completely set the terms of the debate," commented one Republican consultant. As it sought to restore a Democratic congressional majority, the AFL-CIO maintained its alliance with the Clinton administration, an alliance that became much more important to both parties after the 1994 election. Clinton issued an executive order barring companies that hired replacement workers from receiving federal contracts. The order was overturned by the courts, but more helpful was Clinton's successful veto of the TEAM act, a Republican proposal to implement the Dunlop Commission's proposal to revise the Wagner Act's ban on company unions. Although the AFL-CIO campaign failed to restore a Democratic majority, it did succeed in reducing the Republican House majority by nine while the GOP picked up two seats in the Senate. These results fell short of the AFL-CIO's goals, but the dramatic shift to the right presaged in the 1994 election had been stopped. Clinton was reelected while the Republicans sometimes moderated their stances, by going along, for example, with a 90-cent increase in the minimum wage in 1996. Equally important, the AFL-CIO had increased its independent political clout as demonstrated by its success in 1997 in defeating Clinton's bid for renewed fast-track trade authority.[15]

Responding to the new political activism of the labor movement, conservatives attempted to enact legislation they labeled "paycheck protection" to prevent unions from using dues money for political action purposes without prior written permission of members. In 1998, unions used both the mass media and a grassroots door-to-door educational campaign to defeat four ballot initiatives, most notably in California, and stopped legislative enactment in 29 other states and in the Congress. In the Congressional elections that year, the AFL-CIO once again ran a large-scale media campaign and mobilized union activists to campaign in key districts. They further reduced the Republican House majority by another six seats.[16]

Although the AFL-CIO has given priority to its alliance with the Democratic party, the number of unionists and union leaders seeking to break out of the two-party system is growing. These unionists argue that corporation donations to the Democratic party shape that party's actions and that Democrats endorsed by unions often end up voting against labor. In November 1998, the Labor party met at its second convention. The impressive gathering of 1,400 delegates representing 1 million union members heard speeches by presidents of the Steel Workers, Mine Workers, Oil, Chemical, and Atomic Workers, and United Electrical Workers. The convention adopted a five-point program including such issues as a labor bill of rights and national health care and, for the first time, resolved to run candidates.[17]

In recognition of the growing sentiment for a more independent political stance, the AFL-CIO set as a goal getting 2,000 union members to run for office in 2000. In addition, it asserted that it would not limit itself to endorsing Democrats. Endorsement of moderate Republicans in some districts and of radical candidates of the Labor party, New party, and Green party might occur. While the AFL-CIO has become more independent, flexible, and energetic in its approach to political action, its leadership has continued to see an alliance with a Democratic president and Congressional Democrats as the most realistic way to advance the interest of their members and of working people as a whole.[18]

The dramatic campaign of the New Voices leadership captured the imagination of many progressive intellectuals. In the fall of 1996, leading progressive and radical intellectuals organized a teach-in with the labor movement at Columbia University. More than 1,500 attended the well-publicized event and it was followed by similar events at more than 20 campuses. The teach-in movement led to the founding of a new organization, Scholars, Artists, and Writers for Social Justice, aimed at conducting progressive political activity in alliance with the labor movement. The new AFL-CIO leadership has also helped spark a dramatic rise in student activism, with union-related issues the greatest focus of concern. Students involved in the Union Summer campaigns have been one source of this new activism while union-organizing efforts among graduate student assistants are another important source. Students have held sit-ins and rallies at a number of campuses to demand that their universities act against the sweatshop conditions experienced by workers making apparel emblazoned with the names of their universities.[19]

The new AFL-CIO leadership expanded on the tendency of the most liberal unions to ally with the feminist, consumer, and environmental movements. It also continued the alliance with the civil rights leadership that was a hallmark of even the Meany and Kirkland administrations. The AFL-CIO worked closely with the grassroots Jobs with Justice working-class coalitions. The link between unions and university labor studies programs represented another kind of coalition. Labor studies departments not only provide training programs that supplement the unions' own educational activities, but they have helped as well with promoting public understanding of union goals and worked with unions in developing issue-oriented campaigns and coalitions.[20]

While the proportion of workers who are unionized has declined over the past few decades, there has been a progressive alteration in the composition of the unions in the same period. The civil rights and feminist movements have led to gains for women and minorities in employment and a substantial rise in their participation in unions. The Sweeney administration has emphasized increasing the roles of minorities and women in leadership and focused attention on recruiting union members from these segments of the population because of their pro-union leanings. Democratizing the unions, another New Voices goal, represents a bigger challenge. The tradition of relying on a large stratum of full-time, well-paid officials is a substantial obstacle to democratization. Although the new leadership has encouraged activists at the local level, the Sweeney administration tends to emphasize controlled mobilization from the top. The unanimous reelection of the New Voices team at the 1997 AFL-CIO convention was accompanied by a constitutional amendment to extend officer terms from two years to four years, a move that contradicts the goal of democratizing the federation.[21]

The Sweeney administration inherited a foreign policy apparatus closely linked to the U.S. government and to the anticommunist politics of the cold war. Four AFL-CIO international institutes have been conduits for millions of dollars in government funding whose purpose has been to build up anticommunist labor movements around the world. Some prominent AFL-CIO officials and many of the staff members in the AFL-CIO's institutes and international programs are members of the Social Democrats-USA (SDUSA) and the League for Industrial Democracy (LID). Both organizations originated in the socialist movement and emerged as right-wing groups dedicated to anticommunism. Several members of the SDUSA were key members of the Reagan administration's foreign policy team. Although a member of the LID, Sweeney in 1995 joined the Democratic Socialists of America (DSA), a progressive and dovish successor organization of the Socialist party.[22]

Instead of focusing on promoting an anticommunist agenda abroad while pursing liberal reforms at home as did his predecessors, Sweeney's approach to foreign policy stems from his concern about economic inequality and the erosion of good jobs in the United States. He argues that the new globalized economy has led to increased power and profits to corporations but growing inequality at home and a "race to the bottom" for working people around the world as corporations seek the lowest-wage workers. Sweeney maintains: "Increasingly, working Americans understand that it is a threat to their job security and living standards if working people anywhere on earth are forced to do the same jobs for poverty wages."[23]

Sweeney calls on workers to respond to the new globalized economy with increased international solidarity. Workers in different countries working for the same multinational companies or even just working in the same industry should support one another's struggles. There have been several examples of this kind of international solidarity in recent years. When the Teamsters held "Blow the Whistle rallies" against United Parcel Service (UPS) leading up to their 1997 strike, UPS workers in Europe held solidarity rallies. Due to pressure from the Norwegian oil workers' union, Norwegian Statoil recently warned Crown Central Petroleum in Texas to renew normal relations with the U.S. oil union or lose its contract to refine Statoil crude. The HERE organizing campaign at the New Otani Hotel in Los Angeles received support from the Japanese labor movement. The Steelworkers won the Bridgestone-Firestone strike thanks to international solidarity, particularly from the Japanese labor movement. U.S. unions have given as well as received support. There have been demonstrations by U.S. workers at Brazilian and South Korean embassies and consulates in support of unions in those countries. In Mexico, workers in Tijuana's Han Young truck assembly plant won recognition for their independent union thanks in part to demonstrations outside Hyundai showrooms in the United States. A number of U.S. unions are emphasizing cross-border solidarity between Mexican and U.S. workers.[24]

While supporting worker solidarity actions, Sweeney hopes to pressure and convince business leaders into accepting "sensible boundaries" for the global economy. His goal is "a new internationalism that places the weight of U.S. leadership on the side of working people, by making sure fundamental rules govern the global economy, among them common environmental standards, common prohibitions against forced and child labor and against workplace discrimination, common rights of freedom of speech and freedom of association for workers, and common rights for their chosen labor organizations to exist and be free from taint of government or employer control."[25] Sweeney quotes Dean Acheson's phrase about being "present at the creation" of a new international order during the early postwar days. He also takes a positive view of the Marshall Plan. In contrast to leftists, who see the search for U.S. hegemony as the consistent element in U.S. foreign policy since 1945, Sweeney sees the globalization trend of the last 25 years as undermining an international order in which there was shared growth and progress for workers. His goal is thus to update the postwar order to put reasonable limits on the movement of capital and the treatment of workers. The result of the failure to criticize U.S. hegemonic ambitions was evident in the AFL-CIO's condemnation of the Serbs and its silence on the NATO bombing of Yugoslavia.[26]

Although uncritical of NATO, the AFL-CIO tolerated criticism of the bombing by the executive board of the San Francisco AFL-CIO Central Labor Council and the San Francisco chapter of the Labor Council for Latin American Advancement (AFL-CIO). Sweeney has replaced most of the cold warriors in the AFL-CIO's International Affairs Department. Barbara Shailor, the new director of the department focuses her attention on the suffering of workers, especially young women and children, in the developing world who labor in abysmal conditions for minimal compensation and without union protection. Believing that workers should share in the benefits of the global economy, Shailor emphasizes organizing workers into new unions "to bargain collectively with their employers, to speak effectively to their governments, to represent themselves at the new international institutions, and to achieve justice and dignity in their communities the world over." The AFL-CIO is seeking codes of corporate conduct and investment agreements that will strengthen respect for workers' rights. Shailor advocates "frank and open dialog [sic] and a shared understanding of solutions" in the trade secretariats and cross-border solidarity actions. Calling for devoting attention to the "longer term interests of all working people," Shailor wants new rules for the global economy that protect workers and the environment and provide "basic social guarantees."

Although there have been significant changes, the break from past AFL-CIO foreign policy organized to promote anticommunist unions is incomplete. On July 1, 1997, the federation's four international institutes were consolidated with its International Department under a new board of directors to form the Solidarity Center. Although the rhetorical opposition to government-backed unions remains the same as in the past, so does the AFL-CIO's acceptance of government funding of its foreign policy operation. The Solidarity Center is funded by the AFL-CIO, the U.S. Agency for International Development, and the National Endowment for Democracy (NED). The NED is a U.S. government-funded grant-making agency with both labor and business representatives serving on its board. Shailor does not articulate an anticommunist agenda as did prior AFL-CIO international affairs directors, but one has to expect that the conservative agencies that are funding the Solidarity Center will strive to keep the car running down the same old road of training anticommunists. Shailor asserts that the AFL-CIO is "uniquely positioned to provide leadership and a vision for the international trade union movement" because its unions represent more workers employed by multinationals than any other labor federation. Given the long period of decline in labor's position in the United States and its search for a new philosophy, more humility seems appropriate.[27]

The AFL-CIO does not have direct responsibility for collective bargaining, but the unions that promoted the New Directions leadership have also undertaken new initiatives in collective bargaining. While the 1980s was a time of defeat and retreats, the 1990s were a period of regrouping, some important fight-backs, and some historic victories. Although there have also been major defeats in recent years, the victories of the UAW in its dispute with General Motors over outsourcing and of the Teamsters in its 1997 dispute with United Parcel Service over part-time, low-paid work loomed large. By challenging and defeating the UPS management's strategy of promoting part-time job classifications to increase profits and keep the workers divided, the Teamsters called into question the whole corporate campaign of reducing the number of good jobs in the country. The employer tactic of replacing strikers had been so effective that labor observers had expressed doubts about whether strikes could be effective in the new conditions. Not only did these strategically and tactically well-timed strikes prove that strikes can sometimes succeed, they also won wide public sympathy. The majority of the public was concerned about the widening inequality in the United States and sympathized with unions as one group attempting to address the problem. By showing they could make advances for their members and broaden their base of popular support at the same time, the UAW and Teamster strikes improved the climate for organizing by all unions.

Although the Teamsters victory over UPS was the most important strike victory of recent decades, the 1998 election of James Hoffa, Jr., to that union's presidency was a setback for the New Voices trend. Ron Carey and his reform administration had been a key supporter of the New Voices insurgency. Carey was vulnerable because he had relied in his 1996 reelection campaign on those soulless consultants who have been the bane of American politics since the 1970s. The ensuing violations of the fundraising rules for the government-supervised election led to Carey's removal from office and disbarment from running for reelection. Violations by the Hoffa campaign did not lead to sanctions. Hoffa had the support of nearly 90 percent of top union officials in the 1998 election and defeated a late-starting campaign by reformer Tom Leedham by a 55 to 39 percent margin.

Despite his father's record of militancy as well as misconduct, Hoffa's election symbolized the importance of money and name recognition in American political life as compared with the pull of progressive ideals. Those Teamsters voting for Hoffa were not merely voting for a symbol of a time when their union was more powerful but were voting for the tradition, very strong in the United States, of a leader who does it for you rather than with you. Hoffa's victory represented the continuing demobilization of the majority of American trade unionists. The significant vote for the rank-and-file candidate, the base of power achieved by progressives at the local level, and the continuing independent activity of Teamsters for a Democratic Union put limits on Hoffa. Hoffa listed organizing the unorganized as one of his priorities, but it seemed likely that he would give little support to the membership-based organizing campaigns of progressive local unions. Facing significant economic challenges in representing members without a clear alternative to the strategic vision of his progressive predecessor, it is unclear whether Hoffa will be able to turn back the clock to the more conservative politics of top-level deal-making.[28]

Despite the loss of an important ally in Ron Carey's ouster, the Sweeney administration has consolidated its position. Despite its failure thus far to spark a mass organizing drive and foreign policy actions such as implicit support for NATO's bombing campaign, the new AFL-CIO leadership is taking shape as a left-center coalition similar to that which governed the CIO in the period between 1935 and 1946. Shortly after Sweeney's election, the left-oriented 1199 National Health Service Employees Union accepted Sweeney's invitation to rejoin the AFL-CIO. At its 1997 convention, the AFL-CIO unanimously voted to remove the anticommunist clause from its constitution.[29] Many left-minded sixties activists found their way into the labor movement and have become part of the leadership structure of the AFL-CIO and its affiliates. Like most radical academics who came to political consciousness in the 1960s, many labor activists of the sixties generation also have held on to the radical politics they learned in their youth. Members of numerous radical organizations have been active in the labor movement, but no one organization has predominated in influence as the Communist party did in the CIO period. Nevertheless, the influence of left ideas has been profound.

On May 1, 1998, Bill Fletcher, Jr., AFL-CIO educational director, spoke to a joint conference of labor educators about the need to combat neoliberalism. He spoke of the need to face the "realities of class struggle" and to promote a "class consciousness which openly recognizes that the antagonism between capital and labor is built into the very framework of capitalism." Fletcher explained how the AFL-CIO had initiated a program called Common Sense Economics "to promote a dialogue with our members about capitalism." When members ask why they have not heard such presentations before, he tells them to speak with their leaders. To the labor educators, though, he explained: "Our members have been trapped in a cone of silence too long. Many of our leaders, particularly after the purges of the CIO in the late 1940s, deceived themselves into believing that they had a love affair with corporate America."[30] The inclusion of left-minded unionists like Fletcher in the AFL-CIO's leadership structure is indicative of the emergence of a left-center coalition.

Philosophically, Sweeney still adheres to a class-partnership model. "It wasn't always like this," Sweeney argues. "We had a better labor-management relationship in the 1950s and 1960s. There was a spirit of government, business, and labor working together in the interest of working families. We have to restore that kind of philosophy."[31] Despite this ideological orientation, Sweeney's goals remain progressive ones. In the heyday of the left-center coalition in the CIO, progressive leaders who allied with the left still hoped for an accommodation with forward-looking corporate leaders. The strength of the left and of the rank-and-file demand for action was such that centrist CIO leaders joined leftists in leading progressive struggles to organize unions, increase wages, and promote social programs in the political arena.

Will a left-center coalition orientation become consolidated? The goals of the AFL-CIO provide an agenda for progressive changes, but they can only be accomplished by the mobilization of a mass movement. Ad hoc mobilizations and staff-centered organizing will not lead to a mass movement. The decisive question is the democratization of the unions. The involvement of the rank and file in decision-making in their unions and the involvement and decision-making of rank-and-file workers, both union and nonunion, in organizing campaigns is necessary. Historically, the inspiration for rank-and-file organizing and democratization has come from the left. The inclusion of left-wingers in the official structure of the AFL-CIO and of several of its affiliates has led to many new progressive ideas and initiatives. It will take the further strengthening of the left at the rank-and-file level to inspire a mass movement and to provide a solid ally to the New Voices leadership as it seeks to accomplish its ambitious progressive agenda.

NOTES

1. Taylor E. Dark, *The Unions and the Democrats: An Enduring Alliance* (Ithaca, N.Y.: Cornell University Press, 1999), 15. *Statistical Abstract of the United States,* 2001, Table No. 637.

2. Martin Halpern, "Taft-Hartley and the Defeat of the Progressive Alternative in the UAW," *Labor History* 27 no. 2 (Spring 1986): 204–226.

3. Beth Sims, *Workers of the World Undermined: American Labor's Role in U.S. Foreign Policy* (Boston: South End Press, 1992).

4. See Chapter 6.

5. Dark, *The Unions and the Democrats,* 141–57. See Chapter 7.

6. Dark, *The Unions and the Democrats,* 158–83. See Chapter 7.

7. Harold Myerson, "A Second Chance: The New AFL-CIO and the Prospective Revival of American Labor, " in Jo-Ann Mort, ed., *Not Your Father's Union Movement: Inside the AFL-CIO* (London: Verso, 1998), 1–26; Taylor E. Dark, "Debating Decline: The 1995 Race for the AFL-CIO Presidency," *Labor History* 40 (August 1999): 323–44; Dark, *The Unions and the Democrats,* 158–83.

8. Dark, "Debating Decline;" Juan Gonzalez, "An Interview with John Sweeney," *Not Your Father's Union Movement,* 224; Richard Bensinger, "When We Try More, We Win More," *Not Your Father's Union Movement,* 37–40.

9. Juan Gonzalez, "Interview with John Sweeney," 224; AFL-CIO, *Work in Progress,* April 26, 1999, <http://www.afl-cio.org/publ/workin.htm>.

10. Diane E. Lewis, "Labor ranks swelled by 101,000 last year," *Boston Globe,* January 26, 1999, <http://www.boston.com:80/dailyglobe2/026...anks_swelled_by_101_000_last_year+.shtml.> (Lexis-Nexis, accessed September 19, 2003); "Union membership rises by 100,000 in 1998," CNN interactive, January 26, 1999, <http://cnn.com:80/US/9901/26/union.membership.ap/index.html>

11. Martin Halpern, "Coalition Politics and the Unionization of the Ford Motor Company," unpublished manuscript, 1999.

12. Harold Myerson, "Caretakers Take Charge," *LA Weekly,* February 26–March 4, 1999, <http://www.laweekly.com/ink/99/14/powerlines-myerson.shtml>.

13. Michael Eisencher, "Critical Juncture: Unionism at the Crossroads," <http://www.natcavoice.org/un/f/unionism.htm>.

14. Kim Moody, "Up Against the Polyester Ceiling: The 'New' AFL-CIO Organizes—*Itself!*" *New Politics* 6, no. 4 (new series), whole no. 24 (Winter 1998), <http://www.wpunj.edu/~newpol/issue24/moody24.htm>; Richard Bensinger,

"When We Try More, We Win More," *Not Your Father's Union Movement*, 37–40; Steve Early, "Membership-based Organizing," in Gregory Mantsios, ed., *A New Labor Movement for the New Century* (New York: Monthly Review Press, 1998), 82–103.

15. Dark, *The Union and the Democrats*, 170–75, 184–87.

16. International Association of Machinists, "'Paycheck Deception' Flops in 33 States," Faxlink, January, 21, 1999, <http://www.iamaw.org/departments/communications/faxlink01_21_99.htm>.

17. Tony Mazzochi, "Building a Party of Our Own," *A New Labor Movement*, 243–54; "Labor Party Adopts Plan to Run Candidates," November 17, 1998, John Logan to H-Labor@H-NET.MSU.EDU, November 18, 1998.

18. Moody, "Up Against the Polyester Ceiling"; Gonzalez, "Interview with John Sweeney," 225. See Chapter 9 for the results of the AFL-CIO's actions in the 2000 election.

19. Steven Greenhouse, "Activism Surges at Campuses Nationwide, and Labor Is at Issue," *New York Times*, March 29, 1999, A14.

20. Jill Kriesky, ed., *Working Together to Revitalize Labor in Our Communities: Case Studies of Labor Education-Central Labor Body Collaboration* (Orono, Maine: University and College Labor Education Association, 1998).

21. The topic of diversity is discussed in several articles in *A New Labor Movement for a New Century*. Moody, "Up Against the Polyester Ceiling."

22. Sims, *Workers of the World Undermined*; Dark, *The Unions and the Democrats*, 183.

23. John J. Sweeney, "Afterword," *A New Labor Movement*, 334.

24. Matt Witt and Rand Wilson, "Part-Time America Won't Work," *Not Your Father's Union Movement*, 183. The Paper Workers and the Oil, Chemical, and Atomic Workers unions merged their organizations in January 1999 to form PACE. "Pace-setting Union Merger Boost US and Global Labour," ICEM Update, No. 2, January 7, 1999, <http://www.icem.org/update/upd1999/upd99–2.html>; Juan Gonzalez, "Interview with John Sweeney," 227; John J. Sweeney, "The New Internationalism," Remarks to the Council on Foreign Relations, April 1, 1998, <http://www.aflcio.org/publ/speech98/sp0401.htm>. Japanese Trade Union Confederation (RENGO), "We'll Boycott the Use of Hotel 'The New Otani,'" July 17, 1997, <http://www.jtuc-rengo.or.jp/english/htmls1/interact/newotani.html>. After the Teamsters and their progressive allies secured an agreement with Royal Dutch Ahold on a corporate code of conduct, it joined with the U.S. United Food and Commercial Workers and unions from Holland, the Czech Republic, and Singapore to form a World Ahold Union Council. Andy Banks, "New Voices, New Internationalism," *A New Labor Movement*, 280–81, 296–99.

25. John J. Sweeney, Remarks to the Economic Strategy Institute Conference, April 16, 1997, <http://www.aflcio.org/publ/speech97/sp0416.htm>; John J. Sweeney, Comments, World Economic Forum, Davos, Switzerland, January 31, 1998, <http://www.aflcio.org/publ/speech98/sp0131.htm>; Sweeney, "The New Internationalism.

26. "AFL-CIO Condemns 'Ethnic Cleansing' in Kosovo, Protests Murders of Labor Leaders by Serbs," AFL-CIO Press Release, April 1, 1999, <http://www.aflcio.org/publ/press99/pr0401.htm>. The AFL-CIO endorsed NATO expansion in 1998. AFL-CIO Executive Council Statement on NATO Expansion, January 30, 1998, <http://www.aflcio.org/publ/estatements/jan98/csnato.htm>.

27. Jim Smith, Can Labor Meet the Challenge," <http://www.igc.org/lalabor/labor_challenge.html>;Barbara Shailor, "A New Internationalism: Advancing Workers' Rights in the Global Economy," in Jo-Ann Mort, ed., *Not Your Father's Union Movement* (London: Verso, 1998), 145–55; Sims, *Workers of the World Undermined*, 11.

28. "Leedham Issues Statement on Teamster Election," December 5, 1998, <http://ww.igc.org/tdu/html/leedham_statement.html>; William Serrin, "The Teamsters Turn Back the Clock," *New York Daily News* Online, December 9, 1998; "Hoffa: Looking for traces of the father," CNN, December 6, 1998, <http://www.cnn.com/US/9812/06/hoffa.father>; "Teamster Reformers Vow to Continue Fight for Strong Democratic Union," December 5, 1998, <http://www.igc.org/tdu/html/tdu_statement.html>. For background on the Teamsters for a Democratic Union, see Dan La Botz, *Rank-and-File Rebellion: Teamsters for a Democratic Union* (London: Verso, 1990).

29. Dennis Rivera, "Labor's Role in the Political Arena," *A New Labor Movement*, 233; Fred Gaboury, "AFL-CIO convention charts path to future," *People's Weekly World*, October 4, 1997, <http://www.hartford-hwp.com/cp-usa/archives97/97–10–04–1/html>.

30. Seth Wigderson, "May Day Speech on Class by Bill Fletcher AFL-CIO Director Ed.," in H-LABOR, <h-labor@msu.edu>, June 10, 1998, archived at <gopher.h-net.msu.edu>. Speech given May 1, 1998.

31. Juan Gonzalez, "Interview with John Sweeney," 225. See Moody, "Up Against the Polyester Ceiling."

CHAPTER 9

Gore or Nader?
Progressives, Radicals, Labor, and the 2000 Election

Why was Republican George W. Bush able to become president in 2001 even though he received only 48 percent of the vote in the year 2000 election and 543,895 votes fewer than Democrat Al Gore? The first answer that may come to mind is that the Supreme Court did it. Many scholars view the Court's action to stop the Florida recount as partisan maneuvering by the Court's Republican majority rather than a decision rooted in legal precedent or judicial philosophy. The Court's action took place, of course, in the context of the constitutionally mandated electoral college system. Presidential contenders compete in 51 separate contests for electors so that statewide popular vote victories are decisive rather than a national victory. The Supreme Court intervention and the existence of the electoral college system provide two answers to the question of why Bush's minority produced victory. A third explanation revolves around the contention that the 2.7 percent vote for Ralph Nader of the Green party deprived Gore of an electoral college victory. Progressives were sharply divided in the 2000 election campaign. The purposes of this chapter are to evaluate the actual impact of Nader's candidacy in comparison with other independent presidential campaigns but more broadly to assess how labor, progressive, and radical movements coped with the complex political circumstances created by the Clinton presidency and the 2000 election campaign.[1]

There is a long history of dissatisfaction by forces on the left with the choices presented by the Democratic and Republican parties in presidential politics. Socialists and Communists have often entered candidates against what they saw as the two capitalist parties. The high point of the Socialist party vote was Eugene Debs's 6 percent in 1912 and the highest

Communist party (CP) vote was 0.3 percent for William Z. Foster in 1932. The most significant votes for nonsocialist, progressive third-party candidacies were for well-known politicians running as candidates of three distinct organizations each calling itself the Progressive party: former president Theodore Roosevelt in 1912 (28.4 percent), Wisconsin Senator Robert LaFollette in 1924 (16.6 percent), and former vice president Henry Wallace in 1948 (2.4 percent). While each of these campaigns had its distinctive features, Wallace's aroused an emotional campaign by liberal Democrats designed to destroy the third candidacy and only those Democrats associated with the party's popular front-oriented left-wing backed Wallace. Anticommunist liberal Democrats, designating themselves, in Arthur Schlesinger's phrase "vital center" liberals, and the Socialist party, attacked Wallace as a captive of the Communists and claimed Wallace's goal was to defeat Truman.[2]

The Nader campaign of 2000 resembles the 1948 Wallace campaign in a number of respects. Both candidates were broadly respected figures whose candidacies arose from progressive discontent with an incumbent Democratic administration. Large and enthusiastic crowds and some favorable public opinion poll results gave each reason for optimism, but many liberals accused them of aiding reaction, and their actual vote dropped to below 3 percent.[3] There were important differences between the two campaigns, however. The principal issue motivating Wallace's candidacy in 1948 was opposition to the cold war; a secondary focus was civil rights for African Americans. Nader's central point was opposition to corporate economic and political power; a secondary theme was protecting the environment. The Communist party supported Wallace's candidacy but opposed that of Nader.

In 1948 Wallace ran as a candidate who had been closely associated with Franklin Roosevelt and called for a return to Roosevelt's foreign and domestic policies. Truman, an unpopular moderate, also faced a defection on his right as the most obdurate southern segregationists withdrew over the Democratic party's adoption of a strong civil rights plank and fielded a "Dixiecrat" candidate. Truman ignored the segregationist challenge and ran a liberal campaign. He not only embraced the civil rights plank rhetorically, he issued executive orders against segregation in the armed forces and in government contracts. Defying the many experts who predicted an easy Republican victory, Truman successfully reconstituted the New Deal coalition, minus its left wing, and won reelection. Although Gore faced no right-wing defection and responded to the Nader challenge with liberal appeals, his overall message was a mixed one and the New Deal coalition was relatively weaker than it had been in 1948. Equally important, Gore had to contend with an aggressive and sophisticated Republican operation while Truman benefited from the over-confident Republicans' laid-back campaign.

The aftermath of Wallace's weak showing was the consolidation of the cold war red scare, the expulsion of Communist-led unions from the CIO, and the near total isolation of both the Progressive party and the Communist party from the political mainstream. It has yet to be seen if Nader's weak showing will lead to his and the Greens' isolation from the political stage, but, given the absence of the central unifying thread of anticommunism in both domestic and foreign affairs so crucial to the isolation of the pro-Wallace left, this seems unlikely.

In the wake of the cold war isolation of not just Communists but the left as a whole, many left activists looked back on the 1948 campaign as a mistake. Those who previously had expressed support for the idea of a new progressive party, whether Communists, Socialists, or liberals, viewed the idea as hopeless in cold war America. The focus of those who remained active was on defending themselves against attacks, regaining constitutional rights, and participating in nonelectoral movements for peace, civil rights, and civil liberties. Only in the 1960s did the left begin a gradual resurgence as a smattering of older left-wing activists were joined by a new younger generation in peace, civil rights, feminist, and insurgent union movements in the 1960s. Although there were many progressive victories in the 1960s due to grassroots activism and support from the administrations of John F. Kennedy and Lyndon B. Johnson, the Vietnam War led to strong discontent among both liberals and leftists. By mid-1967, a plurality of the country viewed the war as a mistake, but the possibility of a significant independent progressive challenge at the presidential level in 1968 fell apart at the 1967 New Politics conference. Many progressive activists sought to nominate either Senator Eugene McCarthy or Senator Robert Kennedy as the antiwar candidate of the Democratic party that year. With the assassination of Kennedy, the unreformed Democratic party under Johnson's control nominated Vice President Hubert Humphrey. The only electoral challenges from the left were marginal, state-based Peace and Freedom, Freedom and Peace, and socialist parties which collectively gained just 0.3 percent of the vote. Meanwhile, the right-wing American Independent party campaign of George Wallace, former Democratic governor of Alabama, pulled the political debate to the right and garnered 13.5 percent of the vote.[4]

Although progressives were disheartened by Richard M. Nixon's 1968 victory, the turmoil at that year's Democratic convention led to significant reforms in party procedure. Women and minorities gained proportionate representation as convention delegates, most of whom were to be selected in primaries. In 1972 the Democratic party nominated the candidate of the antiwar movement, Senator George McGovern, a progressive who had written a Ph.D. dissertation on the Rockefeller coalfield wars and supported Henry Wallace in 1948. The AFL-CIO and other pro-cold war Democrats failed to support McGovern, who was able to win just 39 percent of the vote. Although the Nixon campaign's dirty tricks played a role in McGovern's poor showing, most Democrats concluded that a candidate too far to the left could not win the presidency. The low vote of both Humphrey and McGovern in the South in particular set the stage for the Democrats to select Jimmy Carter, a former one-term governor of Georgia, as their nominee in 1976. Carter's mix of social liberalism and fiscal conservatism and his identity as a southerner and a born-again Christian helped him to a narrow victory. His move to the right midway through his presidency caused significant discontent in the liberal wing of the Democratic party. Senator Edward Kennedy made a noteworthy but ultimately unsuccessful challenge in the Democratic primaries. In the general election, progressive environmentalist Barry Commoner ran as the candidate of the newly launched Citizens party but received little attention and few votes. More successful than Commoner was Republican representative John Anderson, who initially opposed Ronald Reagan in his party's presidential primaries and then secured 8 percent of the vote running as a center-right independent. The most successful independent since Teddy Roosevelt in 1912 was Ross Perot. Another former Republican campaigning as a center-right candidate, the billionaire businessperson Perot received 19 percent of the vote in 1992. In the 1996 election cycle, Perot ran again under the banner of the Reform party and received 8.4 percent of the vote. Progressive discontent with the policies of the Clinton administration was growing and Green party nominee Ralph Nader appeared on the ballot in 21 states and the District of Columbia and received 0.7 percent of the vote without campaigning actively.[5]

Rightist and center-rightist presidential independents and third-party candidates have been far more successful than left-of-center candidates in recent years for a variety of reasons. George Wallace had a substantial regional base among whites still committed to segregation. When presidential preference polls showed Anderson drawing sizeable support due to widespread dissatisfaction with the major party choices in 1980, the League of Women Voters invited him to participate in the presidential debates. Anderson appeared in a single debate with Ronald Reagan because Jimmy Carter refused to debate, as he put it, "two Republicans." Ross Perot invested millions from his personal fortune to get on the airwaves, gain media, and secure access to the presidential debates. Independent and third-party candidates of the left and center-left have lacked the sizeable constituency, visibility from having run in a major party's primaries, or monetary resources to make a showing similar to that of Wallace, Anderson, or Perot. A less visible factor is the tendency of large media corporations to treat left-wing movements and proposals as either impractical, marginal, or dangerous. There are, to be sure, sizeable progressive constituencies in the country, but since the early 1930s they have looked to the Democratic party for representation and been unwilling to put themselves at risk from a Republican party usually hostile to their interests.

The Democratic party became the country's majority party when the New Deal social reforms of Franklin Roosevelt consolidated a coalition of trade unionists, low income voters, blacks, Jews, Catholics, and liberals alongside the Democratic party's traditional southern base. Although the Democratic party continues to have a slight lead in voter identification, Republicans made gains beginning as early as the 1938 election on the basis of opposition to the radical sit-down strikes and the Communist role in American political life. Two years later, the Republicans made further gains on the basis of opposition to Roosevelt's foreign policy and, once again, the related theme of anticommunism. The Republican advance on the theme of anticommunism in domestic and foreign policy accelerated during the cold war. Democrats began to lose support among white southerners due to the issue of civil rights as early as the 1948 election, a decline that turned into a decisive shift to the Republicans by the late 1960s. Although the civil rights revolution, the increase in the size of the black electorate, and an increase in the proportion of blacks voting for Democrats benefited the Democratic party, the Republicans gained more among white voters, especially but not exclusively in the South, from their shift away from their historic support for black rights. The themes of a tough cold war foreign policy, anticommunism, southern regional pride, and racial conservatism had greater impact in the arena of presidential politics than in congressional, state, or local politics. In the latter arenas, traditional party identification and economic issues counted for more, and the Democratic party continued to dominate in most election rounds until 1994. Nevertheless, key developments in the post-1968 era in the U.S. economy and culture and in the internal life of the major parties gradually undermined Democratic strength leading to an identity crisis for the party from which it has yet to recover.

The cultural issues are complex. A variety of right-wing campaigns against abortion, gun control, immigrants, gay rights, and the ban on prayer in public schools combined with the development of an infrastructure of well-funded right-wing secular and religious organizations moved the political debate in the country to the right. With the right's success in creating new right-wing constituencies, many Democratic politicians treaded carefully to avoid being forced onto one side or another of the emerging cultural fault line in the country. Despite most Democrats' caution, however, liberal and left forces responded to the right-wing challenges and, on most cultural issues, deflected the right-wing challenges. Although the right has won many initiative campaigns targeted against the growing population of immigrants to the United States from Latin America and, to a lesser extent, Asia, the attacks also stimulated Hispanics and Asian and Pacific Island immigrants to organize, become citizens, and vote. These enlarged voting groups tend to favor the Democrats, especially since the attacks emanate from the political right and often from the Republican party. A similar mobilization and orientation to the Democratic party of gay, lesbian, and bisexual voters has occurred in response to attacks on gay rights.[6] Despite the ferocity of the lobbying and political action work of the National Rifle Association, even here a movement for gun control has gained a substantial following. Although many of the cultural issues arose from right-wing offensives, as was the case with the earlier issue of prohibition, the resulting polarization often led to greater support for social liberalism.

Cultural issues are often intertwined with economic ones. The attack on immigrants, for example, is in many respects an attack on low-wage workers.[7] The intertwining of cultural and economic questions is especially evident in two areas where the Democrats have been drawing new strength—from the women's and environmental movements. Here is where the movements for change were on the offensive. The rise of the feminist movement in the late 1960s and early 1970s led to new pro-women's rights attitudes by most of the public. In the wake of the Supreme Court's decision in *Roe v. Wade*, the right mobilized a constituency that stymied the passage of the Equal Rights Amendment (ERA) and has remained on the attack against women's reproductive rights ever since. Not confining themselves to attacking the ERA and abortion rights, the Republicans made gains among some groups by calling for a return to "traditional family values" and decrying the decline in the supposedly "traditional" family of the male breadwinner and female homemaker. However, the feminist movement has continued to actively defend abortion rights, with the support of the majority of the public, and the feminist sensibility remains a major force in American political life. Despite Republican entreaties, the growth of women's participation in the labor force and the increase in single-parent families continued. Most women workers and single parents reacted negatively to being demonized and appreciated the Democrats' responsiveness to their needs. The alignment of women workers with the Democrats and the Democrats' shift from mixed feelings to a pro-choice commitment led to the development of a sizeable gender gap in favor of Democrats among women voters. Similarly, the rise in the 1970s of a well-organized environmental movement which gained decisive support from a large majority of the public has aided the Democrats because of the Republicans' greater animosity to a large federal government role in the economy, regulation, and limitations on business.

Although the Democrats' gain among women and supporters of environmentalism is significant, there was some erosion of support for the Democrats among workers mobilized against specific environmental projects that might cost jobs. To some white male workers, the Democrats' sensitivity to women, environmentalists, and people of color came at the expense of the Democrats' New Deal commitment to jobs and support to white male workers and their families. Many of the New Deal programs had, indeed, been crafted with the needs of families headed by white male workers in mind. Doubts among working class whites about accepting a broadening of the Democratic vision to be more inclusive stemmed in part from white male fears that they would be hurt by the loss of their privileged position in the labor market. Also contributing to the deterioration in support for the Democrats was a fundamental economic shift that was leading Democratic officeholders away from continuing the traditional economic liberalism that had produced the commitment of most working-class people to the New Deal in the first place.

The end of the long postwar boom and the crisis in the economy emerging in the 1969–1975 period combined with the loss of presidential clout in the wake of the Watergate crisis led to an increase in business activism in the political arena in the form of contributions to congressional campaigns of Democrats as well as Republicans and enlarged support for lobbying firms. Right-wing anti-tax campaigns, particularly at the state level, added further pressures on Democrats' economic liberalism while the gradual and, after 1975, accelerating decline of trade unionism, weakened a key source of support for the New Deal approach. All of these factors combined led increasing numbers of Democratic officeholders to conclude that budget constraints and inflationary pressures meant fewer resources were available for social needs. The Democrats' orientation on delivering the goods to its low income constituency declined. As House budget chair Marty Sabo commented in 1993 to Robert Reich, Clinton's secretary of labor, on the increased influence of business on the Democrats: "We're owned by them. Business. That's where the campaign money comes from now. In the nineteen-eighties we gave up on the little guys. We started drinking from the same trough as the Republicans. We figured business would have to pay up because we had the power on the Hill. We were right. But we didn't realize we were giving *them* power over *us*."[8]

The consequences for working people of the economic crisis were not only high unemployment rates during frequent recessions but a long-term stagnation in income that persisted even after profitability was restored. The sharing of the benefits of economic growth characteristic of the New Deal system had come to an end. The gap between the well-to-do and the remainder of the population became an enormous chasm.

Cultural, economic, and foreign policy developments all led to contention within both political parties beginning in the late 1960s. The Republicans resolved their internal conflict by moving significantly to the right. The Democrats' more prolonged internal conflict began with contention over the Vietnam War. Left-liberal New Politics opponents of the Vietnam War angry over the conduct of the 1968 Democratic convention organized the New Democratic Coalition (NDC) to push for party reform and progressivism. The resulting McGovern-Fraser Commission led to rule changes in the party under which most delegates to party conventions are selected in presidential primaries or participatory caucuses and women, minorities, and youth are guaranteed representation. Although McGovern succeeded in winning the Democratic nomination in 1972 with the aid of the New Politics and antiwar movements, his landslide defeat weakened the New Politics group's clout within the party. Remaining one trend within the party, the NDC left-liberals, reinforced by the Democratic Socialist Organizing Committee and by civil rights and women's rights activists, sought to update the party's New Deal liberalism by incorporating the achievement of full equality for minorities and women as central party goals and by replacing the party's cold war commitment to anticommunism with a pro-détente emphasis on peace agreements, nonintervention in the Third World, and shifting funding from defense to domestic needs. Among those opposed to the New Politics were AFL-CIO President George Meany, who remained committed to a strident anticommunism in foreign policy and opposed to any renewal of left-wing influence at home, and Chicago party boss Mayor Richard J. Daley, whose delegation the party refused to seat at the 1972 Democratic convention because of its failure to comply with the rules regarding female and minority representation. Although Meany represented an important magnet of opposition to the New Politics Democrats, many liberal unions cooperated with them and Meany himself still advocated liberal economic policies. The true source of the Democrats' crisis lay in the change in orientation not of its liberal wing but rather in the party leadership and the party's business supporters.[9]

As a major political party seeking to gain election to office, the Democrats espouse a philosophy designed to appeal to people's interests and to their values. Like other major parties in our country's history, it crafts a unifying message while attracting a coalition of interest groups sufficient to win power. While both the message and the coalition of interests have changed over time, the glue that holds the party together is its ability to function as a mechanism for gaining and holding power. This involves in part the self-seeking behavior of individual party loyalists but, more importantly, the ability to "deliver the goods" when in office to its constituent elements. To play in the game of major party politics in the twentieth or twenty-first century, one must have enormous resources to conduct research and develop programs, to get one's message out, field candidates, and run increasingly expensive campaigns. The bottom line reality is that, despite the visibility of officeholders, the control of the Democratic party remains in the hands of those who are trusted by a significant set of business executives with the resources to fund a major party. As Thomas Ferguson and Joel Rogers argue, organized labor, minorities, women, and community activists "have never run the party. They have always occupied the lower rungs of a hierarchy that had other more powerful interests on top—principally capital-intensive and multinationally-oriented big business and its allies among urban real estate magnates, military contractors, and portions of the media." It is these investors in the Democratic party who reacted to the economic crisis that began in 1969 by shifting away from support for New Deal liberalism.[10]

With the party's financial supporters and party leaders seeking a new, less liberal orientation, a number of groups sought to create the philosophy and policy prescriptions to replace New Deal liberalism. After the 1972 election, neoconservative Democrats organized the Coalition for a Democratic Majority (CDM) to push the party to the right on foreign and defense policy and social issues such as busing and welfare. Often allied with the CDM was a group of moderate and conservative southern Democratic elected officials. A number of neoliberal intellectuals emphasized strategies for economic growth rather than redistribution, "market-oriented solutions" and pro-entrepreneurial attitudes rather than support for anti-corporate regulation. Many of these opponents of the New Politics wing of the party and of its traditional liberalism united to form the Democratic Leadership Council (DLC) in 1985. The DLC goal was to move the party to take centrist rather than identifiably liberal positions. After Michael Dukakis's 1988 defeat, the DLC aggressively opposed affirmative action and advocated welfare reform, fiscal responsibility, and getting tough on crime. Bill Clinton became chair of the DLC in 1990. His 1992 election campaign combined DLC themes such as welfare reform alongside a more traditional liberal emphasis on providing jobs by rebuilding the country's infrastructure and national health care. Al Gore likewise was a member of the DLC and, as Ruy Teixeira noted in 2000, "the DLC's fingerprints are all over the current position papers of the Democratic Party." Despite position papers and despite the fact that DLC members were the party's presidential nominees in the last three elections, the DLC failed to outline a coherent public philosophy or program to replace New Deal liberalism. The Democratic party faces a continuing crisis of identity, a crisis that deepened considerably during the presidency of Bill Clinton.[11]

In their compelling chronicle of the Clinton presidency, *Dead Center: Clinton-Gore Leadership and the Perils of Moderation,* James McGregor Burns and Georgia Sorenson argue that Clinton aspired to be a "transforming leader" who produced great and needed changes but instead functioned as a "transactional leader" negotiating, mediating conflicts, tinkering with the status quo, producing at best "incremental" change.[12] Clinton was at his most liberal when it came to selecting the people who would run the government and making affirmations of support for racial equality and abortion rights. Declaring he wanted a cabinet that "looked like America," Clinton appointed significant numbers of minorities and women. Many of his appointees were liberals, but even here Clinton's tendency to be a mediator who avoided conflict meant the abandonment of important progressive allies. Clinton's withdrawal of his nomination of Lani Guinier, the choice of key civil rights groups and a personal friend of his, as assistant attorney general for civil rights in June 1993 disheartened the civil rights community. Clinton advisor George Stephanopoulos recalled that Guinier's appointment was an attempt to "appease our liberal base with appointments because we couldn't deliver on policy."[13]

A few of Clinton's policies involved a centrist compromise between right and left positions, but most represented victories for the right or the left, but more often for the right. There was considerable truth to Jim Hightower's remark that there was nothing in the middle of the road but "yellow stripes and dead armadillos." [14] The liberal victories included the 1993 increase in the earned income tax credit and the associated small increase in the upper income tax rate, the Family and Medical Leave Act, the Brady gun control bill, an executive order to expand the scope of bargaining for federal workers' unions, and the 1996 increase in the minimum wage. The conservative victories included the 1993 passage of the North American Free Trade Agreement (NAFTA), the 1994 anticrime law, and the 1996 welfare reform law. Clinton's defeats were also telling. He failed to meet in any substantial way his 1992 liberal campaign commitments to rebuilding the country's economic infrastructure, investing in education, or providing universal health care. He also failed to deliver on his centrist promise of a middle class tax cut.

Perhaps most critical to understanding Clinton's overall policy direction as right-of-center is economic policy. Clinton decided to give priority to the conservative goal of deficit reduction and to seek only such a program as the rightist Federal Reserve Board chair Alan Greenspan could support. Although Clinton's first budget included two liberal gains of marginally increasing the tax rate on the wealthy and helping the working poor by increasing the earned income tax credit, he sought only a small increase in funding for social investments and even that was lost due to the preference in Congress for deficit reduction. Aware that his policy course was a dramatic departure from past Democratic practice, Clinton shouted to his key advisers during the 1993 deficit reduction battle: "Where are all the Democrats?...We're Eisenhower Republicans here, and we are fighting the Reagan Republicans. We stand for lower deficits and free trade and the bond market. Isn't that great?" Clinton's point, no doubt, was that by putting primacy on fiscal responsibility, he was being like the prudent Dwight Eisenhower, whereas his opponents were irresponsible Reaganites who did not care if they continued driving up the deficit. In a larger sense, however, Clinton's focus on the deficit represented a surrender to the philosophical framework established by the Reaganites.[15]

"The linchpin" of the Reagan revolution in economic policy, argues economist Michael Meeropol, "was the drive to balance the federal budget and cut taxes as a means toward shrinking the role of the federal government in the economy." Limiting the resources of the federal government to what the right views as such necessary matters as defense and crime fighting means restraining or cutting spending on existing social programs and avoiding new social commitments. In the 1993 budget battle, Clinton was constrained by the Reagan framework. In the wake of the 1994 Republican congressional victory and the push to enact their "Contract with America," Clinton's February 1996 proposal for a balanced budget "effectively surrendered to the policies demanded by the Republican majority in Congress." The Reagan Revolution was completed with Clinton's signature on the 1997 budget. When George W. Bush argued in the 2000 campaign for cutting taxes, letting people keep their money, and relying on individuals not government, he was merely espousing the philosophical framework established in the bipartisan balanced budget agreement. Indeed, while Clinton no doubt believed there were important social needs the federal government should meet, he spoke on behalf of the Reaganite philosophical vision when he declared in his 1996 state of the union address, "The era of big government is over."[16]

Although Clinton's rightward movement on budget issues occurred in a series of steps, he was conservative on foreign and defense policy from the outset of his administration. The cold war consensus born during Clinton's childhood came unraveled during the Vietnam War when Clinton was a fervent dove. Clinton's 1980 defeat for reelection as governor of Arkansas occurred in part due to the controversy surrounding the Carter administration sending Cuban refugees to temporary facilities in Arkansas, where disorders ensued. Anticommunist moods in foreign affairs could still play havoc with the electoral success of Democratic politicians. Particularly after Reagan's political success with reasserting anticommunist orthodoxy, Clinton decided to take the foreign and defense issues out of Democratic-Republican competition. His positions on these issues were barely distinguishable from those of George H. W. Bush in the 1992 campaign. Continuing to pursue U.S. global economic hegemony based on the strength of the United States' dominant position in the military sphere meant crippling budgetary constraints and severe limitations on new social reform initiatives.

Clinton's early failure to pass health care legislation was a key turning point. Instead of adopting the liberal approach of a public single payer system, the task force chaired by Hillary Rodham Clinton developed a complex system that incorporated private insurance companies into a managed care system. Fearing that the right-wing would demolish them if they proposed tax increases, the Clintonites included significant cuts in Medicare and Medicaid in their proposal as well as "regional health alliances, contingent premium caps, and all sorts of charges to 'recapture' private-sector health savings for the federal budget." In her analysis of the health care debacle, Theda Skocpol concludes: "So determined was Clinton to avoid the deligitimated subject of 'government,' that he and his advisors could barely acknowledge the government contents of their health care plan to themselves, let alone talk openly and convincingly about them to the American citizenry." The result was a "political boomerang" as the proposal's regulatory complexity gave "right-wing government haters" an effective target and platform. Republicans won control of both houses of Congress for the first time in 40 years in the 1994 bielection, picking up 46 House seats and 12 Senate seats. Turnout was low among Democratic voters and there was also a noticeable shift to the right as the well-financed Republicans campaigned on conservative wedge issues and successfully lambasted an administration that had failed to carry out its promises. Although 1994 was "a relatively good year" for the economy as the nation recovered from the 1990–91 recession, there was only a "minuscule" increase in earnings, a continuation of corporate downsizing, and of the loss of good-paying jobs. Clinton had campaigned against the bad Bush economy, raised expectations, and then failed to meet them.[17]

The mixture of some liberal, some centrist, and several conservative policies added up to an unsatisfactory mishmash rather than a coherent new centrist philosophy. Although the strength of the DLC increased during the Clinton presidency with a political action committee, the New Democrat Network, and a congressional caucus, it was just one party group among several. Rather than leading all segments of his party after the 1994 election, Clinton's main focus became positioning himself for reelection. To this end, he brought Dick Morris, a conservative Republican campaign consultant and analyst of polling data, into his inner circle and embraced Morris's advice to pursue a neutralization and "triangulation" strategy, establishing his own centrist position in opposition to that of liberal Democrats and conservative Republicans. Stephanopoulos, a liberal, notes that Clinton "engaged him [Morris] to run a covert operation against his own White House." The reason for the secrecy became evident when Stephanopoulos and Harold Ickes, Jr., Clinton's deputy chief of staff, finally had a sit-down with Morris and heard the strategy firsthand. Stephanopoulos summarized Morris's pitch:

Neutralization [of the Republicans] required passing big chunks of the Republican agenda: a balanced budget, tax cuts, welfare reform, an end to affirmative action. This would 'relieve the frustrations' that got them elected in 1994 and allow Clinton to 'push them to the right' on 'popular issues' like gun control and a woman's right to choose in 1996. Triangulation demanded that Clinton abandon 'Democratic class warfare dogma,' rise above his partisan roots, and inhabit the political center 'above and between' the two parties.... That meant Clinton had to deliberately distance himself from his Democratic allies, use them as a foil, pick fights with them. Combine these two tactics with a 'strong' foreign policy, a reasonably healthy economy, and public advocacy of issues like school uniforms and curfews that would demonstrate Clinton's commitment to 'values'...and Clinton would win in 1996.[18]

Stephanopoulos described his reaction: "Neutralization sounded like capitulation, and 'triangulation' was just a fancy word for betrayal." Stephanopoulos uses the term "hate" to describe his reaction to Morris. Secretary of Labor Reich commented on his first meeting with Morris: "I came face to face with all I detest in American politics.... To the extent B[ill Clinton] relies on him, he will utter no word that challenges America, no thought that pricks the nation's conscience.... B[ill] will pander to the sub-urban swing [voters], tossing them bromides until they buy him like they buy toothpaste."[19]

Despite Clinton's well-known empathy for others, and his ability to form friendships and be comfortable with all sorts of people, including African Americans, his decision to reach out to Morris stemmed from an obsessive concern with the most narrow conception of his own self-interest. "In a way," Burns and Sorenson conclude, "he had formed his own party of one. Perhaps he could call it the 'centrist' party or the 'triangularist' party. He stood as the one adherent, proselytizer, and intellectual force." In stark contrast with John Kennedy's appeal to voters to elect a Demo-cratic Congress to assist him with his activist reform agenda, Clinton made few public calls for the election of a Democratic Congress and some-times seemed to be discouraging it. "The American people don't think it's the president's business to tell them what ought to happen in a congres-sional election," Clinton remarked in 1996. "A president has to be careful how he makes these arguments to the American people because a lot of time in our history, they would prefer having a president of one party and the Congress the other."[20] While his appearance at fundraisers helped Democratic candidates, Clinton's early fundraising efforts on his own behalf in 1994 dried up sources of donations for congressional candidates and thereby weakened Democratic resistance to the Republican takeover of Congress in 1994. "When Dick Morris commanded a king's ransom for television advertising in 1995," Burns and Sorenson point out, "few thoughts of the consequences for congressional challengers and incum-bents crossed the strategists' minds."[21]

Although Clinton followed Morris's advice to a significant degree, he also went with the proposals of liberals to increase the minimum wage and defend affirmative action. In the run-up to the 1996 election, Burns and Sorenson comment that Clinton "display[ed] an extraordinary brand of leadership-by-followership as he shifted from one tactic to another."[22] What helped Clinton more than anything was the Republicans' overreach-ing themselves on the battle of the budget. As Reich recalled it, the budget battle was *"an idiotic game of bluff. B[ill Clinton] has already lost the real war—the contest over whether balancing the budget is more important than investing in our future. He threw in the towel last June. All that remains is a political game over who appears to have won, how badly the poor get shafted and who gets blamed for this train wreck.*"[23] That the government shutdown fight represented shadow-boxing rather than a turn to a fighting liberalism was evident when Clinton agreed with Republicans on a welfare reform bill that ended the New Deal commitment to the poor. Nevertheless, the AFL-CIO and the leadership of women's and African American civil rights groups continued to back Clinton and the Democratic congressional campaigns of 1996 and 1998. The threatening far right, antilabor, antiabortion, and anti-affirmative action positions of the Republicans had to be opposed with the only viable choices available, the Democrats. Although Clinton won 49 percent of the popular vote in a three-way race and an easy reelection, turnout was the lowest since 1924 and the Republicans retained control of both houses of Congress, though their House majority was reduced by nine seats in 1996 and another five in 1998 when 223 Republicans, 211 Democrats, and one independent Socialist were elected.[24]

Passionately opposed to the right, liberal and African American groups joined Hillary Rodham Clinton in suspecting the drumfire of investigations of the Clinton administration was a "right-wing conspiracy." When the Monica Lewinsky scandal led to Clinton's impeachment, it was particularly liberal and African American groups that came to his defense. In the context of an economic boom that was finally beginning to bring an increase in the incomes of working people, polls showed that the general public opposed the efforts to remove Clinton from office by a two-to-one margin. Most Americans reacted negatively to the Republican and news media focus on what they viewed as the president's private sexual behavior. The Senate rejected the charges against Clinton and the president maintained high job approval ratings throughout his second term. While averse to the Republicans' attack machine, the majority of the public nevertheless personally disapproved of Clinton. Although the right-wing Republicans could claim numerous victories on policy, they had lost the partisan battles to defeat Clinton and to remove him from office and they had made no progress in winning the country to their cultural agenda. In the aftermath of their loss of seats in the 1998 midterm elections, House Republicans forced their unpopular leader, Speaker Newt Gingrich, to resign. The Republicans knew that the public rejected his strident campaign to destroy and command without seeming to care about the consequences to Social Security, Medicare, or education. Though the policy differences remaining between Gingrich and Clinton on the budget had in substance been insignificant, Clinton seemed to care about vital programs the public supported and Gingrich seemed like Scrooge before his transformation.[25]

Republicans aspiring to the presidency in 2000 knew they had to emulate Clinton's caring, not Gingrich's hard edge. If aspirants of both parties focused on appearing to care about the people while tailoring their messages based on polling data, did that mean they stood for nothing in particular? This would prove to be a greater problem for the Democrats than for the Republicans since the Democrats had embraced so much of the Republican agenda during the Clinton presidency. Still rooted in its old base but veering close to its opponents' programs and policies, the Democrats seemed a party in search of an identity.[26]

Although distancing themselves from Clinton's personal behavior, both Bush and Gore sought to position themselves as Clinton-like centrists in the 2000 election campaign. Bush, compared to past Republican presidential candidates, moved to the center rhetorically by campaigning for a *compassionate conservatism* and substantively by promising to be the education president. In most other respects, Bush adhered to traditional Republican themes. He was careful to reassure the religious right about his loyalty, but he de-emphasized their issues when he made centrist appeals to the general public. The center, to be sure, had moved considerably to the right during the Clinton years. Both candidates were for tax cuts, a balanced budget, increased defense spending, a smaller federal government, education reform, a prescription drug program, welfare reform, and protecting Social Security and Medicare. "In many ways," commented Kathleen Frankovic of CBS News, "the candidates were shockingly alike."[27]

There were some specific differences in the plans they proposed. Particularly important was Bush's proposal to provide private Social Security investment accounts, which contradicted his pledge to protect Social Security benefits since the money for the investment accounts had to come from the same pot used to pay the benefits. While of some appeal to the entrepreneurially-minded and younger voters hit hard by the regressive Social Security tax, the Bush proposal caused significant concern among older voters. On the issue of a prescription drug plan for the elderly, Gore proposed a Medicare-based plan while Bush sought to use private insurance companies. On the issues of education, a Patient's Bill of Rights, and prescription drugs, Gore pollster Stanley Greenberg found that 31 percent of respondents thought Gore had the better plans compared with 19 percent for Bush. Yet, Greenberg noted, "half the electorate could not discriminate. That's actually one of the important successes of the Bush campaign." Well-rooted in its right-wing base, the Bush campaign made successful forays into traditional Democratic issues. Nevertheless, Gore appeared to have won a slight advantage overall in the debate on issues. According to Voter News Service exit polls, Gore won majorities among the 62 percent of voters who viewed the economy, education, Social Security, health care, or prescription drugs as the most important issue while Bush had majority support among the 26 percent who thought taxes or world affairs was most important. Respondents favored Bush's Social Security investment idea by about a three-to-two margin but Gore's

Medicare-based prescription drug program by a similar margin. Overall, the 62 percent of respondents who said issues were more important than personal qualities favored Gore by a 55 percent to 40 percent margin.[28]

If in substantive terms, the differences between Gore and Bush on socioeconomic, foreign policy, and defense issues were relatively narrow, three factors appeared to be at work in determining how individual voters made their decisions. First, there were the partisan attachments rooted in the New Deal and cold war eras. For some, these attachments grew from their own direct experience. For others, it was a tradition passed down by parents or other influential older people. The second determinant was the voters' views on racial and cultural issues, values, and identities rooted in the cultural wars that began in the 1960s. Third was their assessment of the candidates as individuals.

To mobilize voters with strong partisan, racial, and cultural attachments, the Gore and Bush campaigns sought to communicate a message that resonated with party tradition and organize an effective get-out-the-vote effort. There were broad areas of agreement between the parties' messages because of Clinton's frequent successes at bipartisan appeals and coalitions and because both campaigns used the rhetoric of "family values" and religiosity previously emphasized by Republicans but appropriated by Clinton. Both parties put together strong get-out-the-vote efforts. Bush's key problem was to keep the Republican loyalties aroused by the culture wars without looking like a negative cultural warrior out-of-touch with tolerant majority views. For the most part, he succeeded. Given the Democrats' identity crisis, the country's divided views about Bill Clinton, and the Nader challenge on the left, Gore's task was more complex: How to arouse the party's low income, labor, African American, feminist, liberal, and environmentalist constituencies while persisting in a centrist appeal to white swing voters at best skeptical about an activist government lending help to the poor and promoting affirmative action.

Gore advisor Carter Eskew remarked: "we were trying to assemble a coalition with a message that had both centrist and populist elements."[29] However, most of Gore's strength came from Democrats, from the New Deal constituencies of unionists, liberals, African Americans, Jews, and low-income voters, and from the new constituencies developing since the 1960s of working women, Hispanics, Asian and Pacific Islanders, and gays and lesbians (Table 1). The overwhelming Democratic orientation of African Americans toward Gore (90 percent) represents a combination of the old New Deal influence plus the impact of the 1960s civil rights upsurge and the Republicans' decision to abandon racial justice. In terms of issues, the highly contentious cultural issues of reproductive choice and gun control cut Gore's way. Sixty percent of respondents favored gun control and 56 percent thought abortion should always or mostly be legal. Those taking liberal positions on these cultural issues favored Gore by a

Table 1
Preference for Gore over Bush in 2000 in Core Democratic Groups

Characteristics	% of all surveyed respondents	% favoring	
		Gore	Bush
Demographic group			
Democrats	39	86	11
union families	26	59	37
income under $30,000*	23	55	40
liberals	20	80	13
African Americans	10	90	9
Jews	4	79	19
working women	31	58	39
Hispanic	7	62	35
Asian	2	55	41
other races (aside from white)	1	55	39
gay or lesbian	4	70	25
Issues			
Support stricter gun control laws	60	62	34
Abortion should be always legal	23	70	25
Abortion should be mostly legal	33	58	38
Help seniors with drugs under Medicare program	57	60	37
Philosophy			
Environment more important than economic growth	46	59	36

* The less than $15,000 and $15-30,000 categories have been combined.

Source: Voter New Service Presidential Election Exit Poll Results, 2000, http://www.cnn.com/ELECTION/2000/epolls/US/P000.html.

wide margin, as did environmentalist voters. In summary, Gore drew his voting strength from partisan Democrats, from populist themes of appeal to the old New Deal coalition, and from supporters of the liberal side in the nation's cultural divide.[30]

The importance of core Democratic constituencies for Gore is evident also in a comparison of his vote in 2000 with that for Clinton in 1996. With a somewhat smaller percentage of the overall vote (48.3 percent compared

Table 2

Comparison of Gore's Support in 2000 with Clinton's Support in 1996 in Core Democratic Groups

Characteristics	1996	2000	1996	2000	1996	2000
	% of all surveyed respondents		% favoring		contribution to total vote	
			Clinton	Gore	Clinton	Gore
Demographic group						
Democrats	39	39	84	86	32.8	33.5
union families	23	26	59	59	13.6	15.3
income under $30,000*	34	23	55	55	18.7	12.7
liberals	20	20	78	80	15.6	16.0
African Americans	10	10	84	90	8.4	9.0
Jews	3	4	78	79	2.4	3.2
working women	29	31	56	58	16.2	18.0
Hispanic	5	7	72	62	3.6	4.3
Asian	1	2	43	55	0.4	1.1
other races (aside from white)	1	1	64	55	0.6	0.6
gay or lesbian	5	4	66	70	3.3	2.8
no gun owner in household	63	52	54	58	34.0	30.2
Issues						
Abortion should be always legal	25	23	69	70	17.5	15.9
Abortion should be mostly legal	35	33	55	58	19.3	19.1
Philosophy						
Government should do more	41	43	72	74	29.5	31.8

* The less than $15,000 and $15-30,000 categories have been combined.

Sources: Voter New Service Presidential Election Exit Poll Results, 2000; <http://www.cnn.com/ALLPOLITICS/1996/elections/natl.exit.poll.index1.html>; <http://www.cnn.com/ALLPOLITICS/1996/elections/natl.exit.poll.index2.html>; <http://www.cnn.com/ELECTION/2000/epolls/US/P000.html>.

Note: The figures in the last two columns were computed by the author from the figures in the first four columns.

with 49 percent), Gore did a little better than Clinton in most of the core Democratic constituencies (Democrats, African Americans, liberals, working women, Asians, and Jews). Moreover, these constituencies represented the same or a larger proportion of the total vote in 2000 than they did in 1996 (Table 2). Gore also received a higher percentage of the vote than did Clinton among gay and lesbian voters who had no guns in their households and among those who thought abortion should be always or mostly legal, but these groups were a somewhat smaller part of the elec-torate in 2000 than they had been in 1996. Voters who thought government should do more increased between 1996 and 2000 and Gore did better than Clinton had among this group. Gore received the same share of the vote of union families as did Clinton (59 percent), but those voters con-tributed more to Gore's totals since they represented a larger share of the electorate in 2000 than in 1996 (26 percent as compared with 23 percent). Gore did not receive as high a proportion of the Hispanic vote as did Clin-ton, but the large increase in the Hispanic vote meant that those voters contributed more to Gore's overall total than they had to Clinton's. One significant area of weakness in Gore's populist appeal was among low-income voters. Gore matched Clinton's share of the vote (55 percent) among voters with an income below $30,000 but, unadjusted for inflation, this income group was a much poorer subset of the population and might have been expected to respond strongly to an effective populist appeal. Overall, however, Gore's 2000 campaign was more effective in mobilizing the Democratic base than Clinton's 1996 campaign. Despite Clinton's renown as a campaigner, his 1996 effort was a centrist campaign with fewer populist themes than Gore's 2000 campaign. Motivated in part by Nader's active campaign on his left, Gore's campaign worked success-fully to mobilize the Democratic base.

What, then, was the impact of Gore's centrism? Gore had to contend with a Republican competing more effectively for votes in the center than had Robert Dole, the 1996 Republican nominee. However, Clinton also had to face Ross Perot, whose appeal, while diminished from 1992, focused on swing voters. Gore appears to have received a smaller propor-tion of the vote due to centrist appeals than had Clinton, receiving a smaller share of the vote of moderates, conservatives, the white religious right, Republicans, gun owners, opponents of abortion, and voters who thought government should do less (Table 3). Gore did slightly better than had Clinton among independents, but this is a category that includes lib-erals and leftists dissatisfied with the Democrats as well as moderates and people on the right. While large numbers embraced Gore's populist mes-sage, few responded to Gore's centrist themes.

The weakness of Gore's appeal to non-core constituencies has led a num-ber of commentators to conclude that the continuing Republican offensive in the cultural wars decisively weakened the Democratic standard-bearer. In his presentation to a conference of Democratic and Republican "insiders" and media people analyzing the 2000 election, Stanley Green-berg noted that the "reasons people gave for voting against Al Gore were heavily concentrated on cultural issues: the positions he took on gay unions, abortions, and guns." When asked to list three reasons for not vot-ing for Gore, Greenberg found that 20 percent of respondents listed his

Table 3

Comparison of Gore's Support in 2000 with Clinton's Support in 1996 in Non-core Democratic Groups

Characteristics	1996	2000	1996	2000	1996	2000
	% of all surveyed respondents		% favoring		contribution to total vote	
			Clinton	Gore	Clinton	Gore
Demographic group						
white religious right	17	14	26	18	4.4	2.5
moderate	47	50	57	52	26.8	26.0
conservative	33	29	20	17	6.6	4.9
Republican	35	35	13	8	4.6	2.8
independent	26	27	43	45	11.2	12.2
gun owner in household	37	48	38	36	14.1	17.3
Issue						
Abortion should be legal						
in few cases	25	27	32	29	8.0	7.8
never	12	13	23	22	2.8	2.9
Philosophy						
Government should do less	52	53	30	25	15.6	13.3

Sources: Voter New Service Presidential Election Exit Poll Results, 2000; <http://www.cnn.com/ALLPOLITICS/1996/elections/natl.exit.poll.index1.html>; <http://www.cnn.com/ALLPOLITICS/1996/elections/natl.exit.poll.index2.html>; <http://www.cnn.com/ELECTION/2000/epolls/US/P000.html>.

Note: The figures in the last two columns were computed by the author from the figures in the first four columns.

support for legalizing gay unions, 19 percent his pro-abortion position, 16 percent his antigun position, and 4 percent his support for affirmative action. In discussing the reasons people gave for voting against Bush, Greenberg highlighted populist attitudes such as opposition to Bush's advocacy of privatizing Social Security and the Republican's favoring of the wealthy. Greenberg acknowledged, however, that "this was a cultural election that defined George Bush as not moderate" on issues such as choice and gun control. Indeed, when one looks at Greenberg's list of the reasons respondents gave for not voting for Bush, there is also a heavy dose of cultural issues—24 percent mentioned Bush's opposition to a woman's right to choose, 16 percent mentioned his poor record on the environment, 10 percent his opposition to sensible gun laws, 8 percent his strong support for the death penalty, and 5 percent his opposition to hate crimes legislation. Greenberg's overemphasis on Gore's rather than Bush's weakness on cultural issues perhaps stemmed from his focus on trying to help Gore win swing voters rather than mobilize the Democratic base. Greenberg commented, for example, that he "discovered in debate prep" that the liberal positions Gore took on cultural issues in the primaries "were views Al Gore felt, believed, and wanted to talk about." Greenberg may have wanted Gore to shy away from an issue like gay civil unions, which is opposed by most voters, but even in this area most express support for laws against discrimination on the basis of sexual preference. The Republican-led cultural offensive has won some elements of the population to its banner but antagonized larger groups.[31]

While Gore had advantages over Bush on socioeconomic issues, cultural issues, and partisanship, and the Gore campaign was at least its rival's equal in the get-out-the-vote effort, Bush was able to draw nearly as many popular votes because of the voters' more positive personal assessment of him as compared with Gore. The evidence for this is clear in public opinion poll data. There were a number of qualities voters recognized and appreciated in Gore. Voters who thought understanding the issues, caring about people, or having experience was the most important quality clearly preferred Gore. On the other hand, Bush had a decided advantage among those who thought honesty, likability, or being a strong leader was most important. The honesty issue appears to have been particularly telling. Respondents more often said Gore would say anything to get elected, attacked his opponent unfairly, or was not honest or trustworthy. For the 35 percent of voters for whom personal qualities were more important than issues, Bush had a 62–35 percent advantage.[32]

There are a variety of factors shaping the public's relatively unfavorable personal assessment of Gore as compared with Bush. The Bush campaign had significantly more money to spend and also benefited from media hostility to the Clinton administration and the Gore campaign. A Pew study found that 80 percent of the media stories on Gore prior to the Democratic convention were negative.[33] To be sure, Bush made misstatements during the campaign and his personal history was quite checkered—his alcoholism, drunk driving conviction, avoidance of service in Vietnam (unrelated to any record of opposition to the war) via elite connections, a business career that included frequent trading on the family name, a failed oil company, a Securities and Exchange Commission investigation for insider trading, and a record as governor of Texas that, after the campaign, Bush campaign officials acknowledged was not defensible. There was little media attention to these stories, however, but rather a constant media focus on Gore's connection with Clinton, the 1996 Buddhist Temple fundraising scandal, and Gore's campaign misstatements. The Bush campaign successfully concentrated on the theme that Gore could not be trusted.

Like Bush, Al Gore, Jr., was the son of a famous father, but in Gore's case the father was known for his liberalism and his courageous opposition to the Vietnam War. With his father facing a difficult reelection battle and perhaps to maintain his own political viability, Gore enlisted in the army after his graduation from Harvard in 1969 and served as a journalist in Vietnam. His father lost his 1970 Senate reelection contest in any case, a defeat that Gore biographer Bill Turque notes "stood for him as a bitter lesson in the perils of staking out too many positions that challenged constituents' core values and beliefs." When Gore entered political life himself with a successful 1976 run for the House of Representatives, it was, Turque points out, "not on Albert Gore's legacy but at a safe distance from it, refining and homogenizing his message for an increasingly Republican state." [34] Gore's foreign and defense policy stances included support for the MX, for the Gulf War, and more generally, for getting over the Vietnam Syndrome. His domestic policy stances included support for the Hyde Amendment banning Medicaid financing of abortions and an attack on Michael Dukakis for being "soft on crime" during the 1988 Democratic primaries. Although Gore wrote an impassioned plea for environmentalism in his 1992 book, *Earth in the Balance,* he was a member of the DLC and a centrist "finger to the political wind" politician. Gore was a key architect of the Clinton presidency and its centrist course. Burns and Sorenson characterize the Clinton leadership system as a "troika" of the president, Hillary Rodham Clinton, and Gore. The vice president met with Clinton for weekly strategy luncheons. At key moments, Gore weighed in with support for Clinton's triangulation strategy. Although many key advisors, including Reich, Health and Human Services Secretary Donna Shalala, Treasury Secretary Robert Rubin, Housing and Urban Development Secretary Henry Cisneros and staffers Leon Panetta, Ickes, and Stephanopoulos, recommended a veto of the welfare reform measure, Gore was among a small group that urged the president to sign it.[35]

Although the Clinton-Gore team had been elected twice and Gore's partnership with the president could not have been closer, the Clinton scandals were an enormous burden for Gore in the 2000 election campaign. Angry at the right-wing Republican attacks on a president who was performing satisfactorily in office, the public was also disappointed in Clinton. Exit polls in 2000 showed that 57 percent of voters approved of Clinton's job performance, but only 36 percent had a favorable opinion of him as a person. Greenberg commented that Clinton's job approval rating and his "personal favorability" rating together explain 62 percent of the variance in the 2000 vote and these two variables were "exactly equal" and opposite in their impact. As Gore advisor Bob Shrum commented, the "Clinton scandals" created a Gore "disadvantage...on the values dimensions, which determined so much of voter choice in 2000." However much he tried to be his own person, Gore was inevitably tethered not only to the Clinton record but to Clinton personally.[36]

Gore's problems were also personal in nature. Republican advisor Karl Rove commented: "One of the problems Gore had was that the Gore campaign didn't seem to know what its center was." Describing one major change in direction, Bob Shrum noted: "Al Gore did something that no one ever does, no front-runner certainly ever does. He changed his [primary] campaign fundamentally in the summer [of 1999]." Just as Clinton's had, Gore's campaign analyzed public opinion polling data and crafted a mix of centrist and populist themes. With the Bush campaign attacking on the issue of restoring dignity and trust in the White House, the mixed messages undermined people's trust in Gore as an individual and thus weakened his overall campaign. Eskew acknowledged that "people perhaps did not understand...and found jarring, and at times even hypocritical" Gore's populism. Eskew characterized Gore as a "techno-populist" who could "sit down and talk to you for four hours about the human genome, but the end of it will be, 'and we've got to make sure these insurance companies don't screw people with this information.'" The appeal of "techno-populism" and of Gore's personal style was limited. After the election, a Democratic consultant who had worked closely with Gore commented to *Nation* writer David Corn: "Gore's biggest problem in the campaign was Gore.... Gore has engendered a mixed personal reaction from people for a long time.... In person, he is low-key, very engaging, funny, thoughtful, great to be around. Place him in front of an audience and it's like a switch flips in his head."[37]

Bill Clinton's unusual effectiveness as a campaigner had enabled him to bounce back repeatedly from numerous personal attacks. The difference between Gore's stiffness and Clinton's ability to communicate that he cared about people thus loomed large. Greenberg, who served as a pollster for both Clinton and Gore, remarked that Gore "didn't have the easy facility some other politicians have of moving into a public space with private values and operating comfortably. He wasn't that comfortable in the public space."[38] Clinton was able, even when conveying a moderate message, to communicate a liberal feeling. Stephanopoulos described a series of meetings of affirmative action supporters with Clinton before a major policy address on the topic. When presidential advisor Erskine Bowles pointed out to Clinton that he was conveying to these advocates his intent "to fully support affirmative action," Clinton replied, "I didn't say that." Stephanopoulos remarked: "His message was clear—even if he didn't want it to be. Clinton's compassion was involuntary, fully felt yet entirely existential, an instinctive empathy so ingrained that he communicated commitment even when he thought he was creating space."[39] Clinton conveyed the same sense of empathy for core Democratic constituencies and for ordinary people in town meetings, debates, campaign appearances, small meetings, and one-on-one encounters. Since voters are selecting an individual for office, considerations of personality and character have always been significant in American politics. Their importance loomed even larger in the 2000 election given the increased media attention to all aspects of a candidate's life and the Republican offensive on the issue of character throughout the Clinton years. For a time, it seemed as if American politics were entirely about one person's personality. As the Clinton era came to an end, what the Democratic party believed in and stood for, beyond appreciating and protecting the only president it had managed to elect in two decades was uncertain.[40]

The Democrats' identity crisis and the emphasis on personality politics by both Clinton and his opponents presented challenges for progressive organizations. Even before their party's crisis, Democratic presidents, like most other officeholders, preferred that progressive activists choose non-confrontational approaches. Franklin Roosevelt issued Executive Order 8802 banning racial discrimination in federal defense contracts to avert the 1941 March on Washington. In his moving call to the nation for moral action against racial discrimination on June 11, 1963, John Kennedy declared that addressing the country's moral crisis "cannot be left to increased demonstrations in the streets." Pressure from the Kennedy administration and others led John Lewis, the spokesperson for the Student Non-Violent Coordinating Committee (SNCC), to revise his speech at the August 27, 1963, March on Washington, a march which Kennedy told civil rights leaders he preferred not take place.[41]

Knowing the attitude of even the most liberal chief executives toward criticism and mass pressure and grateful to have right-wing Republicans replaced by Democrats, many leaders of feminist, civil rights, and environmental groups chose a strategy of cooperation rather than the confrontation that had characterized the Reagan and Bush years. After Gore's defeat, Green party activist Howie Hawkins charged: "The professional liberals who lead the labor, civil rights, environmental, and women's organizations provided political cover for the Democrats during the Clinton administration as it carried out the same corporate agenda that the Republicans support. The liberal lobbies kept their membership bases demobilized during the Clinton administration.... The professional liberals demonstrated that they have more interest in their own career advancement through maintaining friendly ties to the Democratic administration than in advancing issues of concern to their members."[42] Lani Guinier provides a similar but more nuanced critique when she describes how civil rights organizations and the Congressional Black Caucus limited themselves to symbolic protests over Clinton's withdrawal of her nomination:

There was no bottom-up strategy in which civil rights organizations mobilized community pressure and demanded accountability from elected officials within the national government.... My pragmatic friends were no longer convinced that we could effect major change. They did what they were now good at—creating openings for incremental change behind the scenes in legal briefs, in legislative drafts, in little nooks and crannies of influence and employment opportunity.... I too was at least partially seduced by the opportunity for short-term individual success.... I was prepared to be used by powerful decision makers to legitimate safe choices, choices that offered short-term pragmatic advantages but sacrificed long-term principles.[43]

After 12 years of right-wing Republican control of the executive branch, some progressives hoped for good jobs in a Democratic administration. Progressive and left-wing advocates of social change also sought policies that would bring real improvements in people's lives. Social programs and social activism together can increase the power of working people and the oppressed in shaping their own lives.

Was there a demobilization of the progressive forces, a reliance on good contacts to the detriment of social-change activism? In the Clinton administration's first year, civil rights groups organized the Thirtieth Anniversary March commemorating the 1963 March on Washington for Jobs and Freedom. Certainly, the 1993 event was significantly smaller than a similar march a decade earlier when a broad coalition of civil rights, women's, peace, and labor groups joined together to advocate a $5 billion jobs program, a nuclear freeze, passage of the Equal Rights Amendment, and a holiday honoring Martin Luther King, Jr., or, as NAACP leader Benjamin Hooks put it, "the elimination of Reaganism from the face of the earth."[44] In 1993, advocates raised issues on Clinton's agenda such as health insurance for all people, passage of the Brady bill, and full funding of Head Start.[45] Organizers refrained from inviting Lani Guinier to speak because they wanted to avoid an "unnecessary boat rocker" and embarrassing the president at an anticipated meeting.[46] When Clinton vacationed at Martha's Vineyard instead of meeting with march leaders, several speakers criticized the president. Moreover, labor unionists, a sizeable proportion the marchers, carried banners critical of NAFTA and AFL-CIO President Lane Kirkland spoke out for a "trade policy that will uplift human standards rather than destroy them."[47]

Following the march, the civil rights movement entered a period of some disarray with a crisis in the NAACP and an outflanking of the movement within the African American community by Louis Farrakhan's Million Man March, a conservative call for atonement and patriarchal male leadership. With the NAACP recovering from its crisis and a strong institutional base in the Congressional Black Caucus, however, civil rights supporters made effective use of numerous African American representatives and allies within the administration. They were pleased with Clinton's regular appearances in African American settings and frequent socializing with black friends, his travel to Africa, his decision to defend affirmative action and his 1997 Initiative on Race designed to promote racial understanding. Seeing the Republicans' impeachment drive as prejudiced and excessive, African Americans were reminded of the many unfair charges against blacks and rallied to Clinton's defense. Because of Clinton's closeness to the black community, author Toni Morrison called Clinton the country's first black president, an identification Clinton welcomed. Although many black leaders were critical of Clinton's deal with Republicans on welfare reform, aspects of his anticrime legislation, and the neglect of the poor in the booming economy, his sensitivity in other respects to black concerns kept civil rights leaders from any serious break with president. Given Clinton's very high approval rates in the black community, it would be hard to argue that civil rights leaders were out of touch with their constituency during the Clinton years. Although black leftists were highly critical of Clinton, they were swimming against a tide of pro-Clinton sentiment.[48]

Feminist leaders and the pro-choice constituency likewise appreciated Clinton's reversal of Bush's gag rule against abortion counseling at clinics accepting federal funds and the 1994 Violence Against Women Act protecting abortion clinics. During the Reagan-Bush era, Republican attacks on abortion rights led to frequent massive demonstrations in Washington, half a million turning out in 1992. In the more favorable environment of the Clinton years, demonstrations for reproductive rights on this scale did not take place. Nevertheless, feminist leaders pursued a complex strategy that included advocacy behind the scenes as well as mass activism. The National Organization for Women (NOW) continued with independent initiatives such as a march on Washington of 50,000 to protest violence against women in May 1995 and an April 1996 demonstration in San Francisco which drew 13,000 to "Fight the Right" and oppose a California ballot initiative against affirmative action ultimately enacted by the voters.[49]

There were numerous other examples of mass activism during the Clinton years. In response to the explosion of sentiments hostile to gays and lesbians following Clinton's proposal to end the ban on gays in the military, the largest demonstration in U.S. history on behalf of gay and lesbian rights occurred in May 1993, 300,000 by the official count, 1 million according to march organizers. In 1996, the Children's Defense Fund organized a march of 200,000 in an unsuccessful effort to promote increased funding for children's programs and avert injurious welfare reform. After a period of disarray following the Gulf War, the peace movement regrouped in the closing years of the Clinton administration with marches in Georgia against the training of Latin America soldiers in repressive tactics at the School of the Americas and in Washington against NATO's 1998 air war against Yugoslavia. The National Coalition for Peace in Yugoslavia evolved in November 1999 into the National Coalition for Peace and Justice. On Mother's Day 2000, the Million Mom March for gun control mobilized an estimated 750,000. Sparked by ACORN, the Service Employees

International Union, and liberal religious groups, local coalitions for "a living wage" succeeded in getting about 50 communities, including many of the country's largest cities, to adopt living-wage ordinances during the Clinton years.[50]

The anti-NAFTA signs at the Thirtieth Anniversary March were important straws in the wind pointing toward the revitalization of the labor movement. Despite its strong support for Clinton in the 1992 election, the AFL-CIO showed a willingness to criticize Clinton early over his decision to seek passage of Bush's NAFTA proposal. Disappointed at Clinton's failure to follow through on a pledge to add a side agreement protecting workers' jobs before seeking treaty ratification, the AFL-CIO in coalition with environmentalist groups conducted a campaign of demonstrations and lobbying that succeeded in getting most Democrats in Congress to vote against ratification. The Republican takeover of Congress in 1994 sent shock waves through the labor movement. Responding to the turn to the right and to what they saw as weak AFL-CIO leadership, several key union leaders organized an insurgent campaign that resulted in the election of the New Voices team of John Sweeney, Richard Trumka, and Linda Chavez-Thompson to lead the AFL-CIO in 1995.[51]

Under Sweeney's leadership, the AFL-CIO poured resources into organizing, strengthened traditional alliances with civil rights and women's groups, and focused on developing new ties with environmentalists, progressive intellectuals and students. A series of teach-ins with the labor movement brought out thousands of students, faculty, and other progressives on several college campuses beginning in the fall of 1996. A new pro-labor activism developed among students for the first time in a generation. The AFL-CIO employed young activists in Union Summer campaigns to dramatize labor issues and stimulate organizing. In the 1996 and 1998 elections, the AFL-CIO stepped up its role in the electoral arena with issue advertising on television, increased donations to candidates, and mobilizing its own membership for record turnouts of labor voters. On the collective bargaining front, too, a new day began after the retreats of the 1970s and 1980s. Although the overall number of strikes remained low and the unions were unable to enact legislation to ban the business tactic of replacing strikers, some strategically-timed strikes won broad support and resulted in victories. Most notable were the Teamsters 1997 strike against the United Parcel Service and the United Automobile Workers strike against General Motors in 1998. Both highlighted the key issue of the 1990s boom of the need to guarantee secure, good-paying jobs. In the political arena the AFL-CIO continued to ally with Clinton and the Democrats but retained its independent judgment. Thus in 1997 it successfully fought Clinton's attempt to win fast-track trade authority.

The most important mass protest movement of the Clinton years in bringing new issues to the fore in American politics was the antiglobalization campaign organized by labor, left-wing, and environmental organizations. The Seattle demonstration against the World Trade Organization (WTO) in December 1999 captured the imagination of the public and led to widespread support for the notion that corporate-dominated globalization represented a threat to good jobs and living standards, environmental protections, and democracy. A grassroots, left-progressive coalition was emerging that was effectively critiquing the center-right direction in which Clinton and his business allies were taking the country and the world. What was lacking, however, was an alternative progressive-internationalist vision for the world's political economy. The anti-NAFTA campaign contained some anti-Mexican overtones while a campaign to keep China out of the WTO included both anti-Chinese and anticommunist themes. Equally important, the antiglobalization grassroots strategy had no electoral complement. Although the antiglobalization movement and other progressive forces conducted protests at the Republican and Democratic conventions in 2000, a split developed between those who sought independent electoral alternatives and those who thought the Democrats needed to be supported against the antilabor and antienvironmentalist Republicans.[52]

Most progressive movements did not become demobilized during the Clinton years. They made use of contacts within the Clinton administration as best they could, criticized it when they disagreed, mobilized on many new fronts, and won several important victories. The sense that a "better world is possible," a slogan of the antiglobalization movement, led many progressive activists to overcome their disappointment with the Clintonite-led center-right orientation by fashioning new electoral instruments.

Whether emphasizing lobbying elected officials and executive branch officials or a new grassroots activism, progressive organizations were searching during the 1990s for a way to break out of the two-party electoral system under which the power of money held ever-increasing sway over elected officials. Although shying away from the radical step of establishing a new party, the AFL-CIO sought to enhance unions' role in the political process by calling for 2,000 unionists to seek electoral office in 2000. At the congressional level, however, only nine unionists sought election and only one was successful. Similarly, NOW's exploration beginning in 1990 of the possibility of creating a third party, the Twenty First Century party, bore no fruit. Several progressive electoral formations did emerge, however. The New party emphasized building local bases and fusion with major party candidates to avoid the *wasted vote* stigma. A U.S. Supreme Court decision in 1997 against fusion was a big blow to this strategy. The New party disbanded as a national organization, but some state organizations continued to function. In New York, which does allow fusion, the Working Families party has a base in some progressive unions and succeeded in winning permanent ballot status in 1998. In the 2000 election, it focused on an "early and enthusiastic endorsement" of Hillary Clinton but also endorsed the Gore and Lieberman ticket.[53] The Labor party has emphasized building a grassroots base within the labor movement, but its decision to continue delaying the running of candidates over a long period has undermined its vitality despite the holding of some impressive gatherings. Like the New party, the Green party has also emphasized building a local base, but it displayed far less concern about dividing the progressive vote and with building a labor base. The Greens have elected candidates in a number of progressive enclaves. At the same time, the Greens felt to make a leap to being a well-known alternative to the two-party "duopoly," a national presidential campaign was necessary. Nader's modest 1996 campaign on the Green banner achieved some media recognition and 685,000 votes, most from non-Green members. A full-fledged campaign could get an alternative message before the voters and significantly build the party's base. Nader agreed to run a full-fledged 50-state campaign in 2000.[54]

As the 2000 election approached, the AFL-CIO as a federation, most AFL-CIO unions, the National Education Association, and most progressive organizations decided to once again back the Democrats. The United Automobile Workers and the Teamsters initially withheld their endorsement of Gore and had friendly conversations with Nader. Teamster President James R. Hoffa, Jr., who had replaced Sweeney ally Ron Carey as union head, attended both the Democratic and Republican conventions. The UAW eventually endorsed Gore in August and the Teamsters did so in September. The AFL-CIO played a central role in the Gore campaign in providing funds and getting out the vote. Two small unions, the United Electrical Workers and the California Nurses Association, supported Nader. The list of progressive organizations endorsing Gore included NOW, the National Abortion Rights Action League, the Sierra Club, and the League of Conservation Voters. Many progressive and radical activists and intellectuals either endorsed or looked favorably upon the Nader campaign. Nearly 300 scholars and writers signed a pro-Nader ad circulated on the Internet. Reflecting the division among their readers, left-liberal journals like the *Nation,* the *Progressive, Mother Jones, Z,* and the *American Prospect* included articles for and against both Nader and Gore. Although the Greens were a small party rather than a merger of some of the largest liberal organizations in the country, as was true of the Progressive party in 1948, Ralph Nader's stature meant viability for the Greens' attempt to run a national campaign.

In a career that began in the mid-1960s, Ralph Nader has played a unique role in American politics as a public interest advocate and organizer. Numerous public interest organizations that he initiated or sponsored continue to function as advocates for the consumer and the general public. Nader and Nader-sponsored groups staffed by Nader's Raiders educated the public, lobbied legislators and government regulators, succeeded in passing legislation and improving regulations, and won lawsuits on behalf of groups victimized by corporations. Nader became both well-known and trusted by a large segment of the public. For example, when shown a list of groups making statements on the fuel and energy shortage in 1975, 32 percent of poll respondents said that they "would be most inclined to believe" a statement on the rise in gas prices issued by Nader's organization, a higher figure than that for the Federal Trade Commission and the Department of Commerce combined. Beginning in the late 1970s, the well-funded corporate offensive against liberal legislation and regulations made the successes harder to come by. Gradually, Nader came around to the idea of entering the political arena as a candidate for president.[55]

In his memoir of the 2000 election campaign, Ralph Nader emphasizes how the two parties have become more similar over recent years. "Politics, as it is practiced [by the major parties] is the art of having it both ways. One party—the Democrats—regularly says all the right things about campaign finance reform but does nothing. The other party—the Republicans—rarely says the rights thing about the corruption of our elections and does nothing." Nader sees the major party conventions as "entertainment extravaganza" devoid of meaning. He notes that "even when the press does its job, nothing changes" in part because 90 percent of congressional districts are dominated by one party. Nader supports the demonstrations in the streets at the 2000 major party conventions as well as the "shadow conventions" organized by Ariana Huffington but regards the rallies as "harmless venting of steam." Corporations have so much power, including the power to manipulate the ideas most people hear about, that "alienation, withdrawal, and powerlessness" increase and voting declines. The progressive caucus at the Democratic convention, Nader remarks, had too little support to even get their proposals for universal health care, moratoria on the death penalty and on missile defense development, and fair trade debated by the platform committee.[56]

After mentioning the impact in saving over one million lives of his own leadership of the struggle for auto safety regulation, Nader argues that the 1960s and early 1970s were the years of the "outsiders" when the "system worked—government responded to an engaged citizenry." But "somehow that spirit...slipped away, and big business stepped in again to seize more influence on our government.... both Democrats and Republicans have drawn so closely to the monied, corporate interests that the citizens are shut out."[57]

Nader sees "the beginning of the end for progressive Democrats" coming around 1980 as Tony Coehlo, House Democratic fundraiser, persuaded the Democratic party that it could get money from big business just like the GOP. He concludes that "the pro-labor, New Deal Democratic Party was dying." Under Reagan, the Democrats were "morphing into the Republicans to form one corporate party feeding on the same corporate cash, but still sprouting two heads, each wearing different makeup." Democrats "ran away from the word 'liberal'...[a] semantic shift [that] reflected a fundamental abandonment."[58]

Nader's campaign focused on what's wrong with America—the over-weening domination of the big corporations—but not on a clear program of change. Since the late 1960s, data from the National Election Survey indicate that most Americans think the U.S. government is run for the benefit of "a few big interests" rather than for the good of the people.[59] Perhaps Nader's hope was that focusing on that one critical issue—serving the people rather than the corporations—he would stimulate a tide of grassroots activism that would propel a dramatic rise in the polls and his entry into the presidential debates. Once there, there is no telling what might happen. Despite having dropped out of the 1992 race and reentered it, as a participant in three-way presidential debates, Ross Perot had legitimacy and received 19 percent of the vote. As an honest, smart, knowledgeable, progressive critic of corporate power, Nader's debate performance might have propelled him into contention for the presidency.

If the majority of Americans agree about the core problem of governance, there is no clear agreement on what to do about it. The implicit vision of the Nader campaign was that "small is beautiful" and "less is more." Jesse Lemisch supported Nader's candidacy but criticizes him for a "puritanical asceticism that romanticizes hardship, scarcity, localism and underdevelopment." To back up this characterization, Lemisch cites "Nader's mind-boggling revival of the Jeffersonian romance of the yeoman farmer" and a Nader "anecdote about the desirability of mud huts for Egyptian peasants." Nader running mate Winona LaDuke, Lemisch argues, seeks "to be both a feminist and be content with traditional gender roles" but ends up with "traditionalism, essentialism, and the subordination of women." Lemisch cites LaDuke's interview with *Ms.* in which she asserts that her native community (the Anishinaabe) "got the confusion about [gender] roles all worked out a long time ago."[60]

In her interview with *Ms.*, LaDuke emphasized a multi-issue approach to women's issues, mentioning the living wage, health care, welfare reform, and domestic violence, violence in the community, and the "toxins getting into breast milk." Her comments on the feminist movement's focus on reproductive rights were negative ("I hate that kind of forced prioritizing") and she avoided saying whether she was for or against *Roe v. Wade.*[61]

Nader supporter Thomas Harrison notes that during the 2000 election campaign Nader "rarely spoke about racism, hardly ever mentioned homophobia and consistently went out of his way to avoid using the word abortion." In his 1996 campaign, Nader had made an infamous remark disparaging a Green party proposal for same-sex marriage as "gonadal politics" and focused exclusively on economic issues. In 2000 he spoke out on other issues more frequently.[62]

As a well-known and highly esteemed individual, Nader represented an attractive alternative to Bush and Gore for many. Despite the lack of media attention, exclusion from the presidential debates, and limited funding, Nader was able to mount a significant campaign with a "small army of 150,000 volunteers."[63] The most successful part of the campaign was a series of super-rallies attended by 5,000 to 20,000 supporters who paid for their admission to the event. This was very much in the tradition of the Wallace campaign. In both 1948 and 2000, commentators acknowledged that major-party candidates would not be able to draw paying crowds as large as those drawn by Wallace and Nader. In contrast to the fall-off in attendance at Wallace's events as the election approached, Nader continued to draw large crowds down to the wire. Confounding the usual pattern of third-party public opinion polling, Nader's numbers rose in the last two months of the campaign even if they did not rise to the high figures recorded early in 2000 before the campaign was underway in earnest.[64]

The widespread appeal of the Nader campaign contributed in some measure to the Gore campaign's emphasis on populist themes. Not content with drawing support toward the Gore campaign by tilting to the left rhetorically and to some degree programmatically, Gore supporters conducted sustained attacks on Nader reminiscent of those directed at Wallace half a century ago. During the Democratic convention, James Carville, former adviser to Bill Clinton, told one meeting, "Anyone who votes for Ralph Nader is voting for (Supreme Court Justices) Antonin Scalia and (Clarence) Thomas." Democratic chair Ed Rendell told reporters the he was afraid the Republicans would start funding Nader. Leaders of labor unions vacillated between sensible pragmatic appeals to progressives and personal attacks on Nader's character. There were also actions by labor and liberal groups against Nader supporters. The Sierra Club censured a board member who identified his affiliation when he endorsed Nader. The AFL-CIO's Champaign County Central Labor Council in Illinois censured its vice president and COPE Director for making a personal statement supporting Nader.[65]

Many Democrats contended that defeating Gore was Nader's purpose. They charged, for example, that Nader focused his final campaign push in the battleground states where pulling votes from Gore could spell the defeat of the latter's candidacy. Michael Moore, who campaigned for Nader, lends support to the Democrats' accusation in *Stupid White Men* when he reports a shift away from the Molly Ivins strategy of strategic voting for Nader where the state outcome was not in play.

Gore was imploding—and Nader voters everywhere were like rats jumping off a sinking ship.... It appeared he would not get the 5 percent necessary to receive federal matching funds in the next election.

Things at Nader central went crazy. A decision was made to disavow the Ivins plan and go out on a second tour—of states where Gore might win or lose by a percentage point, and Ralph's presence would make all the difference.... It was a bold in-your-face strategy that said to the Democrats, "You have deserted your base. You are no longer Democrats. It is now time you were taught a lesson." Nothing like a switch to the buttocks from Headmaster Nader![66]

Moore reports that he refused to join a Nader campaign tour of the battleground states. Nevertheless, he put in an appearance at Florida State University where he told students that while as someone living in New York, certain to go for Gore, he personally intended to vote for Nader, they should not "listen to me, do what you think is best." Moore would "think no less of you if you feel you have to vote for Gore."[67]

Although Moore is probably accurate in his report of a change in the character of discussion in the Nader campaign, Nader staffers responded that they had never endorsed the Ivins strategy of encouraging a vote for Nader only in noncompetitive states. In assessing the Democrats' accusation, Micah Sifry notes that in the last two weeks of his get-out-the-vote push, Nader spent 60 percent of his time in states that were not in contention. His goal in the run-up to the election, Sifry effectively argues, was to maximize the Green vote, not to defeat Gore.[68]

Nevertheless, there is a significant degree of truth to the Democrats' charge. Nader's campaign throughout the election season focused more of its anger and criticism on Gore and the Democrats. In an appearance on *Meet the Press* and in an interview with the *American Prospect*, Nader indicated a lack of concern with the outcome of the Bush-Gore contest and an apparent preference for defeating Gore: "The Democrats really do need a cold shower."[69] Disappointment with the Democrats' conservative drift was understandable and the argument that one should vote for a candidate with a progressive agenda and record rather than for the lesser evil was sensible. Putting one's primary fire against the Democrats because they, too, had become a corporate party was quite harmful. It contributed to the tendency among voters in general to see little difference between Bush and Gore and thereby helped Bush to get away with positioning himself as a center-right candidate. Nader's campaign did not expose or emphasize Bush's far-right ties or commitments. Nader supporters were right to reject Democratic anger against Nader for entering the race and "stealing" votes. Democratic anger against Nader for letting Bush off the hook and focusing mostly on Gore's weaknesses was legitimate.

The role of the left in the 2000 election campaign was substantial, but leftists were no more unified than were progressives or liberals. Although there was no unified left strategy, leftists played a substantial role in the

Nader campaign and in the grassroots campaign on Gore's behalf as well. There were also three left-wing parties fielding presidential candidates, polling a total of 17,775 votes.[70] A number of left-wing groups viewed the Nader candidacy positively. Among the several hundred intellectuals signing an ad endorsing Nader were numerous prominent leftists. With some of its members supporting Gore, some Nader, and some David McReynolds, the Socialist party candidate, the Democratic Socialists of America (DSA) endorsed no presidential candidate. Setting it sights on building "anti-corporate movements which are capable of winning reforms which empower people," the DSA was critical of Gore's "centrist, neo-liberal politics" while hoping that Nader's campaign might "harness the energy of the protests in Seattle and Washington against the WTO and IMF." Nevertheless, the DSA leadership thought it was "understandable" that "DSA members with ties to mass constituencies will engage in pragmatic lesser-evilism and hold their noses and vote for the Democrat."[71] The CP supported Gore and criticized the Nader candidacy as divisive. Regarding Bush's centrism as "only an image," the CP believed he represented a "grave danger" of a right-wing assault on labor, social programs, and justice in the courts. In favoring Gore, the CP emphasized his liberal stances while acknowledging it had "sharp differences" with him on such "vital issues" as the death penalty, welfare reform, NAFTA, and the WTO. It was critical of Nader's campaign strategy and tactics and his neglect of issues of race and gender equality, raising the minimum wage and labor law reform.[72] Although the Nader campaign and, to a lesser degree, the Gore campaign put forward a number of left-influenced ideas, the key strategic concept of the left-center coalition as the means for achieving progressive advance in U.S. politics was missing from the discussion.

The controversy over Nader's impact on Gore recalls similar discussions about Wallace's impact on Truman in 1948. Wallace biographer Norman Markowitz concluded that the former vice president "probably cost Truman New York, Maryland, and Michigan."[73] Of course, Wallace, like most election observers, thought a Truman victory unlikely. Did Wallace and his supporters prefer a Dewey victory, as many observers charged, or were they indifferent? In mid-1947, prior to Wallace's decision to run, Communist party leader Eugene Dennis addressed labor and progressive fears of a victory of the Republicans, "the main party of monopoly reaction." Sharing those fears, Dennis nevertheless argued, "we cannot be indifferent to what the consequences would be for the people if Big Business were to continue its control of the Government through the Democratic Party and the Truman Administration if it continues, as it probably will, on its present reactionary course."[74] Wallace took a similar stance, equally opposed to both parties, when he announced for president: "There is no real fight between a Truman and a Republican. Both stand for a policy which opens the door to war in our lifetime and makes war certain for our children."[75] As the election campaign developed, Progressive party candidates withdrew from several congressional races to aid in the election of such Democratic liberals as Hubert Humphrey and Helen Gahagan Douglas, but the party made no gestures to aid Truman. On election night, Wallace rejected the suggestion of several of his advisors to include words of congratulations in a telegram to Truman after the latter's victory. "Under no circumstances will I congratulate that son of a bitch," Wallace remarked. Wallace was bitter over his own poor showing and over the many Democratic attacks on him. Two weeks after the election, however, Wallace, like many other Progressives, took credit for Truman's liberal campaign and turn away from conservatism. "It was our all-out fight for the progressive cause which was the chief moving force in causing the American people to reverse their fatally reactionary 1946 trend. They voted for the Democratic candidate for President only after we forced him to compete with us on the same program."[76] Although Wallace's presence in the race did move Truman to run a more liberal campaign and made it impossible for Republicans to label the president soft on communism, commentators tended to focus on Wallace's weak showing and thus added the label of "failure" to the earlier ones, "spoiler" and "captive of the Communists." Wallace and the Progressive party were isolated.

Democratic partisans and many analysts attached the label of spoiler to Ralph Nader in 2000. Many added the label failure, too, since Nader's vote was only a little more than half of the 5 percent goal his campaign had set so it would secure public financing for 2004. Of course, it was the Democrats who were bitter in 2000 since their candidate was kept out of the White House. Since political analysts know that Nader is to the left of Gore and Gore is to the left of Bush, many made the assumption that Nader voters would all have gone to Gore if Nader had not been on the ballot. Certainly, the whole attack on the Nader campaign by progressive supporters of Gore and much of the media that he was taking votes from Gore and thereby helping Bush and spoiling the election were all based on this, to be sure, accurate understanding of the political spectrum. Voter choice, however, involves much more than sticking a pin into a drawing of the political spectrum. Yet, in a review of the 2000 election for the *Political Science Quarterly*, Erickson speculates that, without Nader in the race, Gore would have won by at least a 51–49 percent popular vote margin and a "decisive Electoral College edge." How does he reach this conclusion? He guesses that, without Nader in the race, Gore would have run a more centrist campaign like Clinton's in 1996 and gained more votes in the center "but lost votes on the Left."[77] Another possible impact of a Nader pull-out that Erickson fails to consider is an increase in the influence of Pat Buchanan, the Republican right-winger who captured the Reform party nomination. Buchanan's anticorporate demagogy might have been much more effective in pulling the political debate to the right without the authentic anticorporate Nader in the race.

Speculating about what might have happened if Nader were not on the ballot might appear to Nader partisans or a neutral observer as an aggressive discounting of the Greens' and Nader's determination to run. There were pressures on Nader to pull out of the race, however, and even some Nader partisans such as Michael Moore urged him to reach some accommodation with Gore in the campaign's final stages. Given the stridency of Democratic post-election attacks on Nader for having put Bush in the White House, it is helpful to examine what voters said they would have done in the event of a two-way race.[78]

Responses to hypothetical questions need to be treated a bit more skeptically than responses to other poll questions. Responses to this particular question need especially to be treated with caution. One peculiarity of the responses is that 2 percent of those preferring Bush in a two-person race were respondents who said they had actually voted for Gore while 1 percent of those who would prefer Gore in a two-person race said they had voted for Bush! Equally odd, about 1 percent of those who had voted for one of the two major-party candidates said they would not have voted in a two-candidate race. Republican strategist Karl Rove commented more specifically on the Nader voters: "I know that...the polls say the Nader voter would have voted for Gore, but that's because they're civically responsible individuals answering those questions, and they lie. I think that Nader energized a group of voters who otherwise would have sat on the sidelines."[79] Both mistaken responses and untruthful ones, of course, enter into survey data. Nevertheless, there is one final reason for doubting responses to the two-party presidential race query. The question disguises the fact that everyone knew that, in terms of who was going to win and become president, it *was* a two-person race. A better question would be to ask all respondents to rank order their choices for president. This would give readers information not only on what Nader and other minority party voters would do in the absence of their choice, it would also provide a better indication of the full scope of support for those candidates. We would thus have an idea of how the voting might go under the system of immediate runoff voting (IRV) used in Australia, Ireland, and some U.S. jurisdictions. Although there were numerous newspaper opinion pieces and news stories during the campaign explaining IRV, polling agencies, which conducted dozens of surveys each day of the campaign, chose not to ask presidential preference questions in this manner. The practical implications of asking the question might have been substantial. If Nader's first-round support had jumped up to 15–20 percent, then he would thereby have met the 15 percent standard for inclusion in the debates set by the Presidential Debate Commission.

Despite the flaws in the question, let's apply the "what if" percentages to Nader's national vote totals (ignoring the changes in what some of the

Gore and Bush voters said they would do). According to Voter News Service exit poll data, 47.7 percent of those who voted for Nader would have selected Gore if that had been a two-way race, 21.9 percent would have voted for Bush, and 30.5 percent would have abstained.[80] Gore's national popular vote lead over Bush would have increased by 743,803 votes and his share of the two-party vote would have increased from 50.27 to 50.62 percent. The impact on the electoral college suggested by what exit poll respondents told voters is far less certain, however.

There were only two states, Florida and New Hampshire, in which the vote for Nader exceeded Bush's margin of victory over Gore. A number of observers have remarked that Bush's Florida victory margin of 537 votes would certainly have been overcome if the 97,488 Nader voters had found themselves having to choose between Gore and Bush. Some scholars jump to this conclusion based on the national exit poll responses to the two-person race question. *Florida* exit poll respondents, however, differed from the national sample in their responses. Floridians said they would have voted for Bush 49–47 percent in a two-person race. In the hypothetical two-person race, both Gore and Bush drew 1 percent of their support from Nader voters and 1 percent of their vote from their major-party rival's voters. As Moore commented in *Stupid White Men*, aware of the closeness of the race, Florida Nader supporters worried about a Bush victory were deciding to vote for Gore at an increasing rate in the days leading up to the election. With an essentially even split in Florida among those who ended up actually voting for Nader between Democratic- and Republican-leaning voters, Nader's hypothetical absence from the race would not have tipped the Florida results.

In New Hampshire, Bush won by 7,211 votes while Nader received 22,198 votes. Exit poll respondents favored Bush 48 percent to 47 percent over Gore in a two-person race (with 4 percent saying they would not vote). Three percent of Bush's hypothetical vote would come from Gore supporters and 2 percent from Nader supporters. Of those saying they favored Gore in the two-person race, 1 percent were Bush voters and 3 percent were Nader voters. Ignoring the odd responses of those Bush and Gore voters who said they would switch to the opposite major-party candidate in a two-person race and applying just the Nader voter responses to the two-person race question yields 8,024 additional votes for Gore and 5,463 additional votes for Bush. The hypothetical scenario thus means the results would have been a bit closer but Bush would still have won New Hampshire by 4,650 votes.[81]

Guessing the impact of Nader's hypothetical absence on the results involves the more complex task of imagining how the campaign might have been conducted. Would Gore have conducted a more centrist campaign and would he have been helped or hurt by such a shift? Would Buchanan have emerged more powerfully as a right-wing populist voice and pull the campaign in a racist, anti-immigrant direction? Such guessing requires imaginative leaps rather than merely a numerical calculation. Most important, the hypothetical question ignores the fact that Nader voters, for the most part, were quite deliberate in their choice and committed to their candidate. One post-election survey of a large nationally representative sample conducted by Simon Jackman right after the election asked Nader voters if they wished they could change their vote "given that the election results are so close." Only 11 percent said yes while 89 percent said no. This survey also found significant soft support for Nader, with 14 percent of Gore voters and 6 percent of Bush voters indicating that they had thought about voting for Nader. A CBS News post-election poll also found nine of ten Nader voters "would stick with him, even knowing what they know now about the closeness of the outcome."[82]

Even if the exit poll data had indicated that hypothetically removing Nader from the race would have resulted in Gore's election, Nader's presence in the race was only one of several variables influencing the race. Cited above were the discrimination and ballot irregularities in Florida, the Supreme Court intervention that prevented a recount, Bush's funding edge and more favorable treatment of him by the media, and negative reactions to Gore's personality. The problem of low voter turnout also looms large.

In contrast to the nearly even split in the vote on election day, polling data indicate a distinct preference of non-voters for Gore. For example, a November 27, 2000, telephone poll conducted by Hart and Teeter for NBC found that 54 percent of those not casting ballots would have voted for Gore as opposed to 36 percent for Bush and 5 percent for Nader.[83] Census Bureau data indicate that voting rates were particularly low among several of the demographic groups tending to support Gore. While 60 percent of all citizens eligible to vote reported voting, only 47 percent of those with a family income below $25,000 voted, 45 percent of citizens who were Hispanics, 43 percent of Asian and Pacific Islanders, 44 percent of the never married and separated, 38 percent of those with less than a high school education, and 36 percent of 18–24-year-olds. The low voter participation rate in the United States compared with many other countries stems in part from registration requirements and the resulting low registration rate. The proportion of registered voters turning out to vote was a respectable 86 percent in 2000 but the proportion of the voting age population registered to vote that year dropped to a new low of 64 percent compared to a figure of 74 percent in 1968, the first year the Census Bureau collected data on registered voters. The turnout of 54.7 percent of the voting age population (citizens and noncitizens) in the 2000 election was marginally higher than the 54.2 percent voting in 1996 but still stood as one of the lowest rates recorded.[84]

The pattern of a low turnout rate among Democratic-inclined voters is a long-standing and well-documented problem on which scholars and activists have focused attention with some success. In the 2000 election cycle, states that had no registration requirement, allowed registration on the day of the election, or conducted the election by mail tended to have high turnout rates. However, the overall downward trend in voter registration is disturbing. More attention by the Democratic party and its supporters to easing voter registration requirements and to conducting voter registration drives might have guaranteed a Gore victory. Reforms such as extending voting time would likely increase turnout, too, as nearly half of the 14 percent of the registered voters who did not vote reported they were too busy, had conflicting work or school schedules, or were out of town at the time of the election. A more inclusive electoral process would tend to aid the Democratic party; it would also make the political system more representative and might lead to less cynicism and distrust.[85]

Voter cynicism was an important problem for the Gore campaign because it provided a favorable soil for Republican charges that Gore was not trustworthy and it made it difficult for Gore to campaign on the administration's economic record. Some commentators regard Gore's failure to campaign on the economy as a crucial blunder leading to his defeat. Despite the economic boom, however, Gore's advisors found that "taking credit for the economy just did not work. It was not believable. In fact, it reinforced the sense that he was exaggerating and taking credit for things that were not real." Gore's inability to run on the economy flowed from the fact that the gap between the wealthy and the rest of the population had grown during the boom and from the fact that the Clinton administration had emphasized its commitment to lessening the role of government. How can politicians who say the government should play a smaller role in our complex economy claim credit for managing it?[86]

Gore's biggest problem overall was that the smaller government line meant that his populism was primarily rhetorical rather than programmatic. Absent programmatic initiatives such as national health care, a living wage, shifting the tax burden to the wealthy, restoring the welfare safety net, or guaranteeing decent jobs to all, Gore's mobilization of low income voters remained weak. According to the National Election Study survey data, those with the lowest incomes were two to three times as likely as high income voters to see no difference between the parties (Table 4). A plan for liberal programs could well have increased Gore's support among the historically Democratically-aligned low income voters as well as among the ideologically committed Democratic constituencies.[87]

Many commentators regard Gore's decision to ask for only occasional campaigning by Clinton as an error given Clinton's record as a superb campaigner. Gore faced the dilemma of trying to benefit from Clinton's high job performance ratings, distance himself from the president's scandals and low personal approval ratings, and appear as a leader in his own right. When Clinton did campaign, his focus was often on himself. More campaigning by Clinton might have created more problems than it was

Table 4
Percentage of Respondents Seeing No Important Differences between the
Democratic and Republican Parties by Income, 2000

Income group	
0-16 percentile	51
17-33 percentile	41
34-67 percentile	33
68-95 percentile	18
96-100 percentile	18
All respondents	33

Source: National Election Study Guide to Public Opinion and Electoral Behavior, table 2B4
<http://www.umich.edu/~nes/nesguide>.

worth. Only 35 percent of exit poll respondents both approved and liked Clinton, while 39 percent disapproved and disliked Clinton.[88]

A more clear-cut case can be made that Gore's attempt to distance himself from the Clinton administration in the Elian Gonzales case did his campaign harm. Although Gore's and Bush's positions were similar, public opinion poll data indicated about 10 percent more respondents disapproved of and viewed as irresponsible Gore's handling of the issue as compared with Bush's. Gore weakened himself particularly among progressives. In reviewing Gore's positions on the issue, Gore advisor Carter Eskew commented: "We managed to take a principled position and make it look both unprincipled and stupid..." The "principle" motivating Gore appears to be anticommunism as Eskew notes that Gore "is much more conservative on foreign policy than many Democrats...He doesn't like the Castro regime." Of course, most politicians and most Americans don't like the Cuban government, but there was majority support for returning Elian to his father in Cuba. Here Gore's conservative anticommunism trumped his family values. Most Americans supported the Clinton administration's policy of returning Elian even though a plurality thought it was principally concerned with improving relations with the Cuban government rather than with Elian's welfare. Residual support for détente plus family values trumped anticommunism for most Americans. Eskew may be right that the perception that Gore was "pandering to Cuban-Americans in Miami" was inaccurate. It is doubtful that he would have been much better off if he had made it clear that anticommunism was of such overriding value that even though he knew he was going to get few votes among right-wing Cubans, their extremist behavior had to be accepted. The alienation among progressives would have been all the greater.[89]

Gore's selection of Senator Joseph Lieberman, one of the Senate's most conservative Democrats, won the plaudits of much of the media and a favorable reaction in public opinion polls but weakened him with liberal voters. Lieberman's campaigning to return to the Senate at the same time that he was running for the vice presidency sent a telling signal of his lack of confidence in the Gore campaign and his lack of concern for winning Democratic control of the Senate. In the case of a Gore-Lieberman victory, Lieberman would have had to resign his Senate seat to assume the vice presidency and Connecticut's Republican governor would have appointed a Republican to replace him. Despite Gore's assertion that he was for the people against the powerful, his selection of Lieberman sent a message to corporate leaders, as Lieberman assured the *Wall Street Journal*, that this was campaign rhetoric that would not affect the way a Gore-Lieberman administration would govern.

If the speculation that Nader's withdrawal from the race would certainly have led to a Gore victory seems doubtful, some other alternative scenarios are worth considering. If Nader had targeted Bush as a danger to progressive values and the interests of ordinary people, he would have weakened Bush's attempt to portray himself as a centrist and helped the public to perceive a significant gap between Bush and Gore. If Nader had muted his criticisms of Gore by calling on him to sharply distinguish himself from Bush and pro-corporate conservative policies, he still might have pulled Gore to the left in a manner similar to what occurred in the actual campaign. Of course, pro-Gore liberals might still be attacking Nader for being a spoiler and add an additional charge, if you know Bush is so bad, why don't you get out of the race and let someone who has a chance of defeating him take the anti-Bush vote? Nader supporters could respond that they wanted voters to hear clear anticorporate and progressive proposals, that it was important to open up the political process to alternative voices to encourage citizen participation in governance, and that the more voters heard exposés of Bush's record and philosophy, the better educated they would be about the issues facing the country.

The Democrats also might have pursued a different strategy, refraining from attacking Nader. Gore could have emphasized Nader's positive role in American political life, stressed that they agreed on many goals, and argued that voting for him as the Democratic standard-bearer was a way to more effectively achieve progress toward those common goals. The Democrats and Gore supporters could have attempted to appeal to Nader partisans as a constituency interested in social change instead of criticized them for wasting their votes and seeking to put Bush in the White House. Some Democrats did attempt this strategy but far more common was the tendency to attack Nader personally and to chastise severely his supporters. A combination of an anti-Bush strategy by Nader and a welcome-the-Greens strategy by Gore might have led to a de facto coalition between the Nader and Gore campaigns.

After the election, the Clinton Justice Department turned aside the NAACP request that it intervene in Florida to address the numerous voting irregularities that particularly affected African Americans. Gore and the Democratic party leadership chose not to contest the Supreme Court's partisan intervention in the 2000 election process. Although the House of Representatives is the body that receives and rules on the Electoral College report, only the Congressional Black Caucus sought to challenge the decision to declare Bush the winner of the 2000 election.[90]

Scholars' attention to the right-wing offensive in the cultural wars has resulted in insufficient appreciation of the fact that there is a clear-cut left-of-center progressive majority on most cultural issues. The offensive by left, labor, and progressive forces on the issue of globalization, moreover, opened up new possibilities for progressive advance. Nader's campaign in 2000, despite its misguided strategy of emphasizing the Greens' criticism of Democrats, further heightened public consciousness of the negative impact of corporate domination of the federal government and the nation's political process. Although the events of September 11, 2001, gave an unexpected boost to the Bush presidency, the Enron and Worldcom corporate scandals also opened up the possibility of a new dialogue on the issues of regulation and control of corporations and centering social and economic policy around the concept of justice for working people.

NOTES

1. Federal Election Commission, 2000 Official Presidential Election Results, updated December 2001, <http://fecweb1.fec.gov/pubrec/2000presgeresults.htm>; Vincent Bugliosi, *The Betrayal of America: How the Supreme Court Undermined America and Chose Our President* (New York: Thunder's Mouth Press, 2001).

2. Edward L. and Frederick H. Schapsmeier, *Prophet in Politics: Henry A. Wallace and the War Years* (Ames: Iowa State University Press, 1970), 189–91.

3. Micah Sifry, *Spoiling for a Fight: Third Party Politics in America* (New York: Routledge, 2001), 204; Martin Halpern, *UAW Politics in the Cold War Era* (Albany: State University of New York Press, 1988), 244–45.

4. U.S. Census Bureau, *Historical Statistics of the United States: Colonial Times to 1970* (Washington, D.C.: Government Printing Office, 1976), 1073.

5. Federal Election Commission, 1996 Presidential General Election Results, http://www.fec.gov/pubrec/presge.htm and 1996 Popular Vote Summary For All Candidates Listed On At Least One State Ballot, updated October 1997, <http://www.fec.gov/pubrec/summ.htm> (accessed December 2002).

6. Virginia M. Abuzzo, "Proposition 22: Unintended Consequences," *Humanist* 60, no. 3 (May-June 2000): 31–32.

7. George Lipsitz, *The Possessive Investment in Whiteness: How White People Profit from Identity Politics* (Philadelphia: Temple University Press, 1998), 48–49.

8. Robert B. Reich, *Locked in the Cabinet* (New York: Alfred A. Knopf, 1997), 91.

9. Kenneth Baer, *Reinventing Democrats: The Politics of Liberalism from Reagan to Clinton* (Lawrence: University Press of Kansas, 2000), 19–24; James MacGregor Burns and Georgia J. Sorenson, *Dead Center: Clinton-Gore Leadership and the Perils of Moderation* (New York: Scribner, 1999), 150–51; John Kenneth White, *Still Seeing Red: How the Cold War Shapes the New American Politics* (Boulder, Colo.: Westview Press, 1997), 168–78; Thomas Ferguson and Joel Rogers, *Right Turn: The Decline of the Democrats and the Future of American Politics* (New York: Hill and Wang, 1986).

10. Ferguson and Rogers, *Right Turn*, 1–9, 143–45.

11. Baer, *Reinventing Democrats*, 22–34; Burns and Sorenson, *Dead Center*, 150–53; Ruy Teixeira, "Beyond the Third Way," *The American Prospect* 11 (August 28, 2000): 56–58.

12. Burns and Sorenson, *Dead Center*.

13. George Stephanopoulos, *All too Human: A Political Education* (Boston: Little, Brown and Company, 1999), 143. In December 1994, Clinton also demanded the resignation of Surgeon General Joycelyn Elders, the former Arkansas health director, after she responded positively at a conference on AIDS to a question about including information about masturbation as a part of sex education. The right wing had targeted Elders, the first African American and second woman to serve as surgeon general, over her outspoken advocacy of school-based health clinics and sex education. Joycelyn Elders and David Chanoff, *Joycelyn Elders, M.D.: from Sharecropper's Daughter to Surgeon General of the United States* (New York: William Morrow and Company, 1996), 322–35; Chester R. Jones, *Dancing with the Bear and the Other Facts of Life* (Pine Bluff, Ark.: Delta Press, 1995), 210–24.

14. Jim Hightower, *There's Nothing in the Middle of the Road But Yellow Stripes and Dead Armadillos* (New York: HarperCollins, 1997).

15. Reich, *Locked in the Cabinet*, 63–64, 71–72, 79; Bob Woodward, *The Agenda: Inside the Clinton White House* (New York: Simon & Schuster, 1994), 165; Burns and Sorenson, *Dead Center*, 110–11.

16. Michael Meeropol, *Surrender: How the Clinton Administration Completed the Reagan Revolution* (Ann Arbor: University of Michigan Press, 1998), 1–6, 233–36, 249–50.

17. Theda Skocpol, *Boomerang: Clinton's Health Security Effort and the Turn against Government in U.S. Politics* (New York: W.W. Norton & Company, 1996), 177–78; Meeropol, *Surrender*, 242–45; Harold W. Stanley, "The Parties, the President, and the 1994 Midterm Elections," Colin Campbell and Bert A. Rockman, eds., *The Clinton Presidency: First Appraisals* (Chatham, N.J.: Chatham House Publishers, 1996), 193–4.

18. Stephanopoulos, *All too Human*, 334–5.

19. Ibid., 338, 377–78; Reich, *Locked in the Cabinet*, 273.

20. David S. Broder, "Does Clinton want to Govern?" *Washington Post*, February 4, 1996, C7, as quoted in White, *Still Seeing Red*, 281. See chapter 5, p. 95 for Kennedy's statement.

21. Baer, *Reinventing Democrats*; Burns and Sorenson, *Dead Center*, 224. Clinton spent nearly $2 million for public opinion polls and focus groups in 1993 alone.

George C. Edwards III, "Frustration and Folly: Bill Clinton and the Public Presidency," in Campbell and Rockman, *Clinton Presidency*, 234.

22. Burns and Sorenson, *Dead Center*, 163.

23. Reich, *Locked in the Cabinet*, 283 (emphasis in original).

24. Gary C. Jacobson, "Impeachment Politics in 1998 Congressional Elections," *Political Science Quarterly* 114, no. 1 (Spring 1999), 31–51.

25. DeWayne Wickham, *Bill Clinton and Black America* (New York: Ballantine Books, 2002), 149–50; U.S. Census Bureau, *Statistical Abstract of the United States*, 2001, Tables No. 616, 617.

26. Jacobson, "Impeachment Politics."

27. Kathleen Hall Jamieson and Paul Waldman, eds., *Electing the President, 2000: The Insiders' View* (Philadelphia: University of Pennsylvania Press, 2001), 123.

28. Jamieson and Paul Waldman, *Electing the President*, 105–8; Voter News Service Exit Polls, 2000, <http://www.cnn.com/ELECTION/2000/epolls/US/P000.html>.

29. Jamieson and Paul Waldman, eds., *Electing the President*, 56.

30. Exit poll data indicated that voters who gave priority to the environment over economic growth were slightly fewer in number than those who took the opposite position (46–48 percent) but this formulation of the issue of environmentalism understates its wide appeal. <http://www.cnn.com/ELECTION/2000/epolls/US/P000.html>

31. Jamieson and Paul Waldman, eds., *Electing the President*, 99–108; Karen Ann Gajewski, "Civil Liberties Watch," *Humanist* 61, no. 1 (January-February 2001): 38–40.

32. Voter News Service Exit Polls, 2000, <http://www.cnn.com/ELECTION/2000/epolls/US/P000.html>.

33. Jamieson and Paul Waldman, eds., *Electing the President*, 69.

34. Bill Turque, *Inventing Al Gore: A Biography* (Boston: Houghton Mifflin Co., 2000), 118.

35. Ibid., 60–89, 118–22, 145–50, 229–39; Bob Woodward, *The Choice* (New York: Simon and Schuster, 1996), 139–40; Burns and Sorenson, *Dead Center*, 219–22, 235; Stephanopoulos, *All too Human*, 419–20. In *Earth in the Balance*, Gore commented, "I have become very impatient with my own tendency to put a finger to the political winds and proceed cautiously." Quoted in Turque, 231. Whatever the potential for a new visionary reformism in his environmental work, Gore's role as vice presidential partner to Bill Clinton saw the old tendency live on.

36. Voter News Service Exit Polls, 2000, <http://www.cnn.com/ELECTION/2000/epolls/US/P000.html>; Jamieson and Waldman, eds., *Electing the President*, 90–92.

37. David Corn, "Al, Don't Run," *The Nation* 273, no. 8 (September 17/24, 2001), 12.

38. Jamieson and Waldman, *Electing the President*, 101.

39. Stephanopoulos, *All too Human*, 372.

40. Jamieson and Waldman, *Electing the President*, 54, 67, 101, 208; David Corn, "Al, Don't Run," *The Nation* 273, no. 8 (September 17/24, 2001), 12.

41. Taylor Branch, *Parting the Waters* (New York: Simon & Schuster, 1988), 840–41, 872–76.

42. Howie Hawkins, "Blame the Democrats, Not the Greens," *New Politics* 31 (Summer 2001).

43. Lani Guinier, *Lift Every Voice: Turning a Civil Rights Setback into a New Vision of Social Justice* (New York: Simon & Schuster, 1998), 139–41.

44. *Washington Post*, August 28, 1983, A1; *New York Times*, late city final edition, August 29, 1983, A12.

45. *Atlanta Constitution*, August 29, 1993.

46. Guinier, *Lift Every Voice*, 137.

47. *Washington Post*, August 29, 1993, A1; *Atlanta Constitution*, August 29, 1993; *Los Angeles Times*, August 29, 1993, 2.

48. *Baltimore Sun*, October 17, 1995, final edition, 1A; Wickham, *Bill Clinton*.

49. *Boston Globe*, November 13, 1989, 1; *USA Today*, April 6, 1992; *St. Louis Post-Dispatch*, April 6, 1992, 1A; *New York Times*, April 10, 1995, A10; *Baltimore Sun*, October 3, 1995, 3A; *Chicago Sun-Times*, October 15, 1995; *New York Times*, April 15, 1996, A12.

50. *Boston Globe*, May 21, 1993, 1; *New York Times*, June 2, 1996, sec. 1, p. 30; SOA Watch Press Release, November 18, 2001, <www.soaw.org/new/pressrelease.php?id_13_>; National Coalition for Peace and Justice statement, November 1999, <http://www.nepj.net/founding.htm>; *Los Angeles Times*, May 12, 2000, B1; *St. Louis Post-Dispatch*, May 15, 2000, A1; Jim Hightower, "Campaign for a Living Wage," *The Nation* 274, no. 12 (April 1, 2002), 8; Eric Roston, "How Much is a Living Wage," *Time*, April 8, 2002, 50–53.

51. Burns and Sorenson, *Dead Center*, 90–91.

52. "Globalization and Democracy" special issue, *Annals*, AAPSS, 581, May 2002; Beverly J. Silver and Giovanni Arrighi, "Workers North and South," in Leo Panitch et al., eds., *Socialist Register 2001* (New York: Merlin Press, 2000), 53–73.

53. Sifry, *Spoiling for a Fight*, 271.

54. Lisa Jane Disch, *The Tyranny of the Two Party System* (New York: Columbia University Press, 2002), 23–14, 146 n. 1.

55. Roper Organization survey, January 11–25, 1975, Roper Report 75–2, Roper Center Public Opinion Online, Accession Number 0112988, Lexis-Nexis.

56. Ralph Nader, *Crashing the Party: Taking on the Corporate Government in an Age of Surrender* (New York: St. Martin's Press, 2002), 8–13.

57. Ibid., 19–20.

58. Ibid., 21–24, 28.

59. The NES Guide to Public Opinion and Electoral Behavior, Table 5a2, <http://www.umich.edu/~nes/nesguide/toptable/tab5a_2.htm>, (accessed February 16, 2002).

60. Jesse Lemisch, "Nader vs. the Big Rock Candy Mountain," *New Politics* 31 (Summer 2001); Jennifer Baumgardner, "Kitchen Table Candidate," *Ms.*, (April-May 2001), 47–53.

61. Jennifer Baumgardner, "Kitchen Table Candidate," *Ms.*, (April-May 2001), 53.

62. Thomas Harrison, "The Democrats: No Way to Fight the Right," *New Politics* 31 (Summer 2001); John Buell, "Reinventing Ralph Nader: Back to the Future," *Humanist* 60, no. 4 (July-August 2000), 40–43.

63. Sifry, *Spoiling for a Fight*, 178.

64. For the rise poll numbers, see Barry C. Burden, "Minor Parties in the 2000 Presidential Elections," <www.fas.harvard.edu/~burdern>.

65. Robert Novak, "From Oval Office to Speechwriting Career," *Chicago Sun-Times*, August 20, 2000, 39; Mike Griffin, "Union Democracy and the AFL-CIO on Trial," *Synthesis/Regeneration* 24 (Winter 2001).

66. Michael Moore, *Stupid White Men* (New York: HarperCollins, 2001), 244.

67. Ibid., 248.

68. Sifry, *Spoiling for a Fight*, 207–10.

69. Robert Kuttner, "Ralph Nader: A Conversation," *The American Prospect* 11, no. 15 (June 19–July 3, 2000), 17; Common Dreams Newsletter, "Transcript: Ralph Nader on 'Meet The Press,' Sunday, May 7, 2000," <http://www.common dreams.org/headlines/050800–03.htm> (accessed December 2002).

70. Federal Election Commission, 2000 Official Presidential Election Results, updated December 2001, <http://fecweb1.fec.gov/pubrec/2000presgeresults.htm>.

71. DSA Statements on the 2000 Election, Before the Vote, n.d., <http://www.dsusa.org/news/2kvote.html>. After the election, the Young Democratic Socialists, while applauding the energetic activism aroused by Nader's campaign among young people, criticized Nader for dividing the progressive vote in swing states and failing to perceive that Bush was a larger evil who had to be stopped. The Young Democratic Socialists argued that Nader's and the Greens' opposition to the mobilization of people of color on Gore's behalf was racist. "Nader, Race, and the 2000 Election: A Post-Election Statement From YDS," <http://www.ydsussa.org/file=stattments/2000electionnader>. An even more extreme post-election comment was DSA Vice Chair Harold Myerson's denunciation of the Greens as the group "most intent on destroying progressive prospects." Harold Myerson, "Greens to Liberals: Drop Dead!" *American Prospect* 13, no. 12 (July 1, 2002).

72. Jarvis Tyner, Report to the National Committee, CPUSA, November 18, 2000, <http://www.cpusa.org/article/articleprint/252>.

73. Norman D. Markowitz, *The Rise and Fall of the People's Century: Henry A. Wallace and American Liberalism, 1941–1948* (New York: The Free Press, 1973), 296.

74. Richard J. Walton, *Henry Wallace, Harry Truman, and the Cold War* (New York: Viking Press, 1976), 257–58.

75. Curtis D. MacDougall, *Gideon's Army* (New York: Marzani and Munsell, 1965), 1:288.

76. MacDougall, *Gideon's Army*, 3:859, 882; Markowitz, *The Rise and Fall of the People's Century*, 293, 296; John C. Culver and John Hyde, *American Dreamer: The Life and Times of Henry A. Wallace* (New York: W.W. Norton & Company, 2000), 501.

77. Robert S. Erickson, "The 2000 Election in Historical Perspective," *Political Science Quarterly* 116 (Spring 2001): 29–53.

78. Moore, *Stupid White Men*, 253–54. On election day, the Voter News Service (VNS), a consortium of several major media organizations, collected self-administered questionnaires in which all respondents were asked, "If these were the only two presidential candidates on the ballot today, who would you have voted for? 1 Al Gore (Dem), 2 George Bush (Rep), 3 Would not have voted for president." Gallop Organization survey for CNN and USA Today, November 1–3, 2000, Roper Center Public Opinion Online, Accession Number 0406443, Lexis-Nexis; ABC Exit Polls, State-by-State Voter Surveys, <http://abcnews.go.com/sections/politics/2000 vote/general/exitpoll_hub.html>.

79. Jamieson and Waldman, eds., *Electing the President*, 207.

80. Burden, "Minor Parties;" Voter News Service Exit Polls, 2000, <http://www.cnn.com/ELECTION/2000/epols/US/P000.html>. Burden had access to the VNS data set and provides more detailed information than available on the Web. The VNS data should be available soon via the Roper Center and the Inter-University

Consortium for Political and Social Research. Barry Burden to Martin Halpern, e-mail, September 7, 2002; personal communication, Leec Shapiro, VNS, September 9, 2002.

81. Presidential exit polls, November 7, 2000, Florida and New Hampshire <http://www.msnbc.com/m/d2k/g/polls.asp?office_P&state>; Federal Election Commission, 2000 Official Presidential Election Results, updated December 2001, <http://fecweb1.fec.gov/pubrec/2000presgeresults.htm>; Moore, *Stupid White Men*, 254. Exit poll data on Nader voters shows widely varying results by state. In Alaska, California, and Oregon, Nader voters reported a sizeable preference for Gore in a two-person race. In Pennsylvania, however, Nader voters preferred Bush by about a two-to-one margin while in New Mexico, there was about a two-to-one preference for Gore. Gerald Pomper applies the national exit poll data instead of the state-based data to conclude that "if Nader had not been on the ballot, Gore would have carried Florida and all the other close states easily." Despite this broad brush generalization, even Pomper's application of the national data yields a change in Florida only. Gerald M. Pomper, "The 2000 Presidential Election: Why Gore Lost," *Political Science Quarterly* 116, no. 2 (Summer 2001), 201–223. The Florida exit poll included 1818 respondents while that in New Hampshire had 1232 respondents. Personal communication, Leec Shapir, VNS, September 11, 2002. Although the number of exit poll respondents who had voted for Nader was small (about 30 in Florida and about 45 in New Hampshire) and conclusions based on them must be viewed cautiously, rejecting them out of hand and substituting the national exit poll data means ignoring the specific state contexts. Ten percent of Florida and 9 percent of New Hampshire exit poll respondents reporting they voted for Perot in 1996 voted for Nader in 2000. (The Perot group was 7 percent of Florida and 8 percent of New Hampshire respondents).

82. Post-Election Survey, Simon Jackman for Knowledge Networks, November 18, 2000, <jackman.stanford.edu/papers/2610tabs.pdf>. Kathy Frankovic reported the CBS findings in NYAAPOR News, Winter 2001 <http://nyaapor.org/winter 01.pdf>, CBS News.com, November 13, 2000, <www.cbsnews.com/stories/2000/ 11/13/politics/main249040.shtml>.

83. Two percent favored other candidates and 3 percent were not sure. Roper Center, Public Opinion Online, Accession Number 0375081, Lexis-Nexis.

84. U.S. Census Bureau, *Voting and Registration in the Election of November 2000*, P20–542, February 2002. Note that the Census Bureau figure in the text is based on self-reported sample data and is higher than the Federal Election Commission (FEC) report based on statistics from state election offices. The FEC reported a 51.3 percent turnout in 2000 and a 49.1 percent turnout in 1996. <http://www.fec.gov /pages/2000turnout/reg&to00.htm>, <http://www.fec.gov/pages/htmlto5. htm>, accessed September 2003.

85. Ibid. See Frances Fox Piven and Richard A. Cloward, *Why Americans Still Don't Vote* (Boston: Beacon Press, 2000).

86. Voter News Service Exit Polls, 2000, <http://www.cnn.com/ELECTION/ 2000/epolls/US/P000.html>; Jamieson and Waldman, eds., *Electing the President*, 90–92.

87. National Election Study Guide to Public Opinion and Electoral Behavior, Table 2B4, <www.umich.edu/~nes/nesguide>.

88. Voter News Service Exit Polls, 2000, <http://www.cnn.com/ELECTION/ 2000/epolls/US/P000.html>.

89. The negative reactions to Gore's actions ranged from 8 percent to 14 percent higher than to Bush's. CNN/USAToday telephone poll, April 24, 2000, Accession Numbers 0357257 and 0357259, ABC News telephone poll, April 6, 2000, Accession Numbers 0355780 and 0355781, NBC News, Wall Street Journal telephone poll, April 29–May 1, 2000, Accession Numbers 0358940 and 0358939, Princeton Survey Research Associates, Newsweek telephone poll, April 6–7, 2000, Roper Center, Public Opinion Online, Lexis-Nexis; Jamieson and Waldman, *Electing the President*, 77–78.

90. Charles P. Henry, *Black Scholar* 31 (June 2001): 18–20.

Conclusion

In calling for an Economic Bill of Rights in 1944, President Franklin Roosevelt articulated a vision of an expanded New Deal that in most respects has yet to be attempted. Given the enormous increase in wealth in our economy in the past six decades, the resources certainly exist to guarantee all the rights for which FDR called, especially the right to a useful job, a decent house, a good education, adequate medical care, and the opportunity to achieve and enjoy good health. A broad-based National Jobs for All Coalition has been conducting an educational campaign for "jobs for all at livable wages" as the centerpiece of "a just society dedicated to meeting human needs." Delivering the alternative State of the Union Address for the Democratic party in January 2002, Representative Dennis Kucinich, then chair of the 57-member Congressional Progressive Caucus, called for the implementation of President Roosevelt's proposal and quoted FDR's observations that "unless there is security here at home there cannot be lasting peace in the world." To develop the political will to achieve a new social contract based on Roosevelt's vision requires developing a positive progressive philosophy of government and overcoming the antigovernment attitudes, market-based individualism, and antiliberalism promoted by corporations in the period since the 1960s. Left and progressive organizations, however, can build on the caring values, egalitarianism, and tolerance that are now the common outlook of the majority of Americans.[1]

To restructure U.S. economic policy around the concept of justice will mean substantially reducing the giant chasm between the rich and the majority, collecting untold billions in unpaid taxes, closing tax loopholes, and increasing tax rates on the wealthy and corporations as well as over-

coming the Reaganite shibboleths against deficit spending and government regulation. The concept of economic justice, however, also means a
restructuring of U.S. foreign and defense policies away from attempting to
maintain global hegemony. The consequences of U.S. imperial overreach
include substantial harm to the domestic economy and the well-being of
most Americans from military expenditures that exceed those of all other
countries combined and "blowbacks," or "unintended consequences,"
such as the expansion of drug trafficking controlled by U.S. allies and ter-
rorist attacks on Americans by those angry at what they see as excessive
U.S. influence or domination of their homelands. A progressive policy
would promote dramatic reductions in the U.S. military budget and the
step-by-step elimination of weapons of mass destruction; the shifting of
development resources to global economic bodies controlled by the world
community rather than just the wealthy countries; and United Nations-
led assurance of human rights for all, especially women and oppressed
minorities. On this basis, the United States can participate in a world
beginning to move to a balanced and equitable development that will promote lasting peace.[2]

Progressives seeking a program of radical change in U.S. policies must
contend with the limitations on our political democracy. The most important such limitations are the corporate domination of opinion-forming
media, the massive requirements for and influence of money in the electoral process, barriers such as registration to high-level voter participation; the winner-take-all electoral system; and the restrictions on fusion
in most states. A number of important initiatives are underway to democratize the electoral system. Democratic legislative reforms include immediate runoff voting, fusion, eliminating registration, making election day a
holiday or increasing the number of voting days, and restoring voting
rights for prisoners and ex-felons. The most important electoral reform of
all, mandating the use of public funds instead of private funds for candidates seeking office, would require a constitutional amendment since the
Supreme Court has made buying power in the system with dollars equivalent to the constitutionally guaranteed right to freedom of speech.[3]

To break the logjam in U.S. politics, progressives in the Democratic
party and in left and independent parties and organizations should form
coalitions to push an agenda that combines support for such key egalitarian and cultural issues as abortion rights, affirmative action, gay and lesbian rights, immigrant rights, environmental and consumer protection,
and gun control with a new focus on enacting the elements of Roosevelt's
Economic Bill of Rights, shifting funds from the military budget to domestic needs and moving toward disarmament, reversing the hegemonistic
foreign policies of recent decades, and democratizing the electoral system.
The formation of a coalition embracing political activists of the Democratic party and left and independent parties may seem unlikely. How-

ever, any one organization or individual political leader can call for such
reforms knowing that they will thereby build on current progressive currents of thought among the American people and promote an understanding of future changes necessary to enrich American democracy and
secure economic and social justice for people in our own country and for
all the others with whom we share the planet.

NOTES

1. James MacGregor Burns, *Roosevelt: The Soldier of Freedom* (New York: Har-
court, Brace Jovanovich, 1970), 425; National Jobs for All Coalition, Year End
Report, July 2000-June 2001, <http://www.njfacorg/AnnualR.htm>; The Guild
Law Center for Economic and Social Justice in Detroit is conducting advocacy work
for the Economic Bill of Rights. See Ashley Summitt, "The Case for an Economic Bill
of Rights," September 5, 2001, <http:www.sugarlaw.org/projects/ecobill/case
forEBR.htm>; Office of Representative Dennis J. Kucinich, press release, January
29, 2002, <http://www.house.gov/kucinich/press/pr-020129-stateoftheunion.
htm>, (accessed December 2002).

2. Chalmers Johnson, *Blowback: The Costs and Consequences of American Empire*
(New York: Henry Holt, 2000).

3. Eric Foner, *The Story of Freedom* (New York: W.W. Norton & Company, 1998),
325; Black Radical Congress, "Racism and the Fight for Democracy," <http://
www.zmag.org/brcelec.htm>.

Bibliography

Bernstein, Carl. *Loyalties: A Son's Memoir.* New York: Simon & Schuster, 1989.

Black, Earl, and Merle Black. *The Vital South: How Presidents Are Elected.* Cambridge: Harvard University Press, 1992.

Blair, Diane D. *Arkansas Politics and Government.* Lincoln: University of Nebraska Press, 1988.

Branch, Taylor. *Parting the Waters: American in the King Years.* New York: Simon & Schuster, 1988.

Buhle, Mari Jo. *Women and American Socialism, 1870–1920.* Urbana: University of Illinois Press, 1983.

Burns, James MacGregor, and Georgia J. Sorenson. *Dead Center: Clinton-Gore Leadership and the Perils of Moderation.* New York: Scribner, 1999.

Capeci, Jr., Dominic J. *Race Relations in Wartime Detroit: The Sojourner Truth Housing Controversy of 1942.* Philadelphia: Temple University Press, 1984.

Chernin, Kim. *In My Mother's House.* New York: HarperCollins, 1984.

Comer, James P. *Maggie's American Dream: The Life and Times of a Black Family.* New York: New American Library, 1988.

Dark, Taylor E., *The Unions and the Democrats: An Enduring Alliance.* Ithaca, N.Y.: Cornell University Press, 1999.

Dennis, Peggy. *The Autobiography of an American Communist.* Westport, Conn.: Hill, 1977.

Ferguson, Thomas, and Joel Rogers. *Right Turn: The Decline of the Democrats and the Future of American Politics.* New York: Hill and Wang, 1986.

Flexner, Eleanor. *Century of Struggle: The Woman's Rights Movement in the United States.* Cambridge, Mass.: Belknap Press, 1959.

Flynn, Elizabeth Gurley. *The Rebel Girl: An Autobiography; My First Life (1906–1926).* New York: International Publishers, 1973.

Gillon, Steven M. *The Democrats' Dilemma: Walter F. Mondale and the Liberal Legacy.* New York: Columbia University Press, 1992.

Ginger, Ann Fagan, and David Christiano, eds. *The Cold War against Labor*. Berkeley, Calif.: Meiklejohn Civil Liberties Institute, 1987.

Gross, James A. *The Reshaping of the National Labor Relations Board*. Albany: State University of New York Press, 1981.

Guinier, Lani. *Lift Every Voice: Turning a Civil Rights Setback into a New Vision of Social Justice*. New York: Simon & Schuster, 1998.

Halpern, Martin. *UAW Politics in the Cold War Era*. Albany: State University of New York Press, 1988.

Healey, Dorothy, and Maurice Isserman. *Dorothy Healey Remembers: A Life in the American Communist Party*. New York: Oxford University Press, 1990.

Jamieson, Kathleen Hall, and Paul Waldman, eds. *Electing the President, 2000: The Insiders' View*. Philadelphia: University of Pennsylvania Press, 2001.

Kaplan, Judy, and Lin Shapiro, eds. *Red Diaper Babies: Children of the Left: Edited Transcripts of Conferences Held at World Fellowship Center, Conway, New Hampshire, July 31–August 1, 1982, July 9–10, 1983*. Somerville, Mass.: Red Diaper Productions, 1985.

Kaufman, Burton I. *The Presidency of James Earl Carter, Jr.* Lawrence: University Press of Kansas, 1992.

Lichtenstein, Nelson. *State of the Union: A Century of American Labor*. Princeton, N.J.: Princeton University Press, 2002.

Liebman, Arthur. *Jews and the Left*. New York: John Wiley and Sons, 1979.

Maier, Mark H. *City Unions: Managing Discontent in New York City*. New Brunswick, N.J.: Rutgers University Press, 1987.

Mantsios, Gregory, ed. *A New Labor Movement for the New Century*. New York: Monthly Review Press, 1998.

Meeropol, Michael. *Surrender: How the Clinton Administration Completed the Reagan Revolution*. Ann Arbor: University of Michigan Press, 1998.

Meeropol, Robert, and Michael Meeropol. *We Are Your Sons: The Legacy of Ethel and Julius Rosenberg*. Boston: Houghton Mifflin Co., 1975.

Moore, Michael. *Stupid White Men*. New York: HarperCollins, 2001.

Mort, Jo-Ann, ed. *Not Your Father's Union Movement: Inside the AFL-CIO*. London: Verso, 1998.

Murphy, Marjorie. *Blackboard Unions: The AFT and the NEA, 1900–1980*. Ithaca, N.Y.: Cornell University Press, 1990.

Nader, Ralph. *Crashing the Party: Taking on the Corporate Government in an Age of Surrender*. New York: St. Martin's Press, 2002.

Nesbitt, Murray B. *Labor Relations in the Federal Government Service*. Washington, D.C.: Bureau of National Affairs, 1976.

Orr, Elaine Neil. *Tillie Olsen and a Feminist Spiritual Vision*. Jackson: University Press of Mississippi, 1987.

Ostrander, Susan A. *Women of the Upper Class*. Philadelphia: Temple University Press, 1984.

Reich, Robert B. *Locked in the Cabinet*. New York: Alfred A. Knopf, 1997.

Roberts, Harold S. *Labor Management Relations in the Public Service*. [Honolulu]: University of Hawaii Industrial Relations Center, 1968.

Robinson, Archie. *George Meany and His Times*. New York: Simon & Schuster, 1981.

Rosenbaum, Herbert D., and Alexej Ugrinsky, eds. *Presidency and Domestic Politics of Jimmy Carter*. Westport, Conn.: Greenwood Press, 1994.

Rubin, Lillian Breslow. *Worlds of Pain: Life in the Working Class Family.* New York: Basic Books, 1976.

Selden, David. *The Teacher Rebellion.* Washington, D.C.: Howard University Press, 1985.

Sifry, Micah L. *Spoiling for a Fight: Third Party Politics in America.* New York: Routledge, 2001.

Sims, Beth. *Workers of the World Undermined: American Labor's Role in U.S. Foreign Policy.* Boston: South End Press, 1992.

Skocpol, Theda. *Boomerang: Clinton's Health Security Effort and the Turn against Government in U.S. Politics.* New York: W.W. Norton & Company, 1996.

Spero, Sterling D. *Government as Employer.* Carbondale: Southern Illinois Press, 1972.

Stephanopoulos, George. *All too Human: A Political Education.* Boston: Little, Brown and Company, 1999.

Thompson, Mindy. *The National Negro Labor Council: A History.* New York: American Institute for Marxist Studies, 1978.

Turque, Bill. *Inventing Al Gore: A Biography.* Boston: Houghton Mifflin Co., 2000.

Walsh, John, and Garth Mangum. *Labor Struggle in the Post Office: From Selective Lobbying to Collective Bargaining.* Armonk, N.Y.: M.E. Shapre, 1992.

White, John Kenneth. *Still Seeing Red: How the Cold War Shapes the New American Politics.* Boulder, Colo.: Westview Press, 1997.

Young, Coleman, and Lonnie Wheeler, *Hard Stuff: The Autobiography of Coleman Young.* New York: Penguin, 1994.

Index

About the Author

MARTIN HALPERN is Professor of History at Henderson State University in Arkansas. He is the author of *UAW Politics in the Cold War Era* and the lead author of *Minority Health in Michigan: Closing the Gap.*